UH... HEY! WAIT FOR MEEE!!

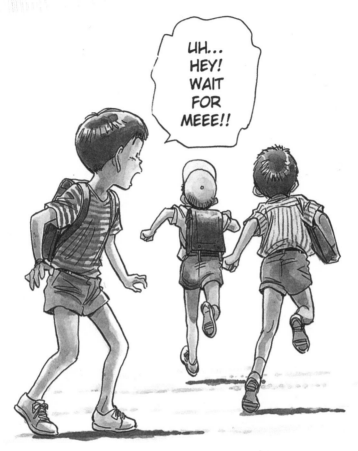

NAOKI URASAWA'S

20th CENTURY BOYS

PROFILES

How did a young boy turn into a terrifying cult leader?! And what kind of world does he rule in the post-apocalyptic future...?!

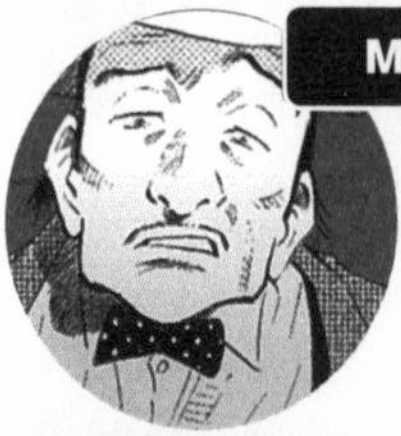

Manjome Inshu

Top cadre of the Friends organization and currently head of the Friendship and Democracy Party.

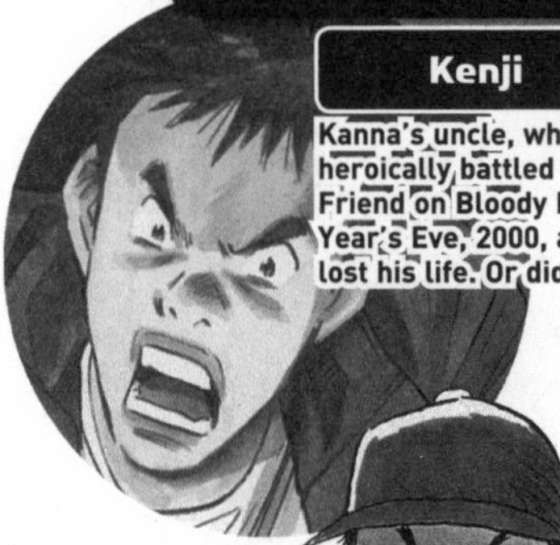

Kenji

Kanna's uncle, who heroically battled the Friend on Bloody New Year's Eve, 2000, and lost his life. Or did he?!

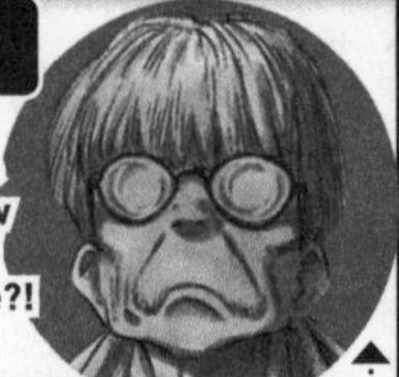

Yoshitsune

Kenji's classmate who heads the underground resistance against the Friends.

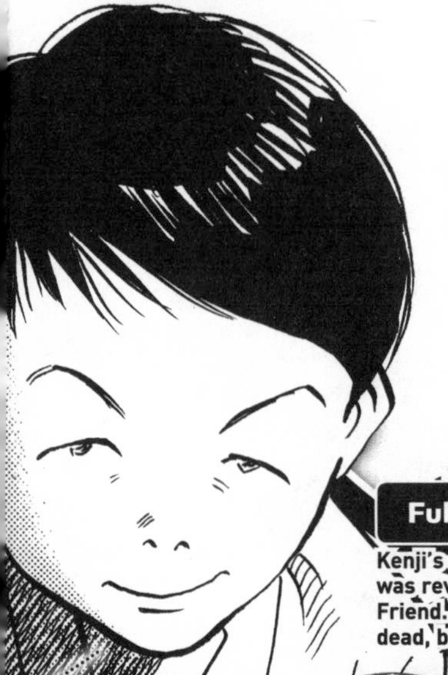

Fukube

Kenji's classmate who was revealed to be the Friend. He was shot dead, but...?!

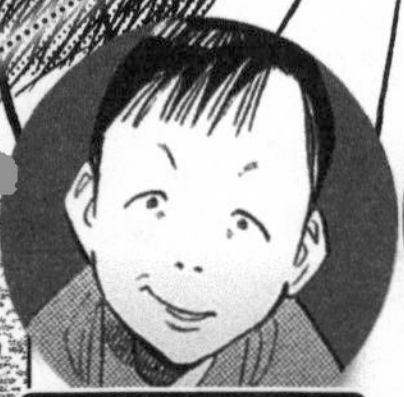

Sadakiyo

Kenji's classmate who always wore a mask and was picked on by other kids.

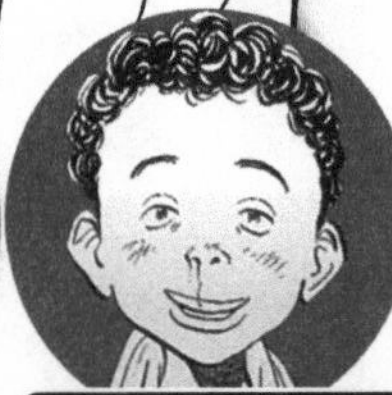

Donkey

Kenji's classmate who became a teacher, but died under mysterious circumstances.

who saved the world and Kenji, who lost his life trying to stop him, is branded a terrorist.

Then in 2014, Kanna is seventeen and determined to avenge her beloved uncle's death. Gathering Kenji's allies around her, she prepares for the final battle, but the Friend is assassinated by one of his own in 2015... Until the day of the Expo 2015 opening

the world for this miracle, the Friend then orders the dispersal of a killer virus around the world, in keeping with the New Book of Prophecy. As a result, the world as we knew it is destroyed...

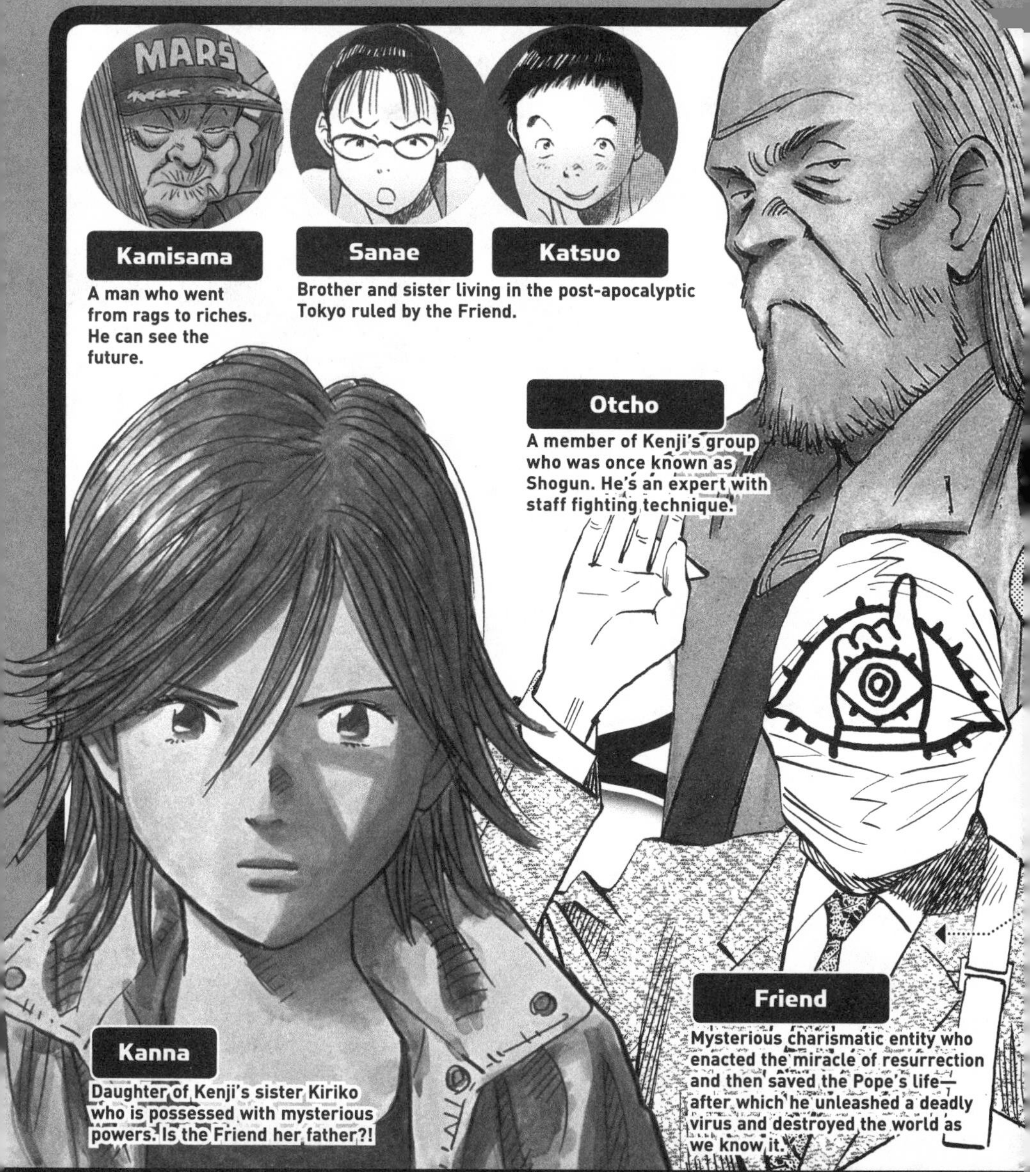
MARS
Kamisama
A man who went from rags to riches. He can see the future.
Sanae
Katsuo
Brother and sister living in the post-apocalyptic Tokyo ruled by the Friend.
Otcho
A member of Kenji's group who was once known as Shogun. He's an expert with staff fighting technique.
Kanna
Daughter of Kenji's sister Kiriko who is possessed with mysterious powers. Is the Friend her father?!
Friend
Mysterious charismatic entity who enacted the miracle of resurrection and then saved the Pope's life—after which he unleashed a deadly virus and destroyed the world as we know it.

The story so far...

In the early 1970s, Kenji and his friends were elementary schoolers who dreamed of the exciting future that awaited them in the 21st century. In their secret headquarters, out in an empty lot, they made up a ridiculous scenario about a League of Evil, whose plan to destroy the world would be thwarted by a group of heroes. They wrote this story in *The Book of Prophecy*.

Later in 1997, the adult Kenji is raising his missing sister's baby Kanna and is shocked when he realizes that a series of ominous incidents is following *The Book of Prophecy*, and that a charismatic leader known only as the Friend seems to be behind it all. By the time Kenji discovers this plot, he has been framed as an evil villain who is plotting to take over the world by spraying a deadly virus! On "Bloody New Year's Eve," the Friend acts the part of the hero

A SUMMARY OF 20

CONTENTS
VOL 16
BEYOND THE LOOKING GLASS

Chap 1: End of the Rainbow 5

Chap 2: A Real Friend 25

Chap 3: Beyond the Looking Glass 43

Chap 4: The Truth of Hanging Hill 61

Chap 5: A Real Ghost 79

Chap 6: Superhuman 97

Chap 7: Friendship Era 115

Chap 8: Pole Vaulter 135

Chap 9: Modern History 153

Chap 10: Kids' Talk 171

Chap 11: Toy Chest 189

NAOKI URASAWA'S 20th CENTURY BOYS

Chapter 1
End of the Rainbow

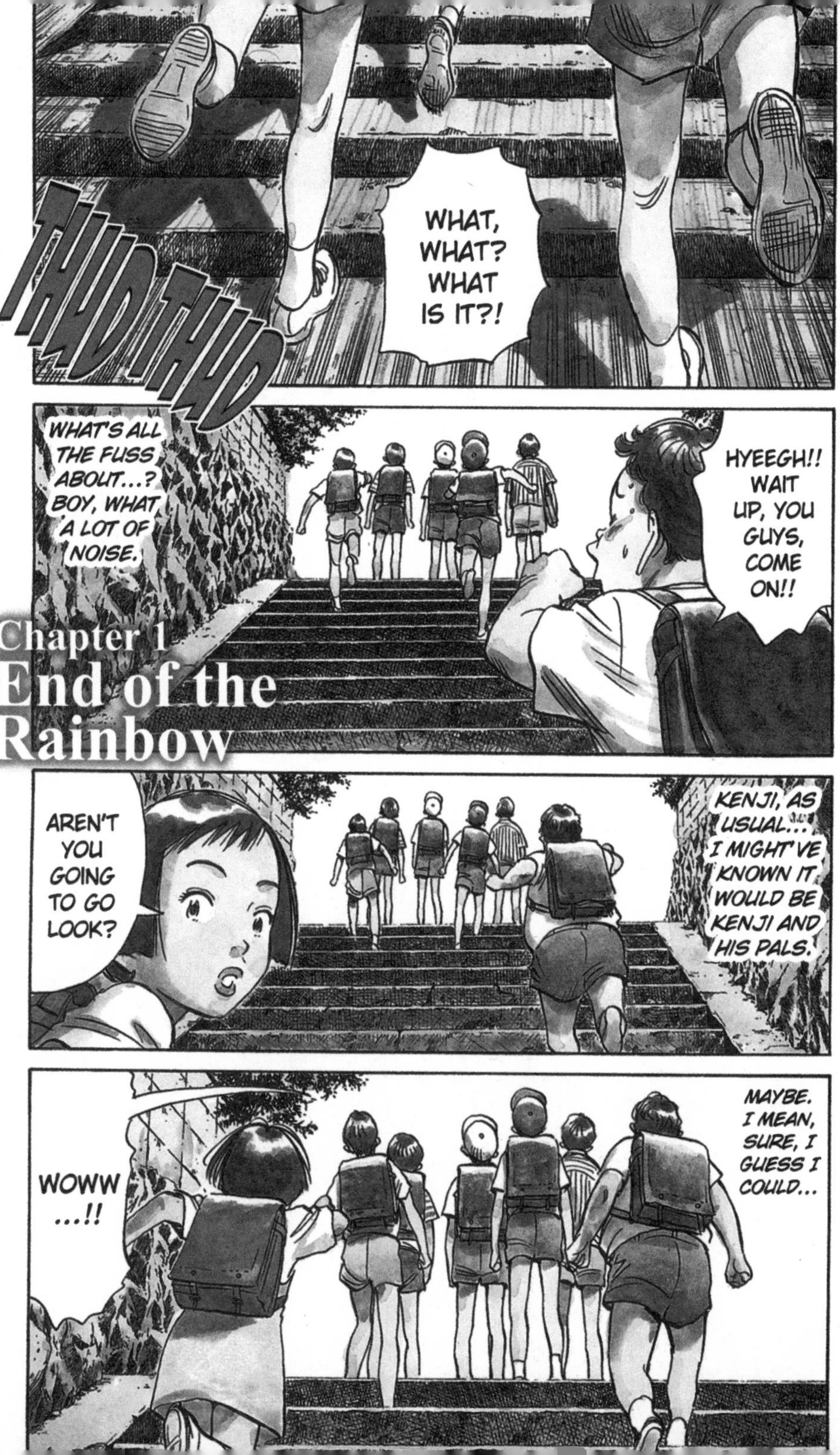
WHAT, WHAT? WHAT IS IT?!
THUD THUD
HYEEGH!! WAIT UP, YOU GUYS, COME ON!!
WHAT'S ALL THE FUSS ABOUT...? BOY, WHAT A LOT OF NOISE.
KENJI, AS USUAL... I MIGHT'VE KNOWN IT WOULD BE KENJI AND HIS PALS.
AREN'T YOU GOING TO GO LOOK?
MAYBE. I MEAN, SURE, I GUESS I COULD...
WOWW ...!!

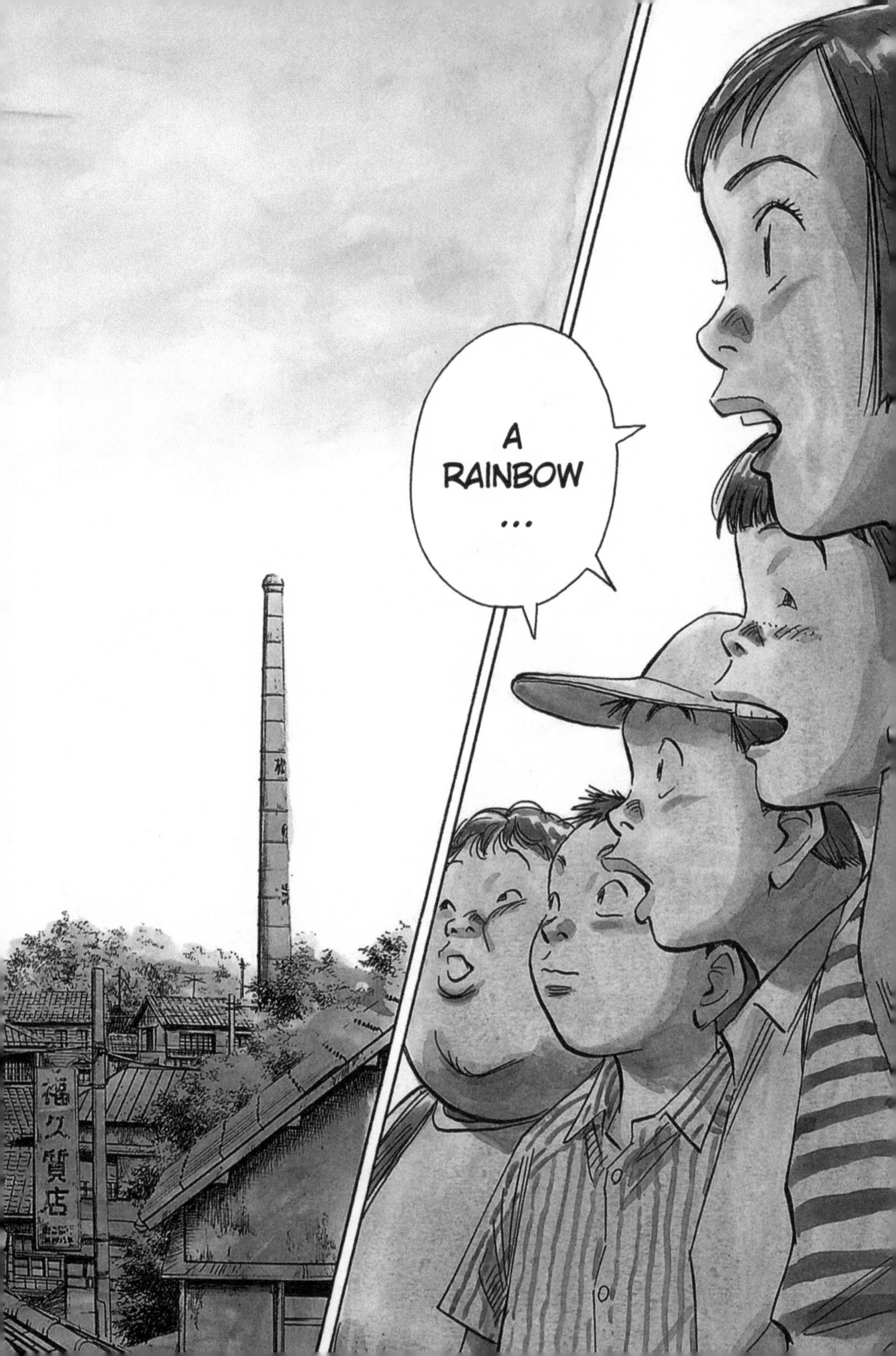
A RAINBOW ...

A RAINBOW...?
THAT'S WHAT THIS
WAS ABOUT? WHO
CARES? DON'T CALL
EVERYBODY OVER
TO SEE A PLAIN OLD
RAINBOW. I MEAN,
WHAT'S SO GREAT
ABOUT THIS? IT'S
JUST A RAINBOW.

Chapter 1
End of the
Rainbow

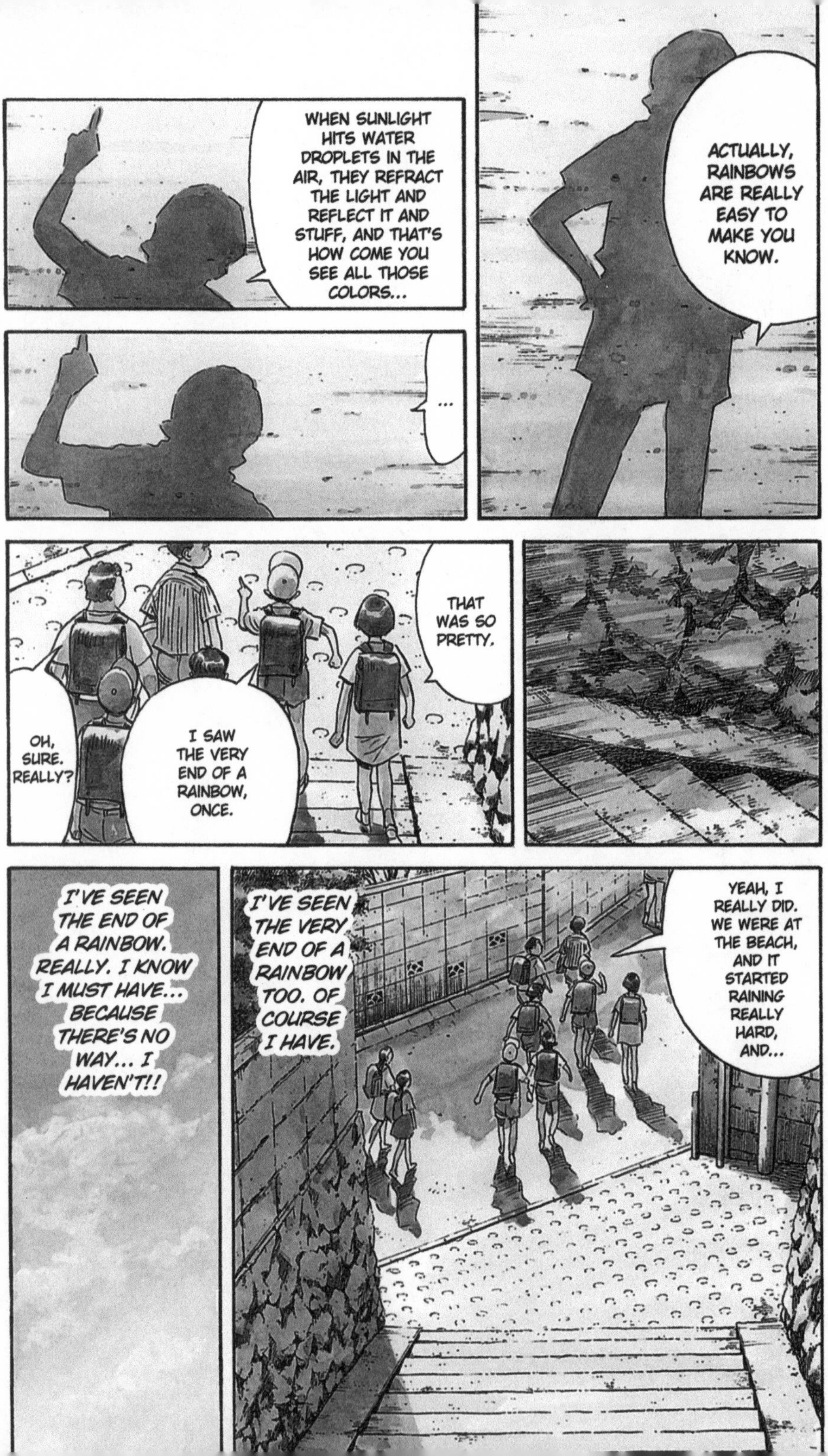

ACTUALLY, RAINBOWS ARE REALLY EASY TO MAKE YOU KNOW.
WHEN SUNLIGHT HITS WATER DROPLETS IN THE AIR, THEY REFRACT THE LIGHT AND REFLECT IT AND STUFF, AND THAT'S HOW COME YOU SEE ALL THOSE COLORS...
...
THAT WAS SO PRETTY.
I SAW THE VERY END OF A RAINBOW, ONCE.
OH, SURE. REALLY?
YEAH, I REALLY DID. WE WERE AT THE BEACH, AND IT STARTED RAINING REALLY HARD, AND...
I'VE SEEN THE VERY END OF A RAINBOW TOO. OF COURSE I HAVE.
I'VE SEEN THE END OF A RAINBOW. REALLY. I KNOW I MUST HAVE... BECAUSE THERE'S NO WAY... I HAVEN'T!!

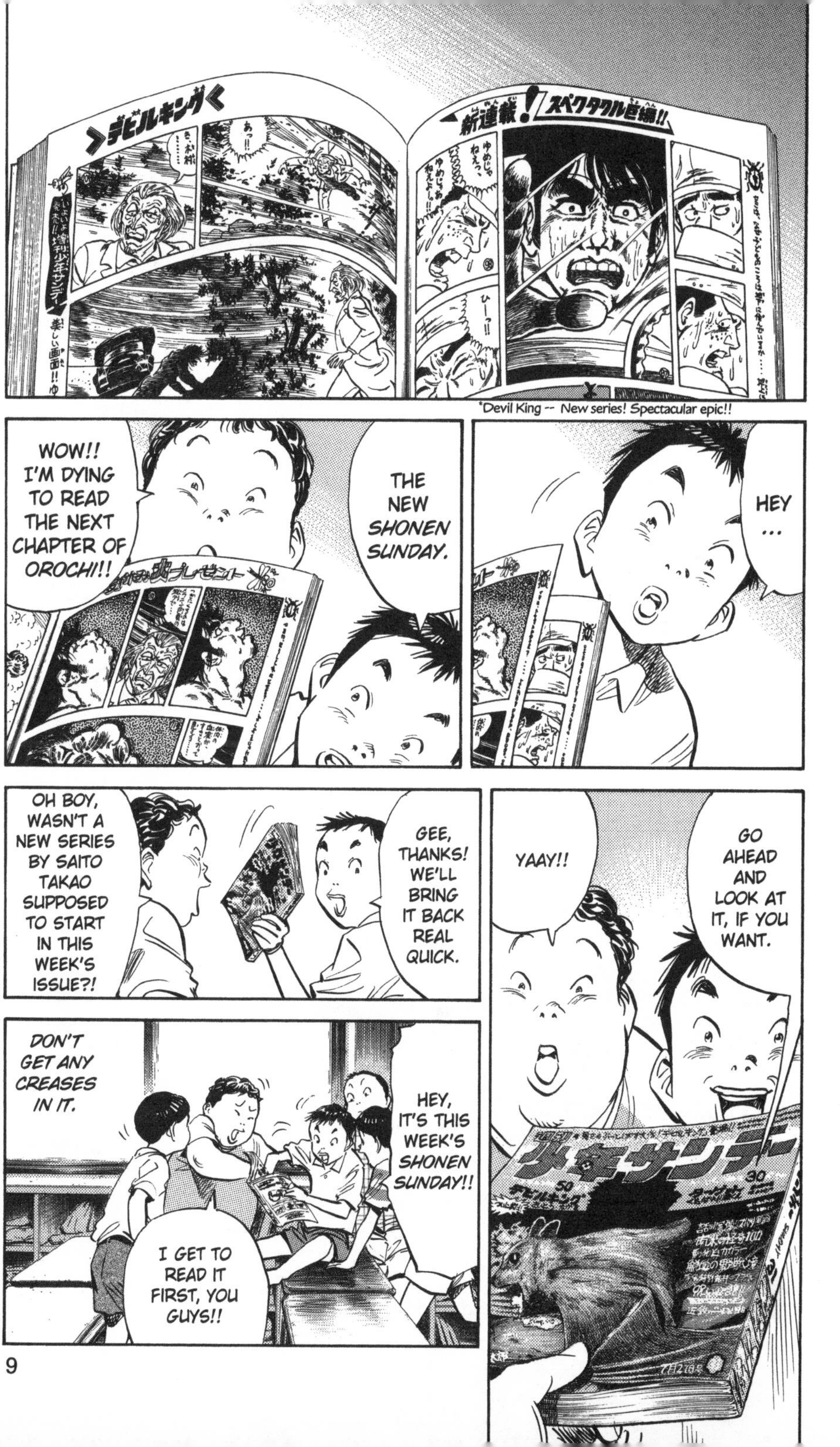
デビルキング
新連載!
スペクタクル巨編!!
あっ…!!
ひーっ!!
*Devil King -- New series! Spectacular epic!!
HEY ...
THE NEW SHONEN SUNDAY.
WOW!! I'M DYING TO READ THE NEXT CHAPTER OF OROCHI!!
GO AHEAD AND LOOK AT IT, IF YOU WANT.
YAAY!!
少年サンデー
GEE, THANKS! WE'LL BRING IT BACK REAL QUICK.
OH BOY, WASN'T A NEW SERIES BY SAITO TAKAO SUPPOSED TO START IN THIS WEEK'S ISSUE?!
HEY, IT'S THIS WEEK'S SHONEN SUNDAY!!
DON'T GET ANY CREASES IN IT.
I GET TO READ IT FIRST, YOU GUYS!!

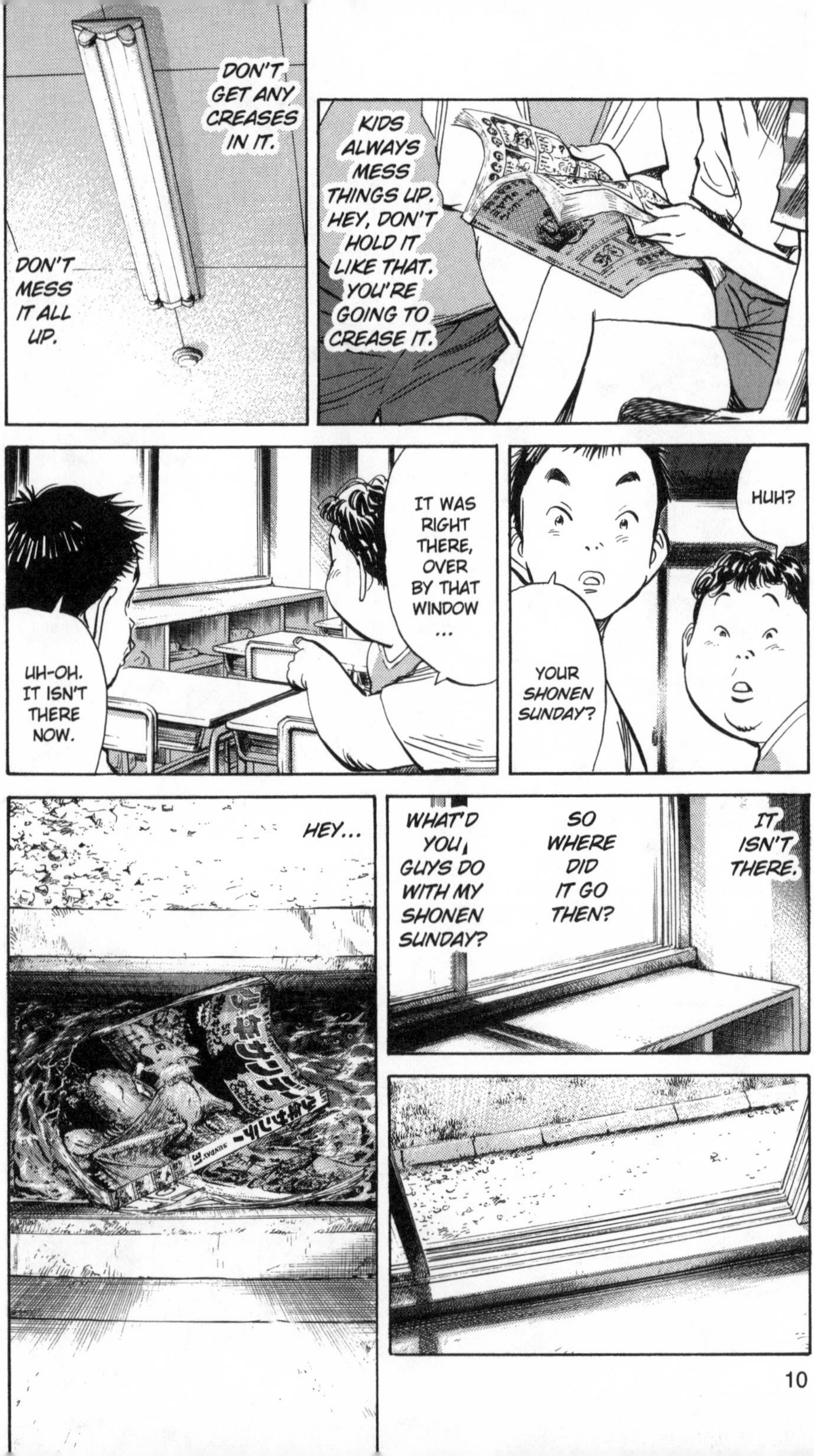
KIDS ALWAYS MESS THINGS UP. HEY, DON'T HOLD IT LIKE THAT. YOU'RE GOING TO CREASE IT.
DON'T GET ANY CREASES IN IT.
DON'T MESS IT ALL UP.
HUH?
YOUR SHONEN SUNDAY?
IT WAS RIGHT THERE, OVER BY THAT WINDOW ...
UH-OH. IT ISN'T THERE NOW.
IT ISN'T THERE.
SO WHERE DID IT GO THEN?
WHAT'D YOU GUYS DO WITH MY SHONEN SUNDAY?
HEY...

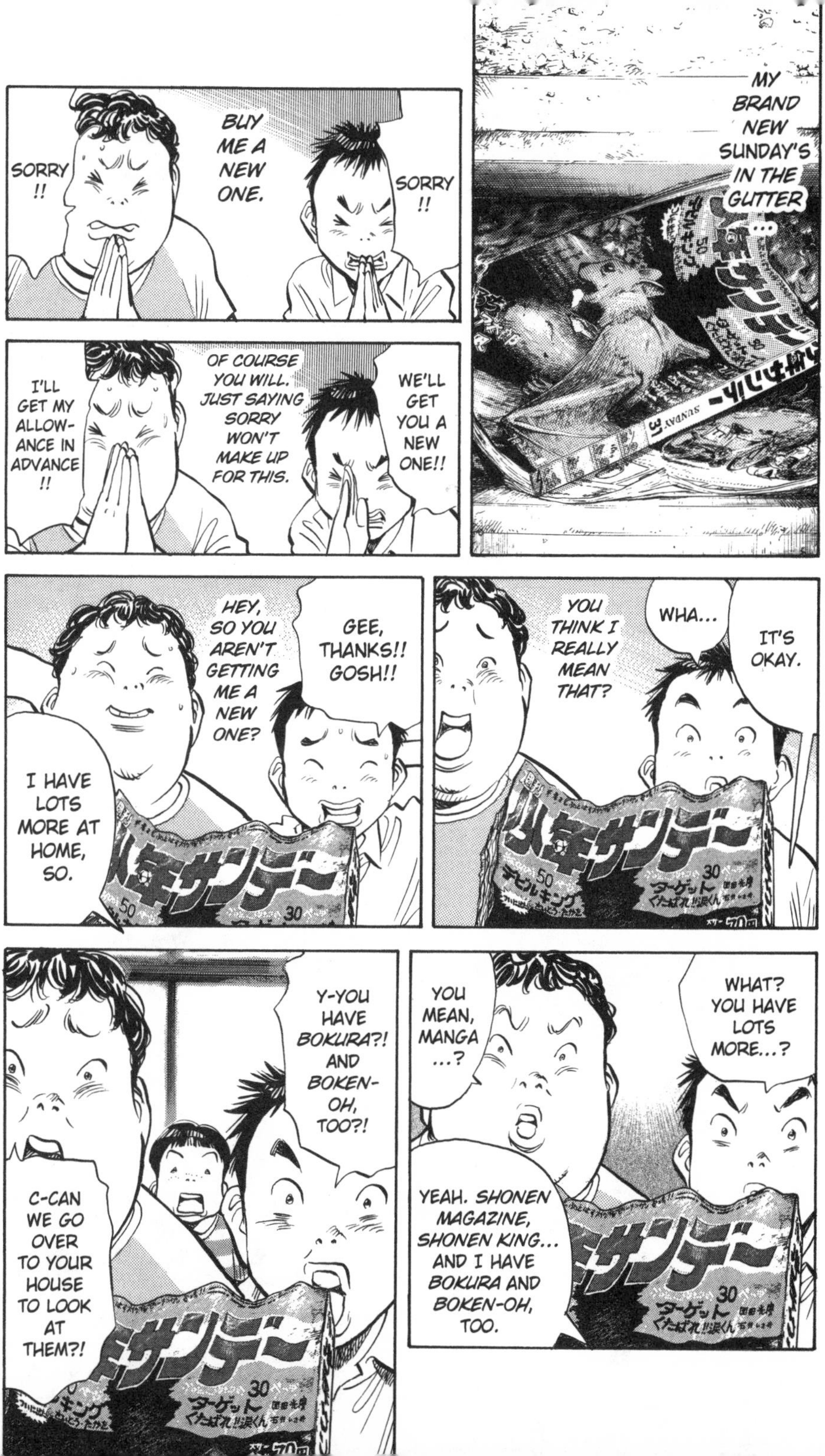
MY BRAND NEW SUNDAY'S IN THE GUTTER...
SORRY!!
BUY ME A NEW ONE.
SORRY!!
WE'LL GET YOU A NEW ONE!!
OF COURSE YOU WILL. JUST SAYING SORRY WON'T MAKE UP FOR THIS.
I'LL GET MY ALLOWANCE IN ADVANCE!!
IT'S OKAY.
WHA...
YOU THINK I REALLY MEAN THAT?
GEE, THANKS!! GOSH!!
HEY, SO YOU AREN'T GETTING ME A NEW ONE?
I HAVE LOTS MORE AT HOME, SO.
WHAT? YOU HAVE LOTS MORE...?
YOU MEAN, MANGA...?
YEAH. SHONEN MAGAZINE, SHONEN KING... AND I HAVE BOKURA AND BOKEN-OH, TOO.
Y-YOU HAVE BOKURA?! AND BOKEN-OH, TOO?!
C-CAN WE GO OVER TO YOUR HOUSE TO LOOK AT THEM?!

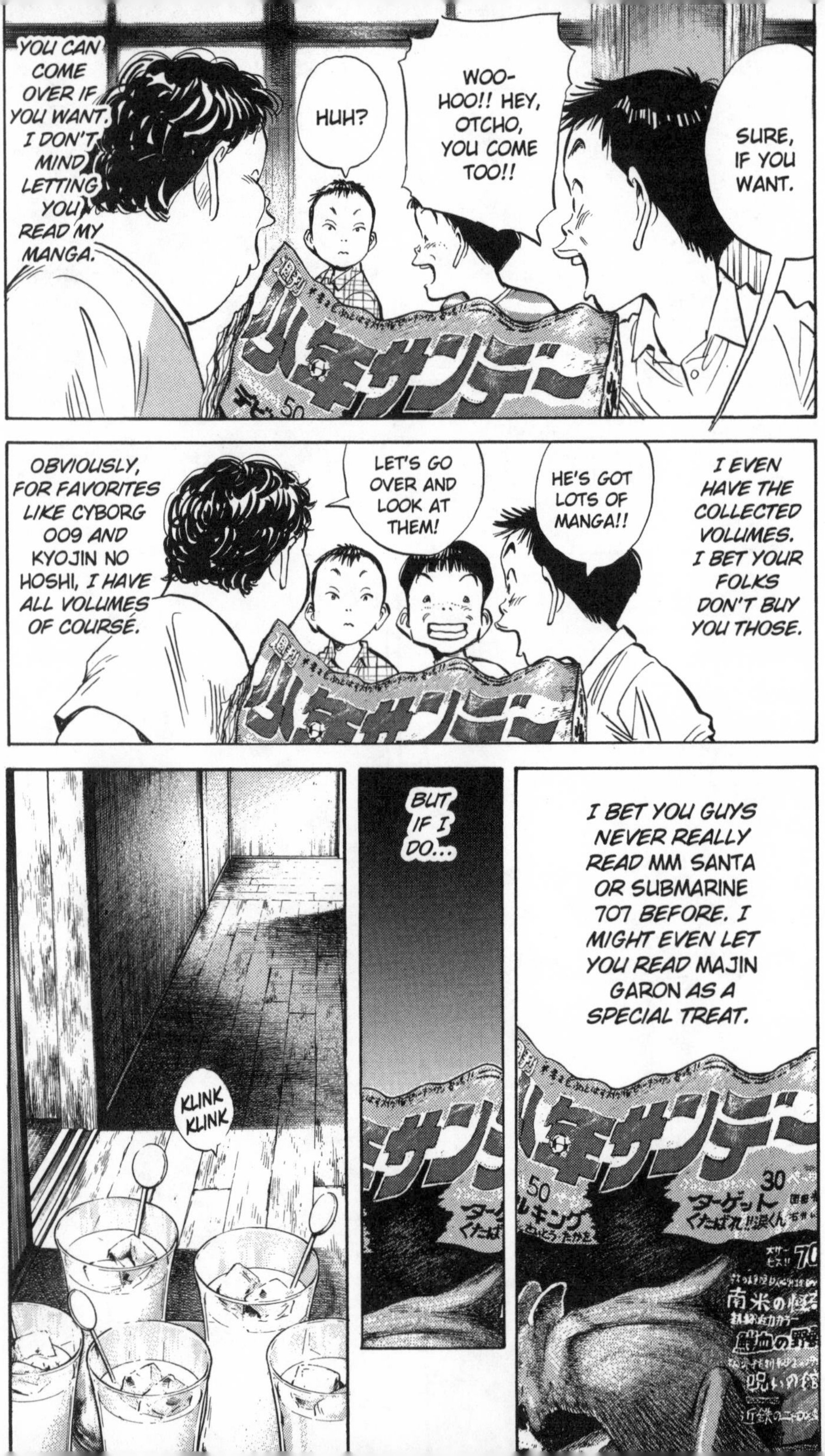
SURE, IF YOU WANT.
WOO-HOO!! HEY, OTCHO, YOU COME TOO!!
HUH?
YOU CAN COME OVER IF YOU WANT. I DON'T MIND LETTING YOU READ MY MANGA.
少年サンデー
I EVEN HAVE THE COLLECTED VOLUMES. I BET YOUR FOLKS DON'T BUY YOU THOSE.
HE'S GOT LOTS OF MANGA!!
LET'S GO OVER AND LOOK AT THEM!
OBVIOUSLY, FOR FAVORITES LIKE CYBORG 009 AND KYOJIN NO HOSHI, I HAVE ALL VOLUMES OF COURSE.
I BET YOU GUYS NEVER REALLY READ MM SANTA OR SUBMARINE 707 BEFORE. I MIGHT EVEN LET YOU READ MAJIN GARON AS A SPECIAL TREAT.
少年サンデー
BUT IF I DO...
KLINK KLINK

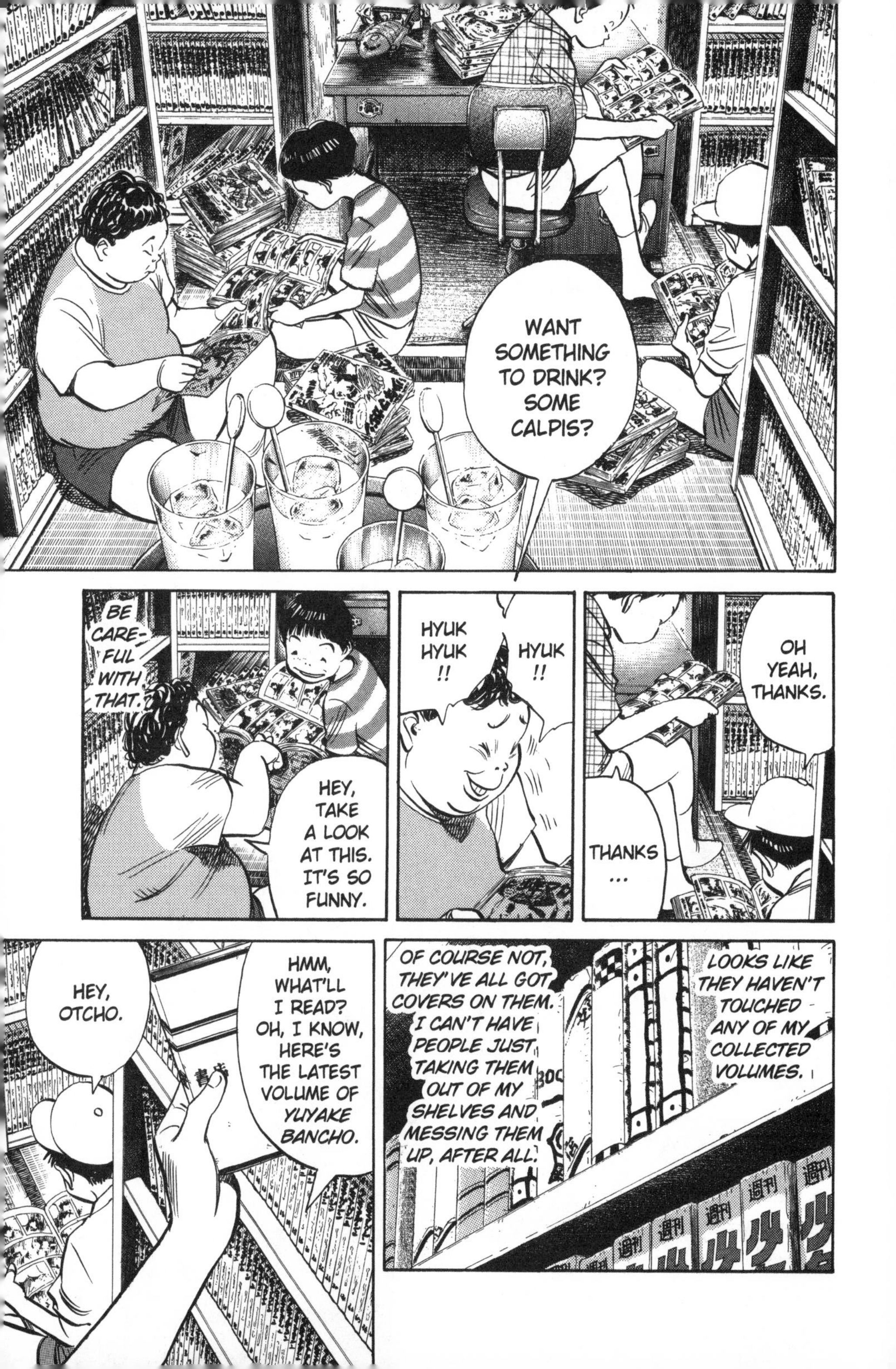
WANT SOMETHING TO DRINK? SOME CALPIS?
OH YEAH, THANKS.
THANKS ...
HYUK !!
HYUK HYUK !!
BE CARE-FUL WITH THAT.
HEY, TAKE A LOOK AT THIS. IT'S SO FUNNY.
LOOKS LIKE THEY HAVEN'T TOUCHED ANY OF MY COLLECTED VOLUMES.
OF COURSE NOT, THEY'VE ALL GOT COVERS ON THEM. I CAN'T HAVE PEOPLE JUST TAKING THEM OUT OF MY SHELVES AND MESSING THEM UP, AFTER ALL.
HMM, WHAT'LL I READ? OH, I KNOW, HERE'S THE LATEST VOLUME OF YUYAKE BANCHO.
HEY, OTCHO.

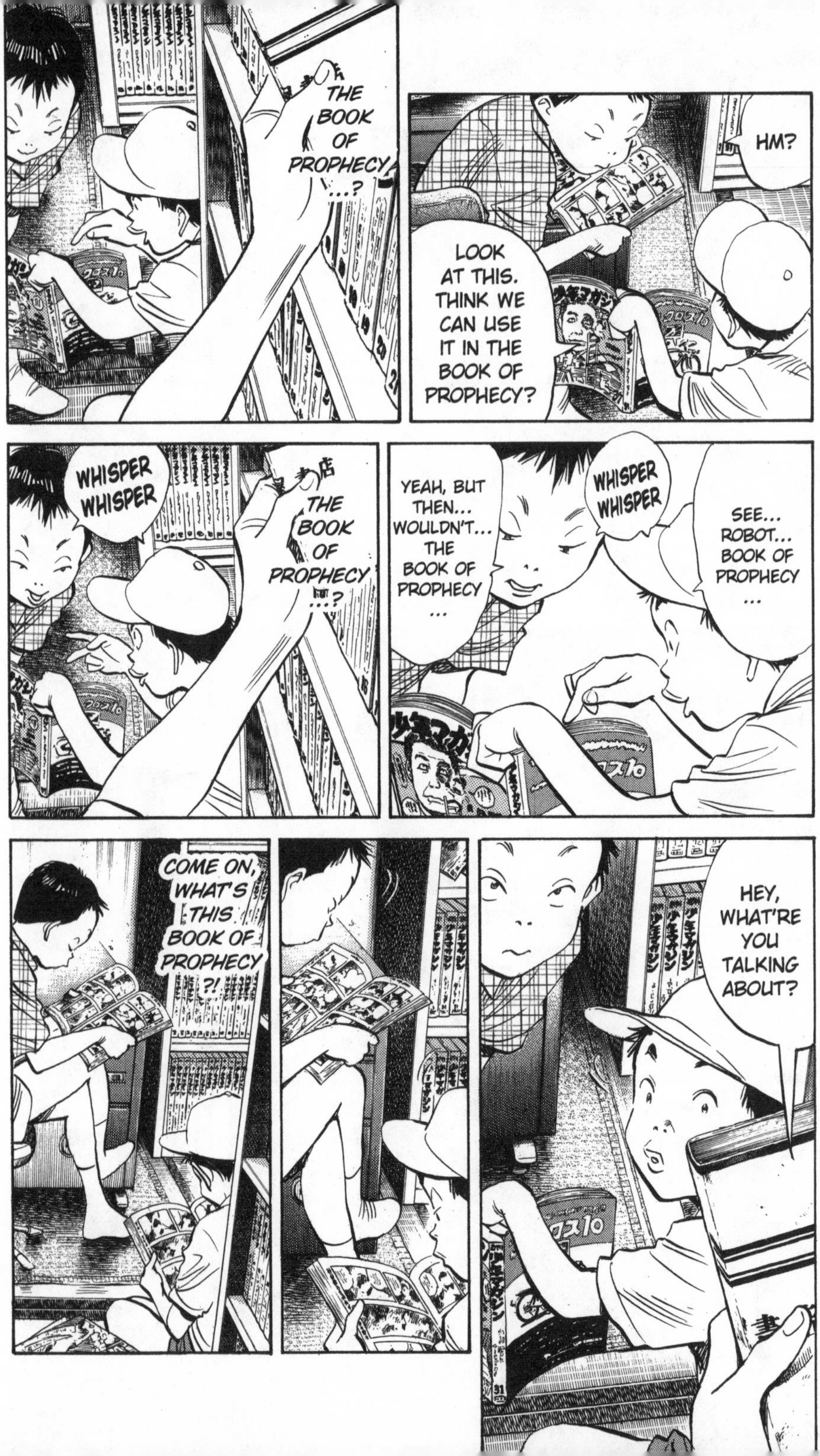
HM?
LOOK AT THIS. THINK WE CAN USE IT IN THE BOOK OF PROPHECY?
THE BOOK OF PROPHECY ...?
SEE... ROBOT... BOOK OF PROPHECY ...
WHISPER WHISPER
YEAH, BUT THEN... WOULDN'T... THE BOOK OF PROPHECY ...
THE BOOK OF PROPHECY ...?
WHISPER WHISPER
HEY, WHAT'RE YOU TALKING ABOUT?
COME ON, WHAT'S THIS BOOK OF PROPHECY ?!

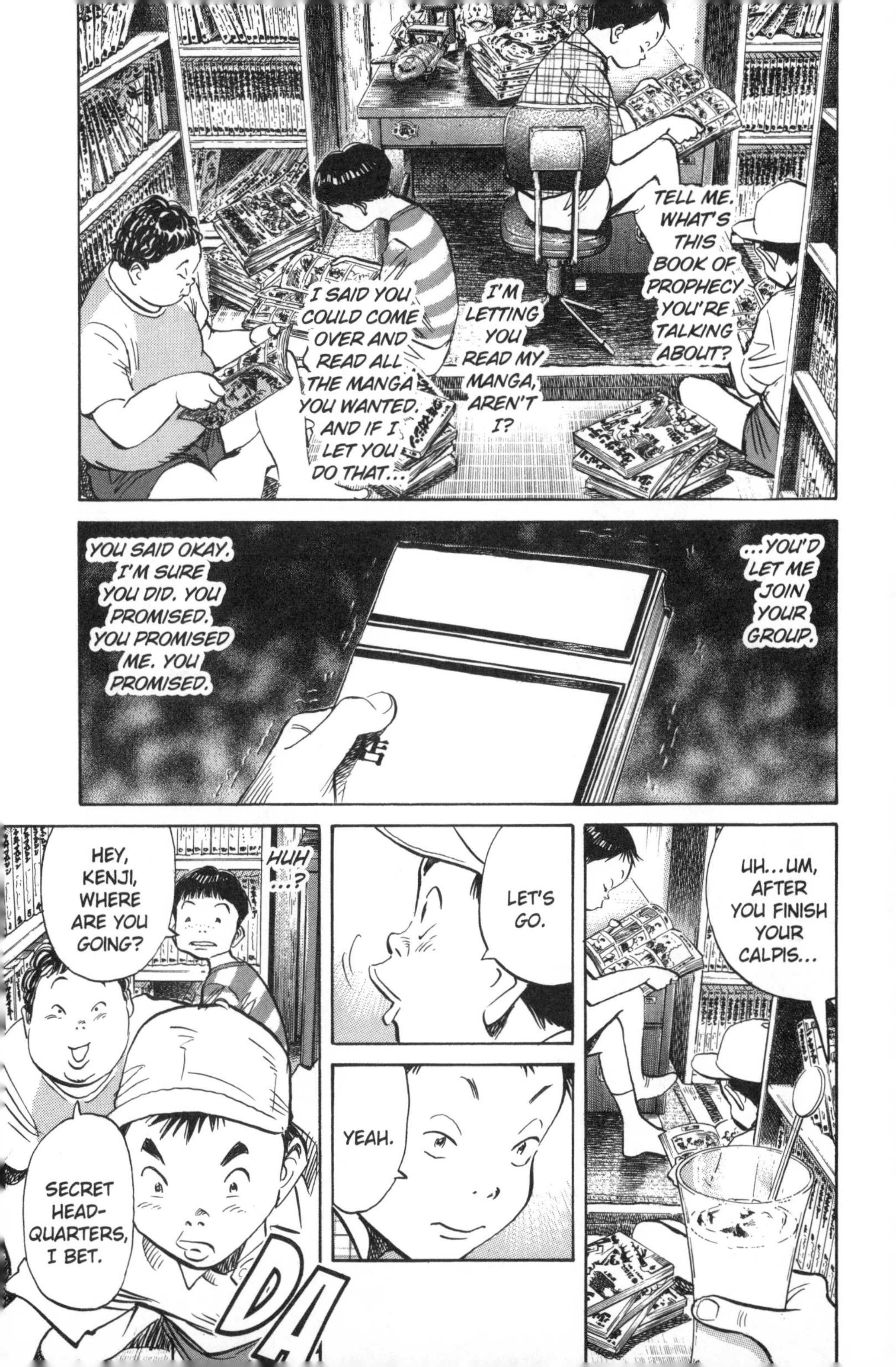
TELL ME. WHAT'S THIS BOOK OF PROPHECY YOU'RE TALKING ABOUT?
I'M LETTING YOU READ MY MANGA, AREN'T I?
I SAID YOU COULD COME OVER AND READ ALL THE MANGA YOU WANTED. AND IF I LET YOU DO THAT...
...YOU'D LET ME JOIN YOUR GROUP.
YOU SAID OKAY. I'M SURE YOU DID. YOU PROMISED. YOU PROMISED ME. YOU PROMISED.
UH...UM, AFTER YOU FINISH YOUR CALPIS...
LET'S GO.
YEAH.
HUH...?
HEY, KENJI, WHERE ARE YOU GOING?
SECRET HEAD-QUARTERS, I BET.
DA

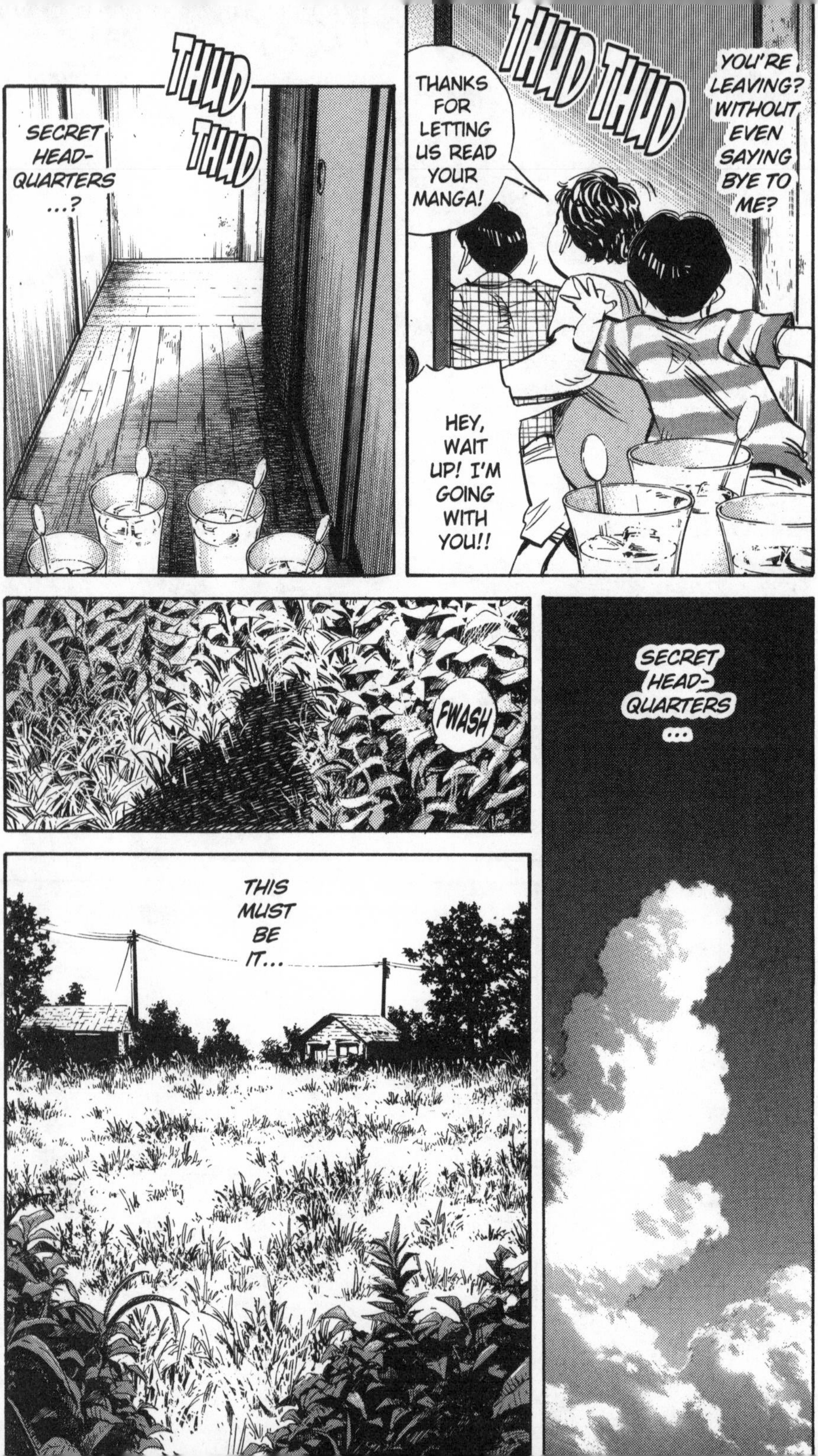
YOU'RE LEAVING? WITHOUT EVEN SAYING BYE TO ME?
THUD THUD
THANKS FOR LETTING US READ YOUR MANGA!
HEY, WAIT UP! I'M GOING WITH YOU!!
THUD THUD
SECRET HEAD-QUARTERS ...?
SECRET HEAD-QUARTERS ...
FWASH
THIS MUST BE IT...

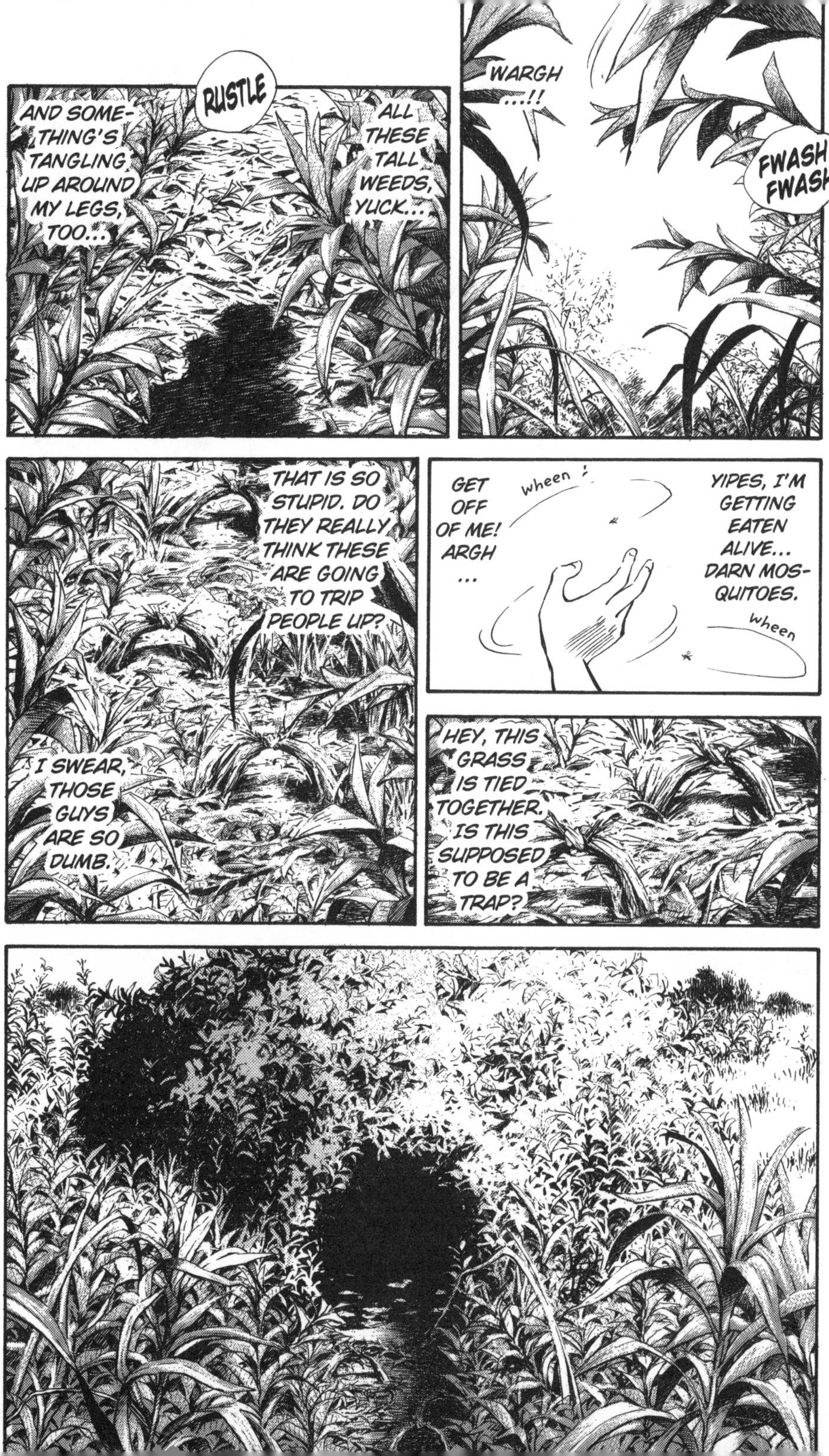
WARGH ...!!
FWASH FWASH
ALL THESE TALL WEEDS, YUCK...
RUSTLE
AND SOME-THING'S TANGLING UP AROUND MY LEGS, TOO...
YIPES, I'M GETTING EATEN ALIVE... DARN MOS-QUITOES.
wheen
GET OFF OF ME! ARGH ...
wheen
HEY, THIS GRASS IS TIED TOGETHER. IS THIS SUPPOSED TO BE A TRAP?
THAT IS SO STUPID. DO THEY REALLY THINK THESE ARE GOING TO TRIP PEOPLE UP?
I SWEAR, THOSE GUYS ARE SO DUMB.

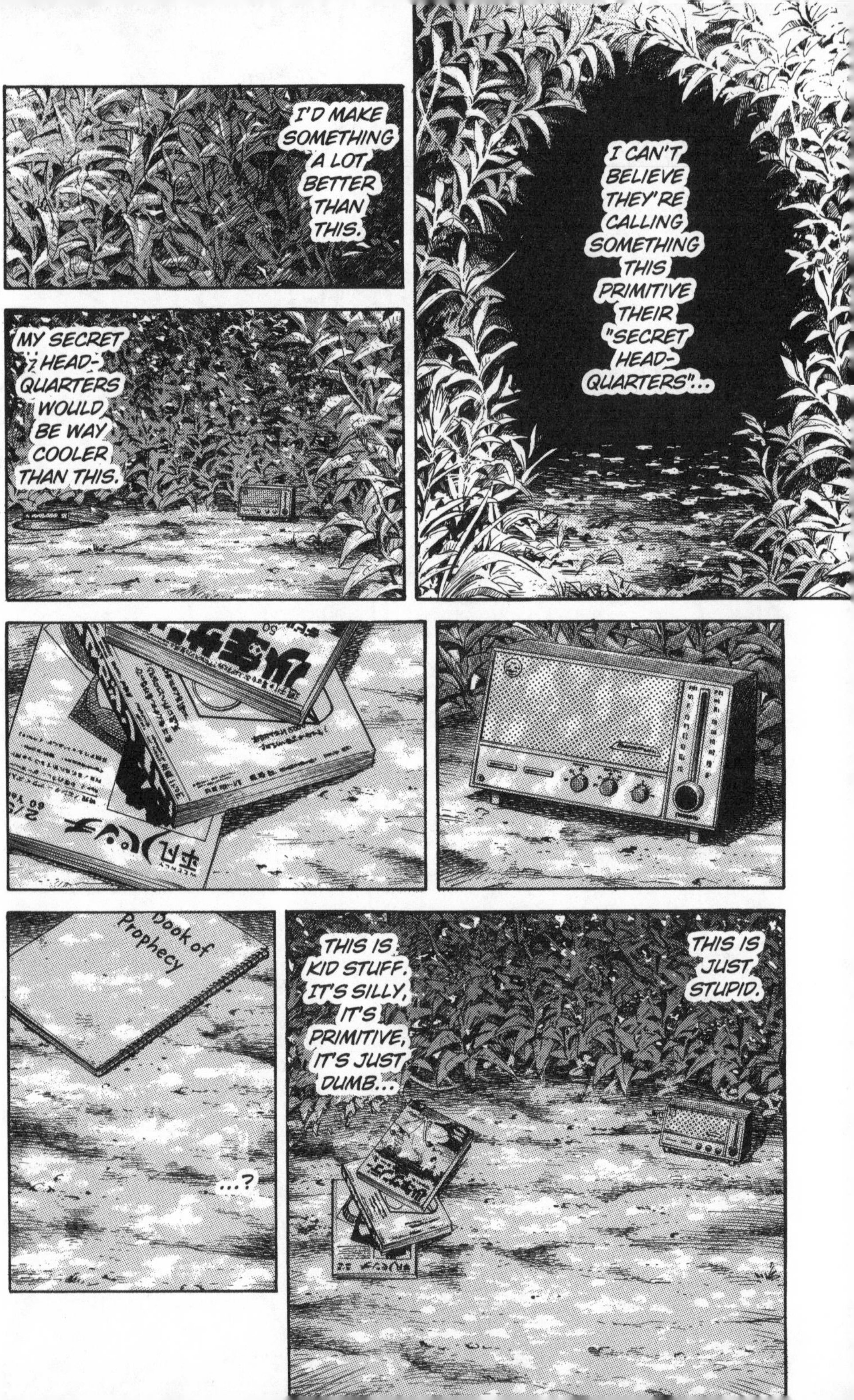
I CAN'T BELIEVE THEY'RE CALLING SOMETHING THIS PRIMITIVE THEIR "SECRET HEAD-QUARTERS"...
I'D MAKE SOMETHING A LOT BETTER THAN THIS.
MY SECRET HEAD-QUARTERS WOULD BE WAY COOLER THAN THIS.
THIS IS JUST STUPID.
THIS IS KID STUFF. IT'S SILLY, IT'S PRIMITIVE, IT'S JUST DUMB...
Book of Prophecy
...?

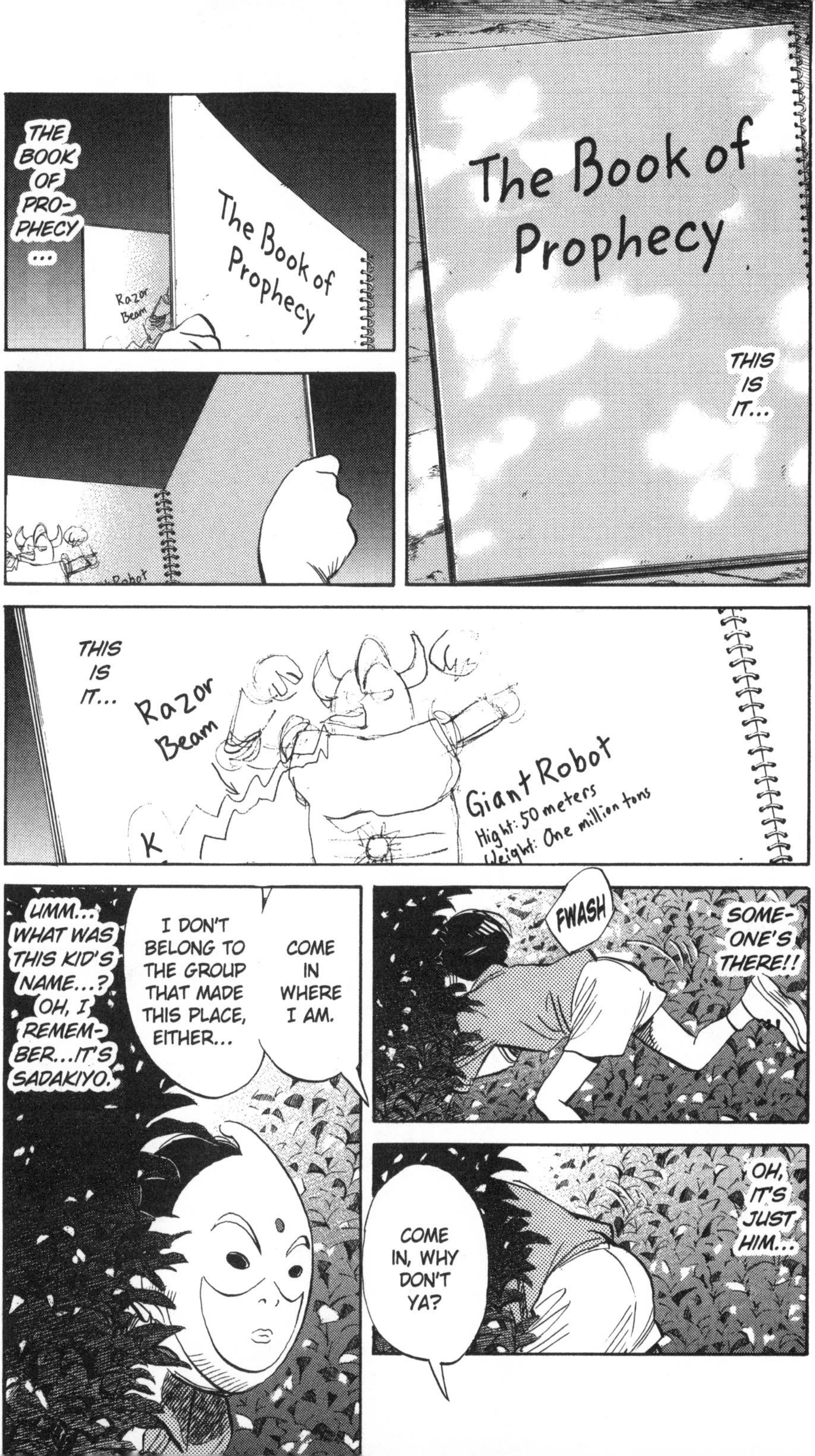
The Book of Prophecy
THIS IS IT...
THE BOOK OF PRO-PHECY...
The Book of Prophecy
Razor Beam
Robot
THIS IS IT...
Razor Beam
Giant Robot
Hight: 50 meters
Weight: One million tons
K
FWASH
SOME-ONE'S THERE!!
OH, IT'S JUST HIM...
COME IN WHERE I AM.
I DON'T BELONG TO THE GROUP THAT MADE THIS PLACE, EITHER...
UMM... WHAT WAS THIS KID'S NAME...? OH, I REMEM-BER...IT'S SADAKIYO.
COME IN, WHY DON'T YA?

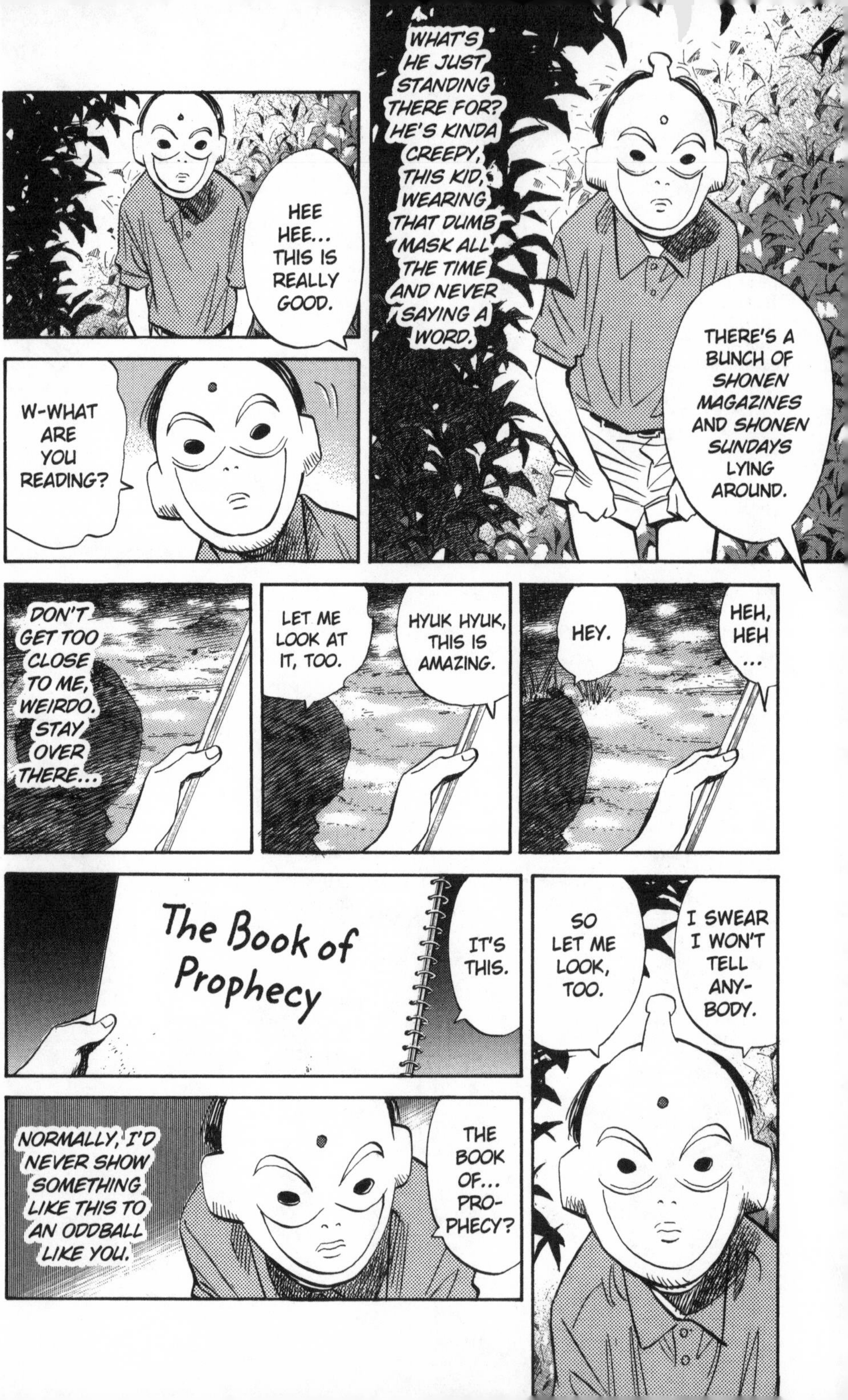
WHAT'S HE JUST STANDING THERE FOR? HE'S KINDA CREEPY, THIS KID, WEARING THAT DUMB MASK ALL THE TIME AND NEVER SAYING A WORD.
THERE'S A BUNCH OF SHONEN MAGAZINES AND SHONEN SUNDAYS LYING AROUND.
HEE HEE... THIS IS REALLY GOOD.
W-WHAT ARE YOU READING?
HEH, HEH ...
HEY.
HYUK HYUK, THIS IS AMAZING.
LET ME LOOK AT IT, TOO.
DON'T GET TOO CLOSE TO ME, WEIRDO. STAY OVER THERE...
I SWEAR I WON'T TELL ANY-BODY.
SO LET ME LOOK, TOO.
IT'S THIS.
The Book of Prophecy
THE BOOK OF... PRO-PHECY?
NORMALLY, I'D NEVER SHOW SOMETHING LIKE THIS TO AN ODDBALL LIKE YOU.

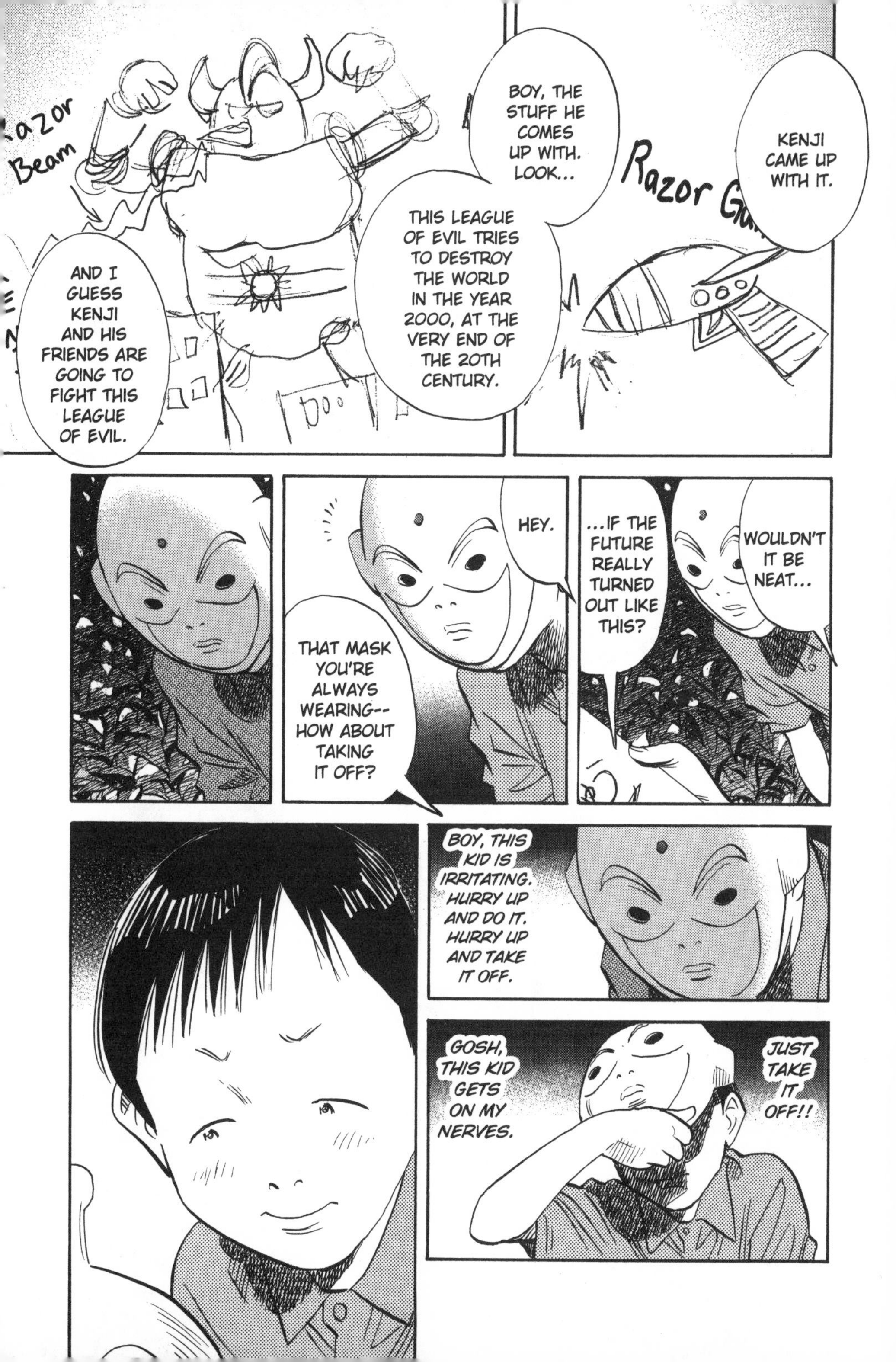
KENJI CAME UP WITH IT.
Razor Gu
BOY, THE STUFF HE COMES UP WITH. LOOK...
THIS LEAGUE OF EVIL TRIES TO DESTROY THE WORLD IN THE YEAR 2000, AT THE VERY END OF THE 20TH CENTURY.
azor Beam
AND I GUESS KENJI AND HIS FRIENDS ARE GOING TO FIGHT THIS LEAGUE OF EVIL.
WOULDN'T IT BE NEAT...
...IF THE FUTURE REALLY TURNED OUT LIKE THIS?
HEY.
THAT MASK YOU'RE ALWAYS WEARING-- HOW ABOUT TAKING IT OFF?
BOY, THIS KID IS IRRITATING. HURRY UP AND DO IT. HURRY UP AND TAKE IT OFF.
JUST TAKE IT OFF!!
GOSH, THIS KID GETS ON MY NERVES.

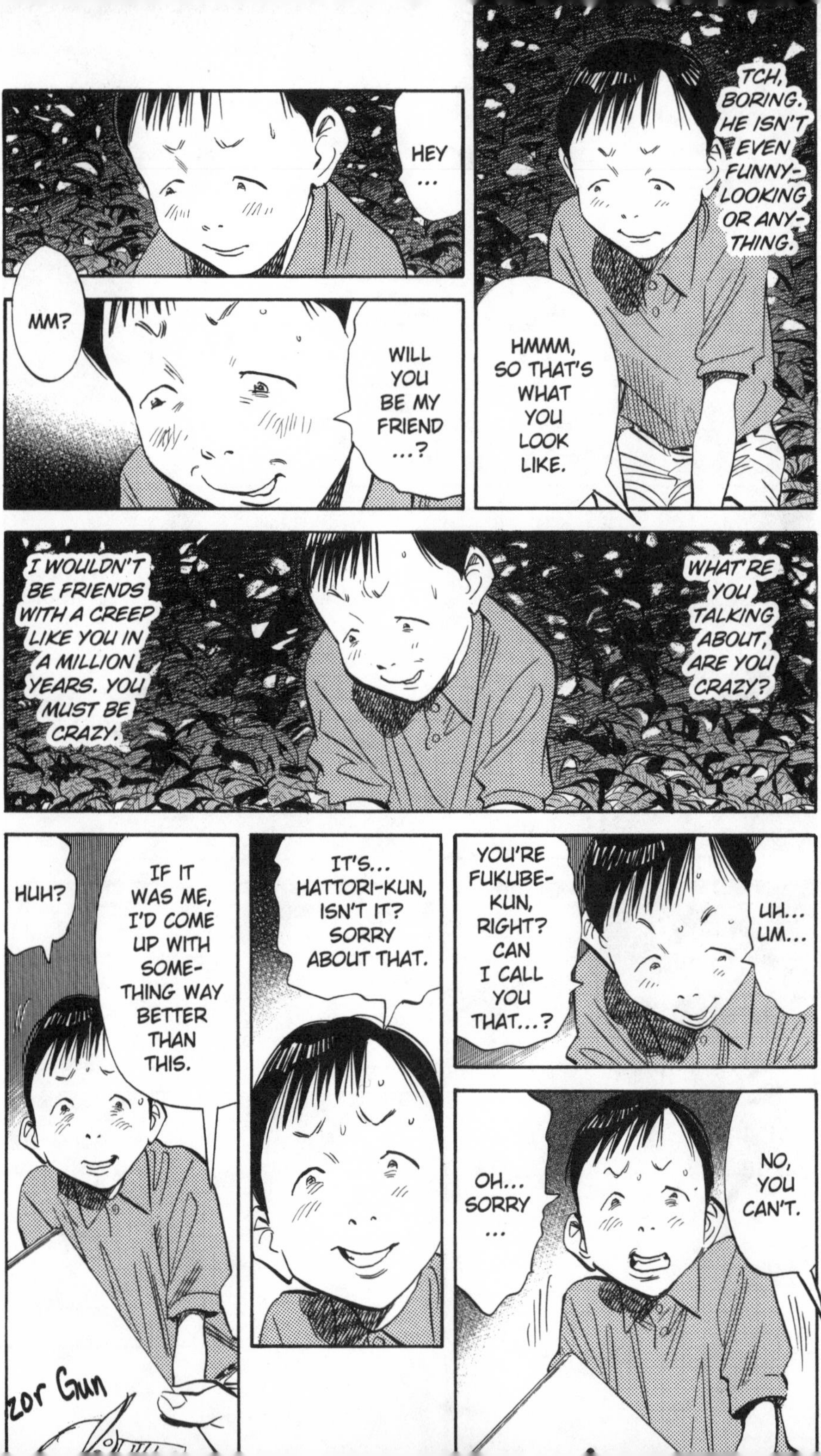
TCH, BORING. HE ISN'T EVEN FUNNY-LOOKING OR ANYTHING.
HMMM, SO THAT'S WHAT YOU LOOK LIKE.
HEY...
WILL YOU BE MY FRIEND...?
MM?
WHAT'RE YOU TALKING ABOUT, ARE YOU CRAZY?
I WOULDN'T BE FRIENDS WITH A CREEP LIKE YOU IN A MILLION YEARS. YOU MUST BE CRAZY.
UH... UM...
YOU'RE FUKUBE-KUN, RIGHT? CAN I CALL YOU THAT...?
NO, YOU CAN'T.
OH... SORRY...
IT'S... HATTORI-KUN, ISN'T IT? SORRY ABOUT THAT.
IF IT WAS ME, I'D COME UP WITH SOME-THING WAY BETTER THAN THIS.
HUH?
zor Gun

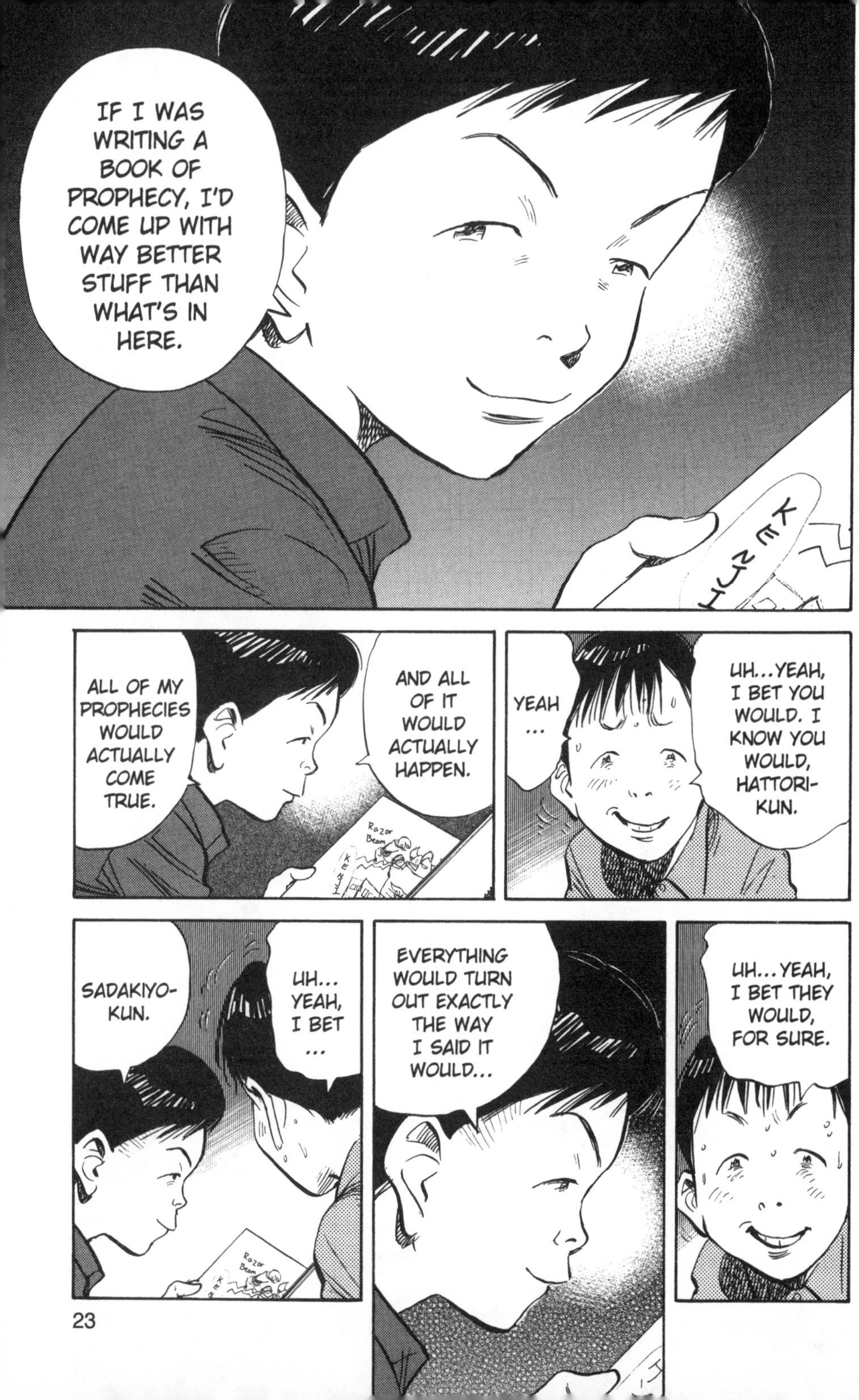
IF I WAS WRITING A BOOK OF PROPHECY, I'D COME UP WITH WAY BETTER STUFF THAN WHAT'S IN HERE.
KENJI
UH...YEAH, I BET YOU WOULD. I KNOW YOU WOULD, HATTORI-KUN.
YEAH ...
AND ALL OF IT WOULD ACTUALLY HAPPEN.
ALL OF MY PROPHECIES WOULD ACTUALLY COME TRUE.
UH...YEAH, I BET THEY WOULD, FOR SURE.
EVERYTHING WOULD TURN OUT EXACTLY THE WAY I SAID IT WOULD...
UH... YEAH, I BET ...
SADAKIYO-KUN.

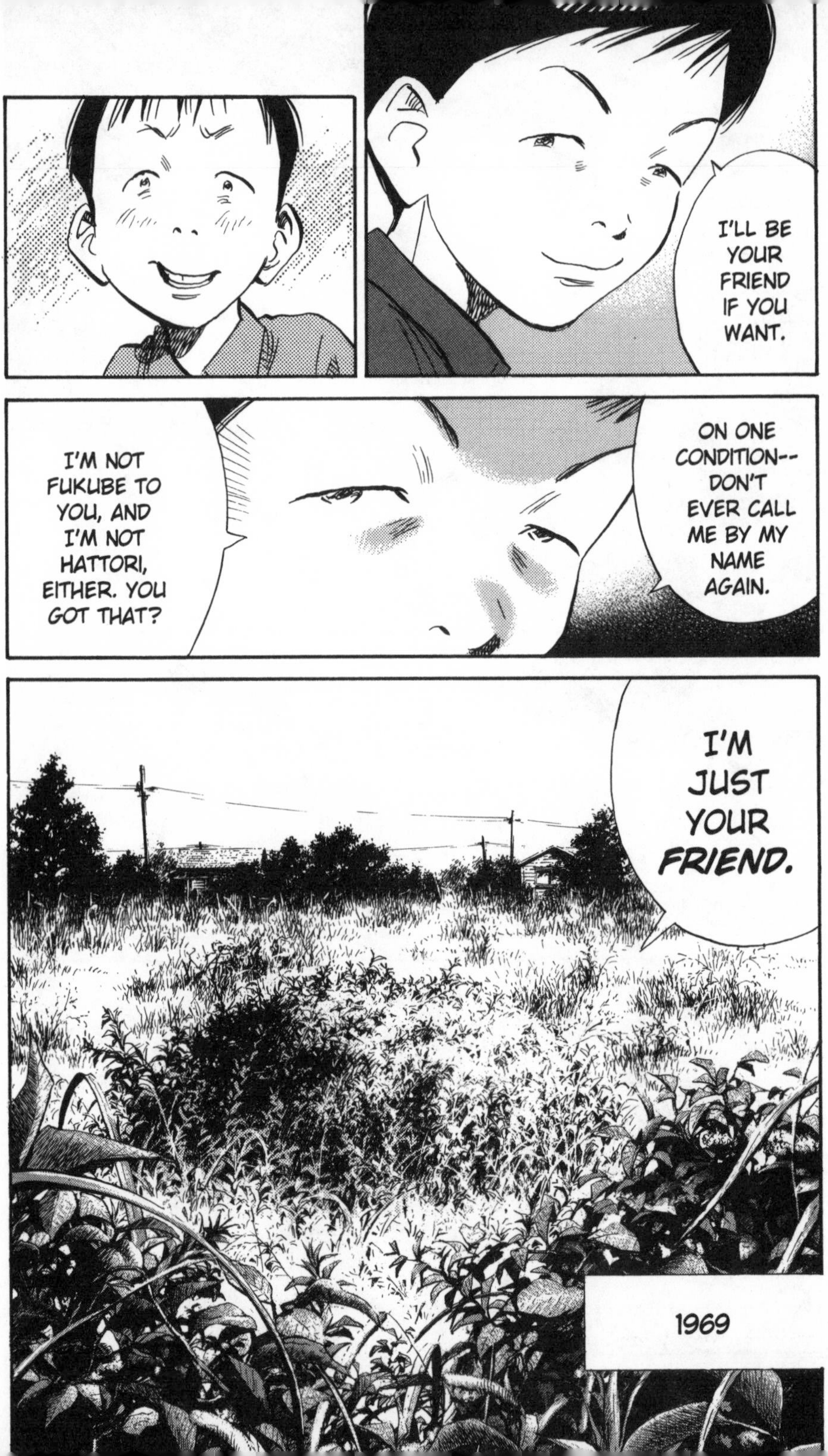
I'LL BE YOUR FRIEND IF YOU WANT.
ON ONE CONDITION--DON'T EVER CALL ME BY MY NAME AGAIN.
I'M NOT FUKUBE TO YOU, AND I'M NOT HATTORI, EITHER. YOU GOT THAT?
I'M JUST YOUR *FRIEND.*
1969

Chapter 2 A Real Friend

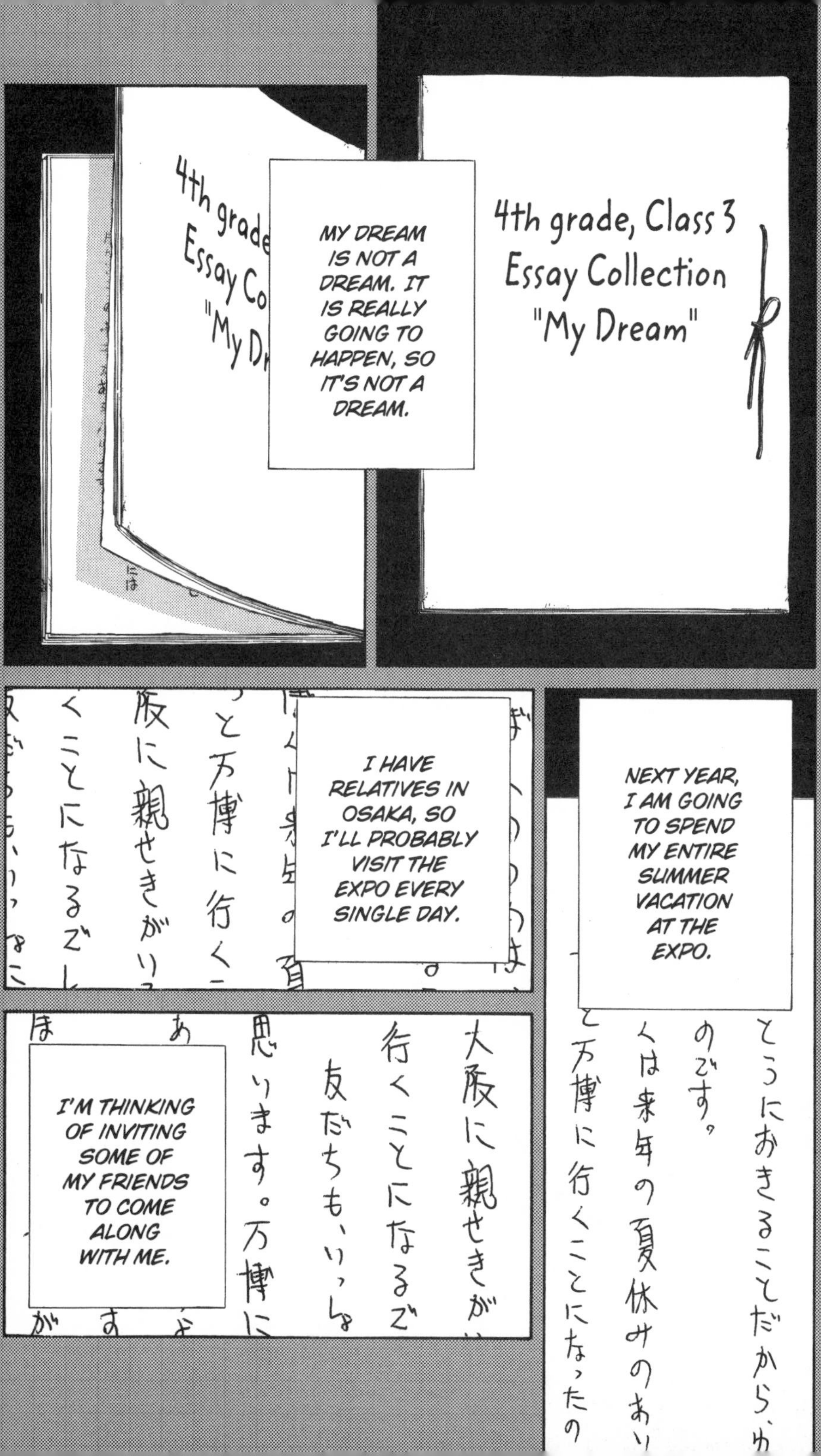
4th grade, Class 3
Essay Collection
"My Dream"
MY DREAM IS NOT A DREAM. IT IS REALLY GOING TO HAPPEN, SO IT'S NOT A DREAM.
NEXT YEAR, I AM GOING TO SPEND MY ENTIRE SUMMER VACATION AT THE EXPO.
I HAVE RELATIVES IN OSAKA, SO I'LL PROBABLY VISIT THE EXPO EVERY SINGLE DAY.
I'M THINKING OF INVITING SOME OF MY FRIENDS TO COME ALONG WITH ME.

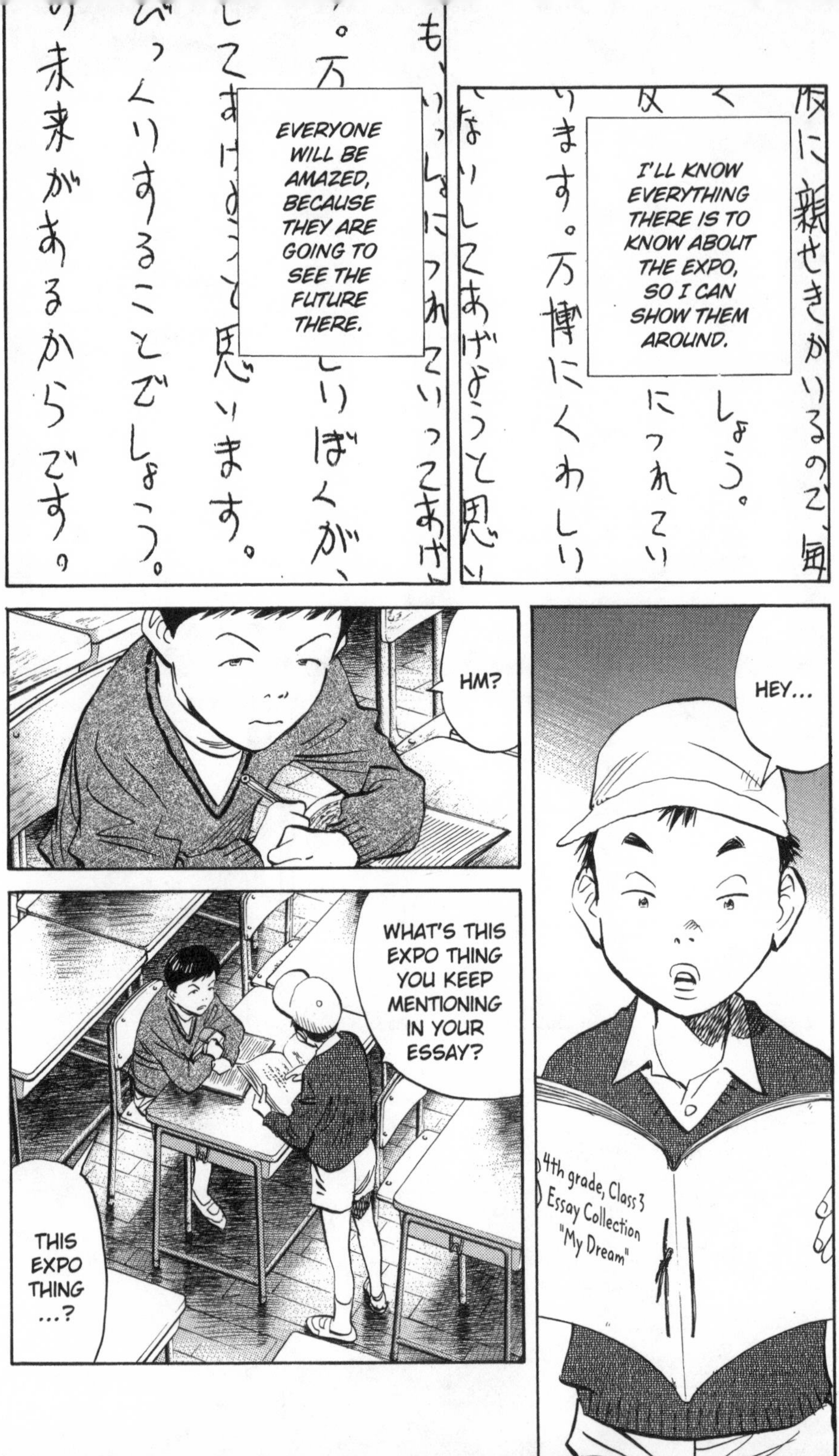
I'LL KNOW EVERYTHING THERE IS TO KNOW ABOUT THE EXPO, SO I CAN SHOW THEM AROUND.
EVERYONE WILL BE AMAZED, BECAUSE THEY ARE GOING TO SEE THE FUTURE THERE.
HEY...
4th grade, Class 3 Essay Collection "My Dream"
HM?
WHAT'S THIS EXPO THING YOU KEEP MENTIONING IN YOUR ESSAY?
THIS EXPO THING ...?

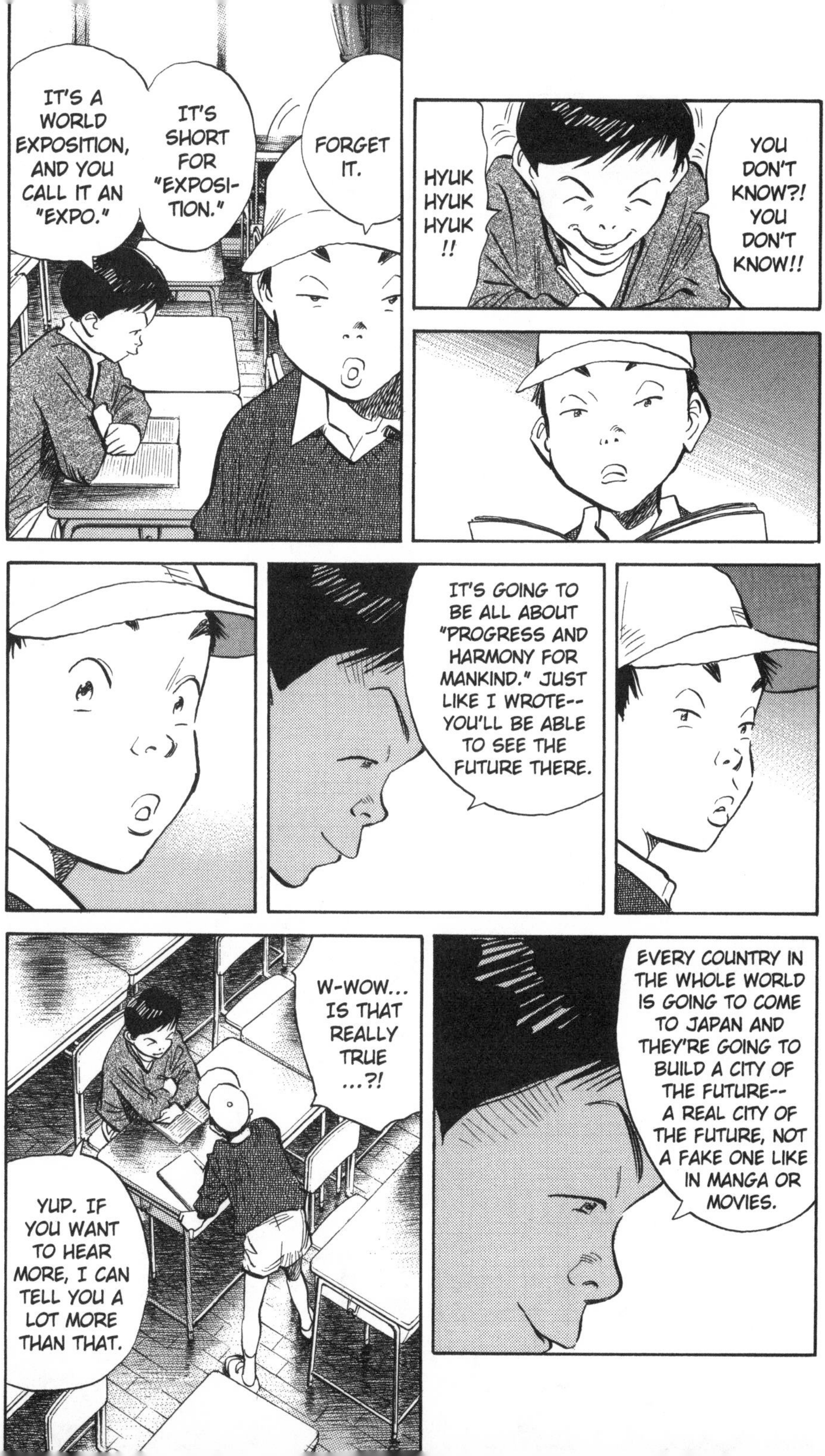

YOU DON'T KNOW?! YOU DON'T KNOW!!
HYUK HYUK HYUK !!
FORGET IT.
IT'S SHORT FOR "EXPOSITION."
IT'S A WORLD EXPOSITION, AND YOU CALL IT AN "EXPO."
IT'S GOING TO BE ALL ABOUT "PROGRESS AND HARMONY FOR MANKIND." JUST LIKE I WROTE-- YOU'LL BE ABLE TO SEE THE FUTURE THERE.
EVERY COUNTRY IN THE WHOLE WORLD IS GOING TO COME TO JAPAN AND THEY'RE GOING TO BUILD A CITY OF THE FUTURE-- A REAL CITY OF THE FUTURE, NOT A FAKE ONE LIKE IN MANGA OR MOVIES.
W-WOW... IS THAT REALLY TRUE ...?!
YUP. IF YOU WANT TO HEAR MORE, I CAN TELL YOU A LOT MORE THAN THAT.

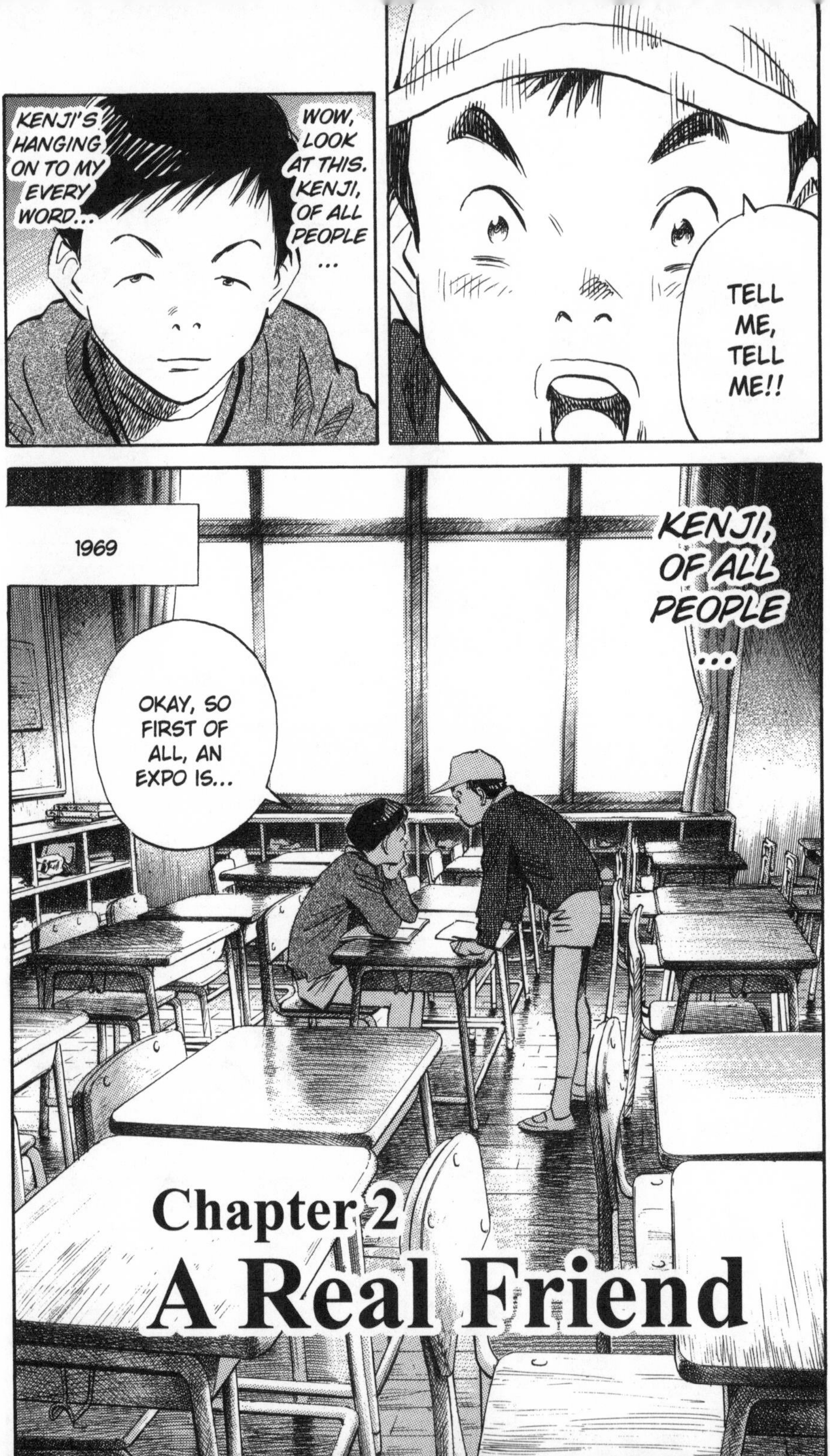
TELL ME, TELL ME!!
WOW, LOOK AT THIS. KENJI, OF ALL PEOPLE...
KENJI'S HANGING ON TO MY EVERY WORD...
1969
KENJI, OF ALL PEOPLE...
OKAY, SO FIRST OF ALL, AN EXPO IS...
Chapter 2
A Real Friend

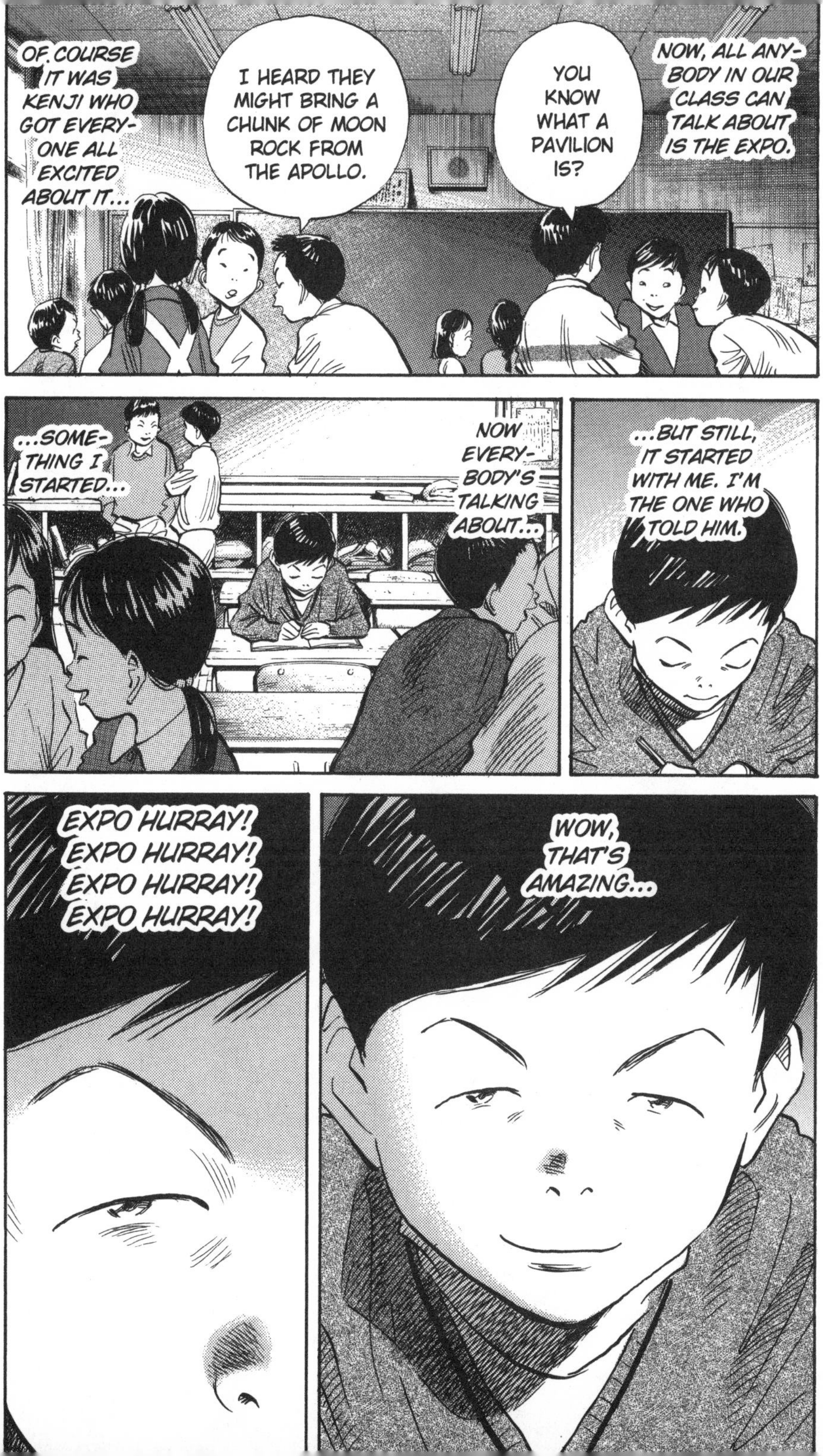
OF COURSE IT WAS KENJI WHO GOT EVERYONE ALL EXCITED ABOUT IT...
I HEARD THEY MIGHT BRING A CHUNK OF MOON ROCK FROM THE APOLLO.
YOU KNOW WHAT A PAVILION IS?
NOW, ALL ANYBODY IN OUR CLASS CAN TALK ABOUT IS THE EXPO.
NOW EVERYBODY'S TALKING ABOUT...
...SOMETHING I STARTED...
...BUT STILL, IT STARTED WITH ME. I'M THE ONE WHO TOLD HIM.
EXPO HURRAY! EXPO HURRAY! EXPO HURRAY! EXPO HURRAY!
WOW, THAT'S AMAZING...

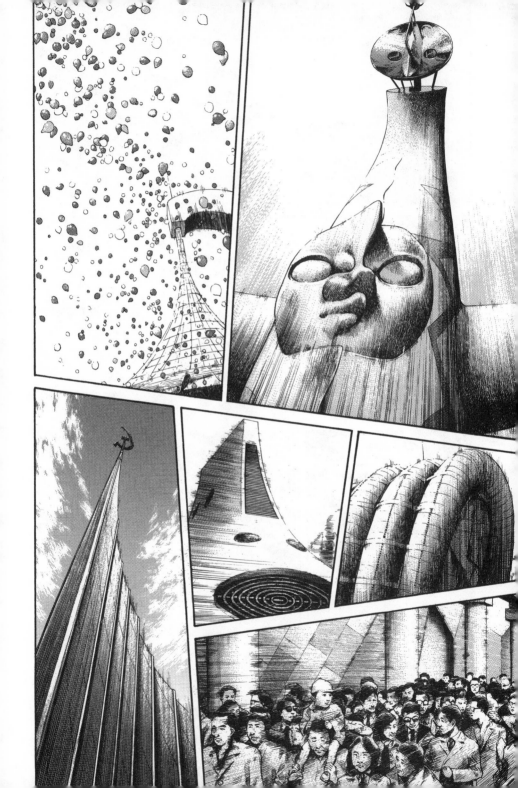

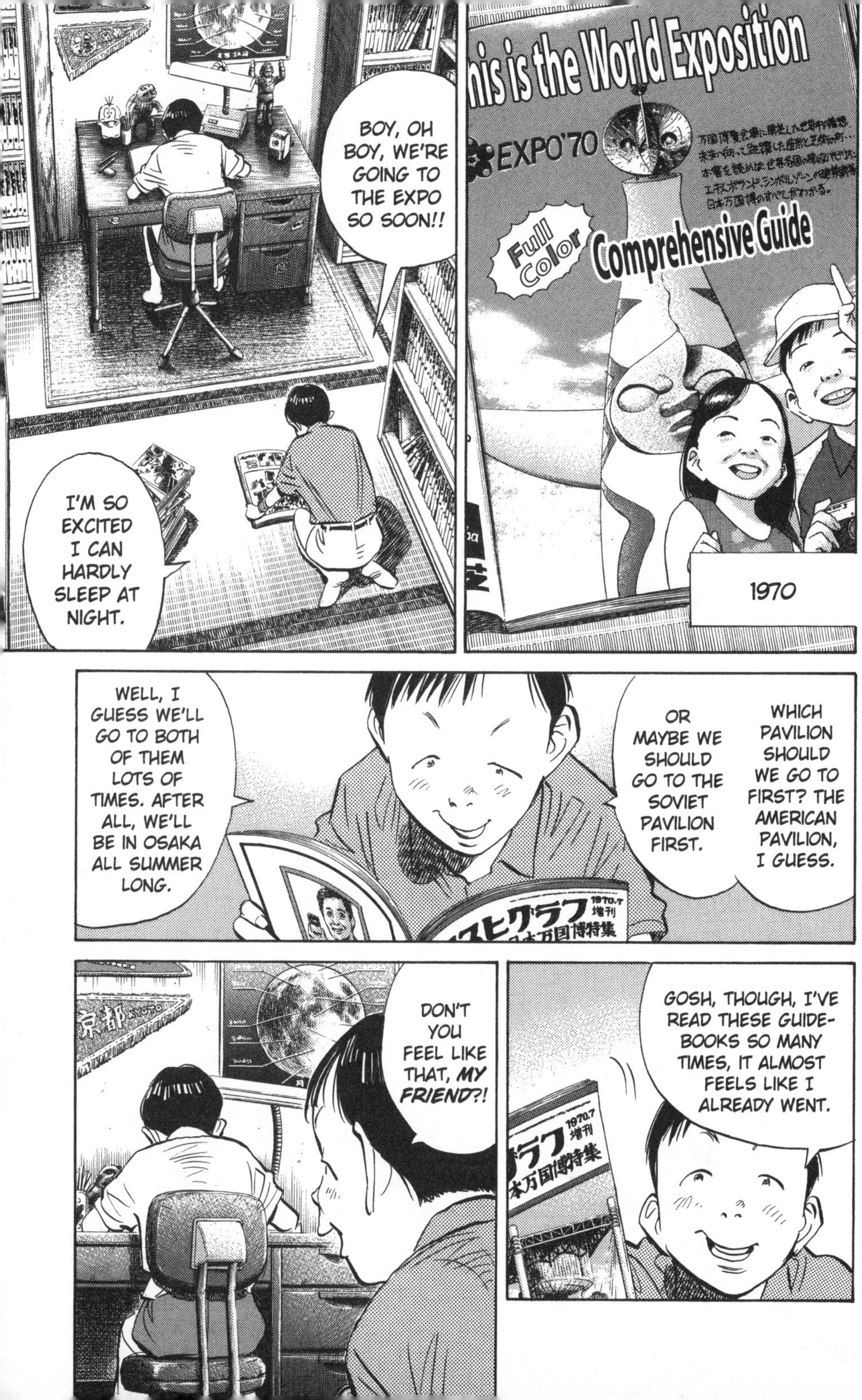

his is the World Exposition
EXPO'70
Full Color
Comprehensive Guide
1970
BOY, OH BOY, WE'RE GOING TO THE EXPO SO SOON!!
I'M SO EXCITED I CAN HARDLY SLEEP AT NIGHT.
WHICH PAVILION SHOULD WE GO TO FIRST? THE AMERICAN PAVILION, I GUESS.
OR MAYBE WE SHOULD GO TO THE SOVIET PAVILION FIRST.
WELL, I GUESS WE'LL GO TO BOTH OF THEM LOTS OF TIMES. AFTER ALL, WE'LL BE IN OSAKA ALL SUMMER LONG.
1970.7 増刊
GOSH, THOUGH, I'VE READ THESE GUIDE-BOOKS SO MANY TIMES, IT ALMOST FEELS LIKE I ALREADY WENT.
京都 KYOTO
DON'T YOU FEEL LIKE THAT, *MY FRIEND*?!

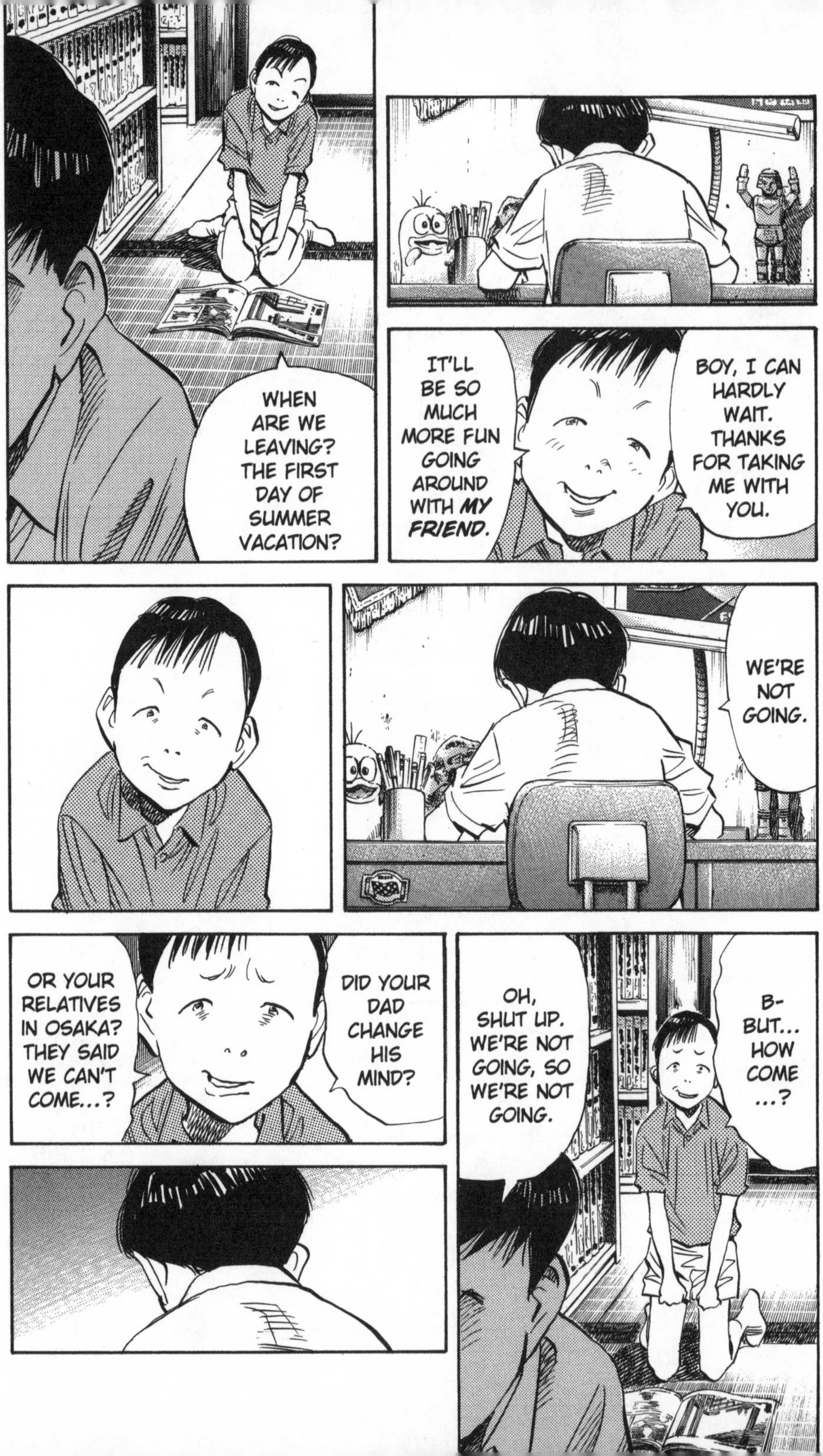
BOY, I CAN HARDLY WAIT. THANKS FOR TAKING ME WITH YOU.
IT'LL BE SO MUCH MORE FUN GOING AROUND WITH *MY FRIEND*.
WHEN ARE WE LEAVING? THE FIRST DAY OF SUMMER VACATION?
WE'RE NOT GOING.
B-BUT... HOW COME...?
OH, SHUT UP. WE'RE NOT GOING, SO WE'RE NOT GOING.
DID YOUR DAD CHANGE HIS MIND?
OR YOUR RELATIVES IN OSAKA? THEY SAID WE CAN'T COME...?

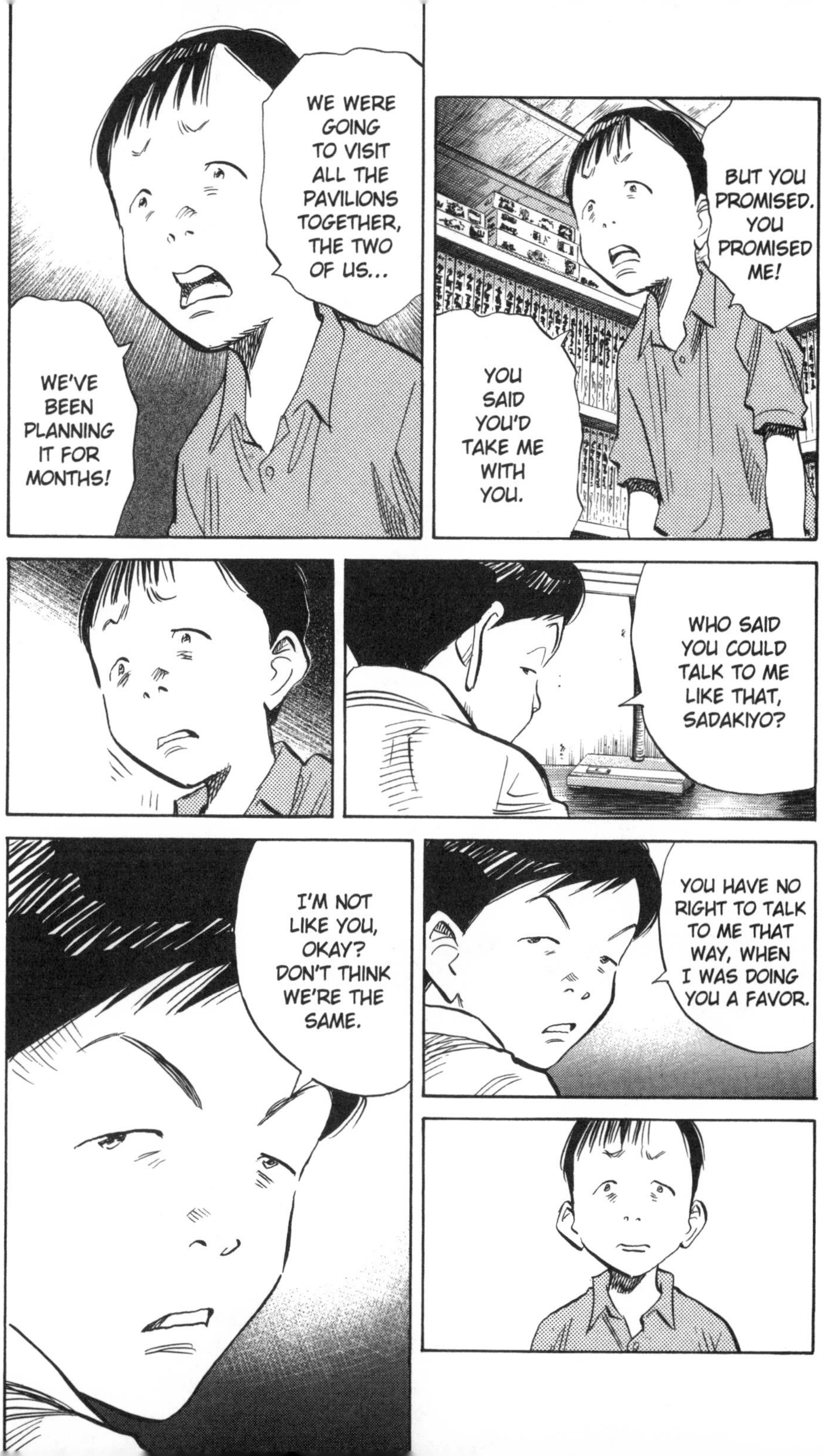
BUT YOU PROMISED. YOU PROMISED ME!
YOU SAID YOU'D TAKE ME WITH YOU.
WE WERE GOING TO VISIT ALL THE PAVILIONS TOGETHER, THE TWO OF US...
WE'VE BEEN PLANNING IT FOR MONTHS!
WHO SAID YOU COULD TALK TO ME LIKE THAT, SADAKIYO?
YOU HAVE NO RIGHT TO TALK TO ME THAT WAY, WHEN I WAS DOING YOU A FAVOR.
I'M NOT LIKE YOU, OKAY? DON'T THINK WE'RE THE SAME.

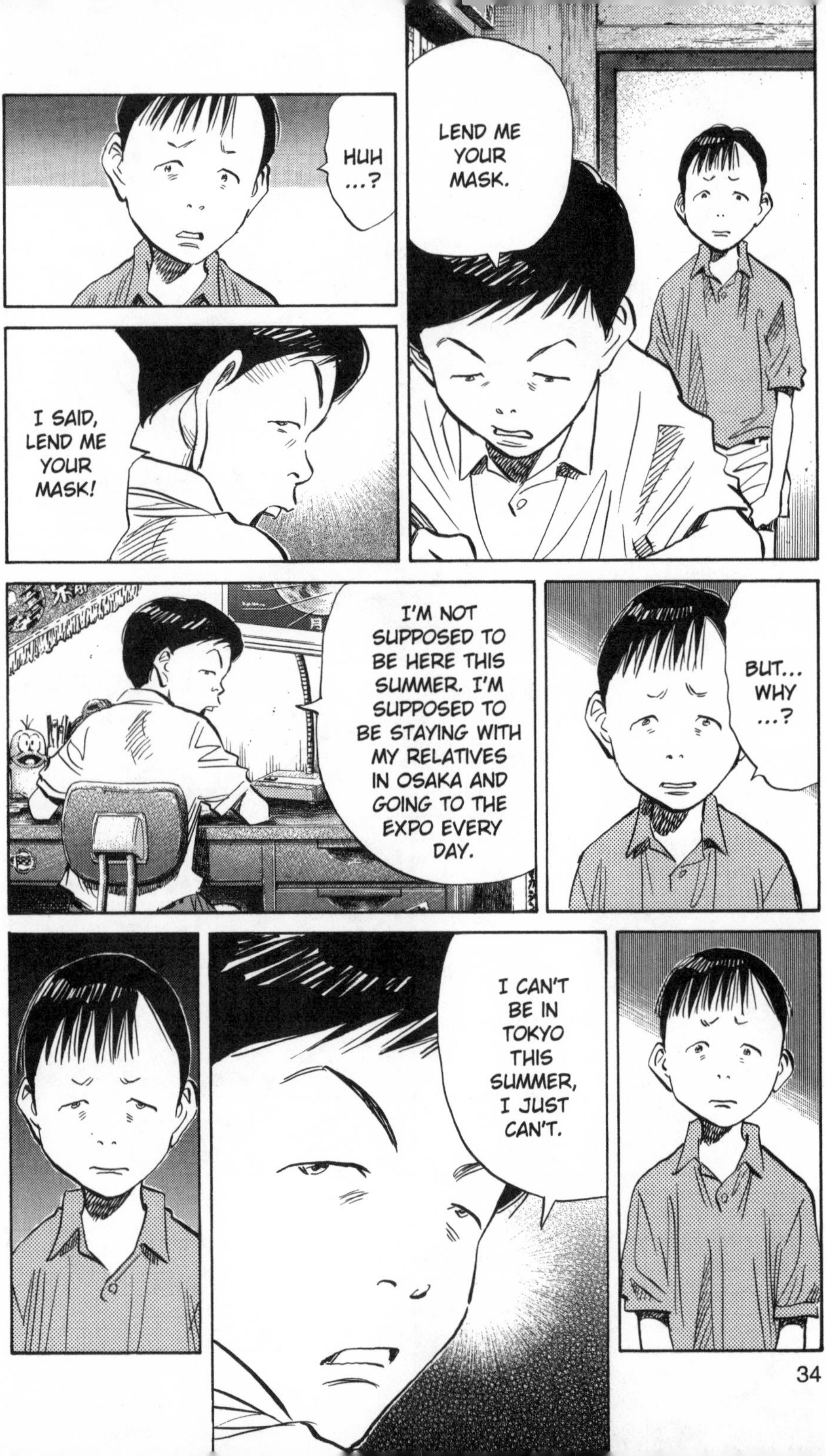

LEND ME YOUR MASK.
HUH ...?
I SAID, LEND ME YOUR MASK!
BUT... WHY ...?
I'M NOT SUPPOSED TO BE HERE THIS SUMMER. I'M SUPPOSED TO BE STAYING WITH MY RELATIVES IN OSAKA AND GOING TO THE EXPO EVERY DAY.
I CAN'T BE IN TOKYO THIS SUMMER, I JUST CAN'T.

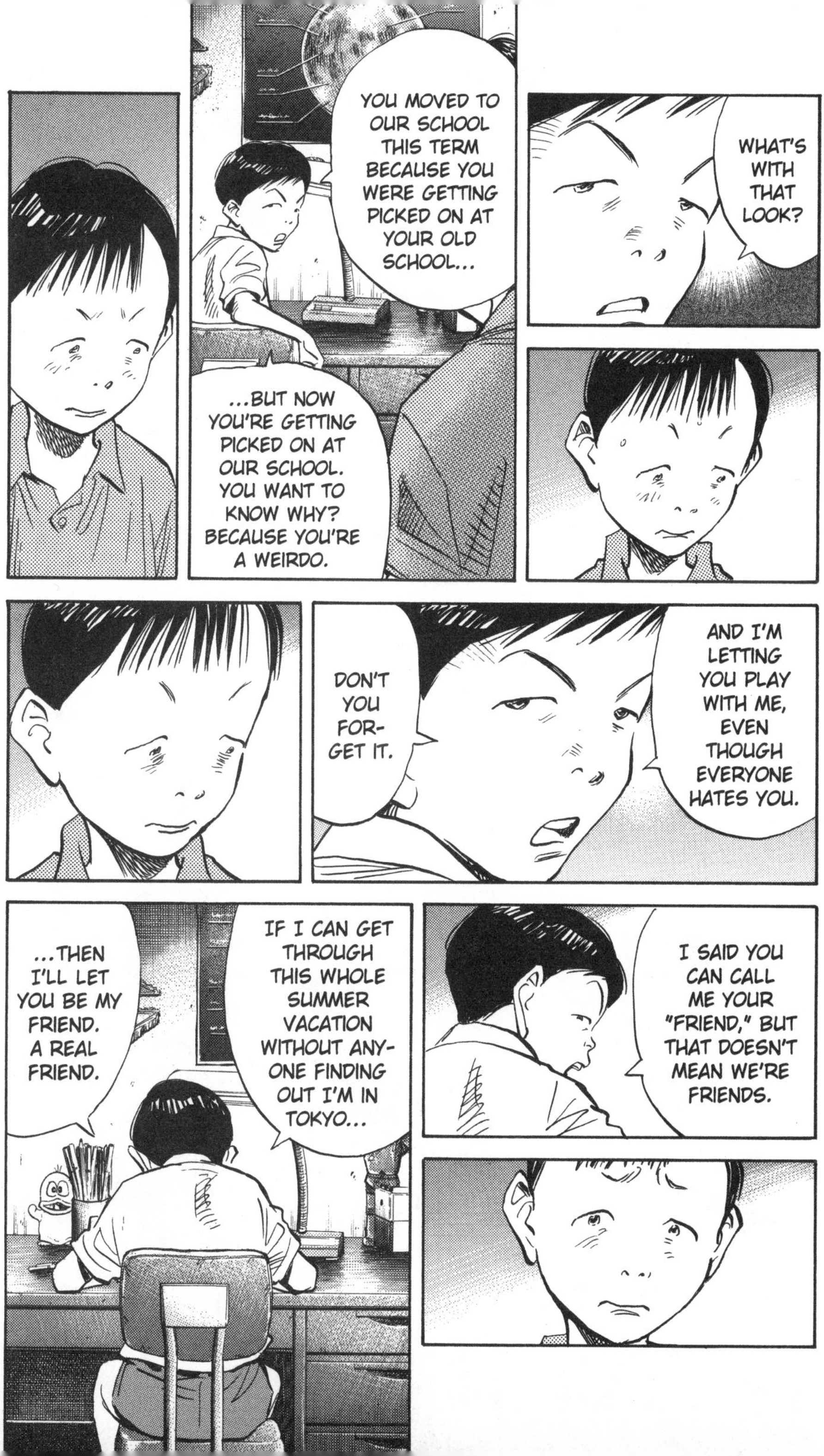
WHAT'S WITH THAT LOOK?
YOU MOVED TO OUR SCHOOL THIS TERM BECAUSE YOU WERE GETTING PICKED ON AT YOUR OLD SCHOOL...
...BUT NOW YOU'RE GETTING PICKED ON AT OUR SCHOOL. YOU WANT TO KNOW WHY? BECAUSE YOU'RE A WEIRDO.
AND I'M LETTING YOU PLAY WITH ME, EVEN THOUGH EVERYONE HATES YOU.
DON'T YOU FOR-GET IT.
I SAID YOU CAN CALL ME YOUR "FRIEND," BUT THAT DOESN'T MEAN WE'RE FRIENDS.
IF I CAN GET THROUGH THIS WHOLE SUMMER VACATION WITHOUT ANY-ONE FINDING OUT I'M IN TOKYO...
...THEN I'LL LET YOU BE MY FRIEND. A REAL FRIEND.

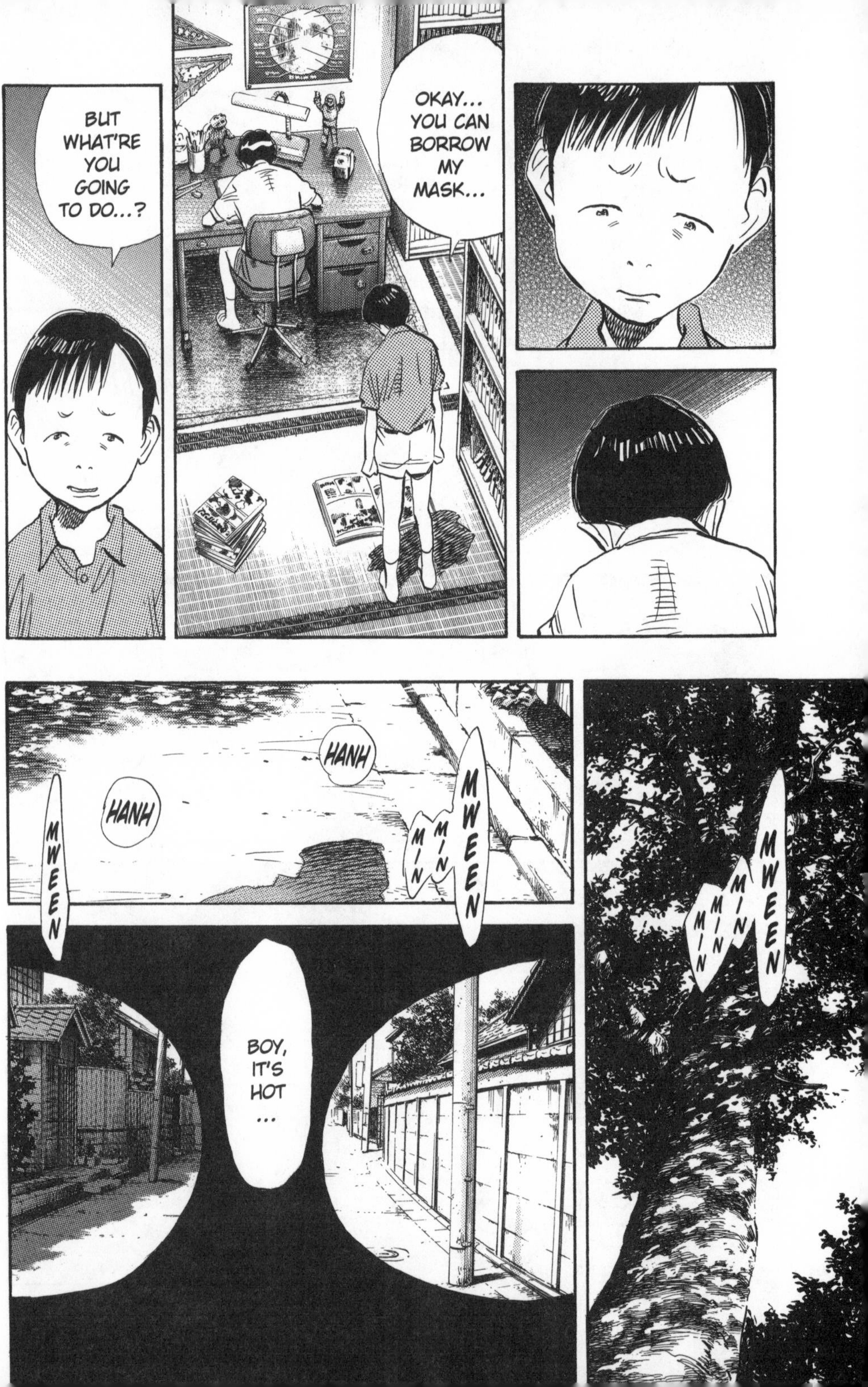
OKAY... YOU CAN BORROW MY MASK...
BUT WHAT'RE YOU GOING TO DO...?
MWEEN
MIN MIN MIN
HANH
MWEEN
MIN MIN
HANH
MWEEN
BOY, IT'S HOT ...

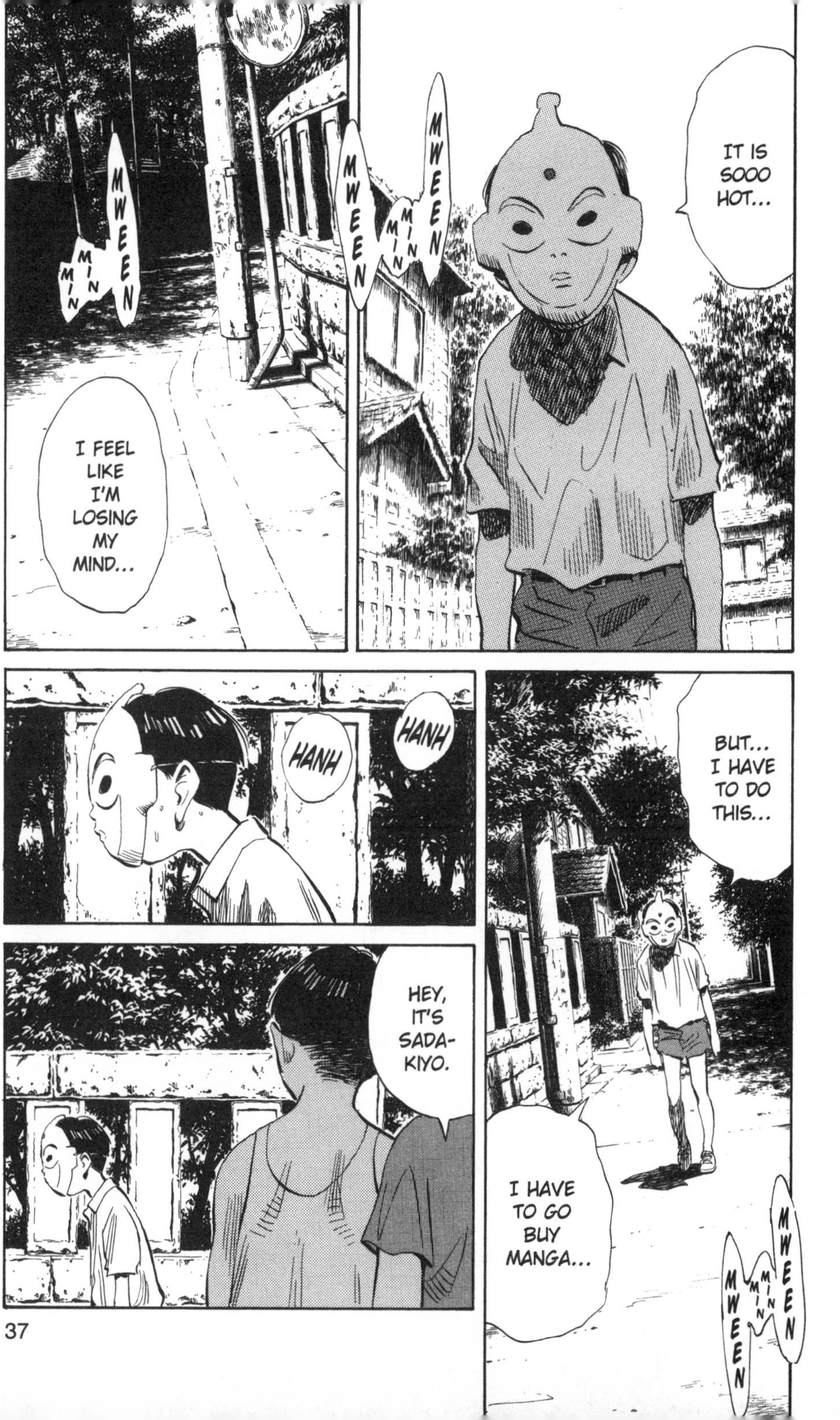
IT IS SOOO HOT...
MWEEN
MIN MIN
MWEEN
MWEEN
MIN MIN
I FEEL LIKE I'M LOSING MY MIND...
BUT... I HAVE TO DO THIS...
I HAVE TO GO BUY MANGA...
MWEEN
MIN MIN
MWEEN
HANH
HANH
HEY, IT'S SADA-KIYO.

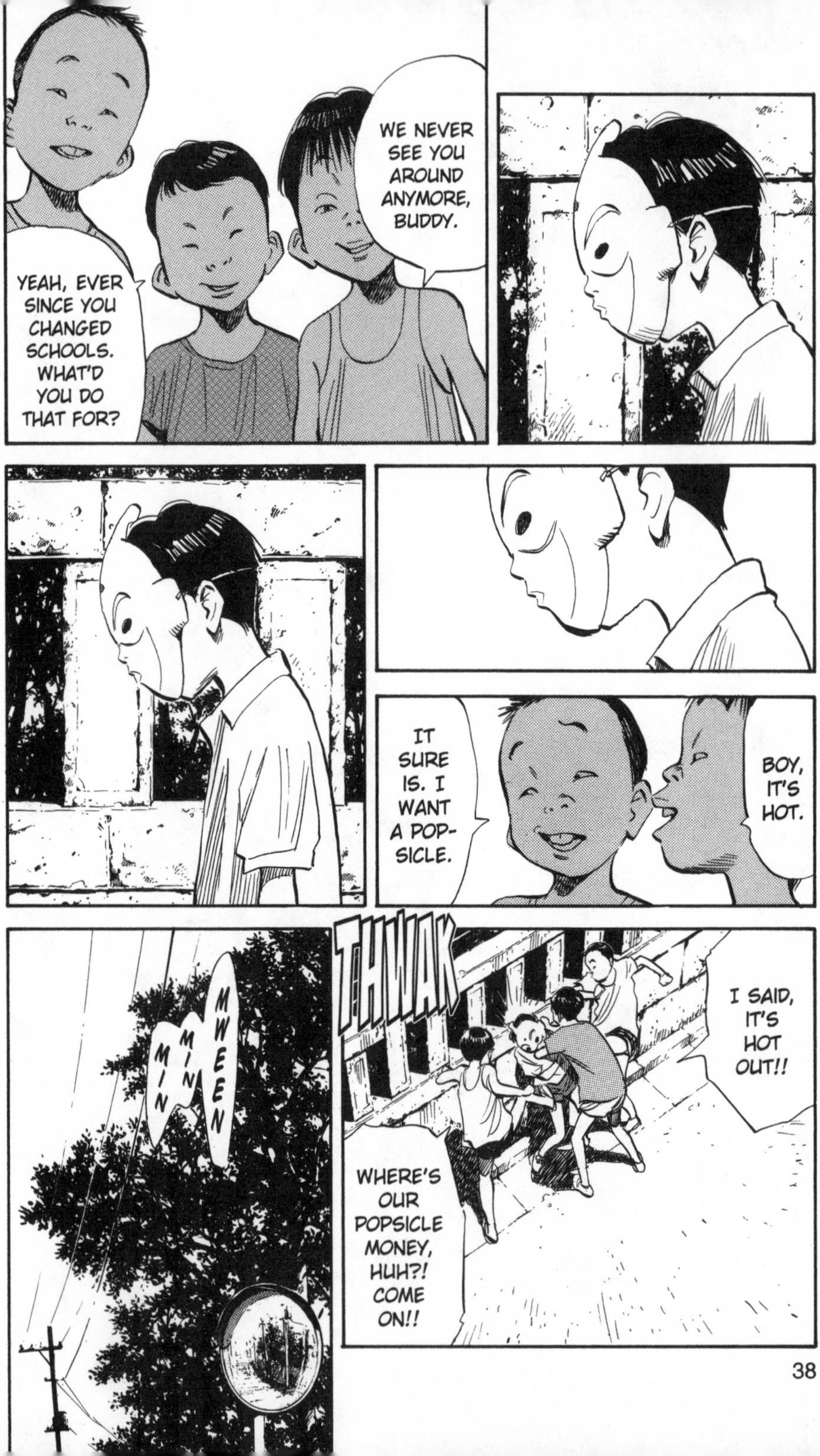

WE NEVER SEE YOU AROUND ANYMORE, BUDDY.
YEAH, EVER SINCE YOU CHANGED SCHOOLS. WHAT'D YOU DO THAT FOR?
BOY, IT'S HOT.
IT SURE IS. I WANT A POP-SICLE.
THWAK
I SAID, IT'S HOT OUT!!
WHERE'S OUR POPSICLE MONEY, HUH?! COME ON!!
MWEEN
MIN
MIN

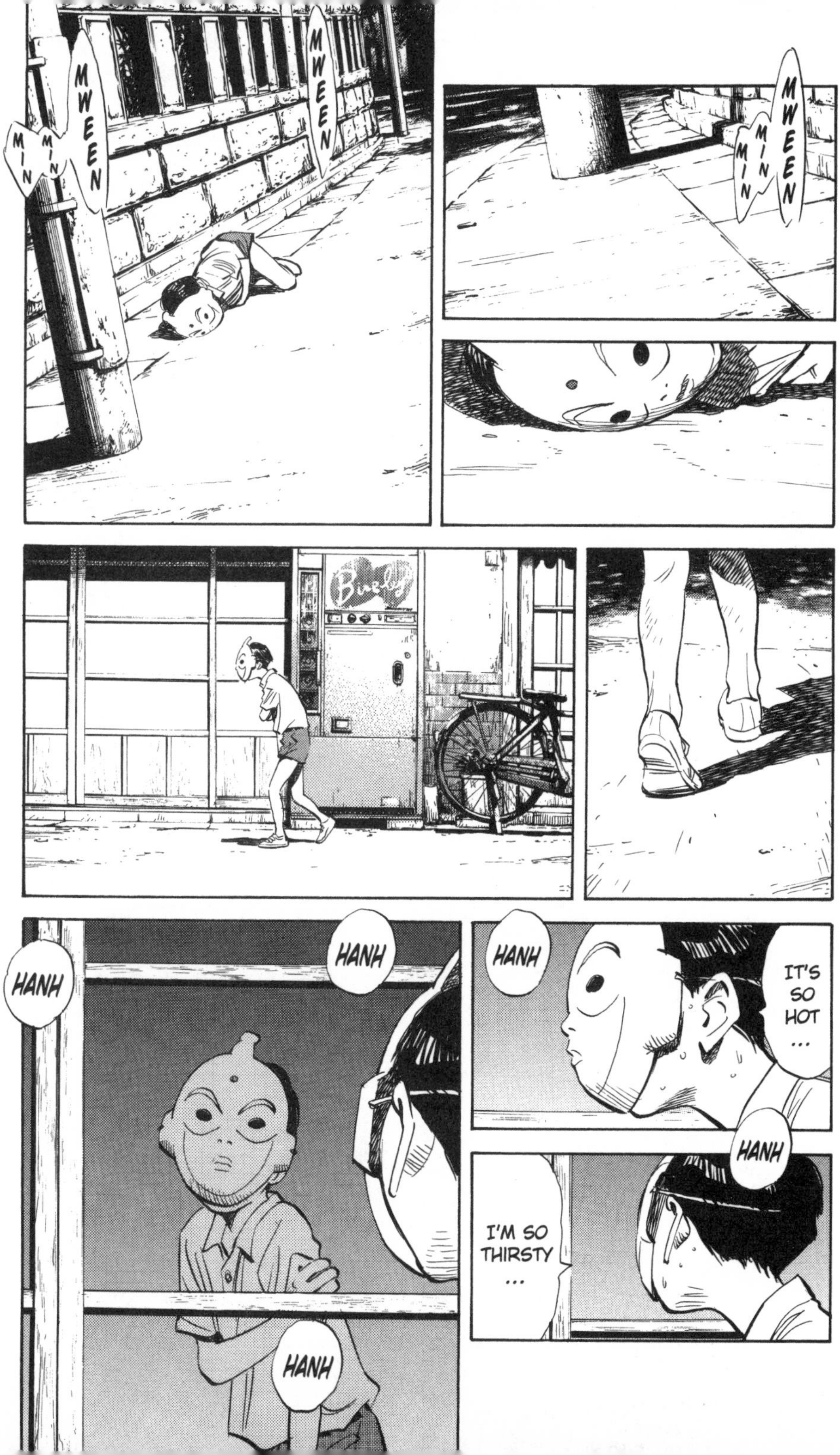
MWEEN
MIN
MIN
MWEEN
MWEEN
MIN
MIN
IT'S SO HOT ...
HANH
HANH
I'M SO THIRSTY ...
HANH
HANH
HANH

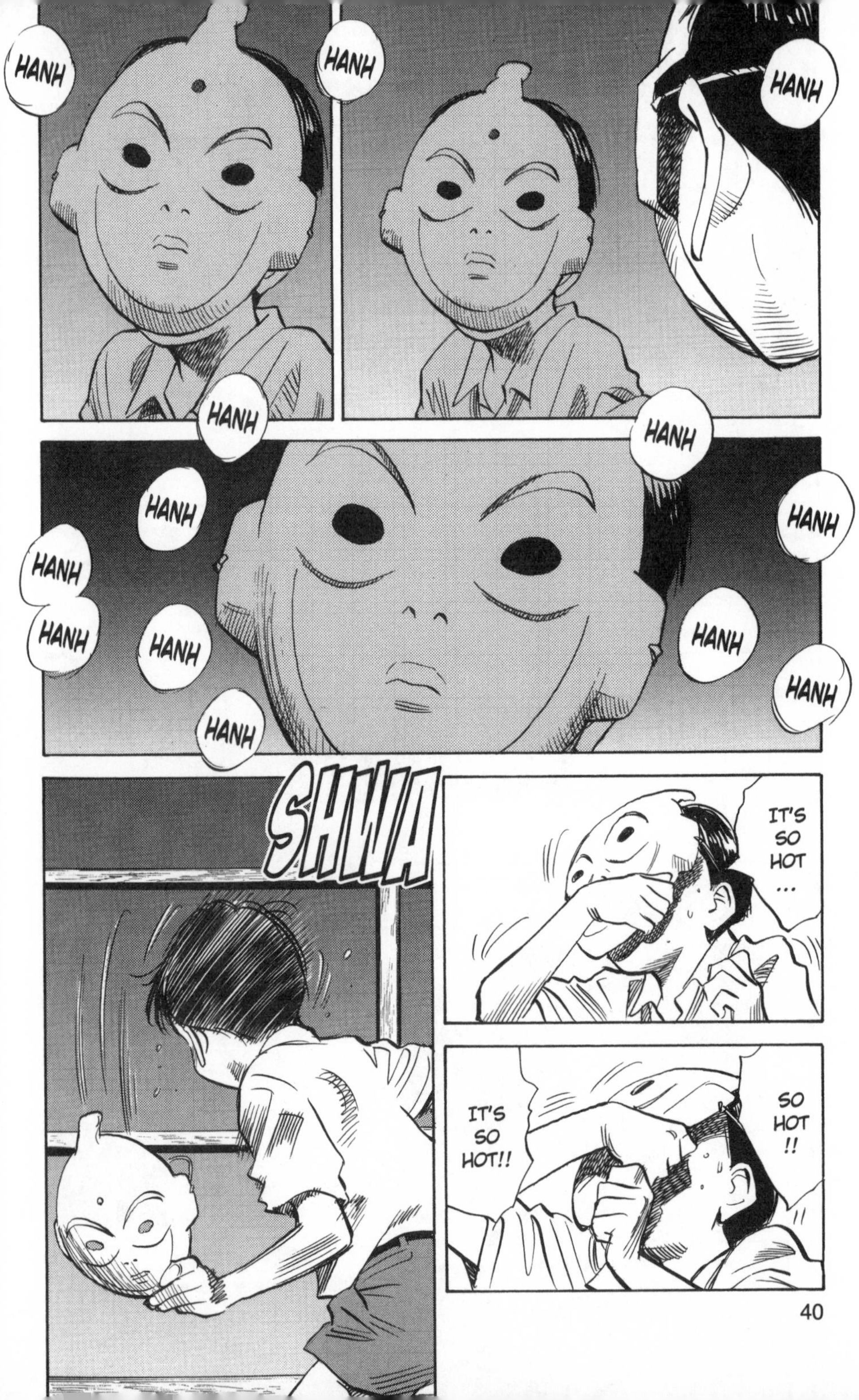

HANH
HANH
HANH
HANH
HANH
HANH
HANH
HANH
HANH
HANH
HANH
HANH
HANH
IT'S SO HOT ...
SO HOT !!
IT'S SO HOT!!
SHWA

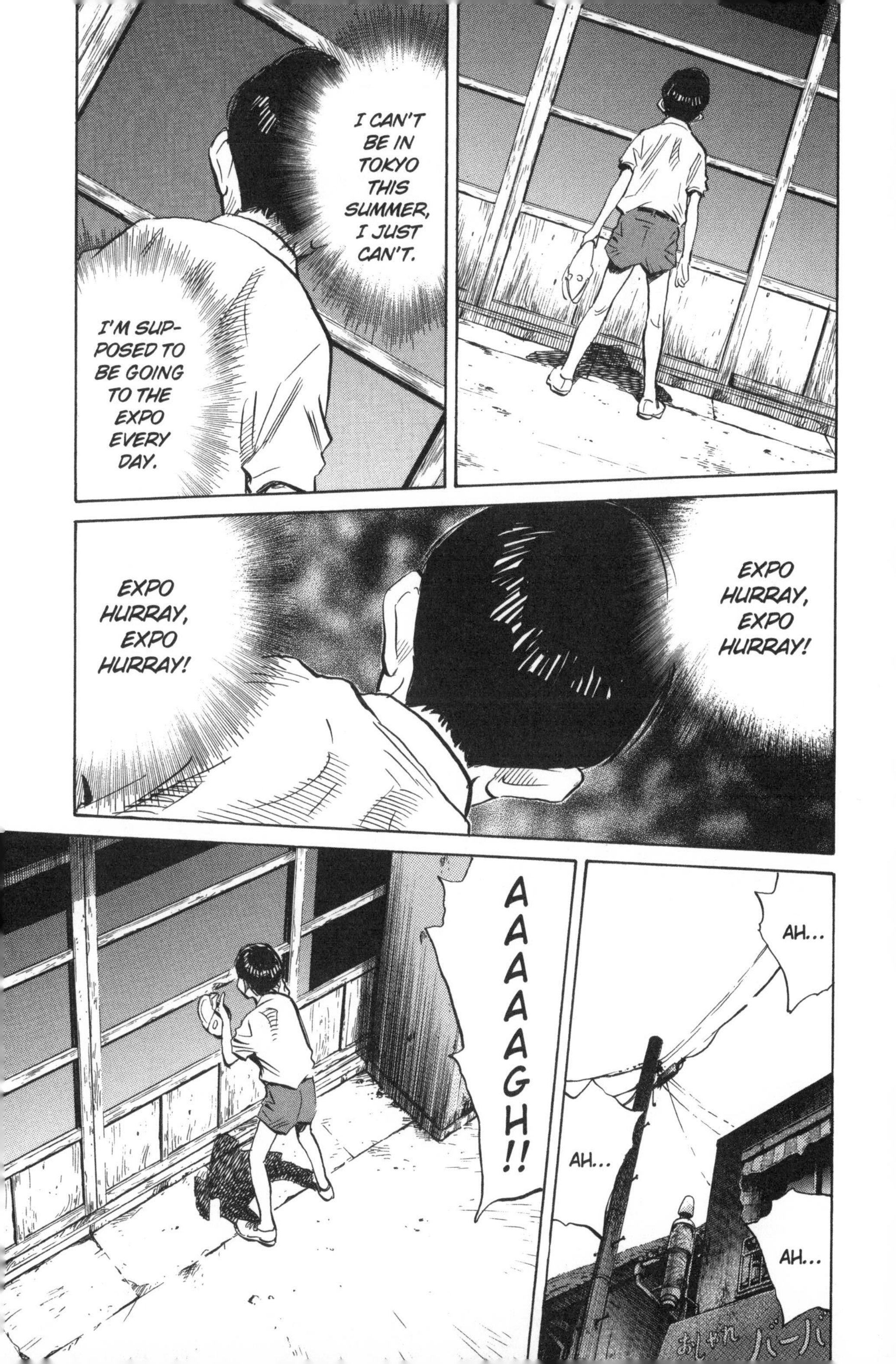
I CAN'T BE IN TOKYO THIS SUMMER, I JUST CAN'T.
I'M SUPPOSED TO BE GOING TO THE EXPO EVERY DAY.
EXPO HURRAY, EXPO HURRAY!
EXPO HURRAY, EXPO HURRAY!
AH...
AH...
AH...
AAAAAAAGH!!

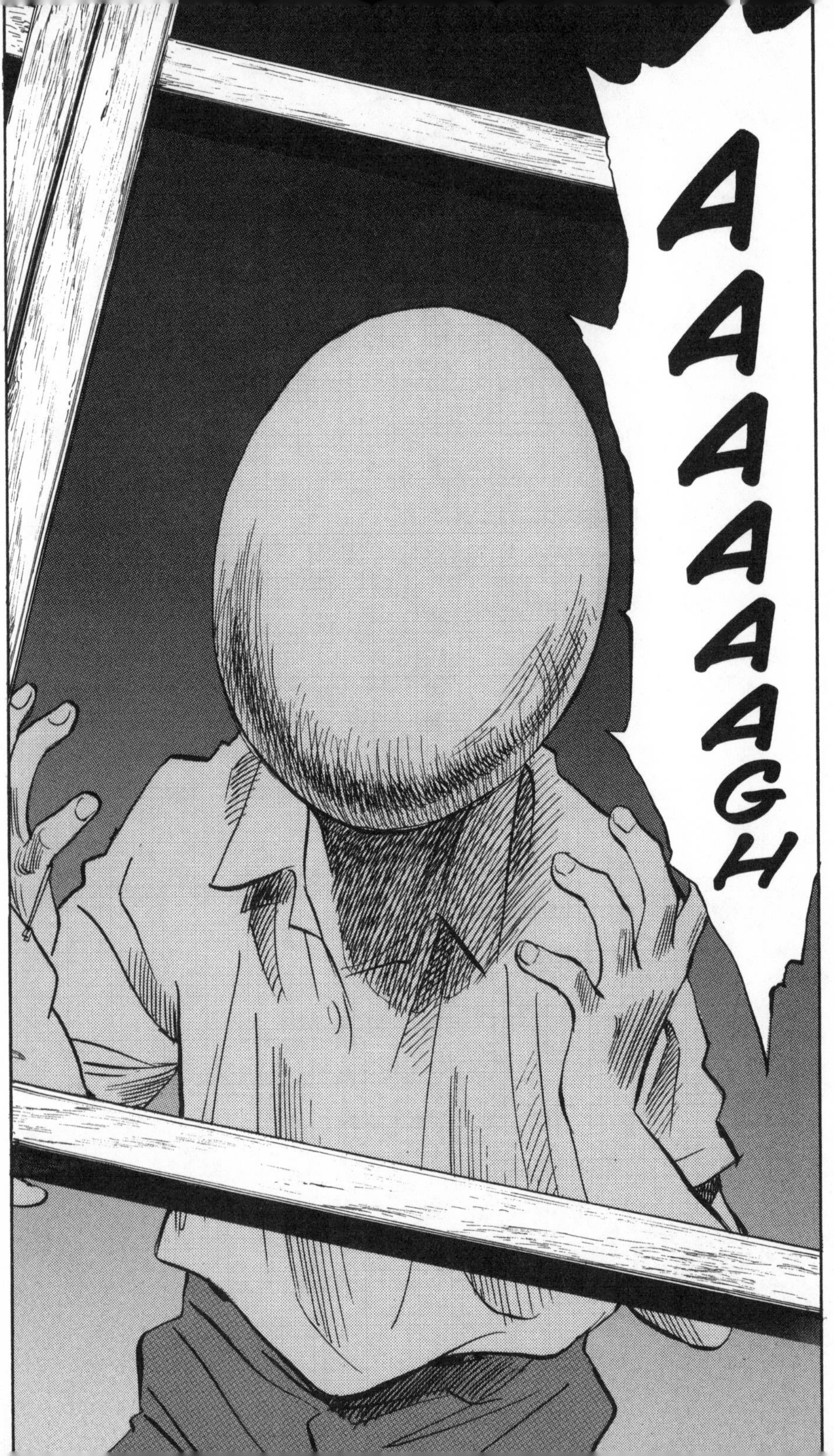
AAAAAAGH

Chapter 3 Beyond the Looking Glass

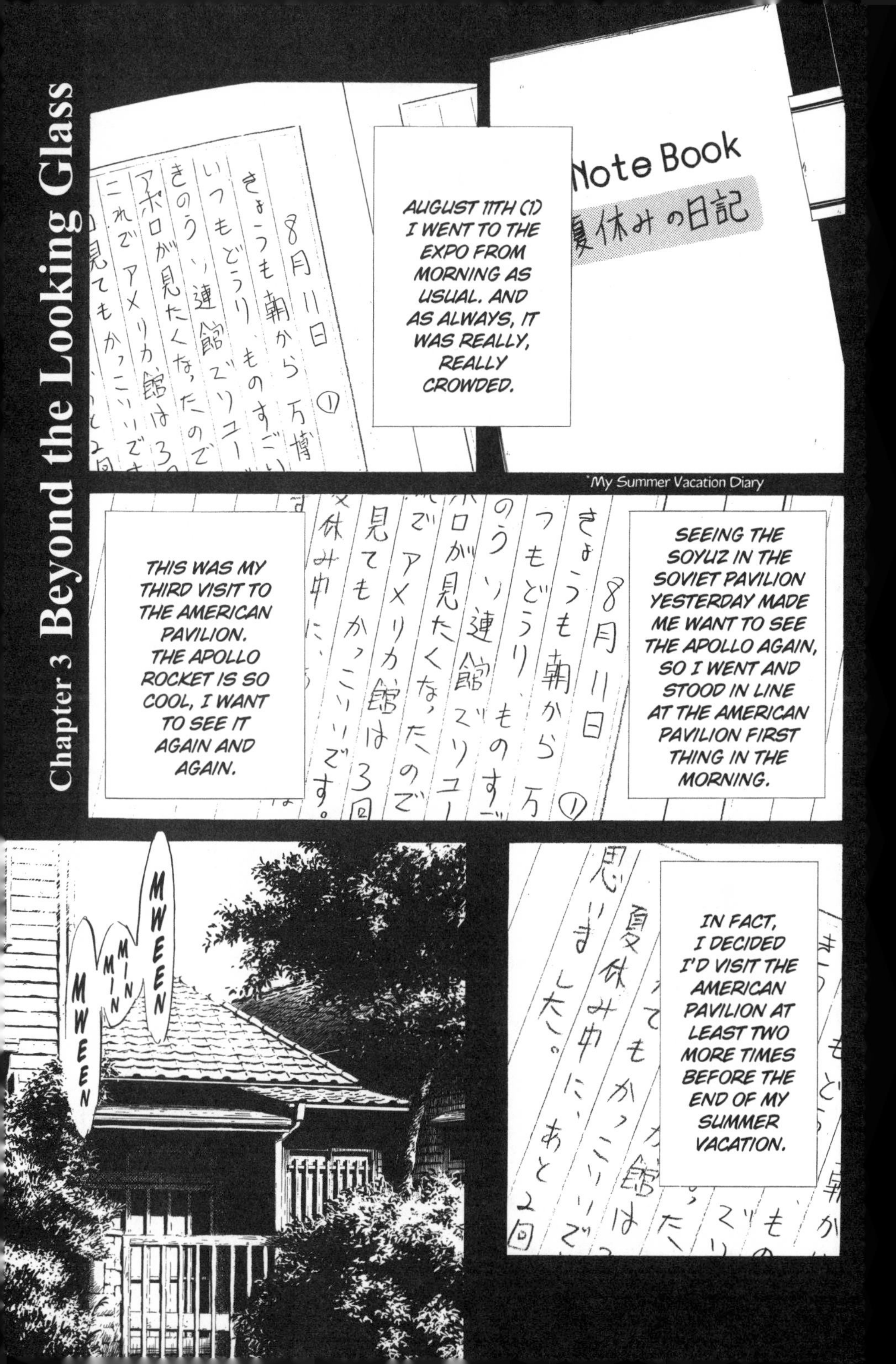
Note Book
夏休みの日記
AUGUST 11TH (1) I WENT TO THE EXPO FROM MORNING AS USUAL. AND AS ALWAYS, IT WAS REALLY, REALLY CROWDED.
*My Summer Vacation Diary
SEEING THE SOYUZ IN THE SOVIET PAVILION YESTERDAY MADE ME WANT TO SEE THE APOLLO AGAIN, SO I WENT AND STOOD IN LINE AT THE AMERICAN PAVILION FIRST THING IN THE MORNING.
THIS WAS MY THIRD VISIT TO THE AMERICAN PAVILION. THE APOLLO ROCKET IS SO COOL, I WANT TO SEE IT AGAIN AND AGAIN.
IN FACT, I DECIDED I'D VISIT THE AMERICAN PAVILION AT LEAST TWO MORE TIMES BEFORE THE END OF MY SUMMER VACATION.
MWEEN
MIN MIN
MWEEN

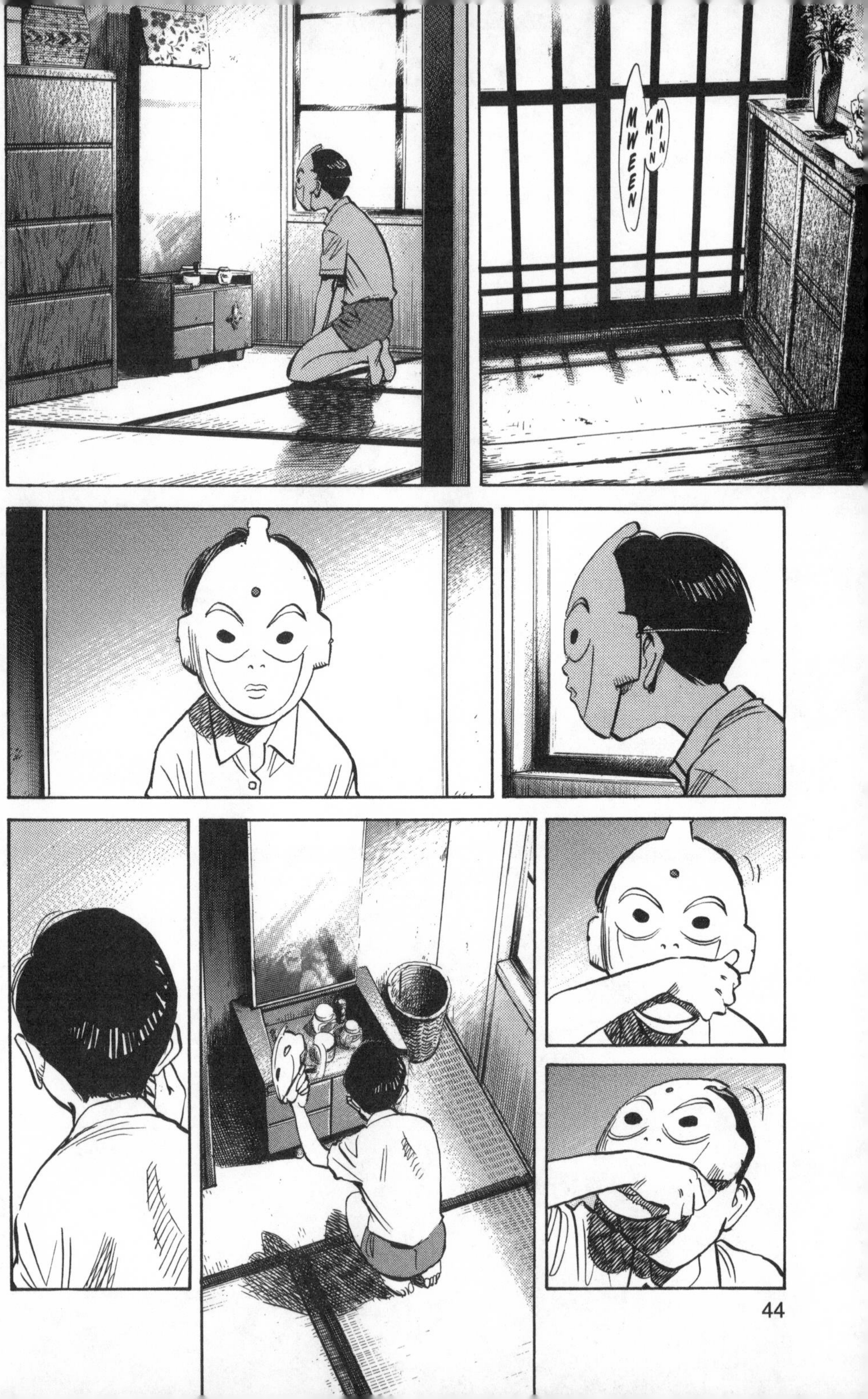
MIN MIN MWEEN

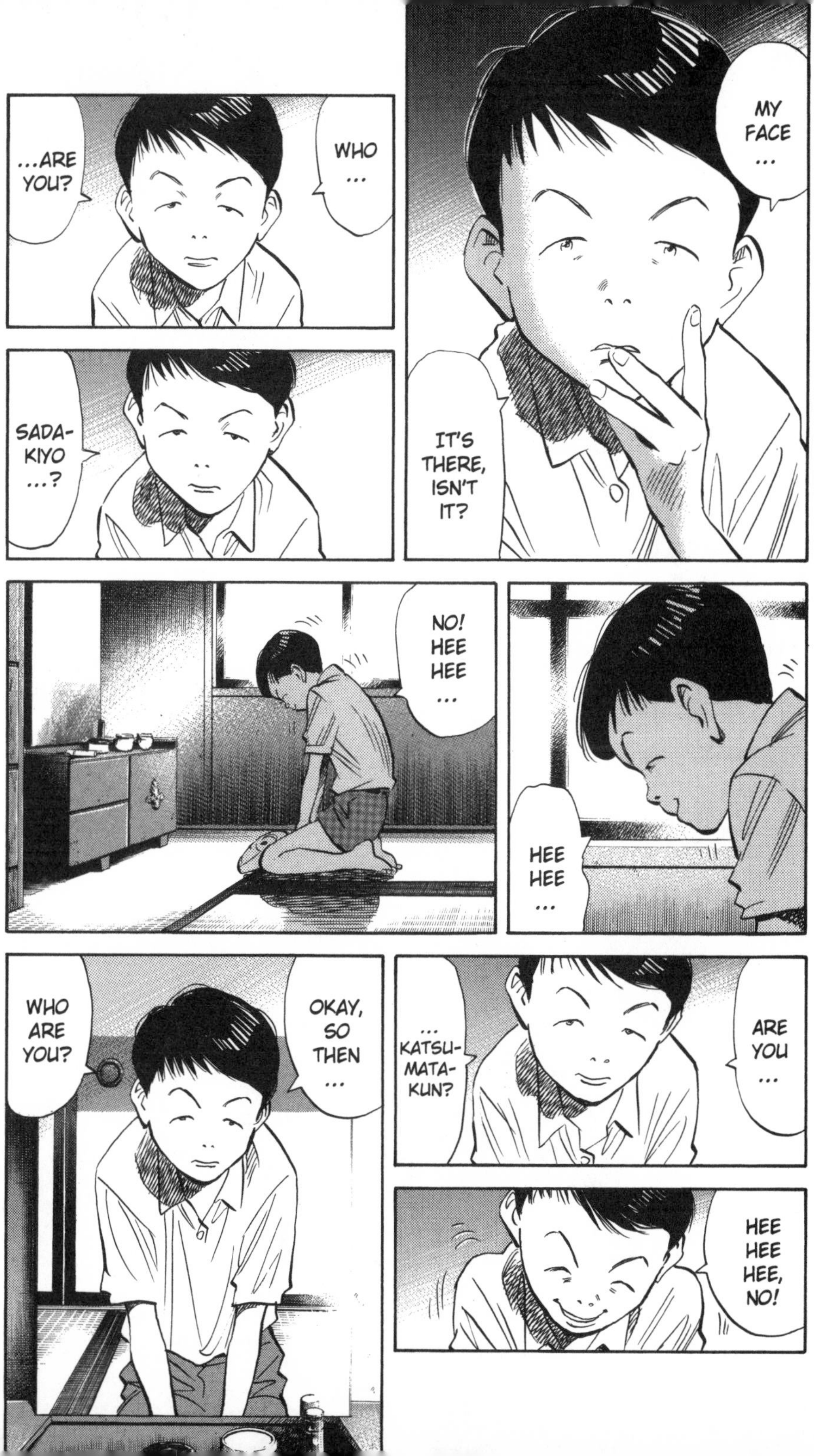
MY FACE ...
IT'S THERE, ISN'T IT?
WHO ...
...ARE YOU?
SADA-KIYO ...?
HEE HEE ...
NO! HEE HEE ...
ARE YOU ...
... KATSU-MATA-KUN?
HEE HEE HEE, NO!
OKAY, SO THEN ...
WHO ARE YOU?

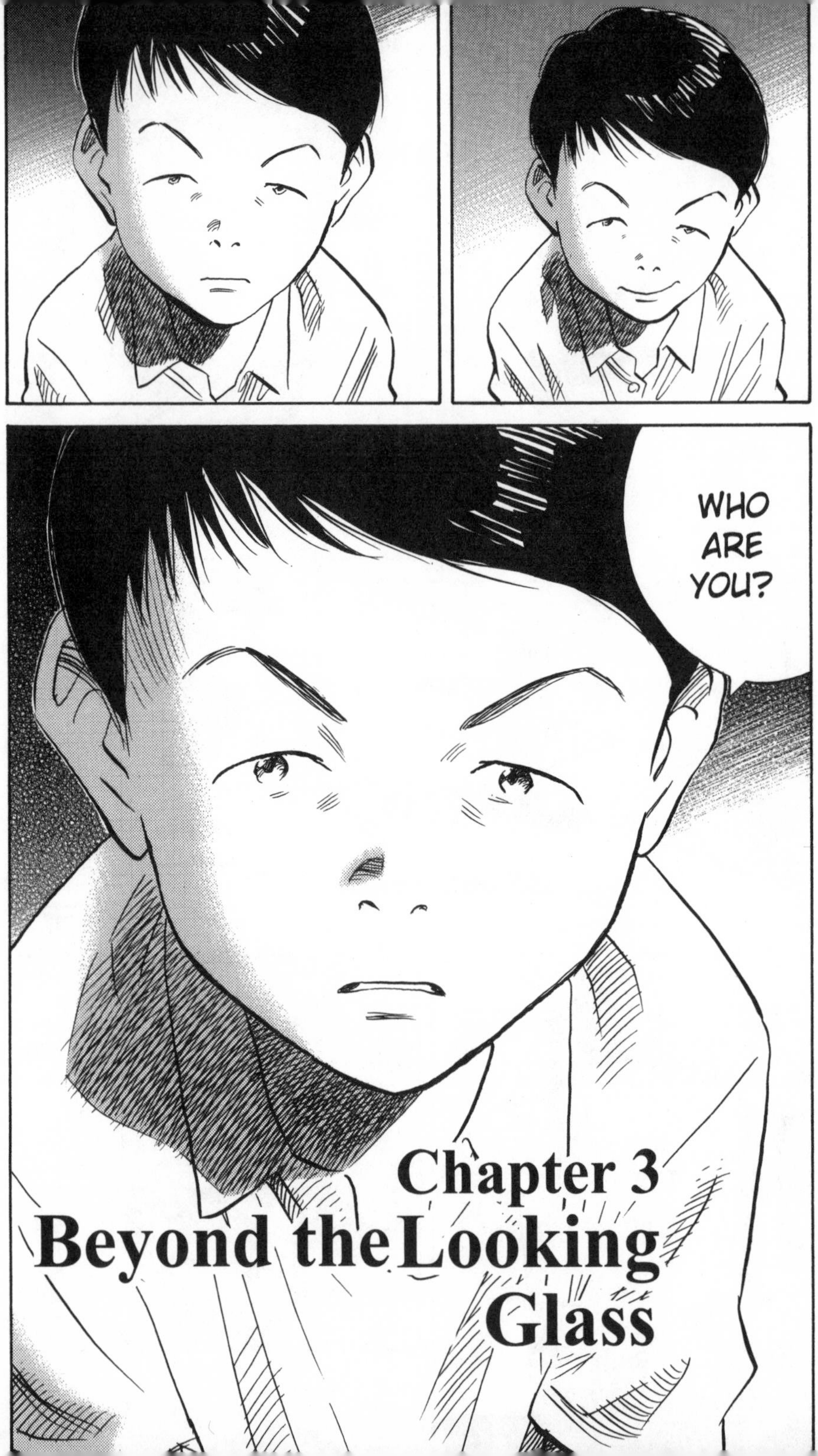
WHO ARE YOU?

Chapter 3 Beyond the Looking Glass

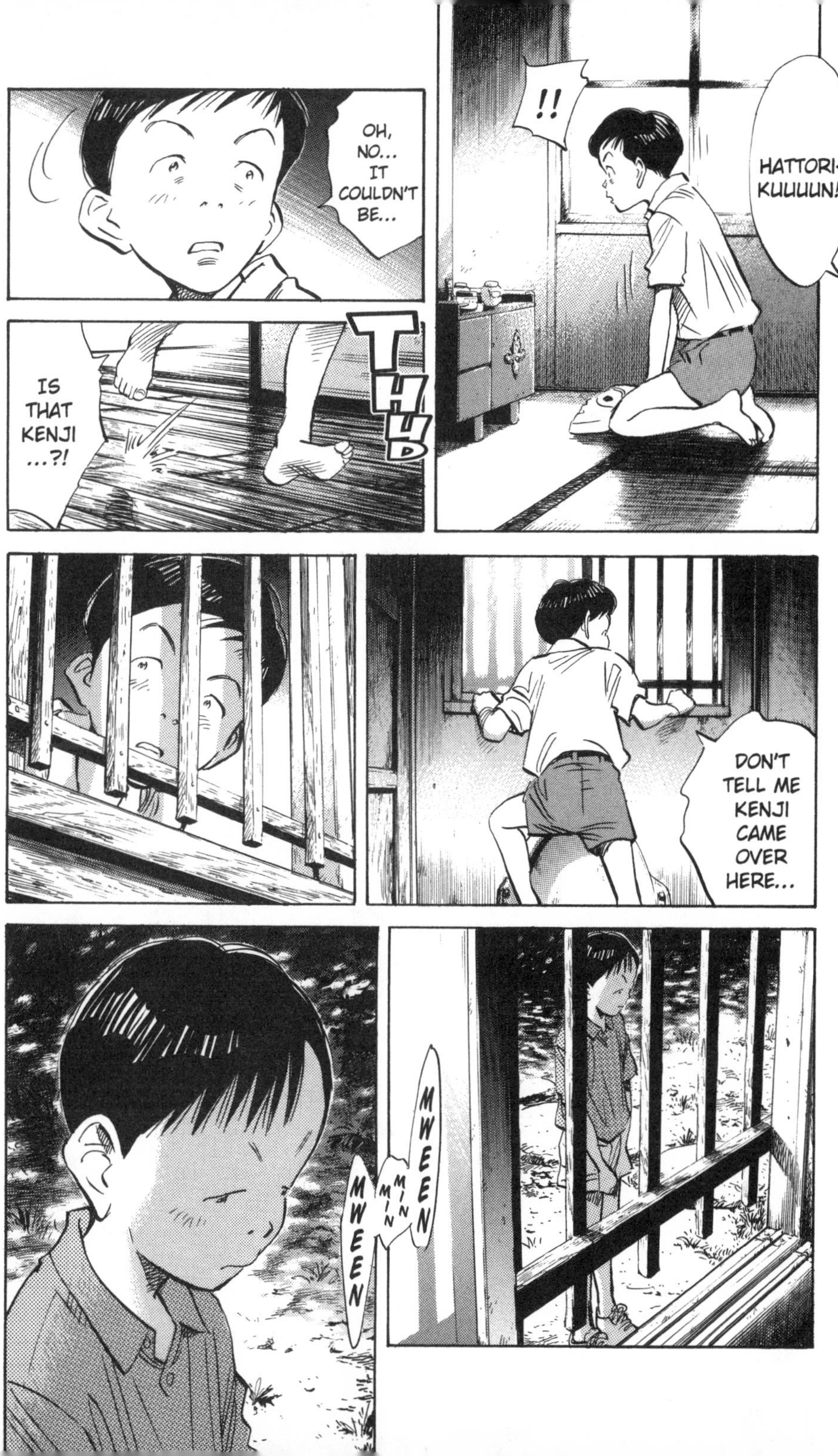
HATTORI-KUUUUN!
!!
OH, NO... IT COULDN'T BE...
THUD
IS THAT KENJI ...?!
DON'T TELL ME KENJI CAME OVER HERE...
MWEEN
MIN MIN
MWEEN

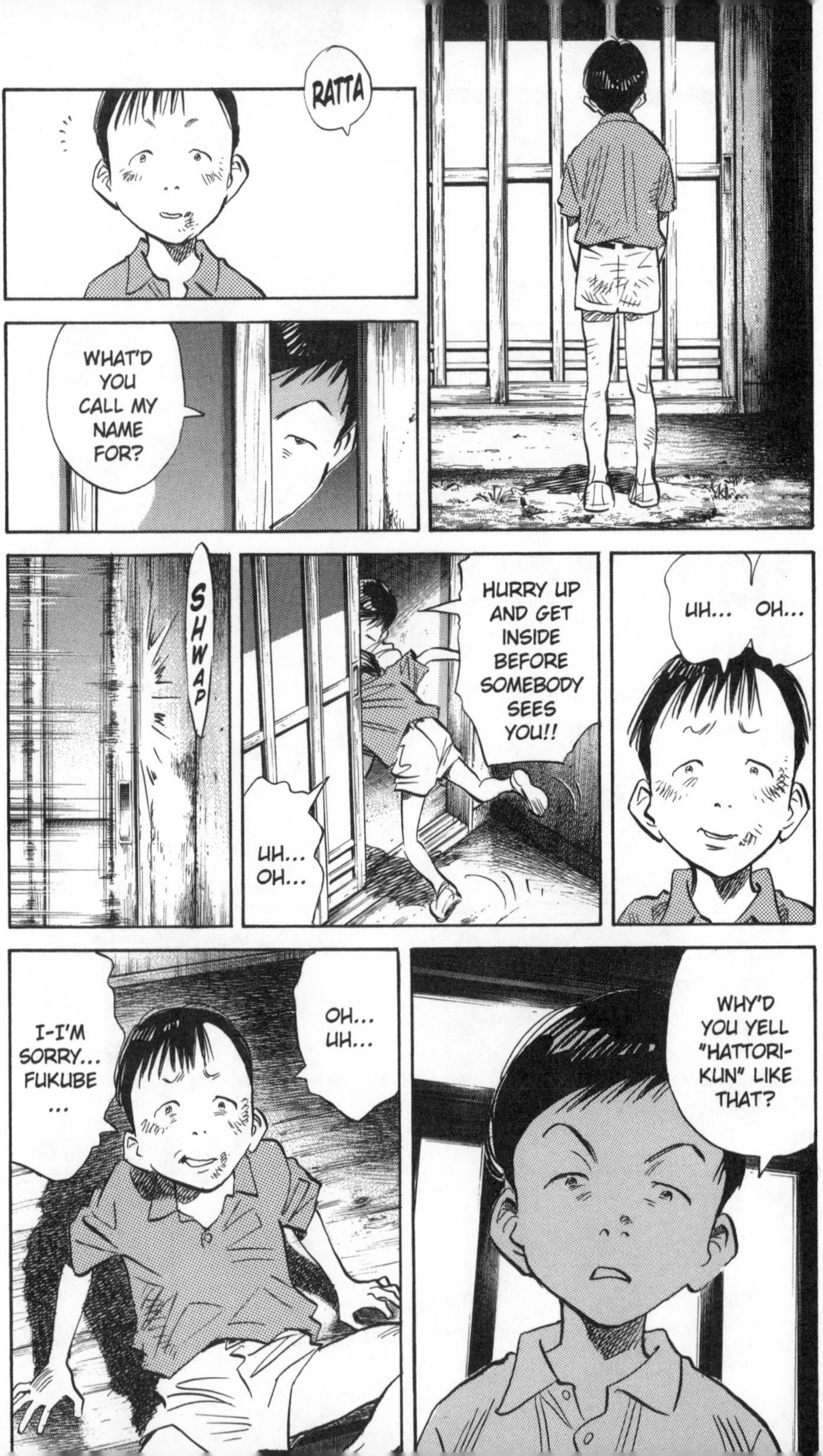
RATTA
WHAT'D YOU CALL MY NAME FOR?
UH... OH...
HURRY UP AND GET INSIDE BEFORE SOMEBODY SEES YOU!!
UH... OH...
SHWAP
WHY'D YOU YELL "HATTORI-KUN" LIKE THAT?
OH... UH...
I-I'M SORRY... FUKUBE ...

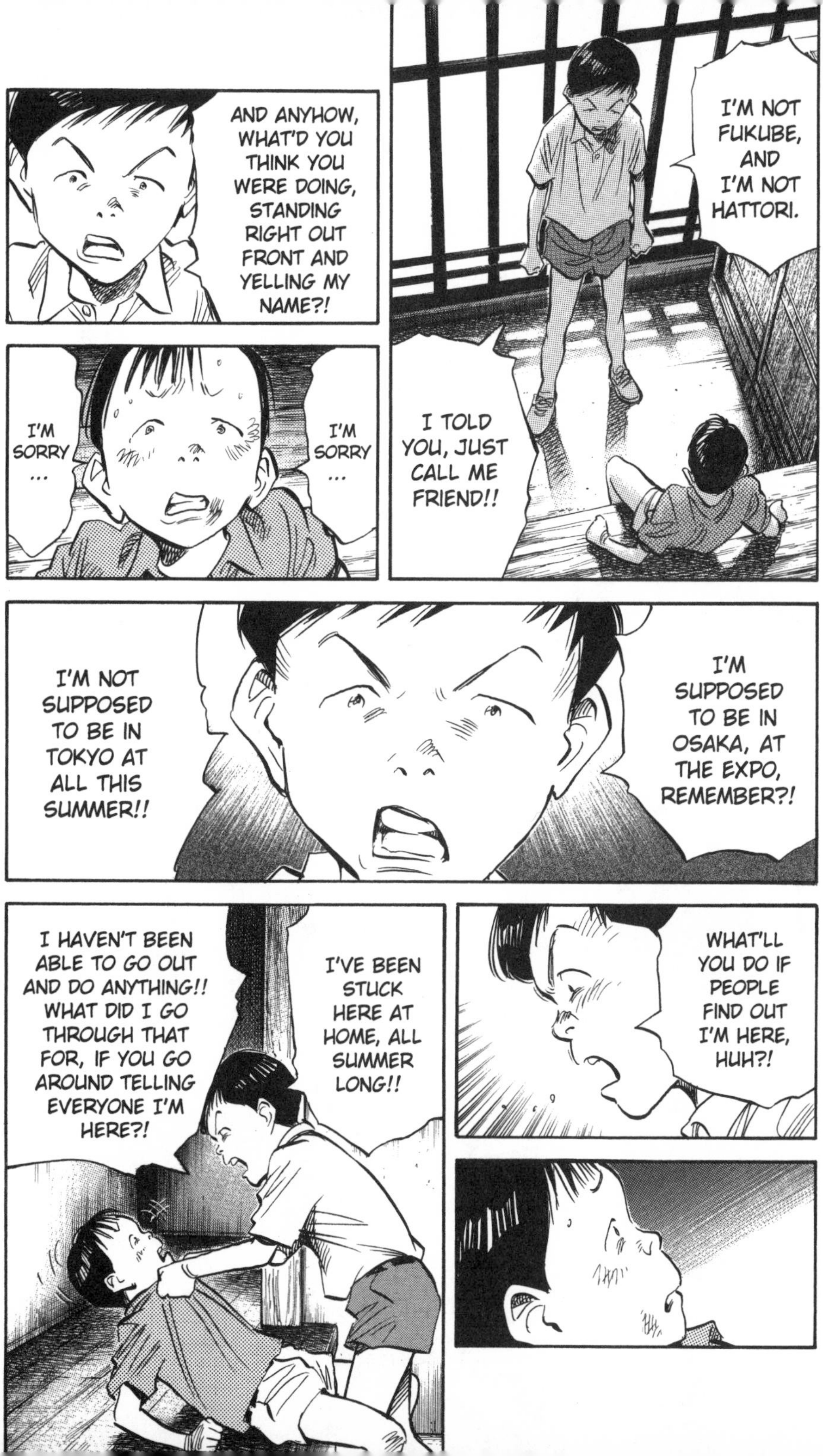
I'M NOT FUKUBE, AND I'M NOT HATTORI.
I TOLD YOU, JUST CALL ME FRIEND!!
AND ANYHOW, WHAT'D YOU THINK YOU WERE DOING, STANDING RIGHT OUT FRONT AND YELLING MY NAME?!
I'M SORRY...
I'M SORRY...
I'M SUPPOSED TO BE IN OSAKA, AT THE EXPO, REMEMBER?!
I'M NOT SUPPOSED TO BE IN TOKYO AT ALL THIS SUMMER!!
WHAT'LL YOU DO IF PEOPLE FIND OUT I'M HERE, HUH?!
I'VE BEEN STUCK HERE AT HOME, ALL SUMMER LONG!!
I HAVEN'T BEEN ABLE TO GO OUT AND DO ANYTHING!! WHAT DID I GO THROUGH THAT FOR, IF YOU GO AROUND TELLING EVERYONE I'M HERE?!

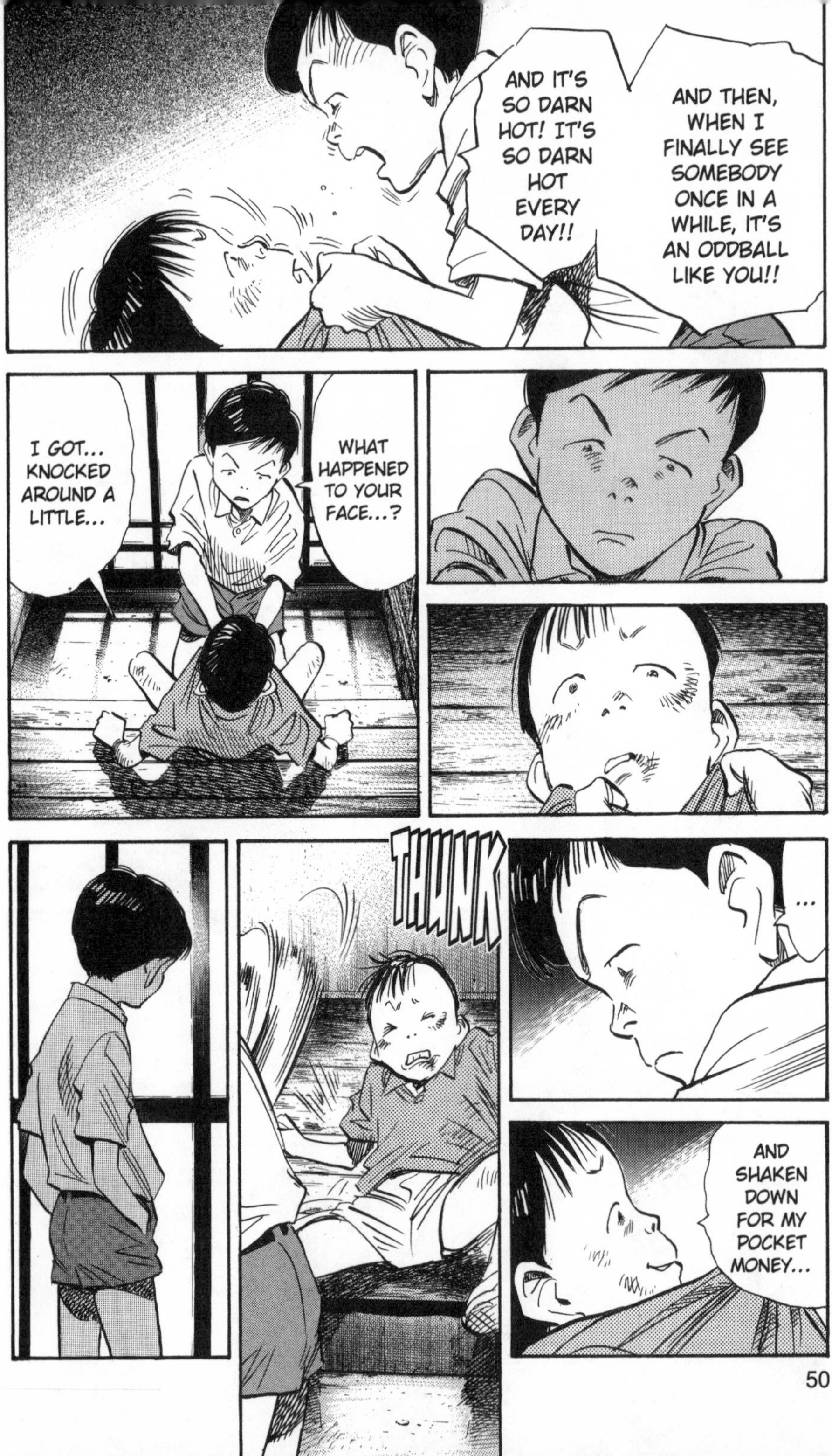
AND THEN, WHEN I FINALLY SEE SOMEBODY ONCE IN A WHILE, IT'S AN ODDBALL LIKE YOU!!
AND IT'S SO DARN HOT! IT'S SO DARN HOT EVERY DAY!!
WHAT HAPPENED TO YOUR FACE...?
I GOT... KNOCKED AROUND A LITTLE...
...
AND SHAKEN DOWN FOR MY POCKET MONEY...
THUNK

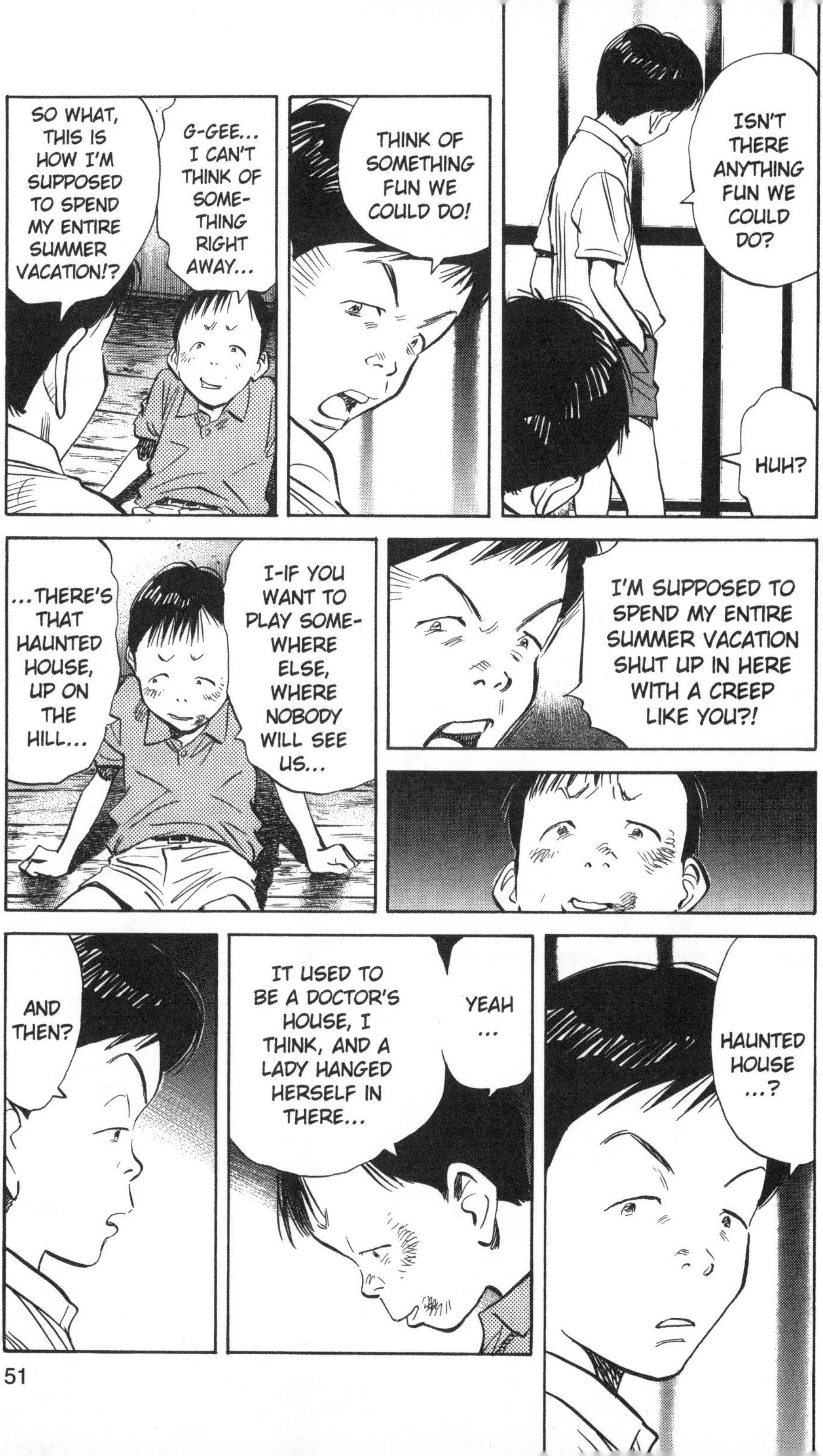
ISN'T THERE ANYTHING FUN WE COULD DO?
HUH?
THINK OF SOMETHING FUN WE COULD DO!
G-GEE... I CAN'T THINK OF SOME-THING RIGHT AWAY...
SO WHAT, THIS IS HOW I'M SUPPOSED TO SPEND MY ENTIRE SUMMER VACATION!?
I'M SUPPOSED TO SPEND MY ENTIRE SUMMER VACATION SHUT UP IN HERE WITH A CREEP LIKE YOU?!
I-IF YOU WANT TO PLAY SOME-WHERE ELSE, WHERE NOBODY WILL SEE US...
...THERE'S THAT HAUNTED HOUSE, UP ON THE HILL...
HAUNTED HOUSE ...?
YEAH ...
IT USED TO BE A DOCTOR'S HOUSE, I THINK, AND A LADY HANGED HERSELF IN THERE...
AND THEN?

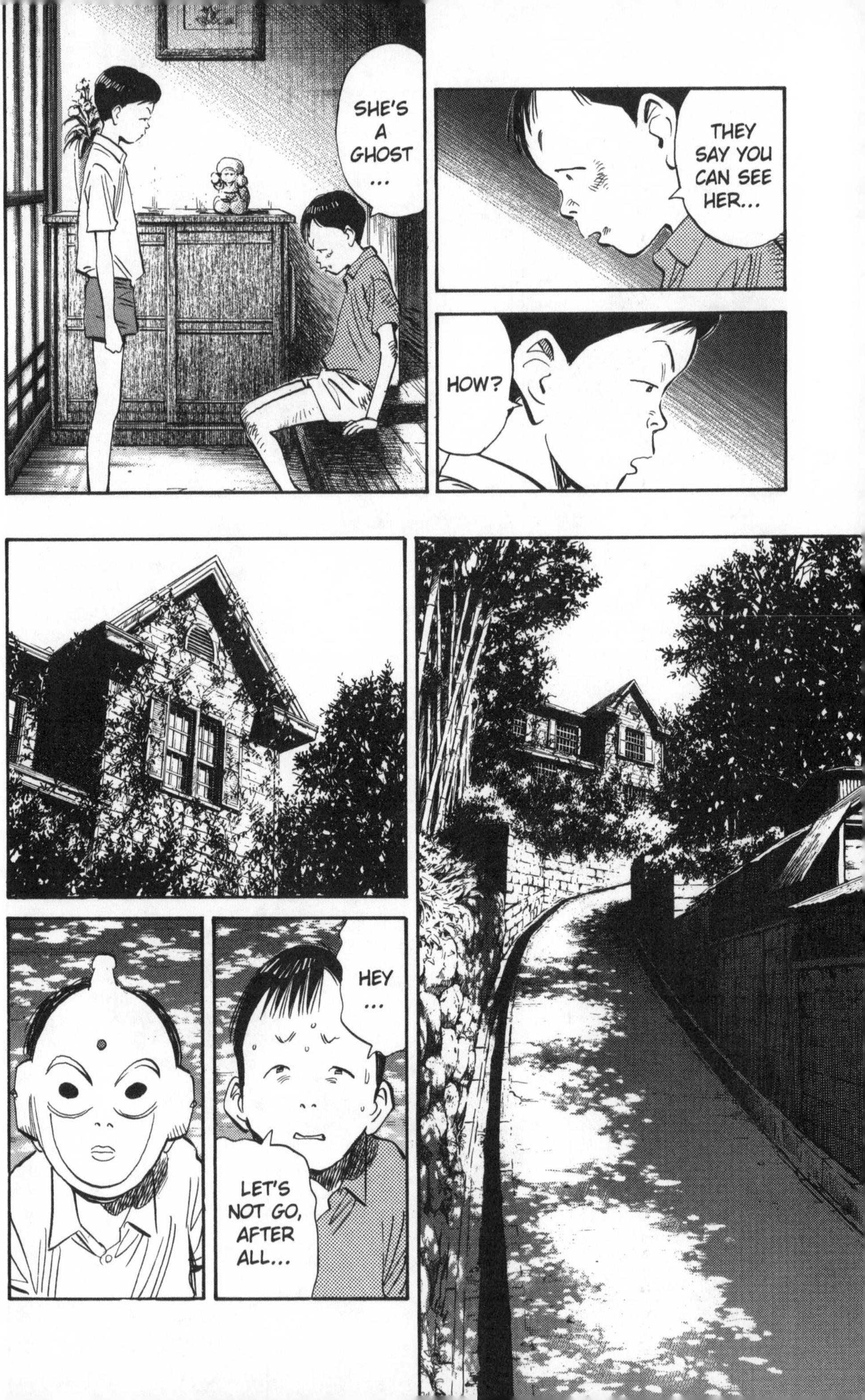
THEY SAY YOU CAN SEE HER...
HOW?
SHE'S A GHOST ...
HEY ...
LET'S NOT GO, AFTER ALL...

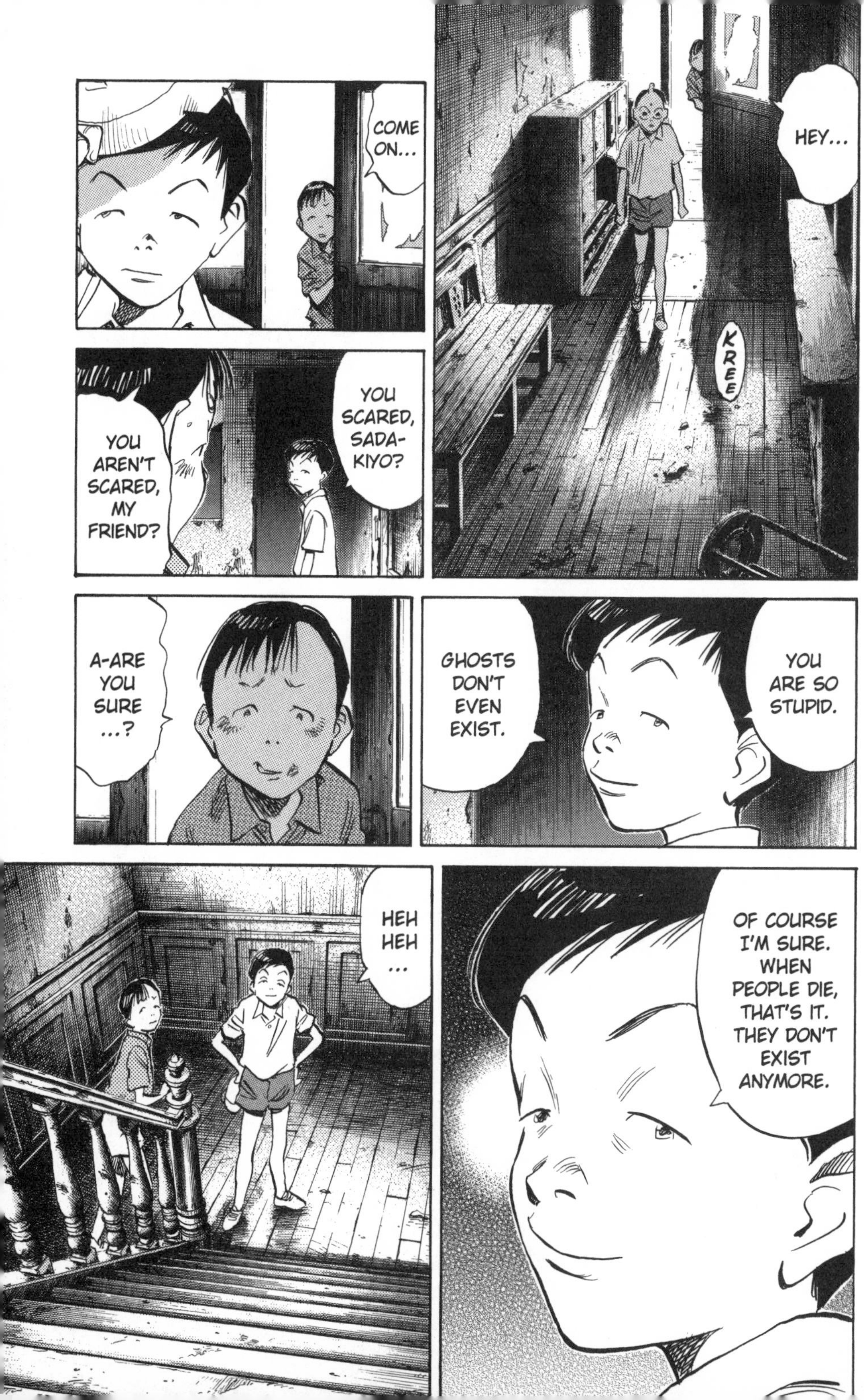
HEY...
KREE
COME ON...
YOU SCARED, SADA-KIYO?
YOU AREN'T SCARED, MY FRIEND?
YOU ARE SO STUPID.
GHOSTS DON'T EVEN EXIST.
A-ARE YOU SURE ...?
OF COURSE I'M SURE. WHEN PEOPLE DIE, THAT'S IT. THEY DON'T EXIST ANYMORE.
HEH HEH ...

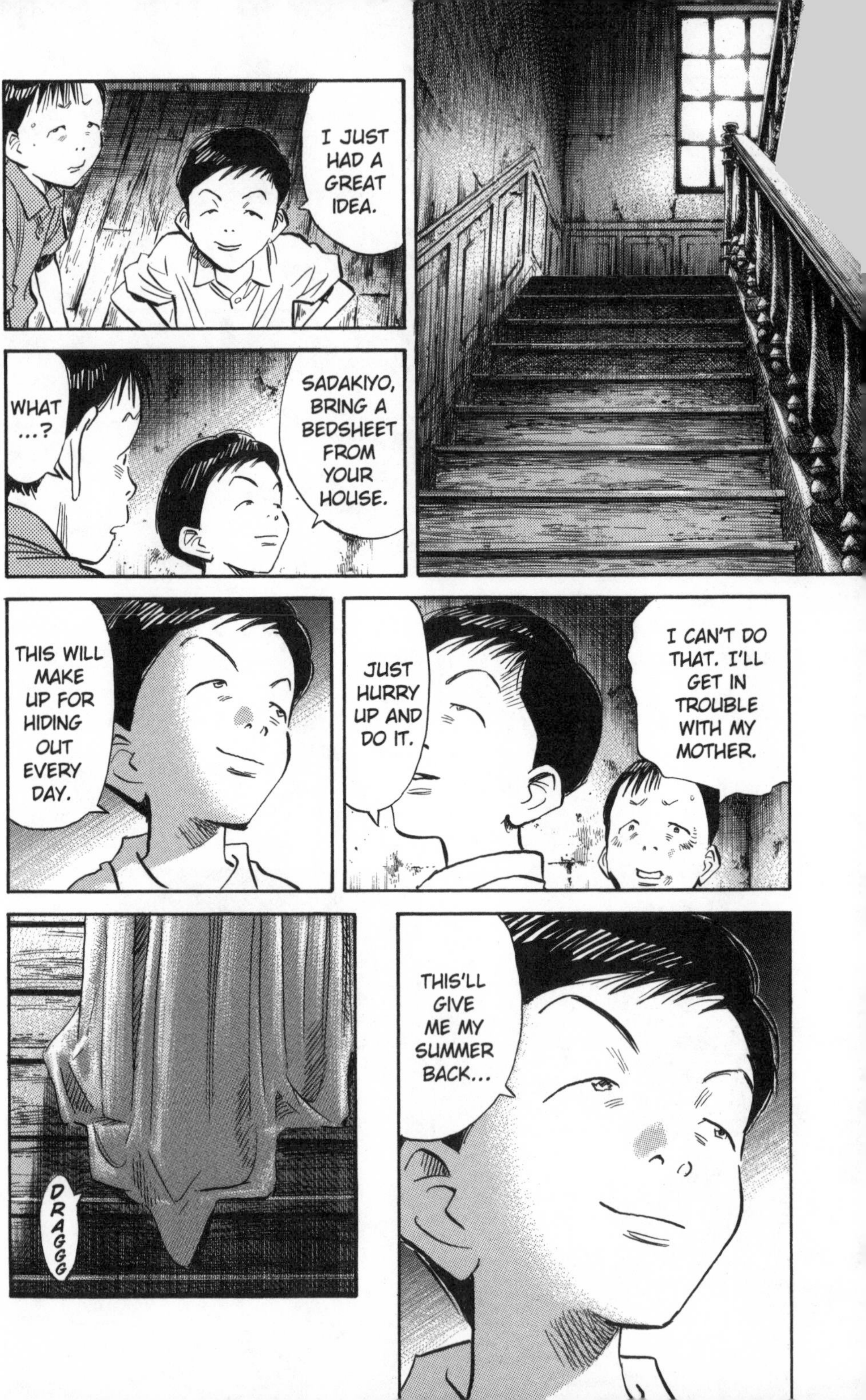
I JUST HAD A GREAT IDEA.
SADAKIYO, BRING A BEDSHEET FROM YOUR HOUSE.
WHAT ...?
I CAN'T DO THAT. I'LL GET IN TROUBLE WITH MY MOTHER.
JUST HURRY UP AND DO IT.
THIS WILL MAKE UP FOR HIDING OUT EVERY DAY.
THIS'LL GIVE ME MY SUMMER BACK...
DRAGGG

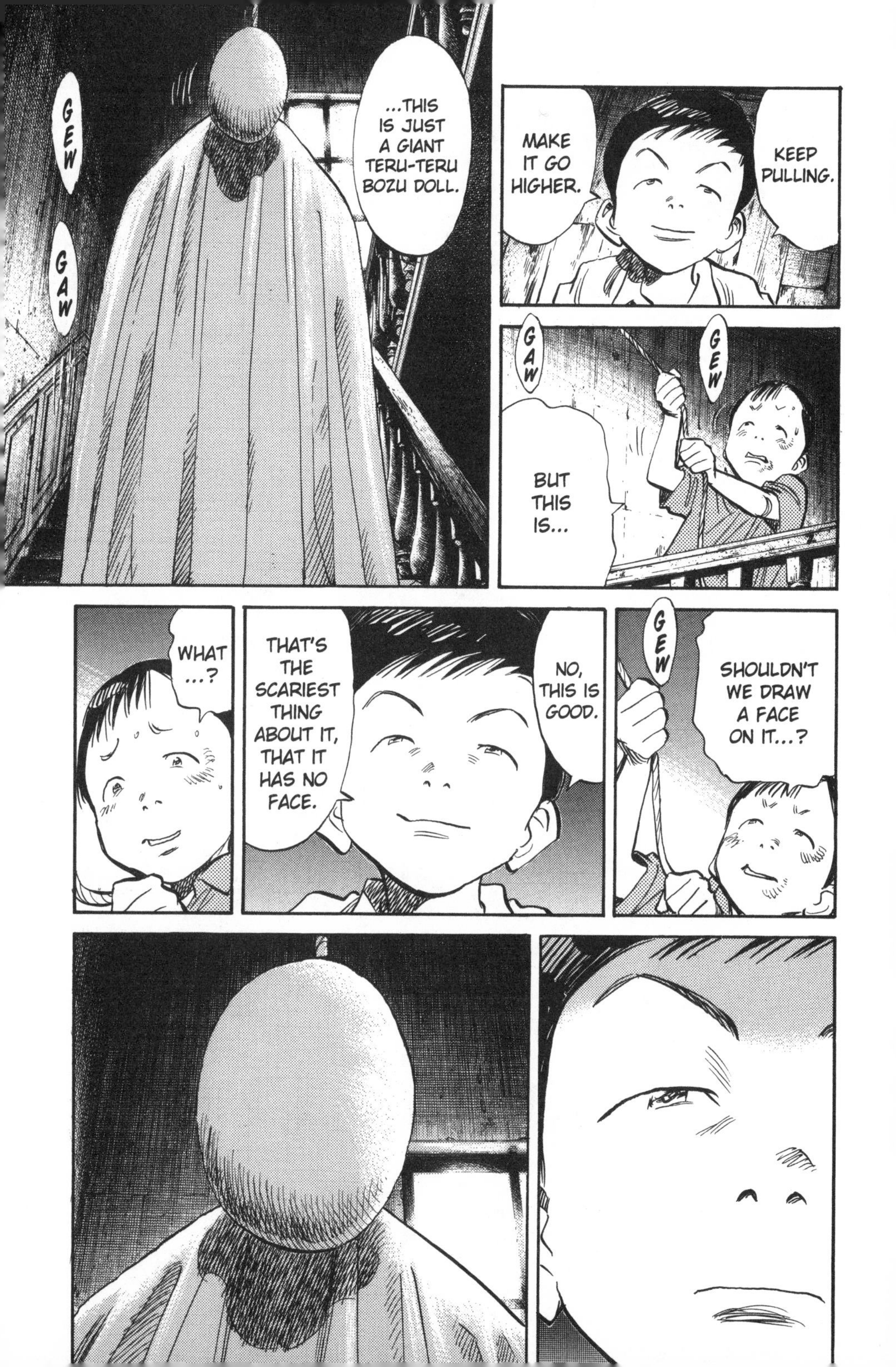
KEEP PULLING.
MAKE IT GO HIGHER.
GEW
GAW
BUT THIS IS...
...THIS IS JUST A GIANT TERU-TERU BOZU DOLL.
GEW
GAW
GEW
SHOULDN'T WE DRAW A FACE ON IT...?
NO, THIS IS GOOD.
THAT'S THE SCARIEST THING ABOUT IT, THAT IT HAS NO FACE.
WHAT...?

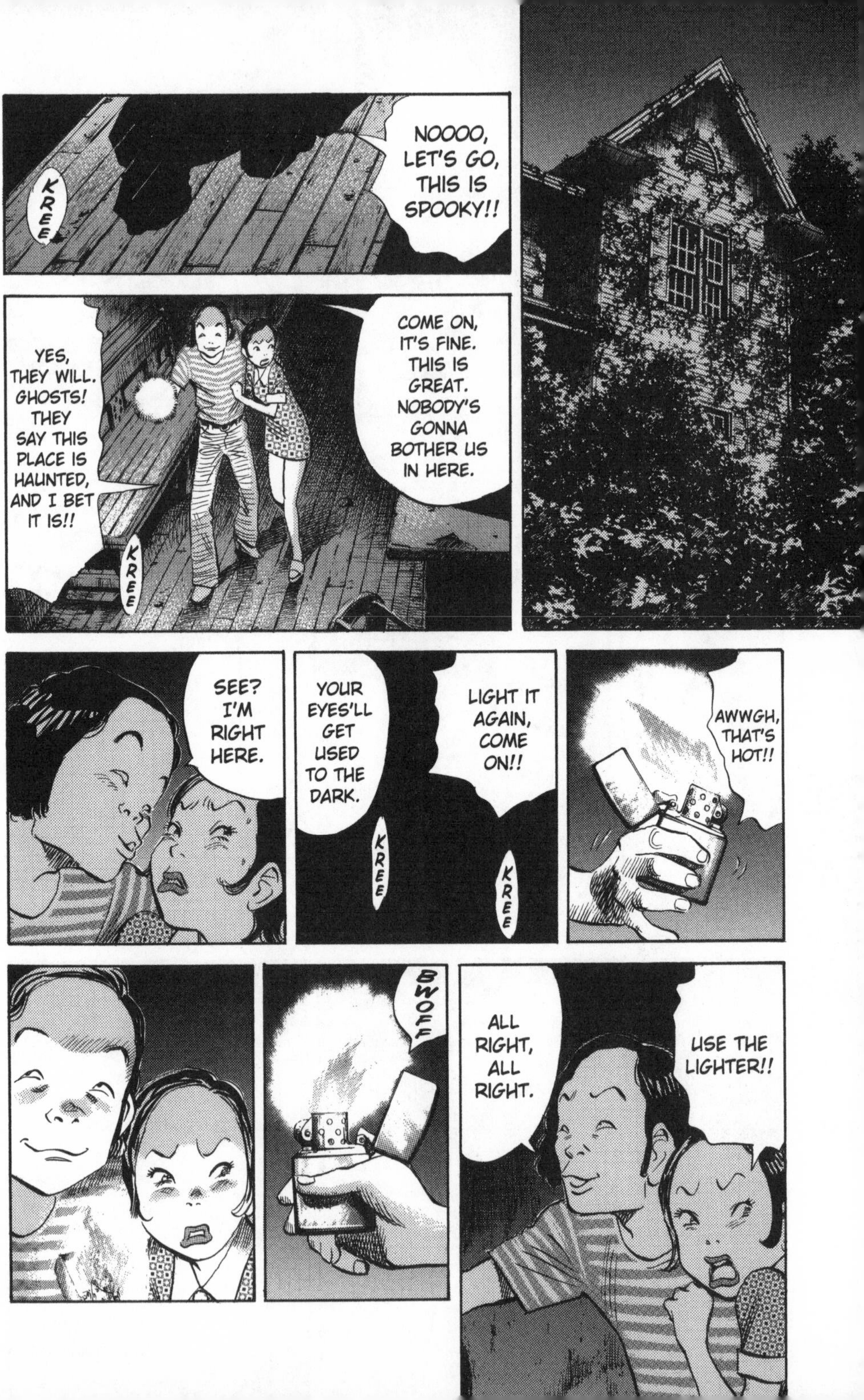
NOOOO, LET'S GO, THIS IS SPOOKY!!
KREE
COME ON, IT'S FINE. THIS IS GREAT. NOBODY'S GONNA BOTHER US IN HERE.
YES, THEY WILL. GHOSTS! THEY SAY THIS PLACE IS HAUNTED, AND I BET IT IS!!
KREE
AWWGH, THAT'S HOT!!
LIGHT IT AGAIN, COME ON!!
KREE
YOUR EYES'LL GET USED TO THE DARK.
KREE
SEE? I'M RIGHT HERE.
USE THE LIGHTER!!
ALL RIGHT, ALL RIGHT.
BWOFF

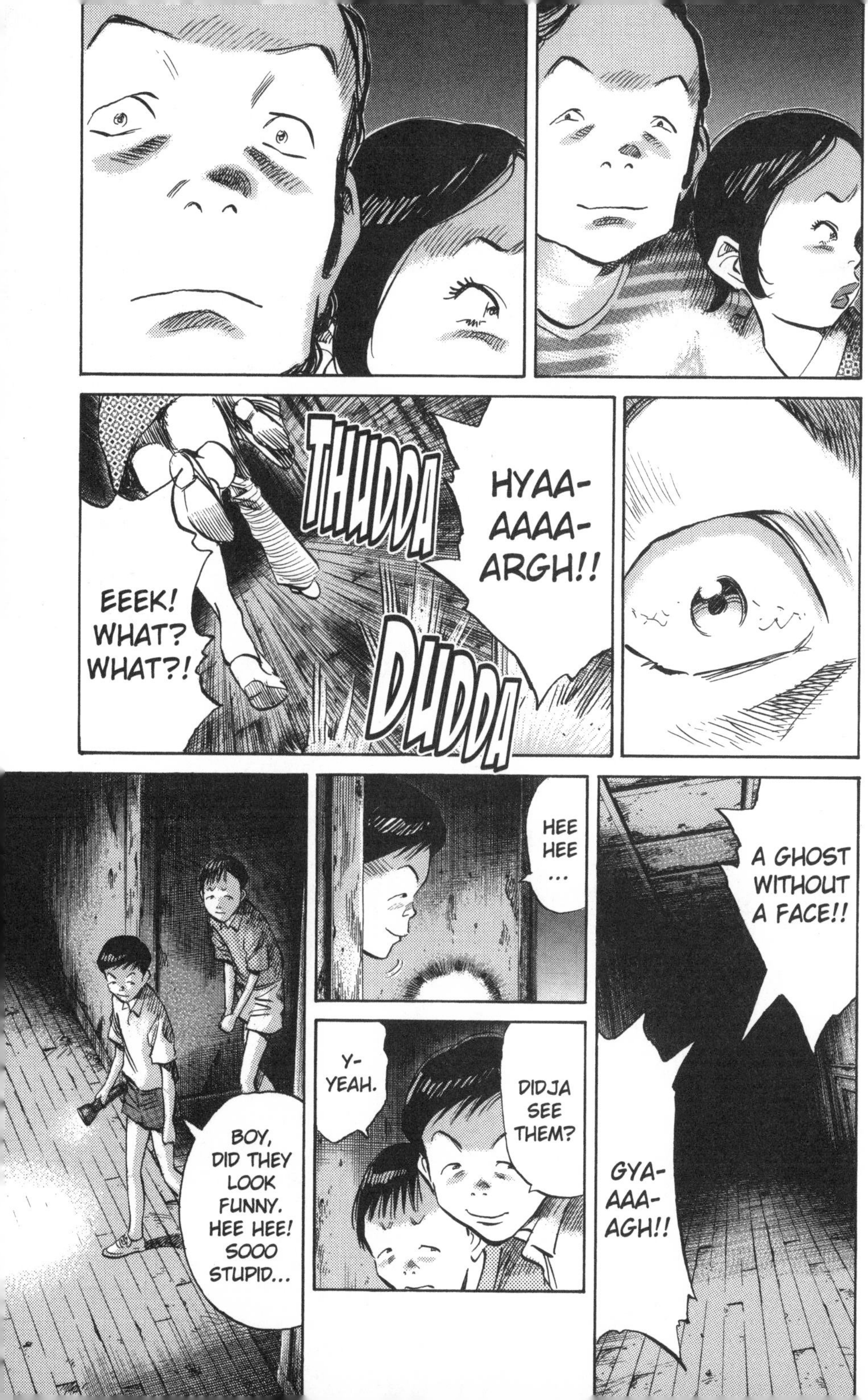
HYAA-AAAA-ARGH!!
THUDDA
EEEK! WHAT? WHAT?!
DUDDA
A GHOST WITHOUT A FACE!!
GYA-AAA-AGH!!
HEE HEE ...
DIDJA SEE THEM?
Y-YEAH.
BOY, DID THEY LOOK FUNNY. HEE HEE! SOOO STUPID...

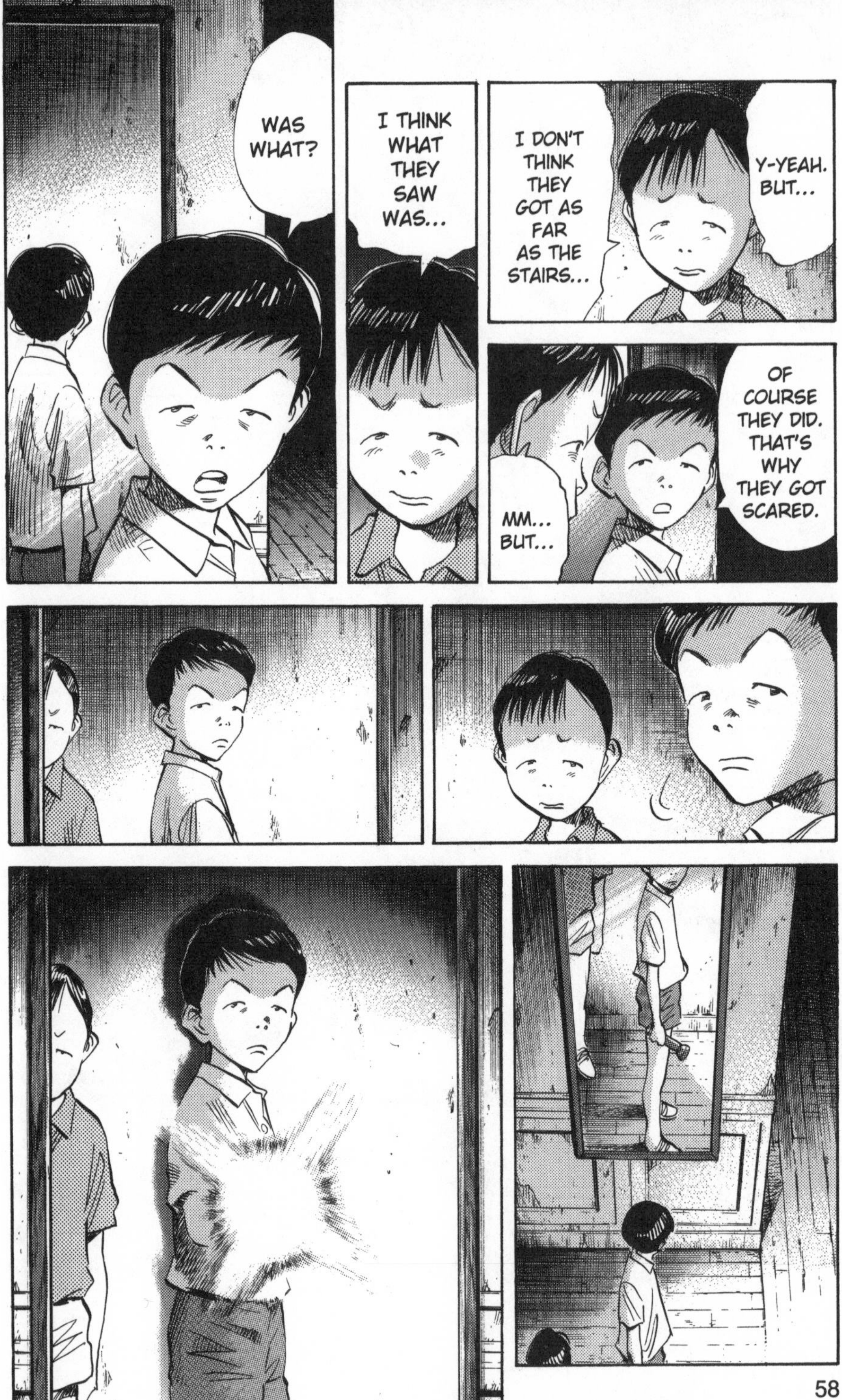
Y-YEAH. BUT...
I DON'T THINK THEY GOT AS FAR AS THE STAIRS...
OF COURSE THEY DID. THAT'S WHY THEY GOT SCARED.
MM... BUT...
I THINK WHAT THEY SAW WAS...
WAS WHAT?

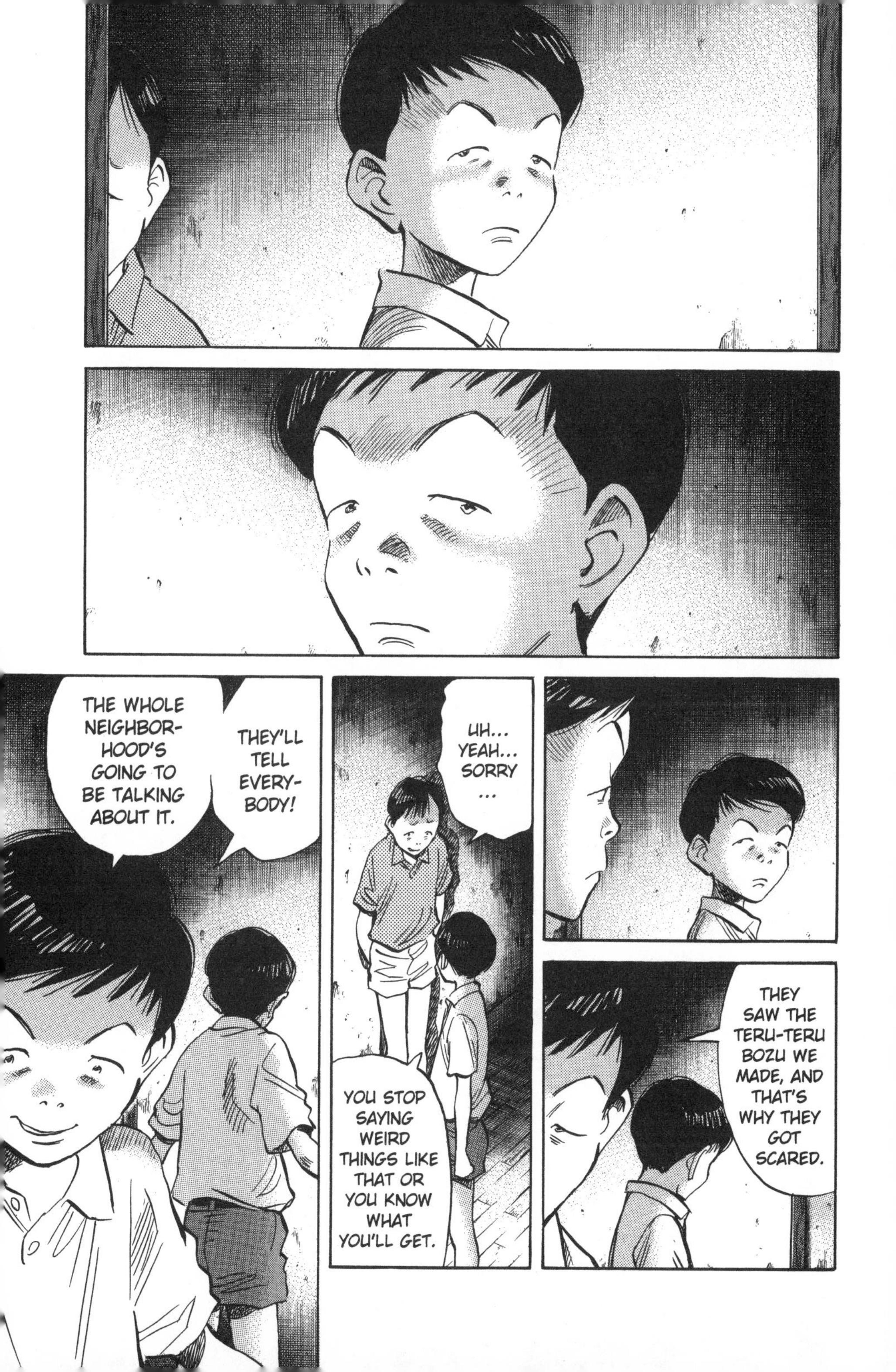
THEY SAW THE TERU-TERU BOZU WE MADE, AND THAT'S WHY THEY GOT SCARED.
UH... YEAH... SORRY...
YOU STOP SAYING WEIRD THINGS LIKE THAT OR YOU KNOW WHAT YOU'LL GET.
THEY'LL TELL EVERYBODY!
THE WHOLE NEIGHBORHOOD'S GOING TO BE TALKING ABOUT IT.

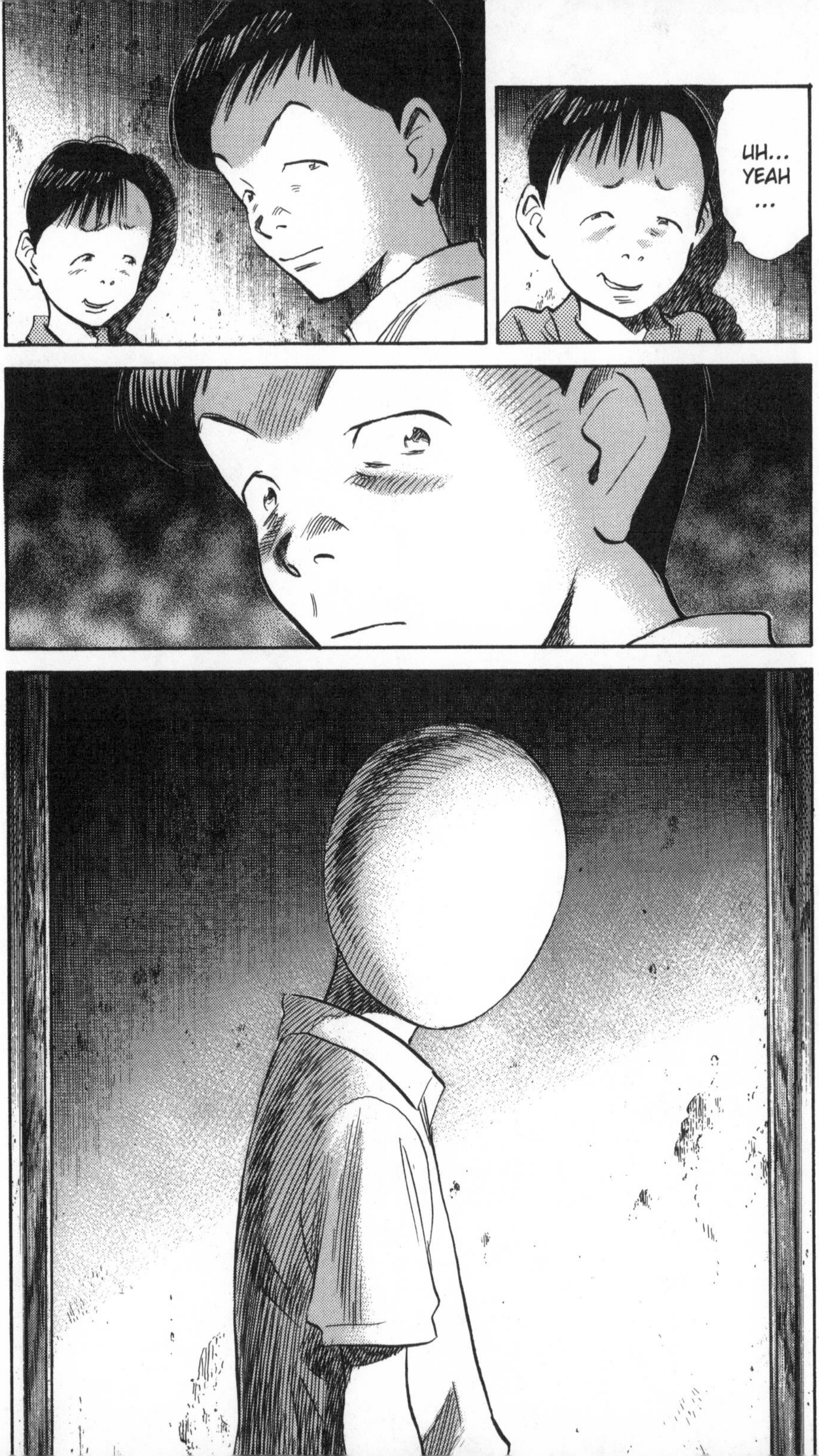
UH... YEAH ...

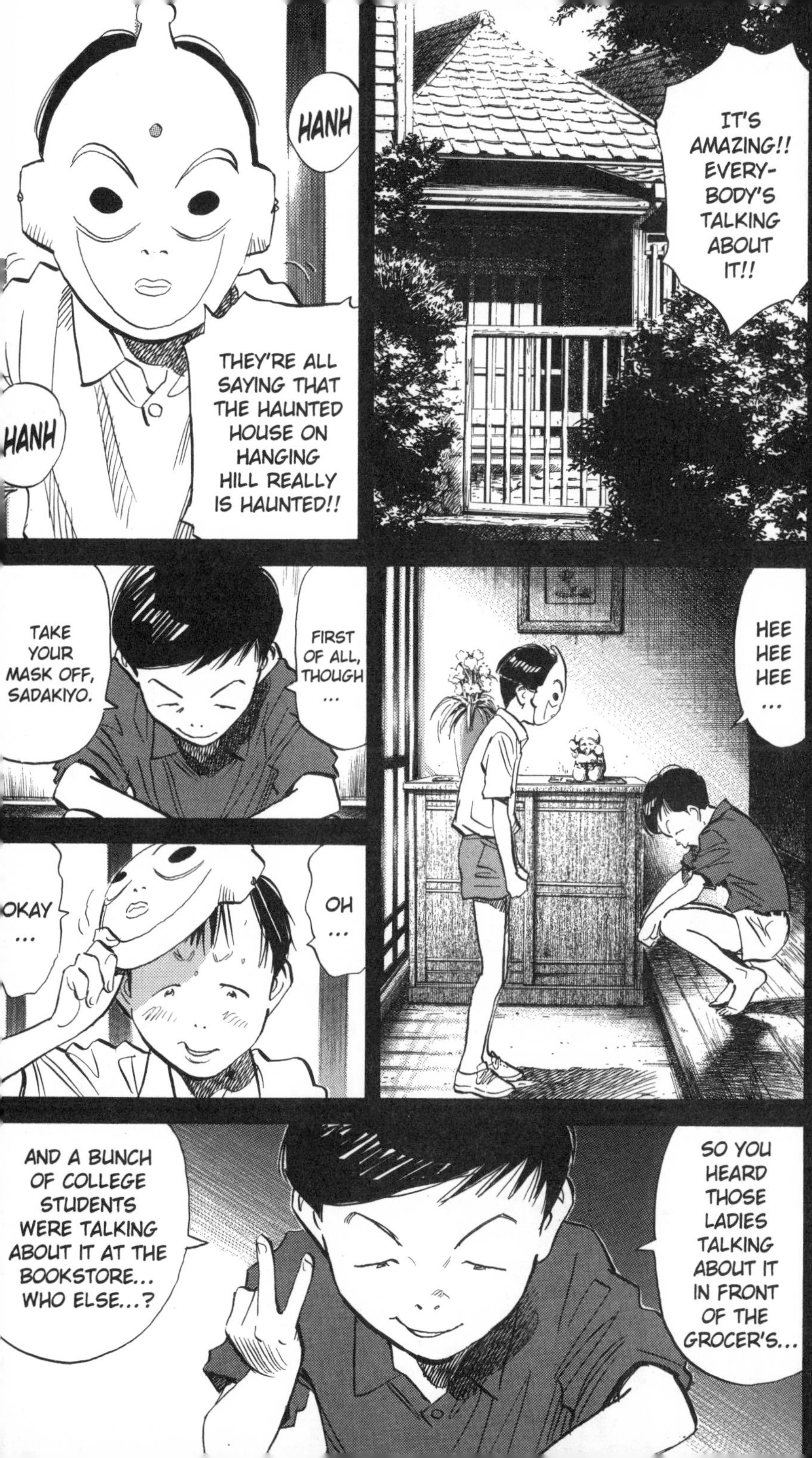
IT'S AMAZING!! EVERY-BODY'S TALKING ABOUT IT!!
HANH
THEY'RE ALL SAYING THAT THE HAUNTED HOUSE ON HANGING HILL REALLY IS HAUNTED!!
HANH
HEE HEE HEE...
FIRST OF ALL, THOUGH...
TAKE YOUR MASK OFF, SADAKIYO.
OH...
OKAY...
SO YOU HEARD THOSE LADIES TALKING ABOUT IT IN FRONT OF THE GROCER'S...
AND A BUNCH OF COLLEGE STUDENTS WERE TALKING ABOUT IT AT THE BOOKSTORE... WHO ELSE...?

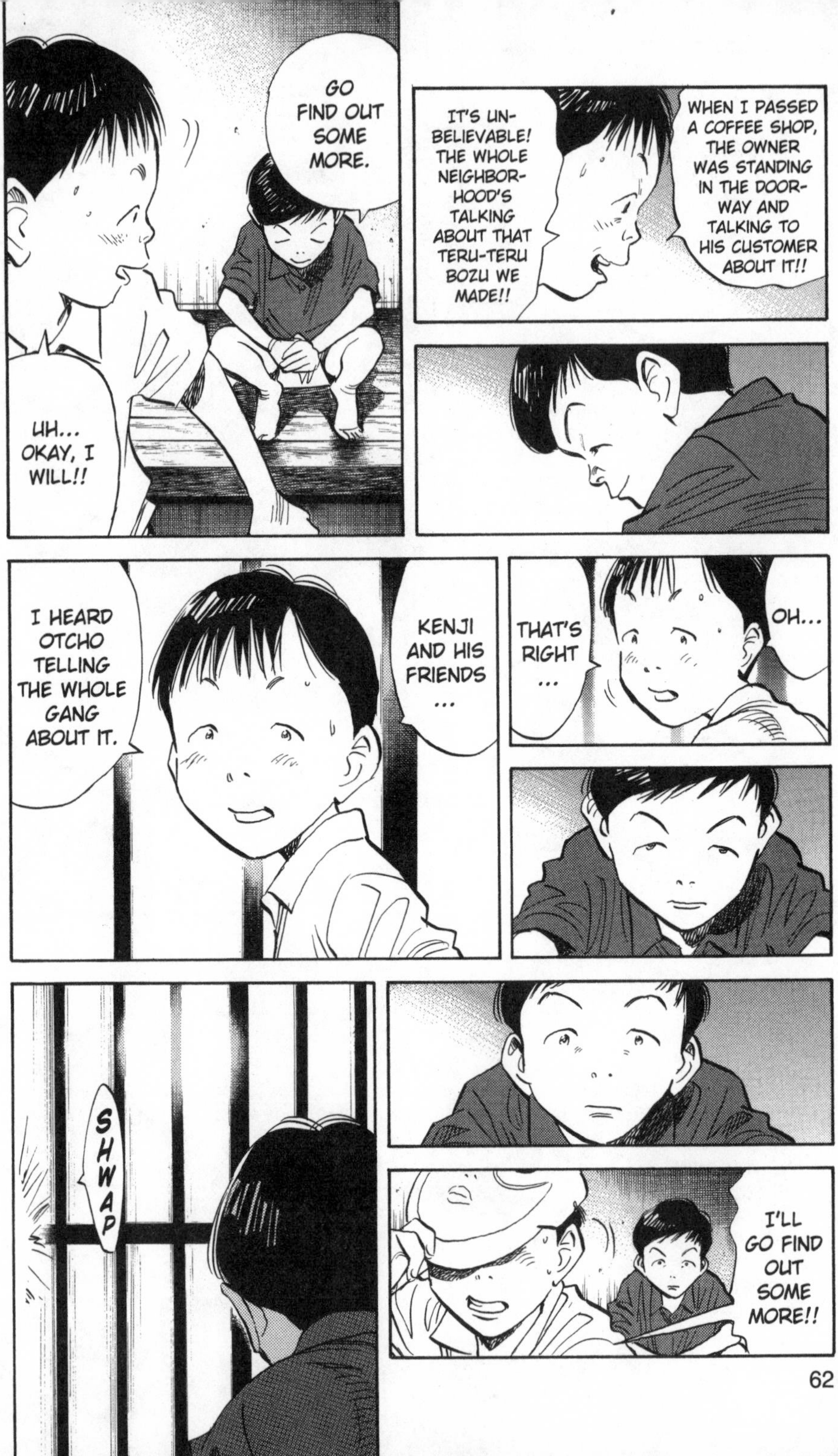

WHEN I PASSED A COFFEE SHOP, THE OWNER WAS STANDING IN THE DOORWAY AND TALKING TO HIS CUSTOMER ABOUT IT!!
IT'S UNBELIEVABLE! THE WHOLE NEIGHBORHOOD'S TALKING ABOUT THAT TERU-TERU BOZU WE MADE!!
GO FIND OUT SOME MORE.
UH... OKAY, I WILL!!
OH...
THAT'S RIGHT ...
KENJI AND HIS FRIENDS ...
I HEARD OTCHO TELLING THE WHOLE GANG ABOUT IT.
I'LL GO FIND OUT SOME MORE!!
SHWAP

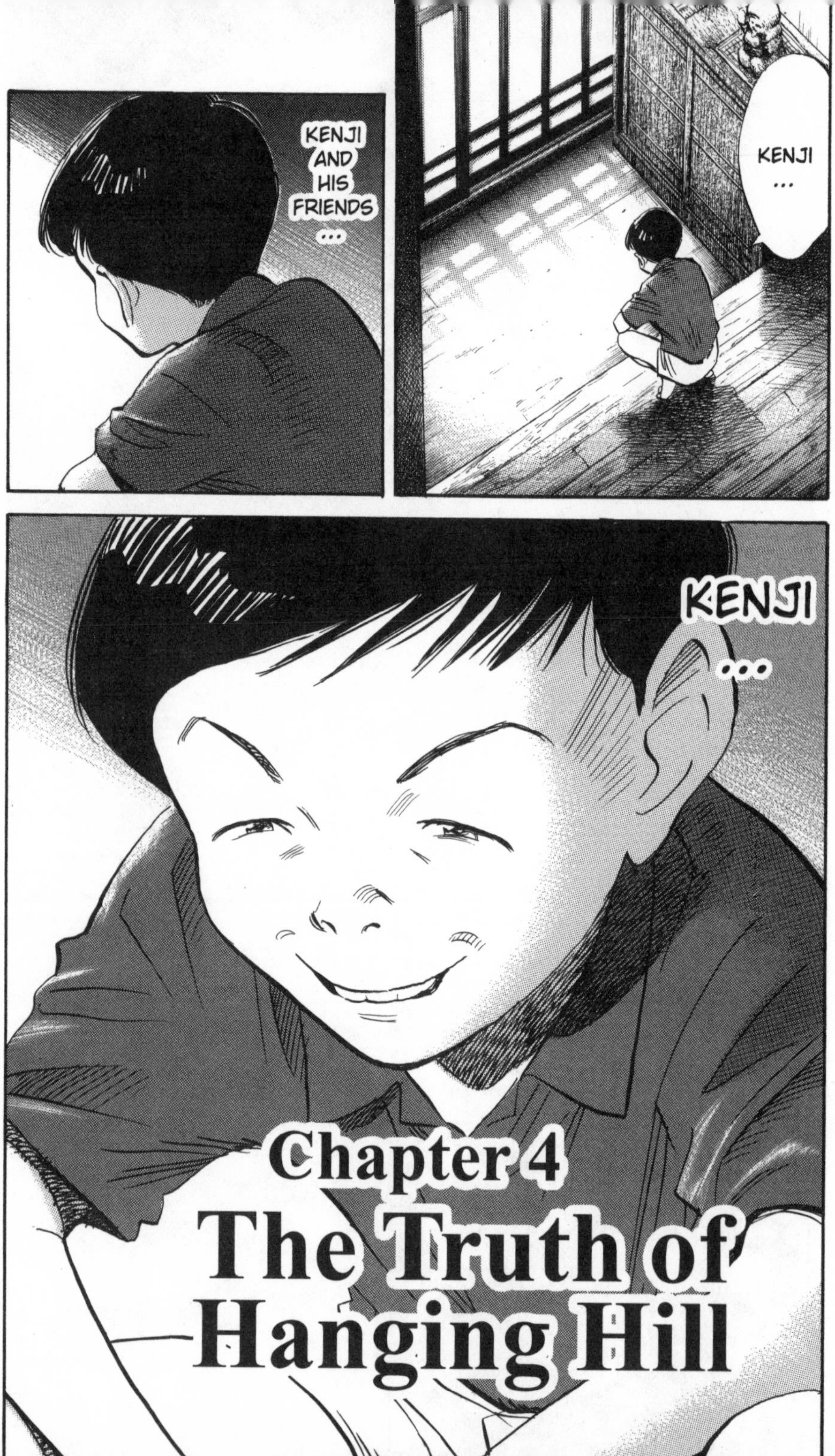
KENJI ...
KENJI AND HIS FRIENDS ...
KENJI ...

Chapter 4
The Truth of Hanging Hill

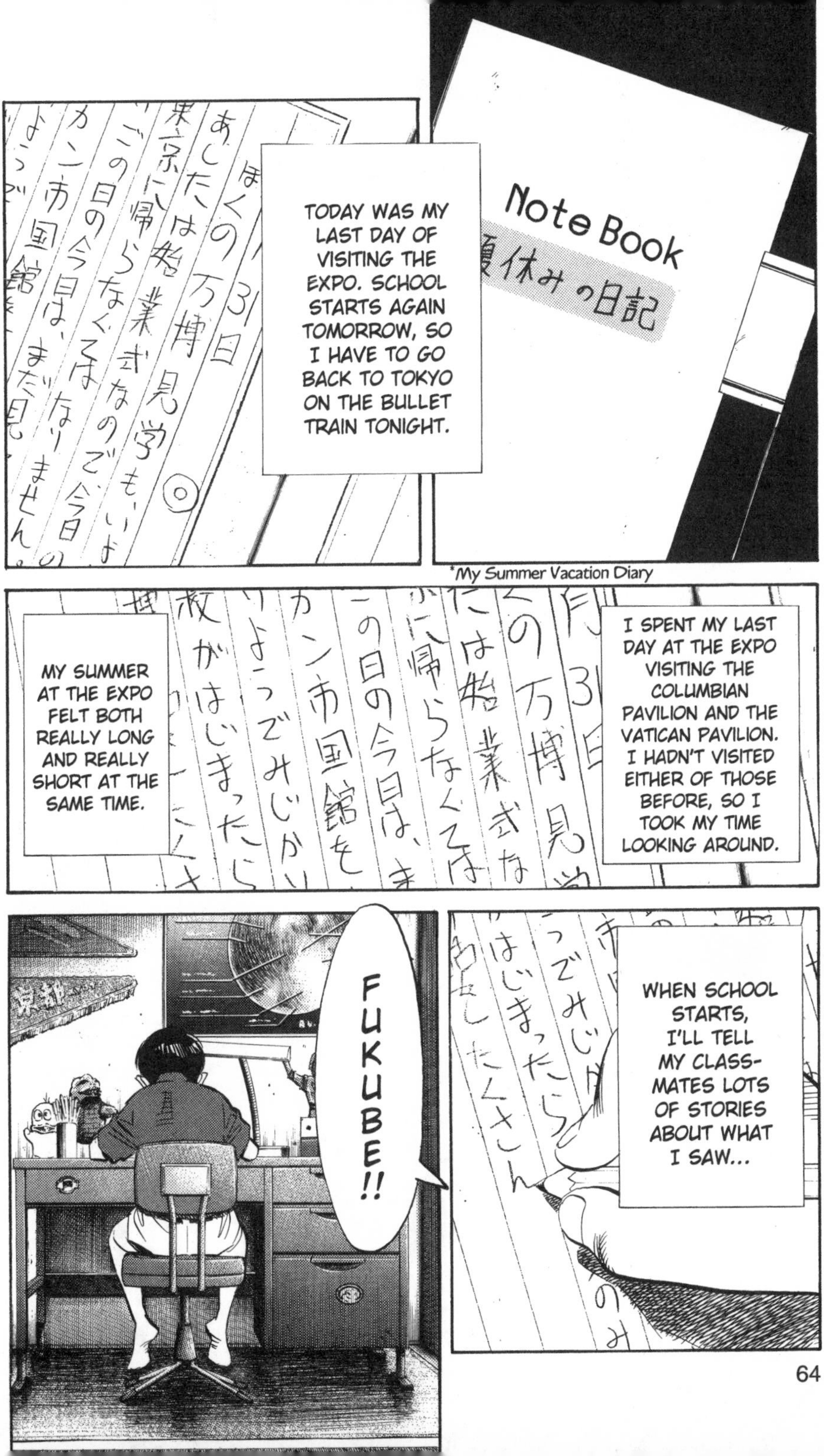

Note Book
夏休みの日記
*My Summer Vacation Diary
TODAY WAS MY LAST DAY OF VISITING THE EXPO. SCHOOL STARTS AGAIN TOMORROW, SO I HAVE TO GO BACK TO TOKYO ON THE BULLET TRAIN TONIGHT.
I SPENT MY LAST DAY AT THE EXPO VISITING THE COLUMBIAN PAVILION AND THE VATICAN PAVILION. I HADN'T VISITED EITHER OF THOSE BEFORE, SO I TOOK MY TIME LOOKING AROUND.
MY SUMMER AT THE EXPO FELT BOTH REALLY LONG AND REALLY SHORT AT THE SAME TIME.
WHEN SCHOOL STARTS, I'LL TELL MY CLASS-MATES LOTS OF STORIES ABOUT WHAT I SAW...
FUKUBE!!

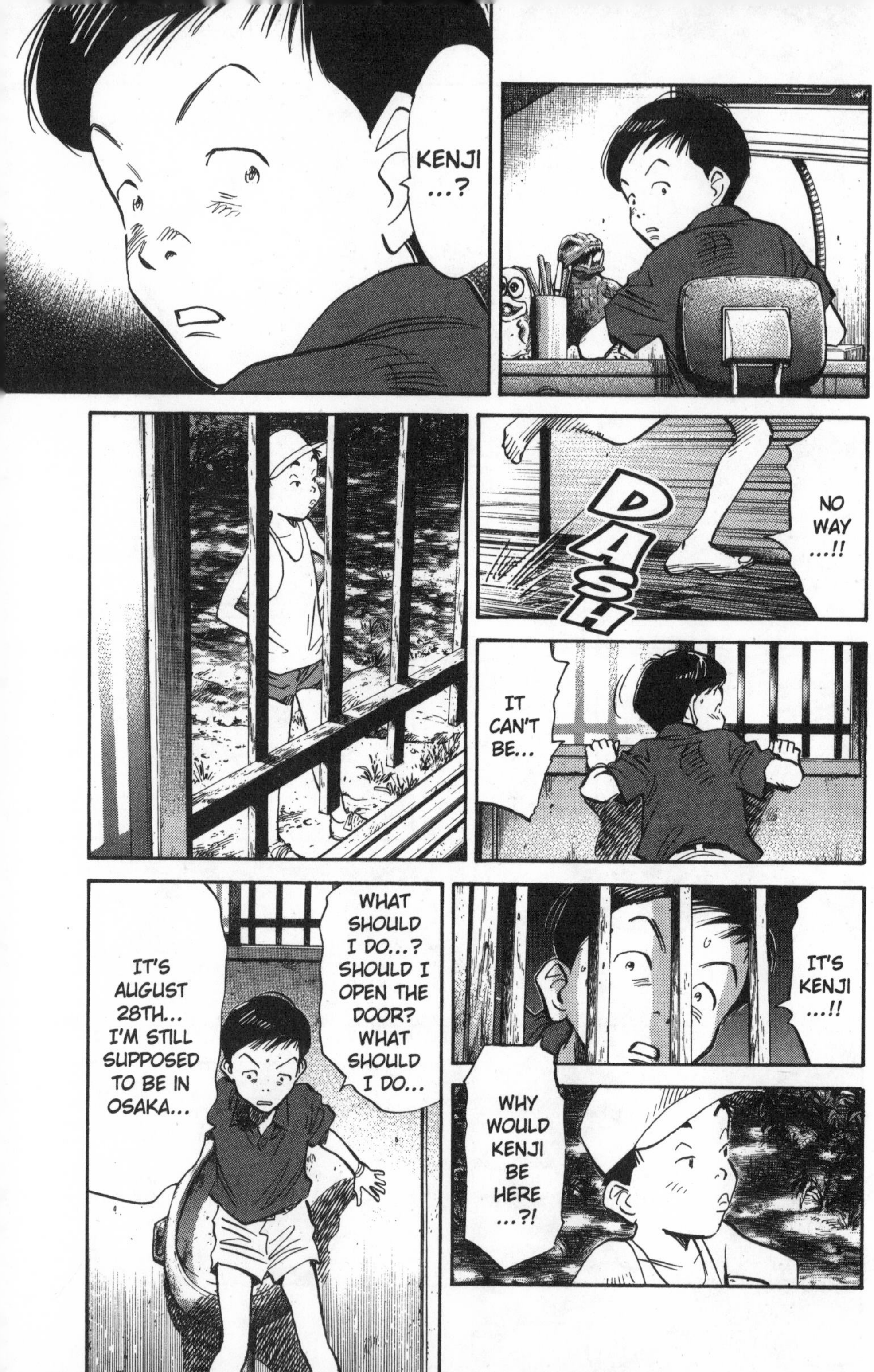
KENJI ...?
NO WAY ...!!
DASH
IT CAN'T BE...
IT'S KENJI ...!!
WHY WOULD KENJI BE HERE ...?!
WHAT SHOULD I DO...? SHOULD I OPEN THE DOOR? WHAT SHOULD I DO...
IT'S AUGUST 28TH... I'M STILL SUPPOSED TO BE IN OSAKA...

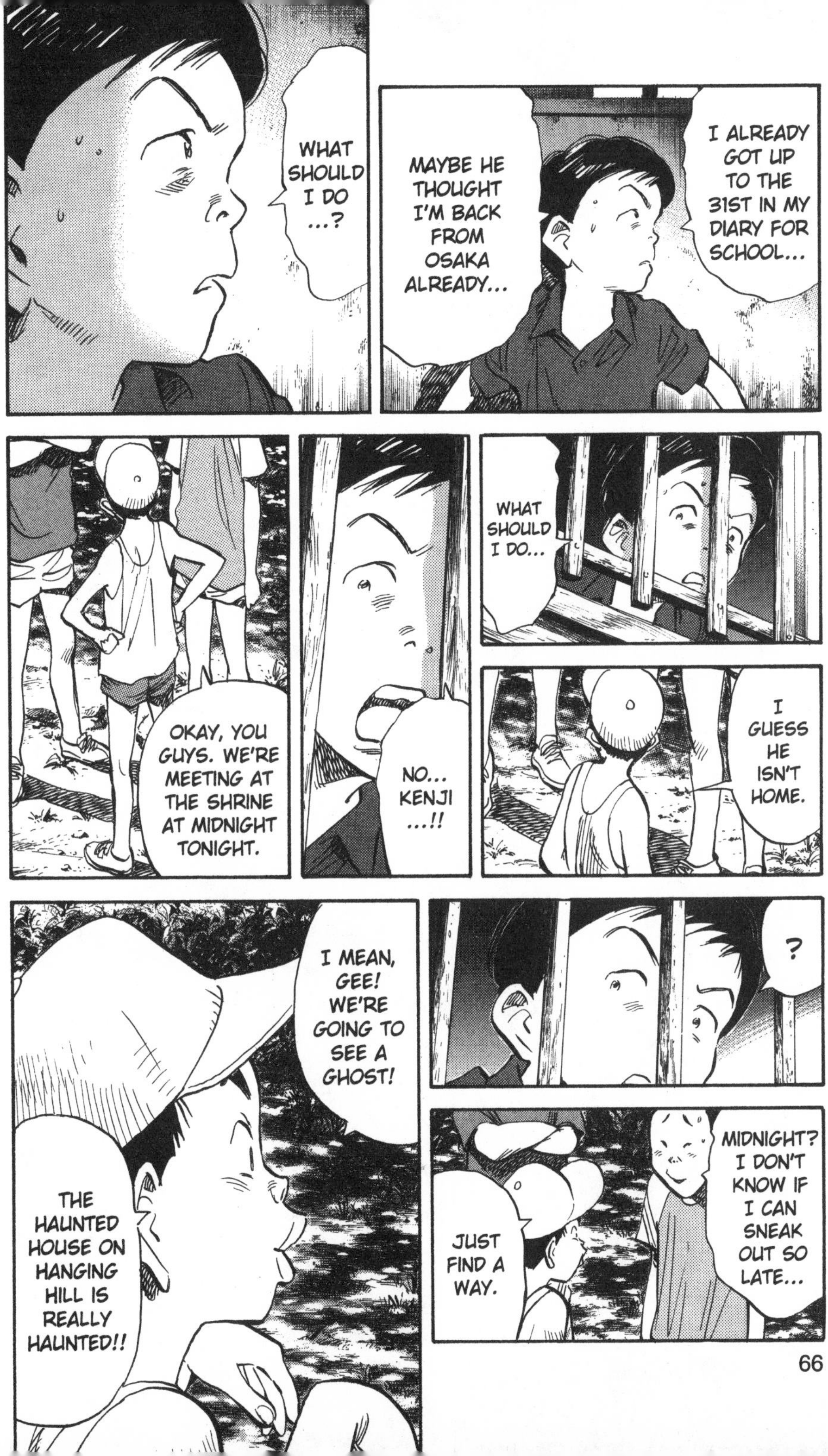
I ALREADY GOT UP TO THE 31ST IN MY DIARY FOR SCHOOL...
MAYBE HE THOUGHT I'M BACK FROM OSAKA ALREADY...
WHAT SHOULD I DO ...?
WHAT SHOULD I DO...
I GUESS HE ISN'T HOME.
NO... KENJI ...!!
OKAY, YOU GUYS. WE'RE MEETING AT THE SHRINE AT MIDNIGHT TONIGHT.
?
MIDNIGHT? I DON'T KNOW IF I CAN SNEAK OUT SO LATE...
JUST FIND A WAY.
I MEAN, GEE! WE'RE GOING TO SEE A GHOST!
THE HAUNTED HOUSE ON HANGING HILL IS REALLY HAUNTED!!

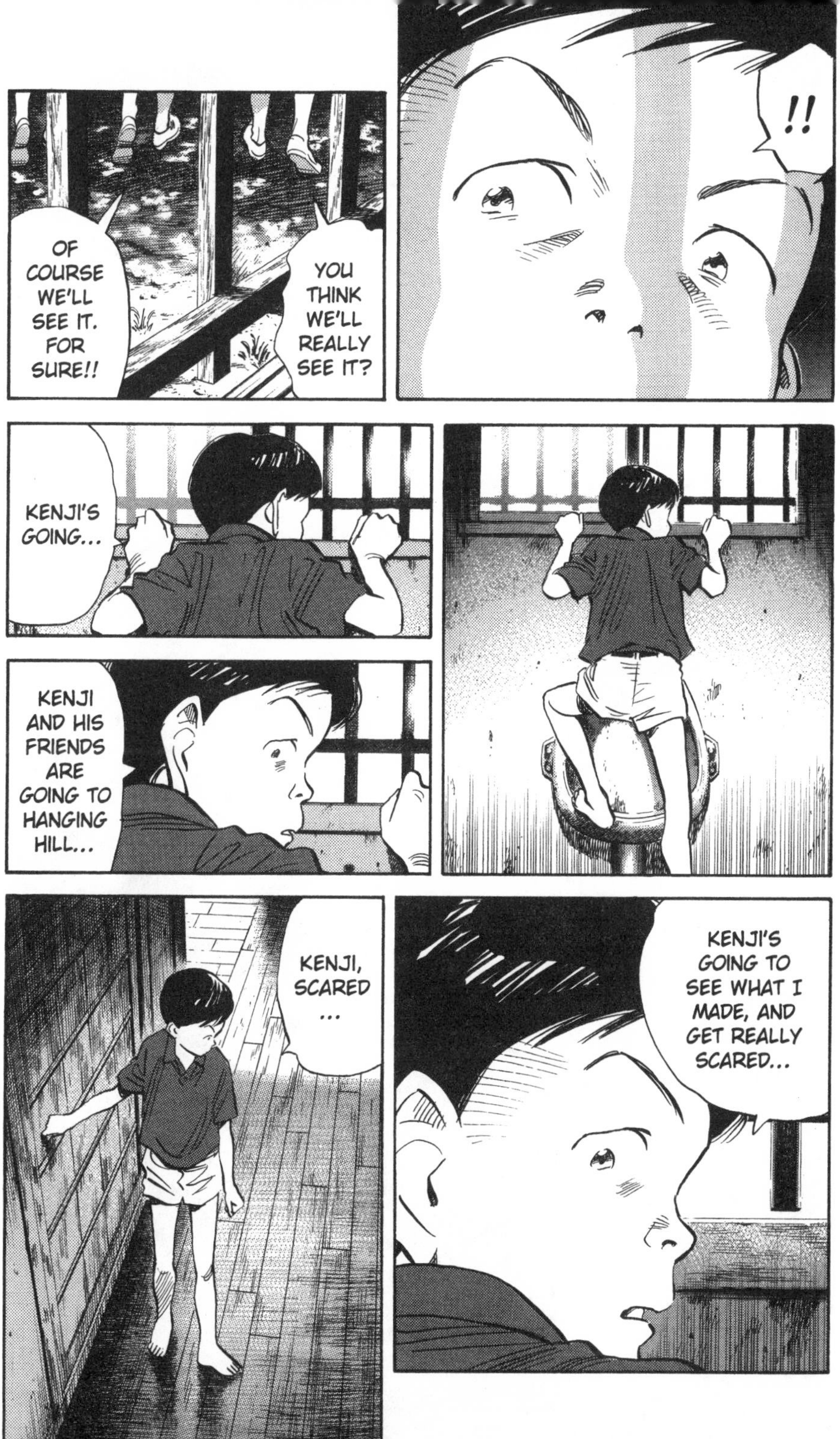
!!
YOU THINK WE'LL REALLY SEE IT?
OF COURSE WE'LL SEE IT. FOR SURE!!
KENJI'S GOING...
KENJI AND HIS FRIENDS ARE GOING TO HANGING HILL...
KENJI'S GOING TO SEE WHAT I MADE, AND GET REALLY SCARED...
KENJI, SCARED ...

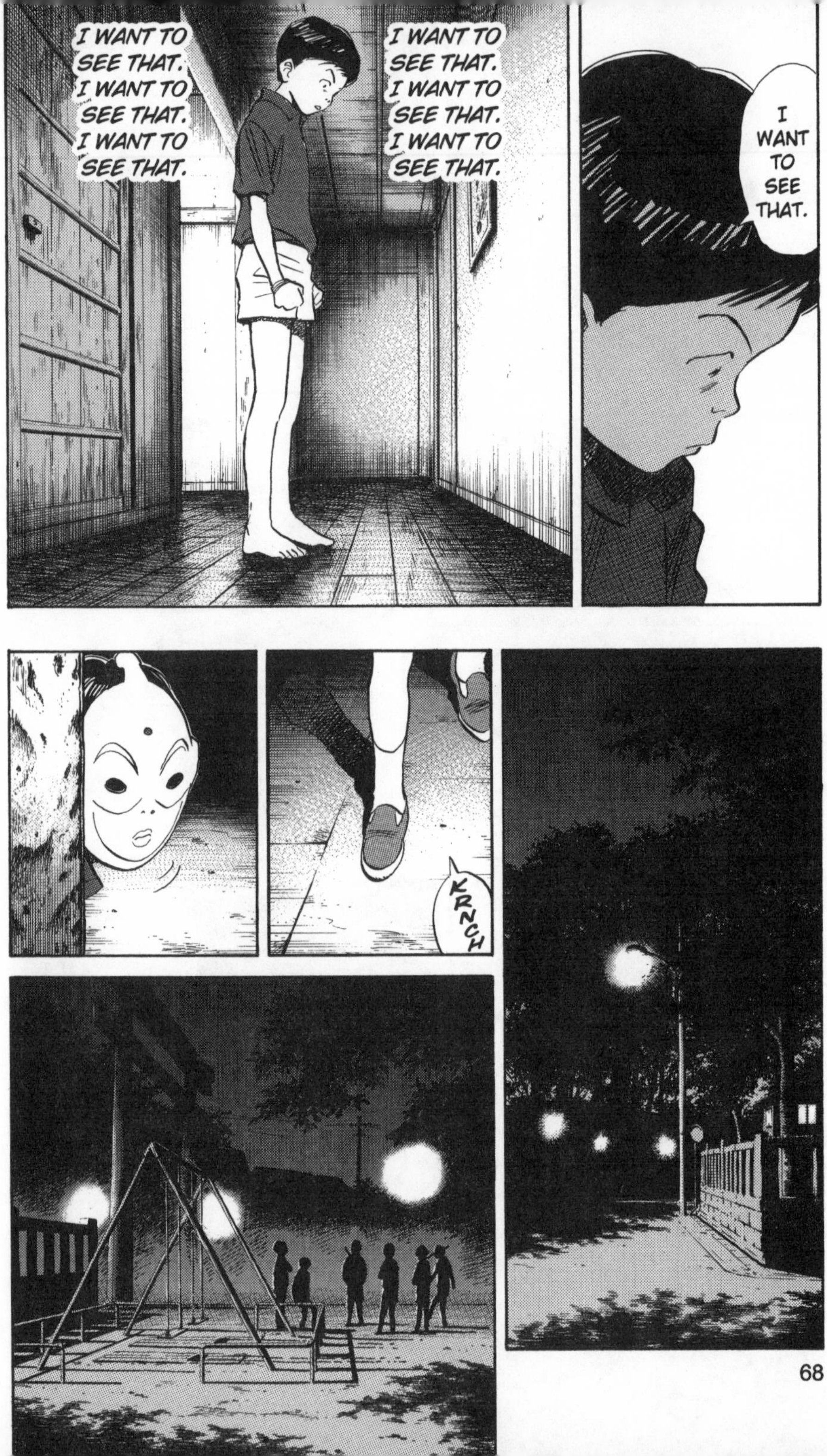
I WANT TO SEE THAT.
I WANT TO SEE THAT. I WANT TO SEE THAT. I WANT TO SEE THAT.
I WANT TO SEE THAT. I WANT TO SEE THAT. I WANT TO SEE THAT.
KRNCH

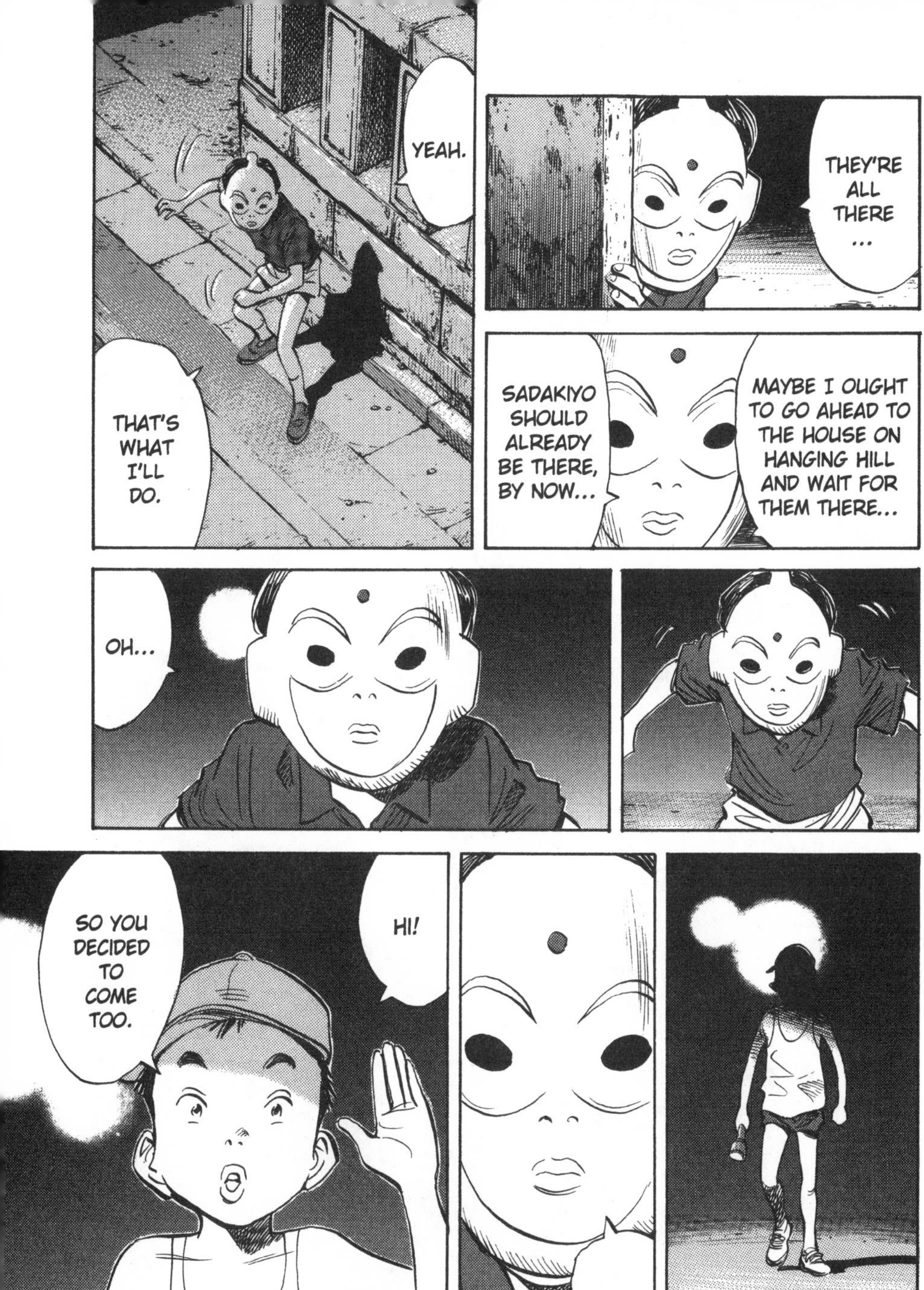
THEY'RE ALL THERE ...
MAYBE I OUGHT TO GO AHEAD TO THE HOUSE ON HANGING HILL AND WAIT FOR THEM THERE...
SADAKIYO SHOULD ALREADY BE THERE, BY NOW...
YEAH.
THAT'S WHAT I'LL DO.
OH...
UH...
HI!
SO YOU DECIDED TO COME TOO.

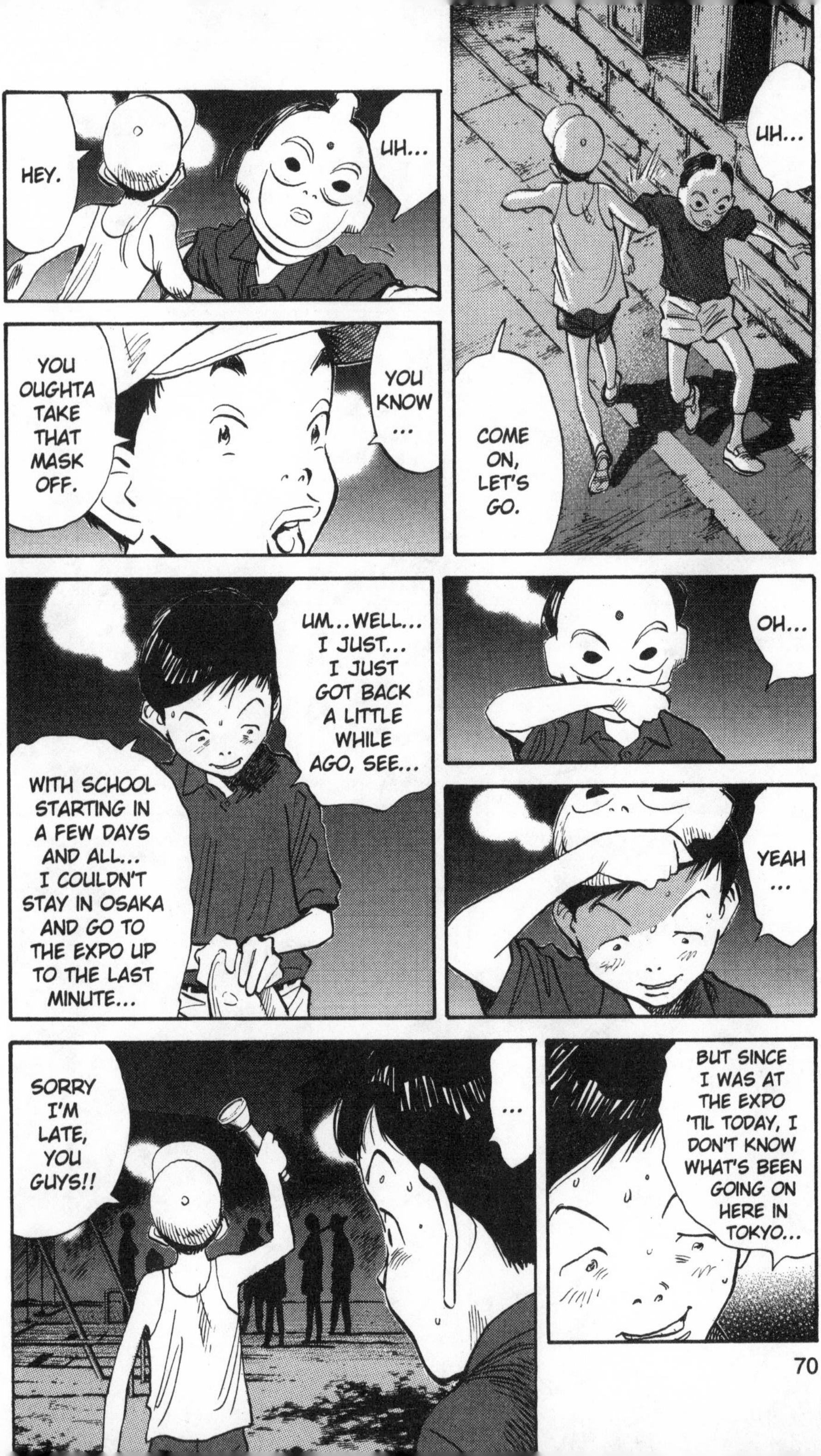
UH...
COME ON, LET'S GO.
UH...
HEY.
YOU KNOW...
YOU OUGHTA TAKE THAT MASK OFF.
OH...
YEAH...
UM...WELL... I JUST... I JUST GOT BACK A LITTLE WHILE AGO, SEE...
WITH SCHOOL STARTING IN A FEW DAYS AND ALL... I COULDN'T STAY IN OSAKA AND GO TO THE EXPO UP TO THE LAST MINUTE...
BUT SINCE I WAS AT THE EXPO 'TIL TODAY, I DON'T KNOW WHAT'S BEEN GOING ON HERE IN TOKYO...
...
SORRY I'M LATE, YOU GUYS!!

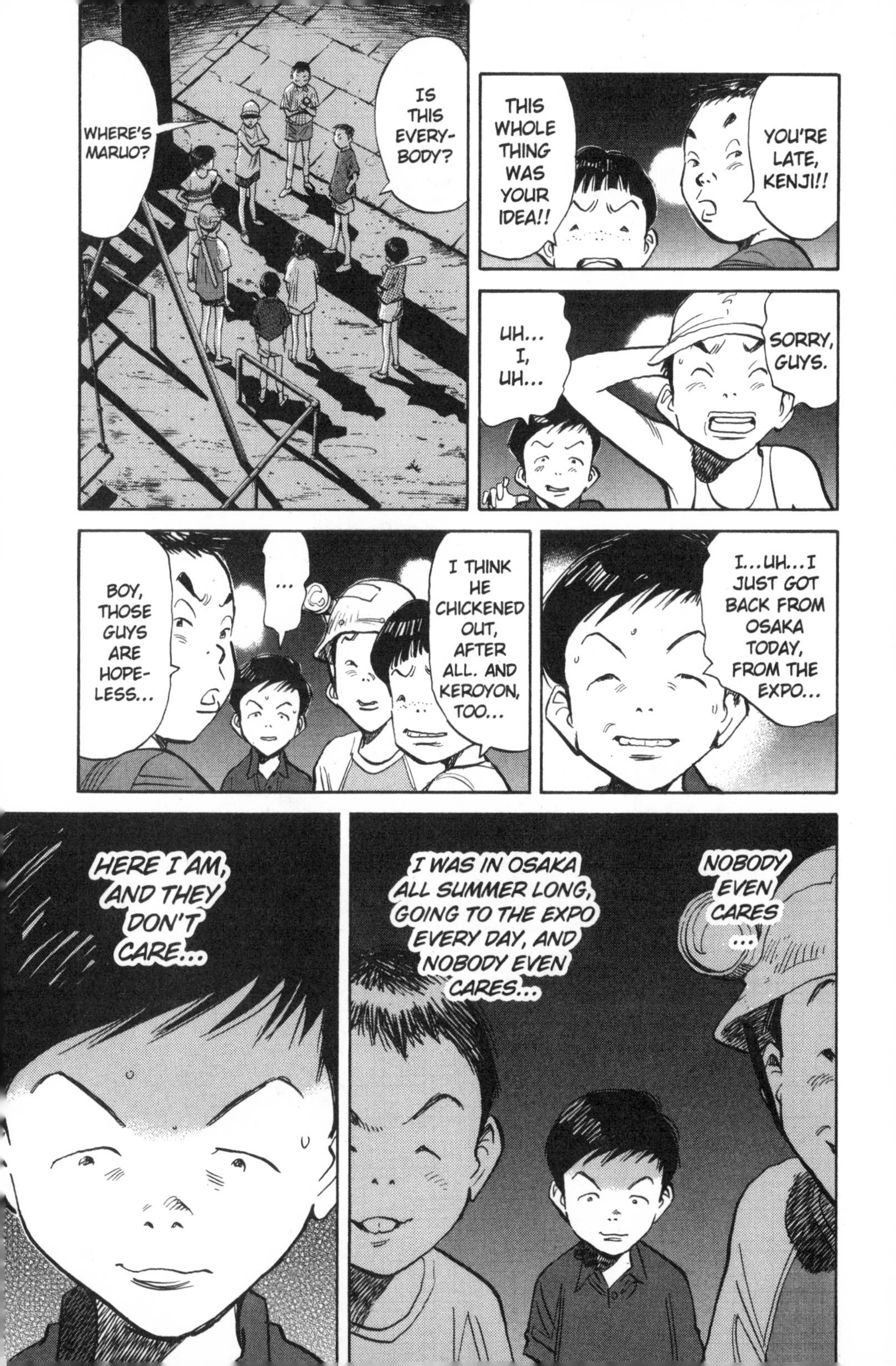
YOU'RE LATE, KENJI!!
THIS WHOLE THING WAS YOUR IDEA!!
SORRY, GUYS.
UH... I, UH...
IS THIS EVERY-BODY?
WHERE'S MARUO?
I...UH...I JUST GOT BACK FROM OSAKA TODAY, FROM THE EXPO...
I THINK HE CHICKENED OUT, AFTER ALL. AND KEROYON, TOO...
...
BOY, THOSE GUYS ARE HOPE-LESS...
NOBODY EVEN CARES ...
I WAS IN OSAKA ALL SUMMER LONG, GOING TO THE EXPO EVERY DAY, AND NOBODY EVEN CARES...
HERE I AM, AND THEY DON'T CARE...

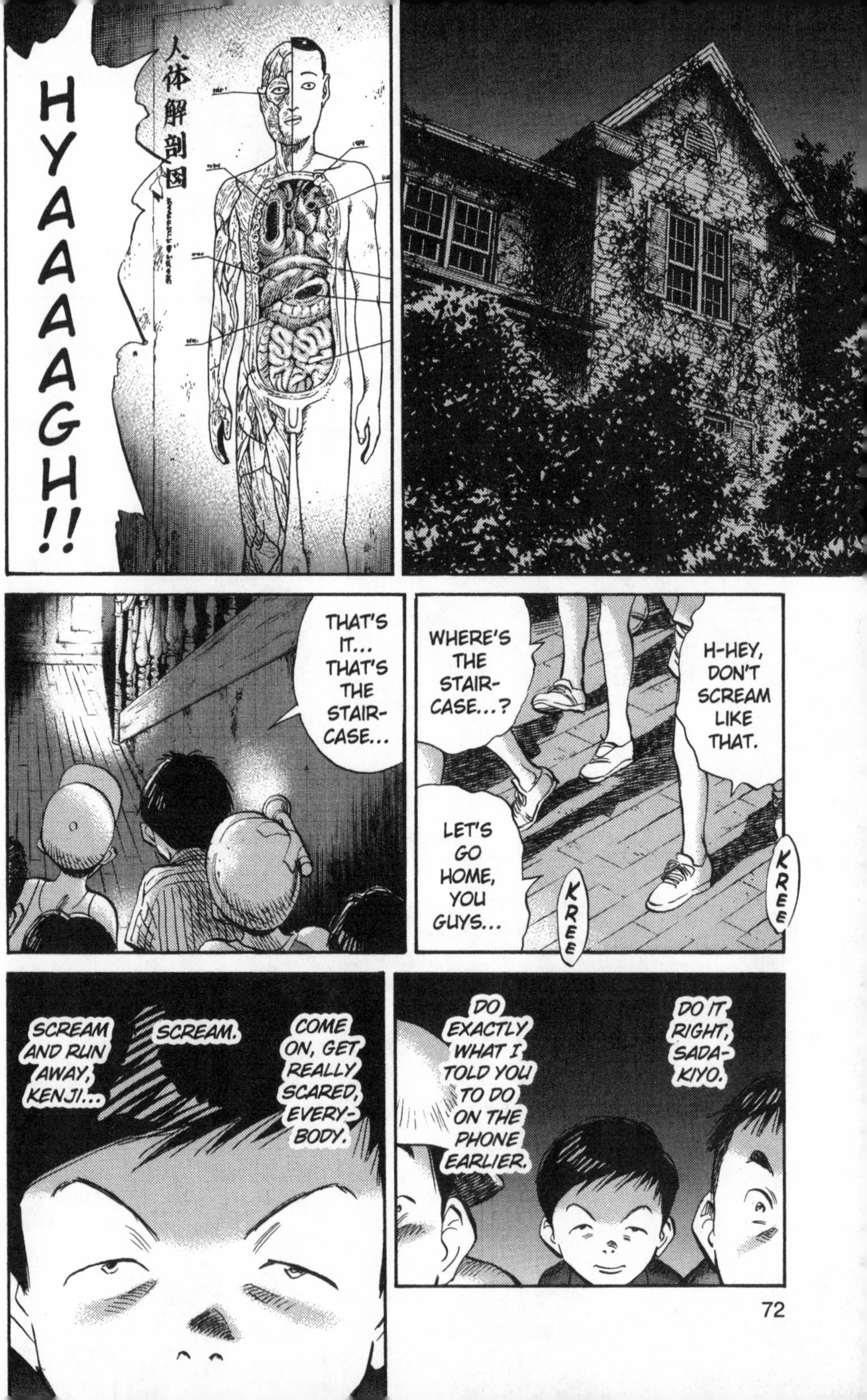
人体解剖図
HYAAAAAGH!!
H-HEY, DON'T SCREAM LIKE THAT.
WHERE'S THE STAIR-CASE...?
LET'S GO HOME, YOU GUYS...
KREE
KREE
THAT'S IT... THAT'S THE STAIR-CASE...
DO IT RIGHT, SADA-KIYO.
DO EXACTLY WHAT I TOLD YOU TO DO ON THE PHONE EARLIER.
COME ON, GET REALLY SCARED, EVERY-BODY.
SCREAM.
SCREAM AND RUN AWAY, KENJI...

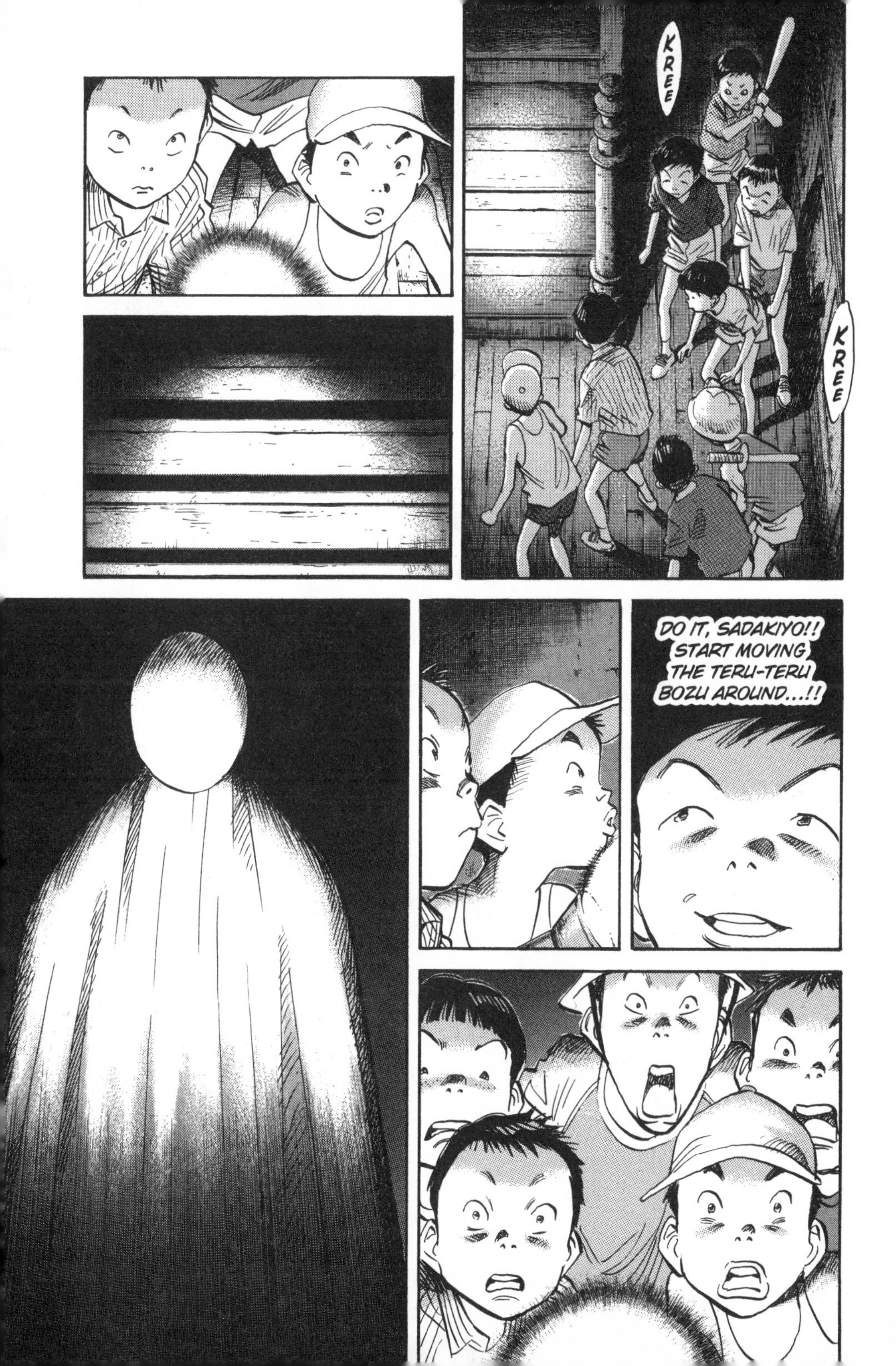
KREE
KREE
DO IT, SADAKIYO!! START MOVING THE TERU-TERU BOZU AROUND...!!

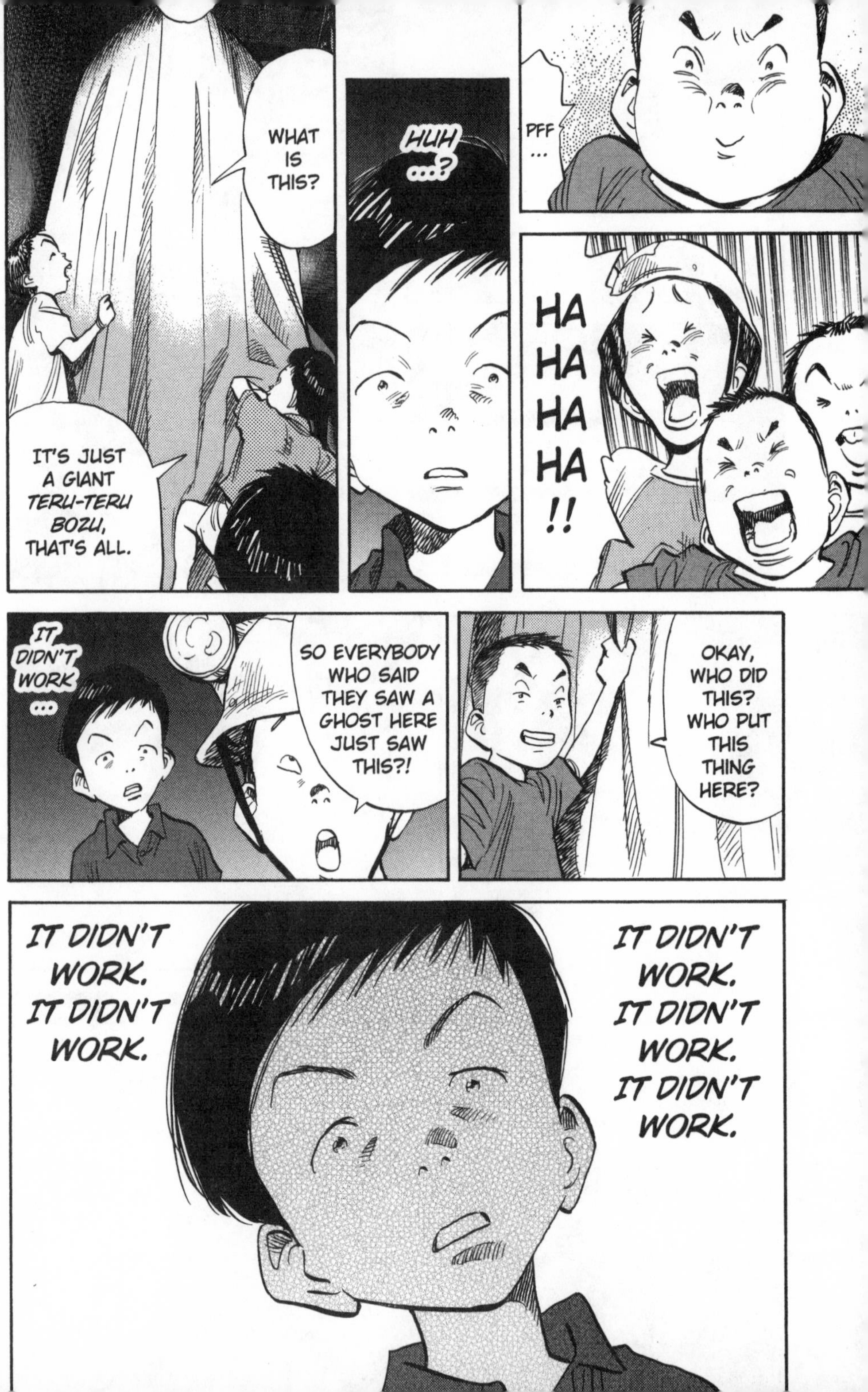
PFF
...
HA
HA
HA
HA
!!
HUH
...?
WHAT IS THIS?
IT'S JUST A GIANT TERU-TERU BOZU, THAT'S ALL.
OKAY, WHO DID THIS? WHO PUT THIS THING HERE?
SO EVERYBODY WHO SAID THEY SAW A GHOST HERE JUST SAW THIS?!
IT DIDN'T WORK ...
IT DIDN'T WORK. IT DIDN'T WORK. IT DIDN'T WORK.
IT DIDN'T WORK. IT DIDN'T WORK.

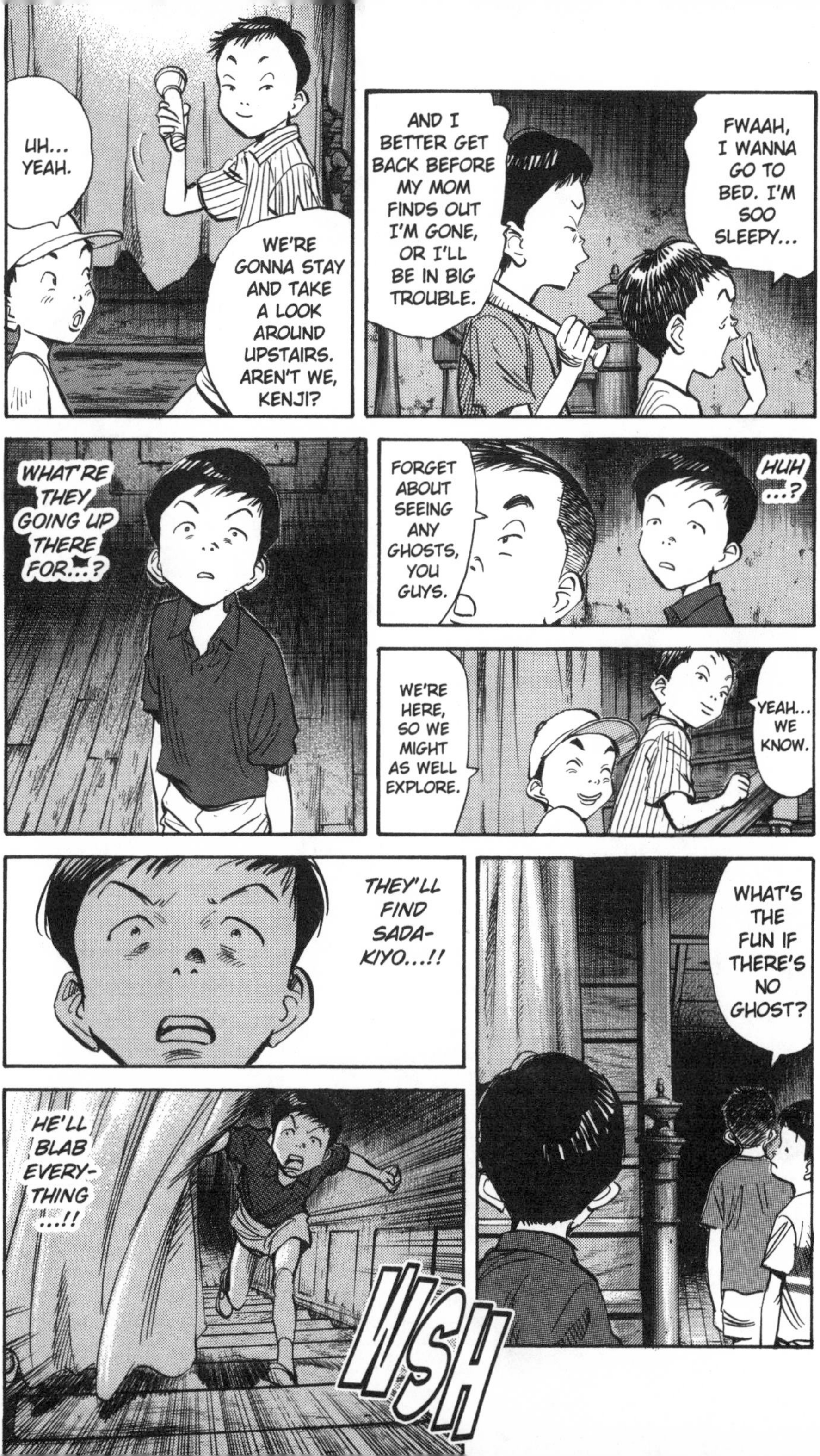
FWAAH, I WANNA GO TO BED. I'M SOO SLEEPY...
AND I BETTER GET BACK BEFORE MY MOM FINDS OUT I'M GONE, OR I'LL BE IN BIG TROUBLE.
WE'RE GONNA STAY AND TAKE A LOOK AROUND UPSTAIRS. AREN'T WE, KENJI?
UH... YEAH.
HUH ...?
FORGET ABOUT SEEING ANY GHOSTS, YOU GUYS.
YEAH... WE KNOW.
WE'RE HERE, SO WE MIGHT AS WELL EXPLORE.
WHAT'RE THEY GOING UP THERE FOR...?
WHAT'S THE FUN IF THERE'S NO GHOST?
THEY'LL FIND SADA-KIYO...!!
HE'LL BLAB EVERY-THING ...!!
WSH

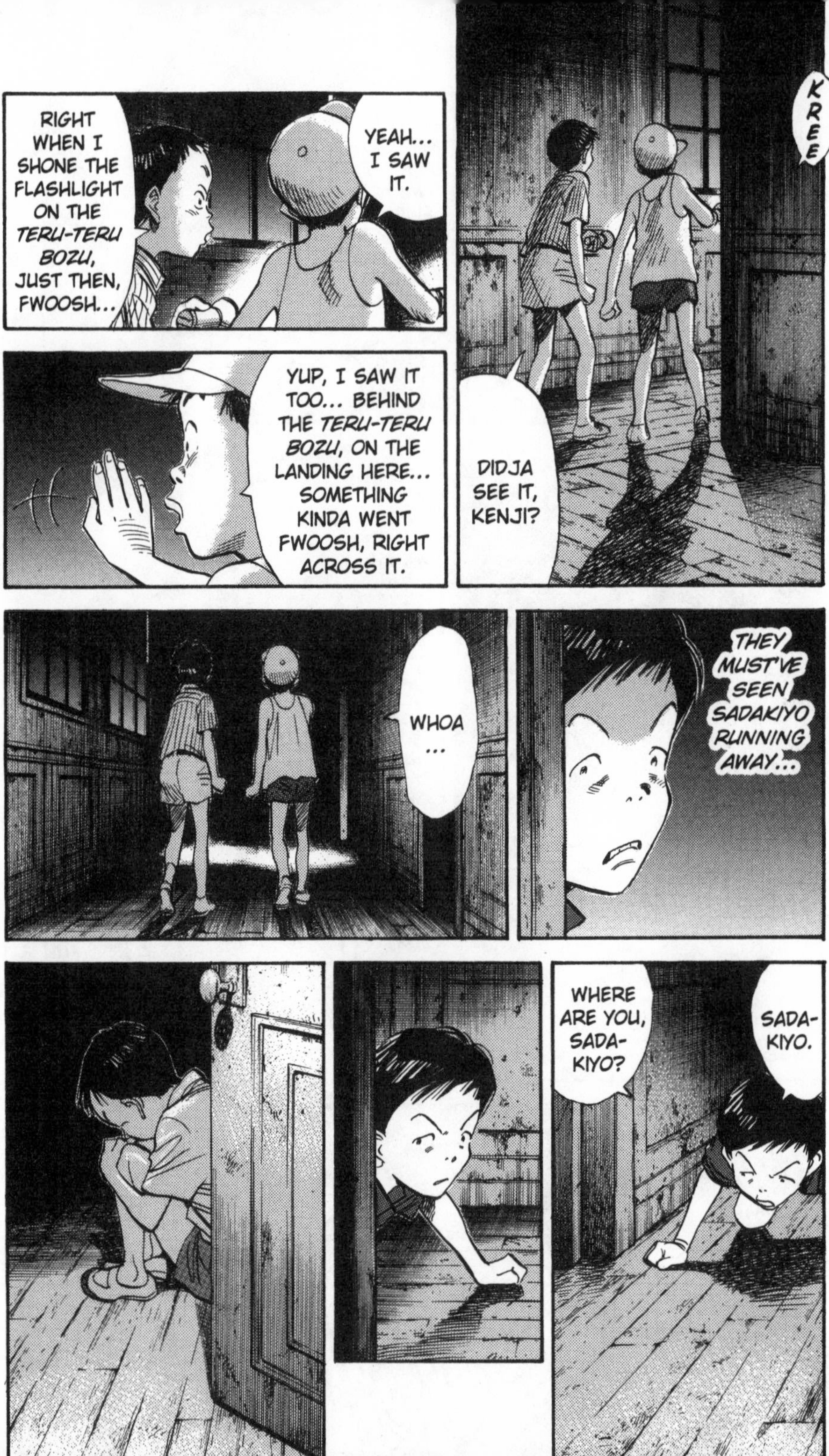
KREE
DIDJA SEE IT, KENJI?
YEAH... I SAW IT.
RIGHT WHEN I SHONE THE FLASHLIGHT ON THE *TERU-TERU BOZU*, JUST THEN, FWOOSH...
YUP, I SAW IT TOO... BEHIND THE *TERU-TERU BOZU*, ON THE LANDING HERE... SOMETHING KINDA WENT FWOOSH, RIGHT ACROSS IT.
THEY MUST'VE SEEN SADAKIYO RUNNING AWAY...
WHOA ...
SADA-KIYO.
WHERE ARE YOU, SADA-KIYO?

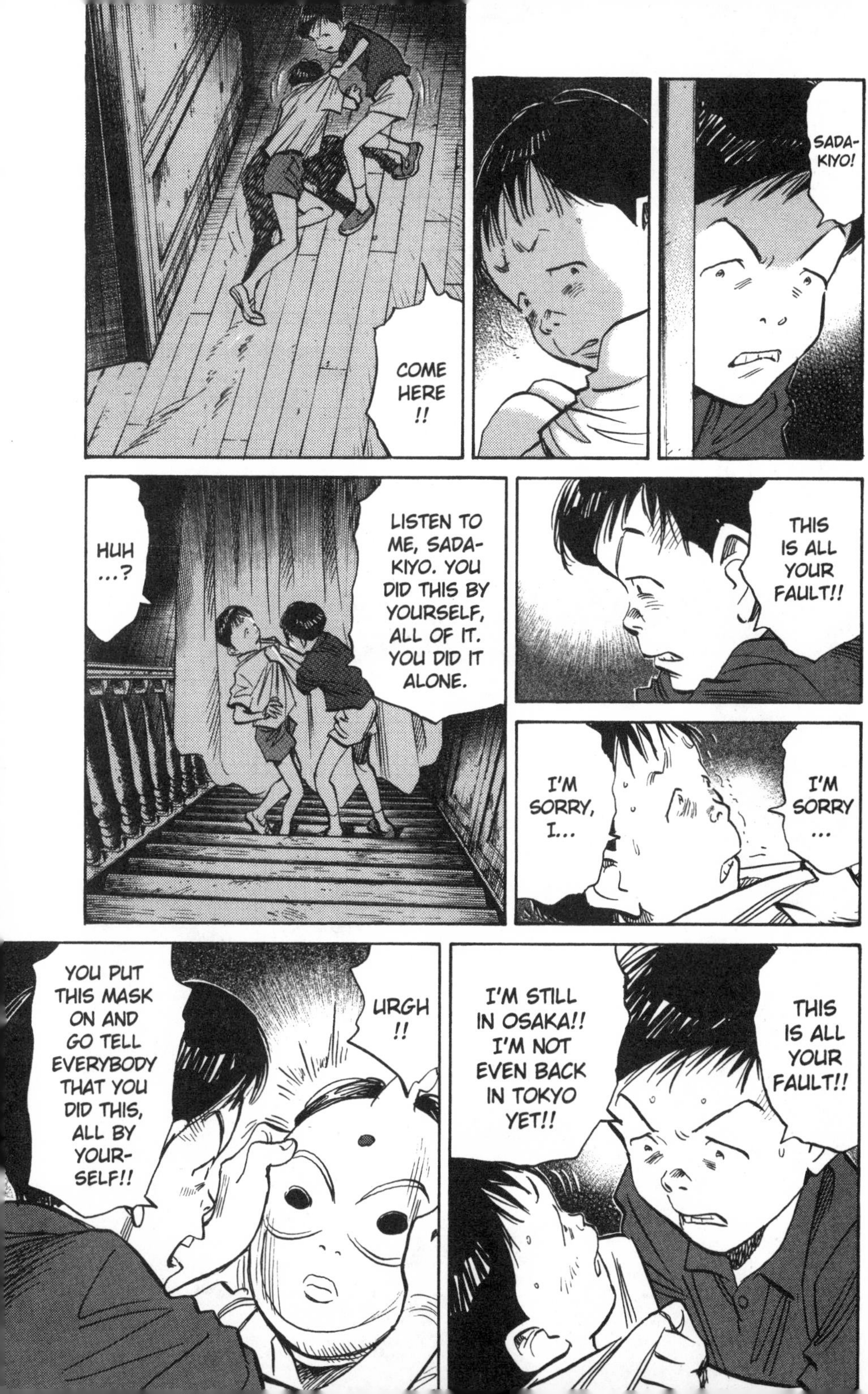
SADA-KIYO!
COME HERE !!
THIS IS ALL YOUR FAULT!!
I'M SORRY ...
I'M SORRY, I...
LISTEN TO ME, SADA-KIYO. YOU DID THIS BY YOURSELF, ALL OF IT. YOU DID IT ALONE.
HUH ...?
THIS IS ALL YOUR FAULT!!
I'M STILL IN OSAKA!! I'M NOT EVEN BACK IN TOKYO YET!!
URGH !!
YOU PUT THIS MASK ON AND GO TELL EVERYBODY THAT YOU DID THIS, ALL BY YOUR-SELF!!

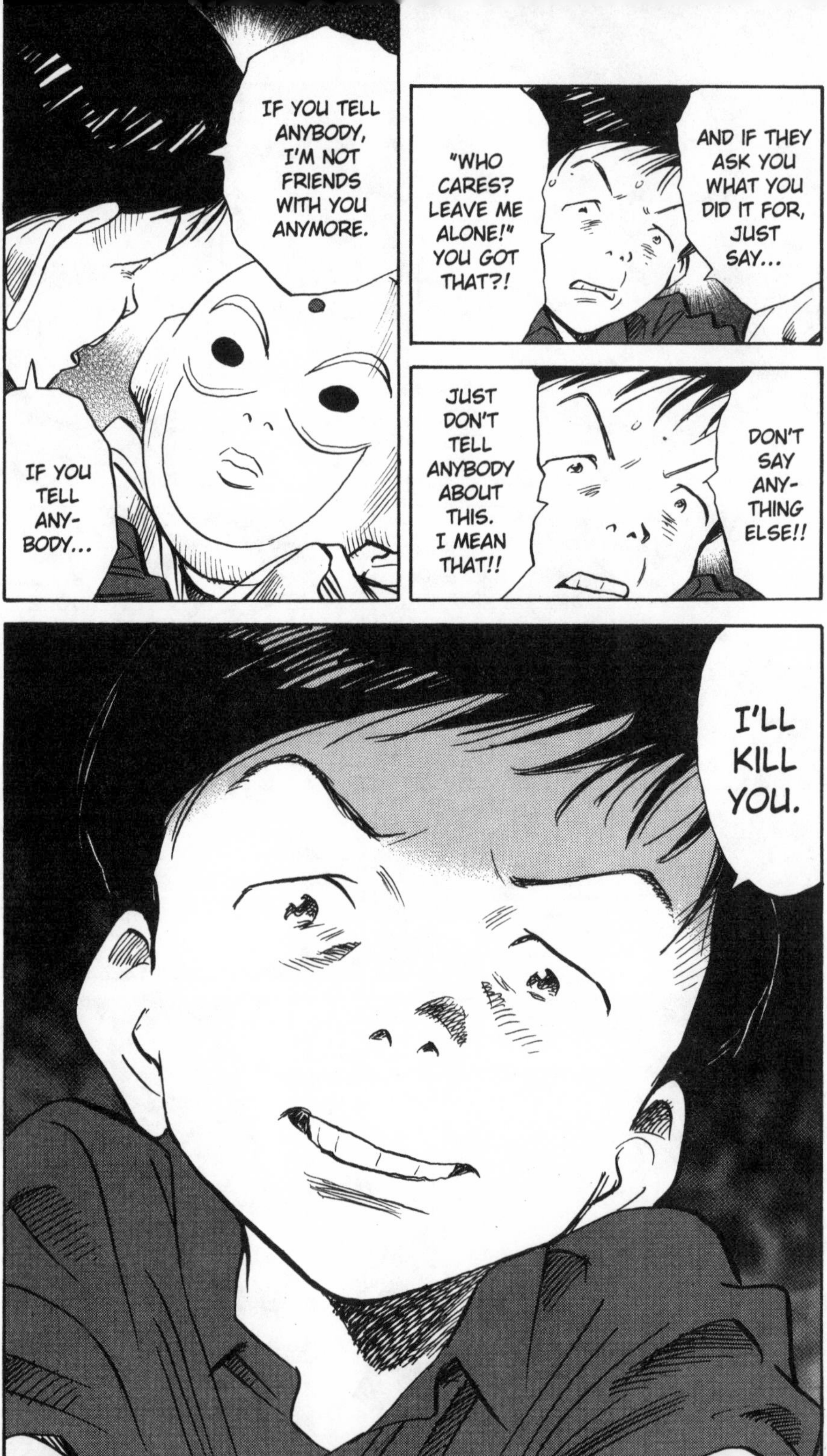
AND IF THEY ASK YOU WHAT YOU DID IT FOR, JUST SAY...
"WHO CARES? LEAVE ME ALONE!" YOU GOT THAT?!
DON'T SAY ANY-THING ELSE!!
JUST DON'T TELL ANYBODY ABOUT THIS. I MEAN THAT!!
IF YOU TELL ANYBODY, I'M NOT FRIENDS WITH YOU ANYMORE.
IF YOU TELL ANY-BODY...
I'LL KILL YOU.

Chapter 5 A Real Ghost

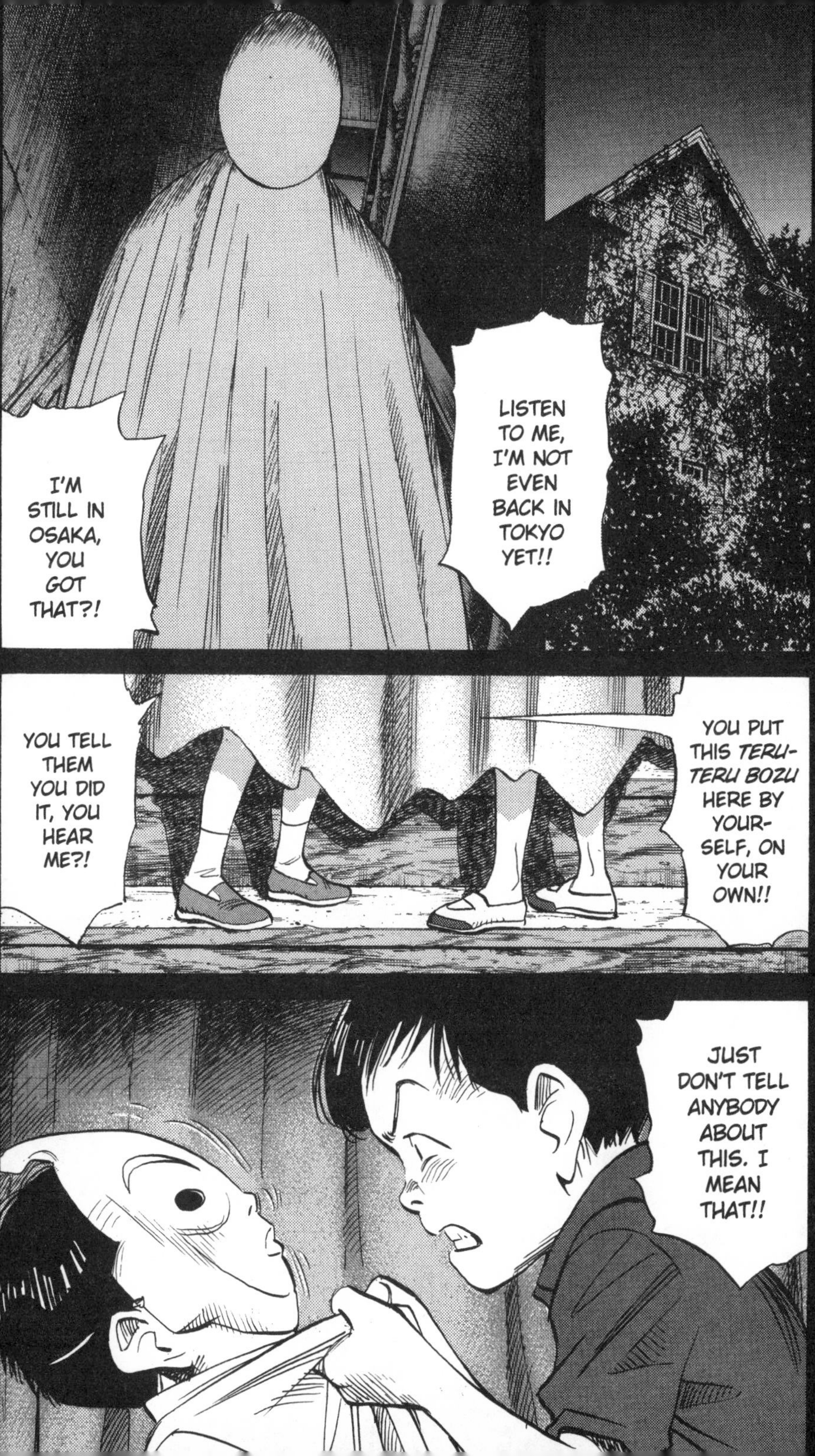
LISTEN TO ME, I'M NOT EVEN BACK IN TOKYO YET!!
I'M STILL IN OSAKA, YOU GOT THAT?!
YOU PUT THIS *TERU-TERU BOZU* HERE BY YOURSELF, ON YOUR OWN!!
YOU TELL THEM YOU DID IT, YOU HEAR ME?!
JUST DON'T TELL ANYBODY ABOUT THIS. I MEAN THAT!!

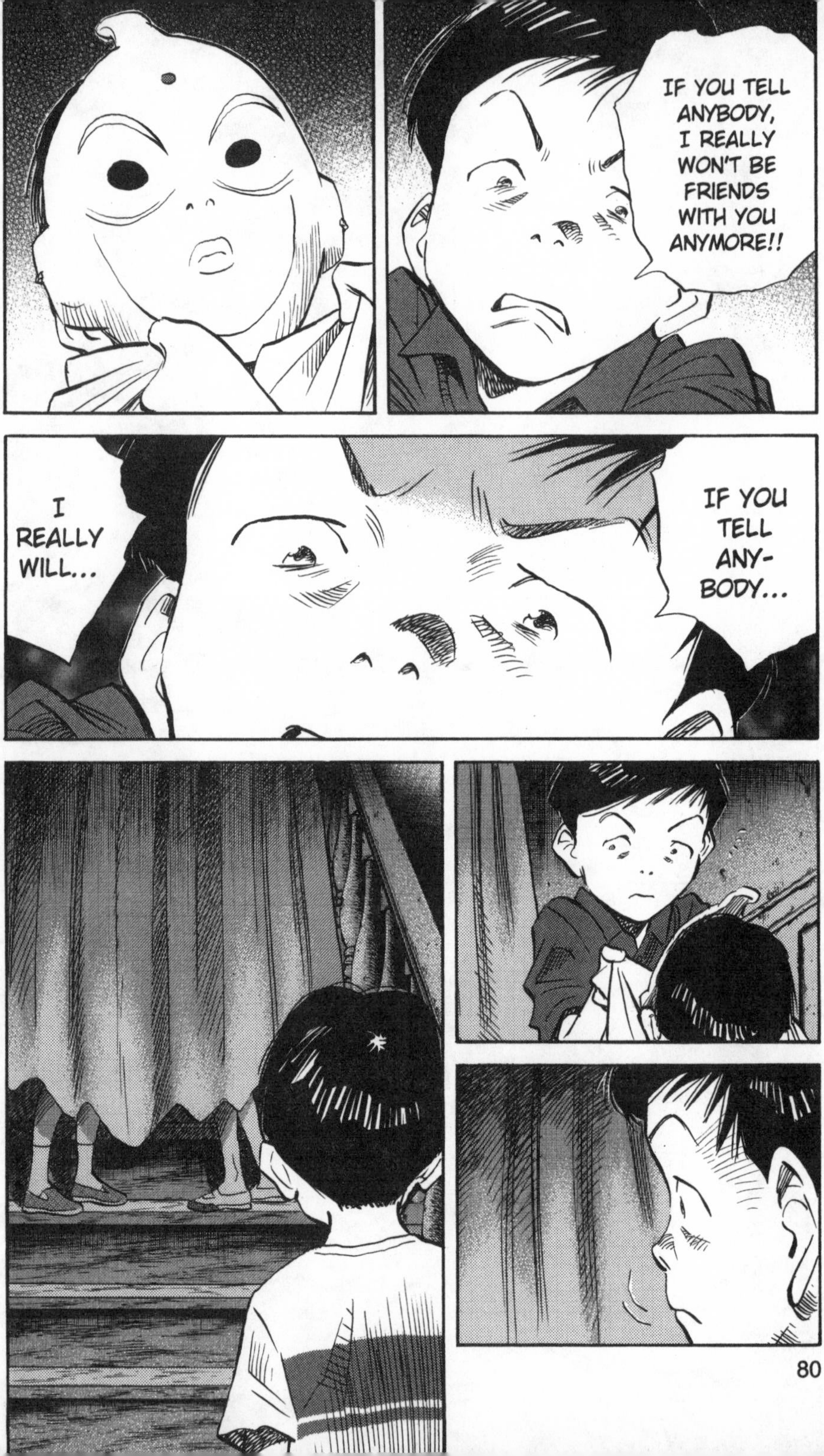
IF YOU TELL ANYBODY, I REALLY WON'T BE FRIENDS WITH YOU ANYMORE!!
IF YOU TELL ANY-BODY...
I REALLY WILL...

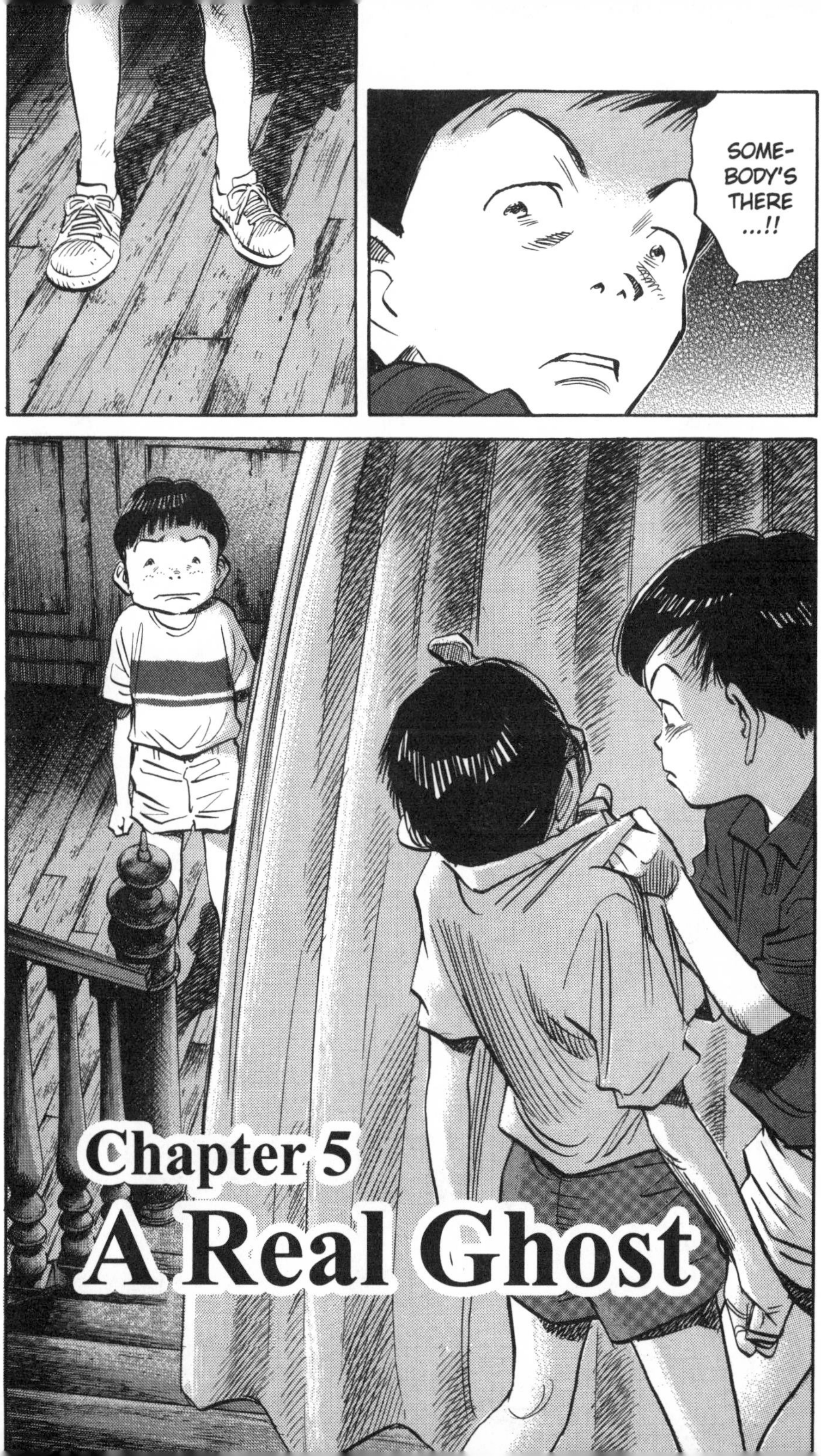
SOMEBODY'S THERE ...!!

Chapter 5
A Real Ghost

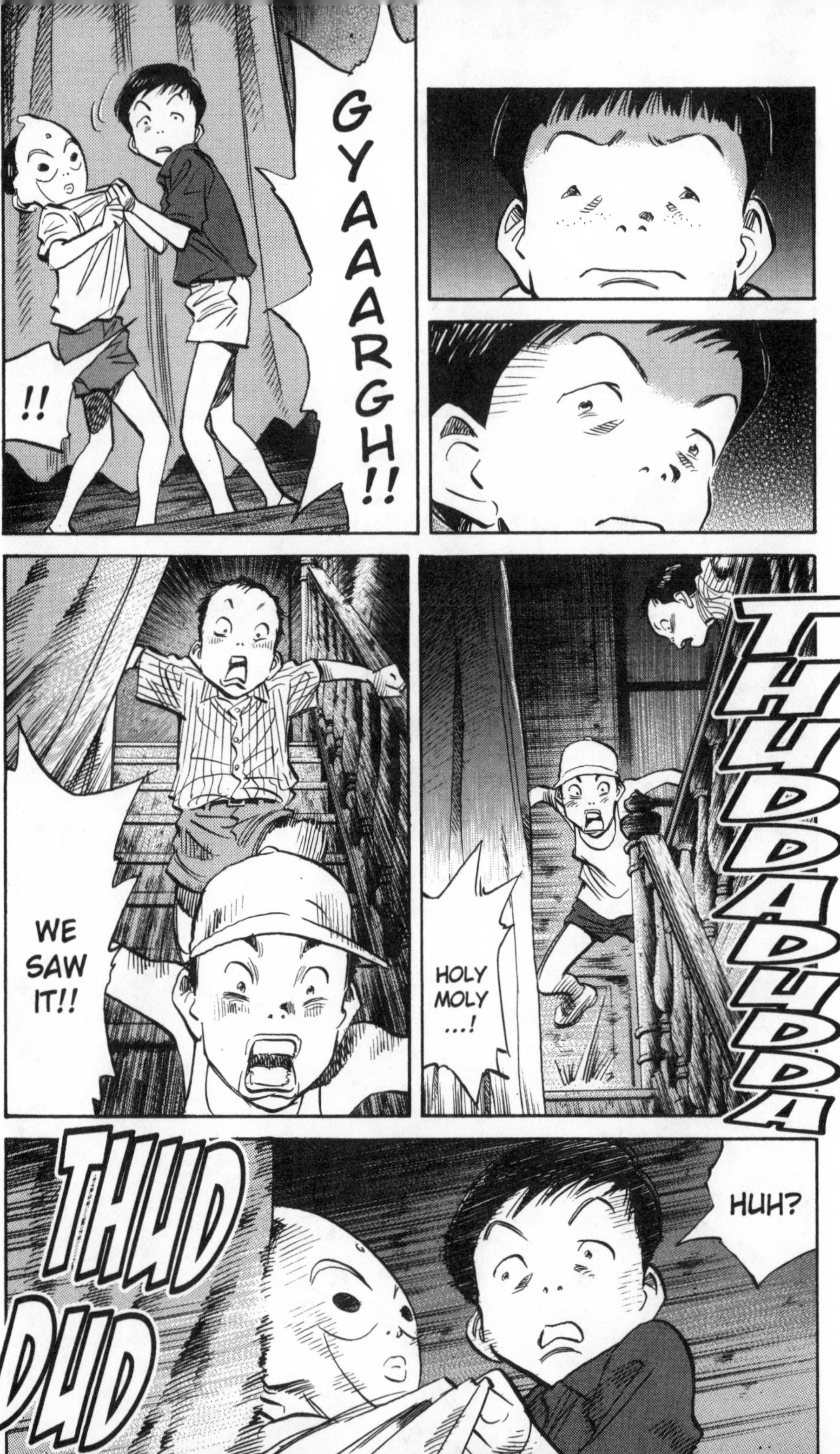
GYAAARGH!!
!!
THUDDADUDDA
HOLY MOLY ...!
WE SAW IT!!
HUH?
THUD DUD

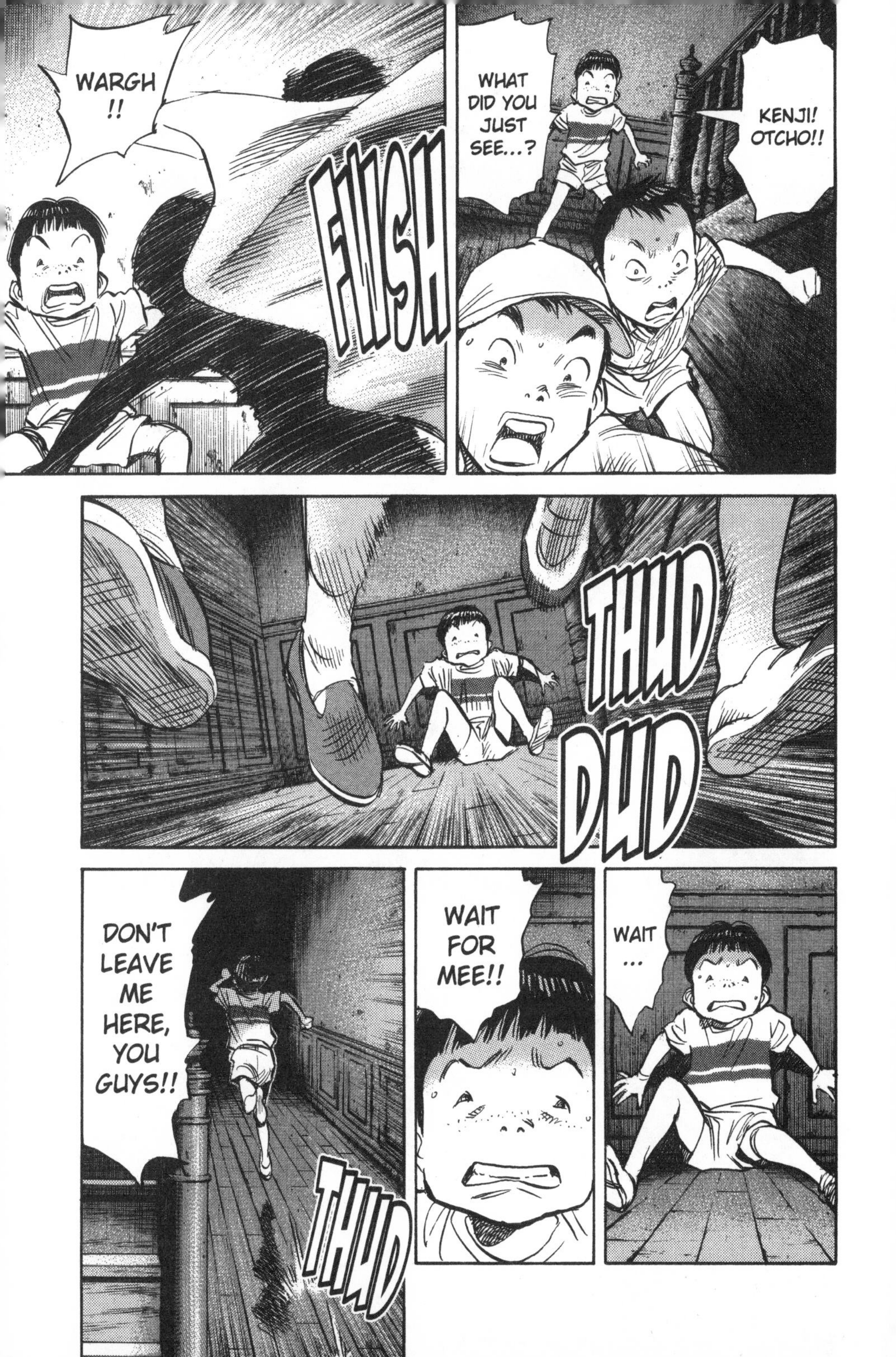
KENJI! OTCHO!!
WHAT DID YOU JUST SEE...?
WARGH !!
FWSH
THUD
DUD
WAIT ...
WAIT FOR MEE!!
DON'T LEAVE ME HERE, YOU GUYS!!
THUD

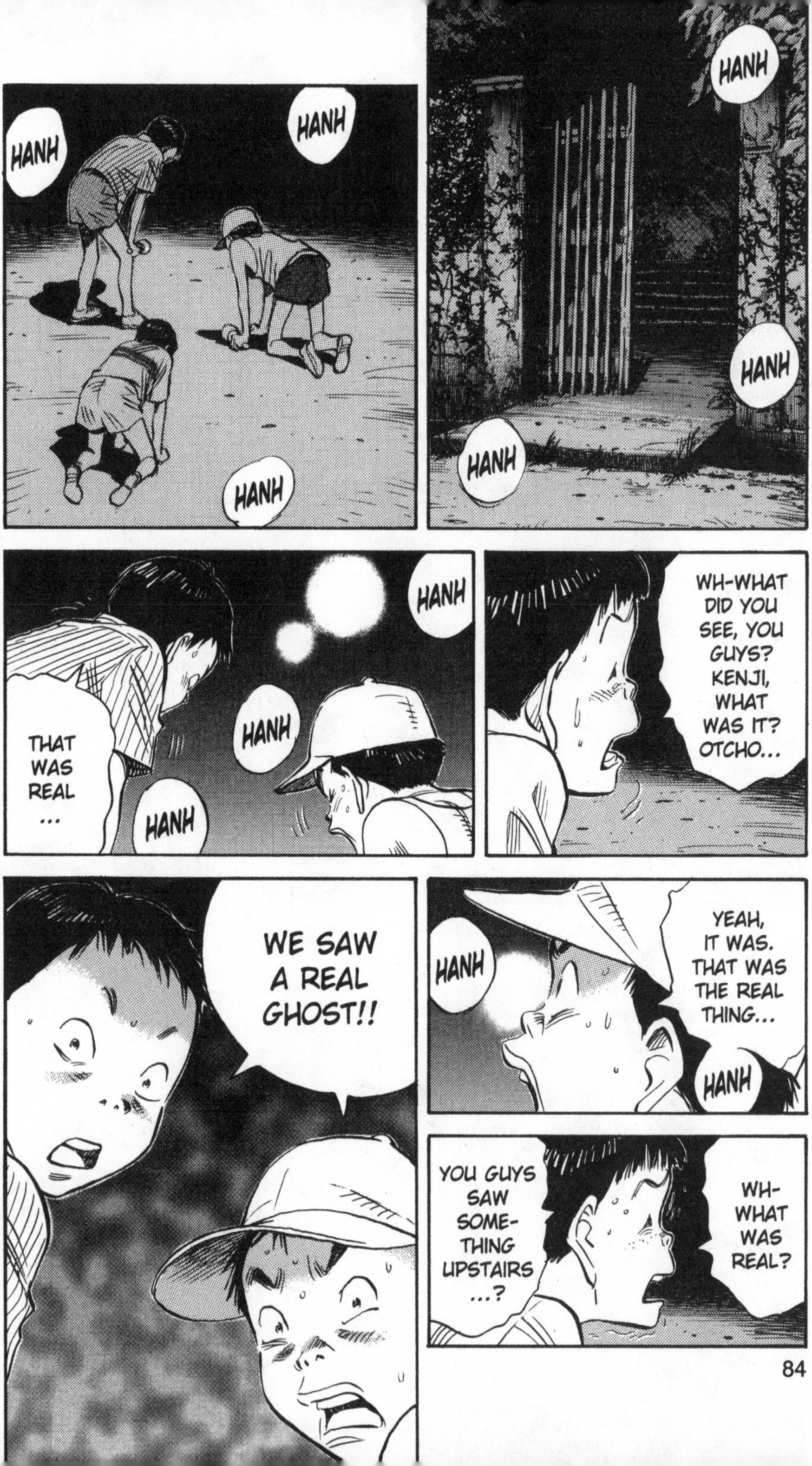

HANH
HANH
HANH
HANH
HANH
HANH
WH-WHAT DID YOU SEE, YOU GUYS? KENJI, WHAT WAS IT? OTCHO...
HANH
HANH
HANH
THAT WAS REAL ...
HANH
YEAH, IT WAS. THAT WAS THE REAL THING...
HANH
WH- WHAT WAS REAL?
YOU GUYS SAW SOME-THING UPSTAIRS ...?
WE SAW A REAL GHOST!!

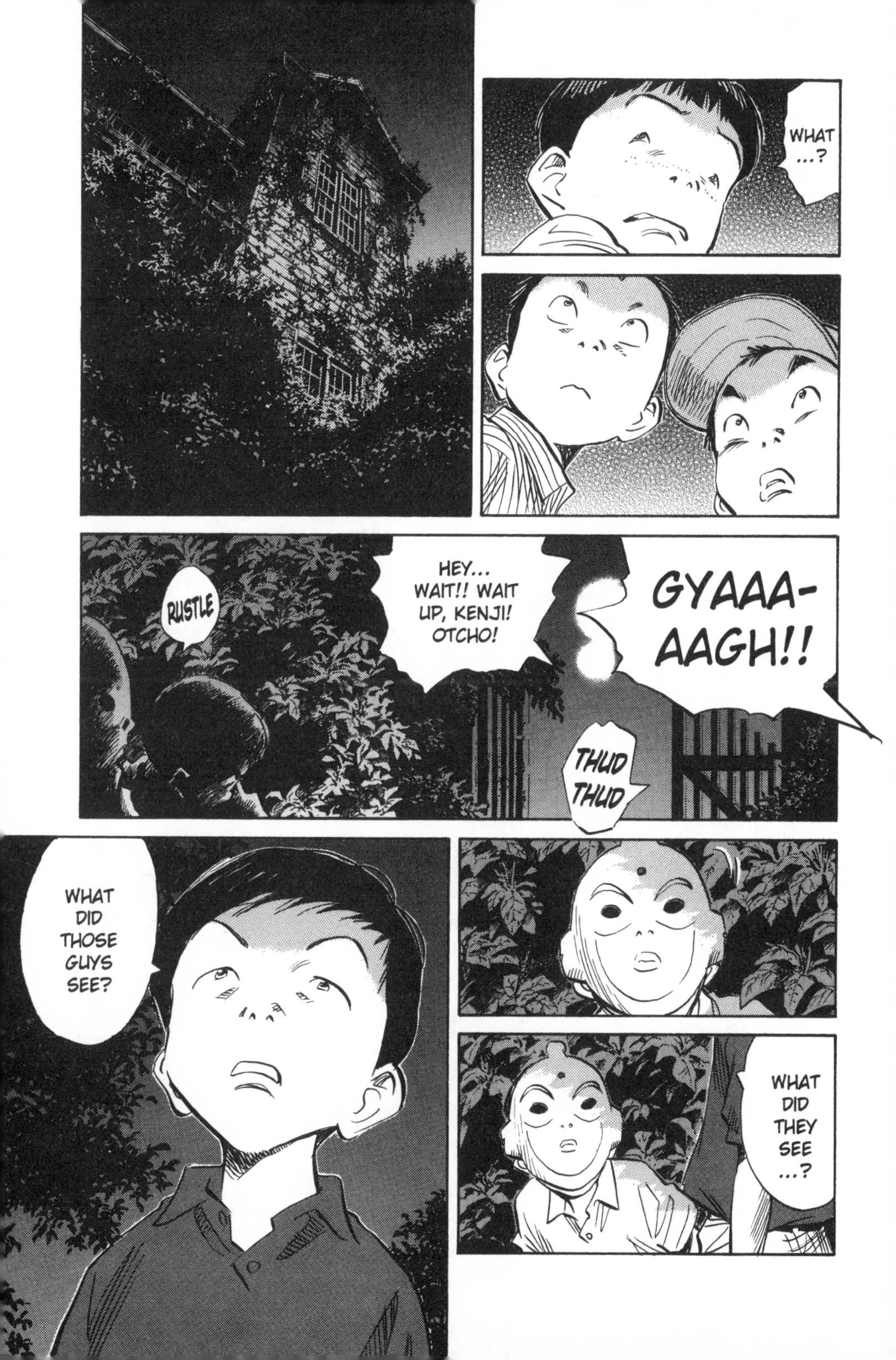

WHAT ...?
GYAAA-AAGH!!
HEY... WAIT!! WAIT UP, KENJI! OTCHO!
RUSTLE
THUD THUD
WHAT DID THEY SEE ...?
WHAT DID THOSE GUYS SEE?

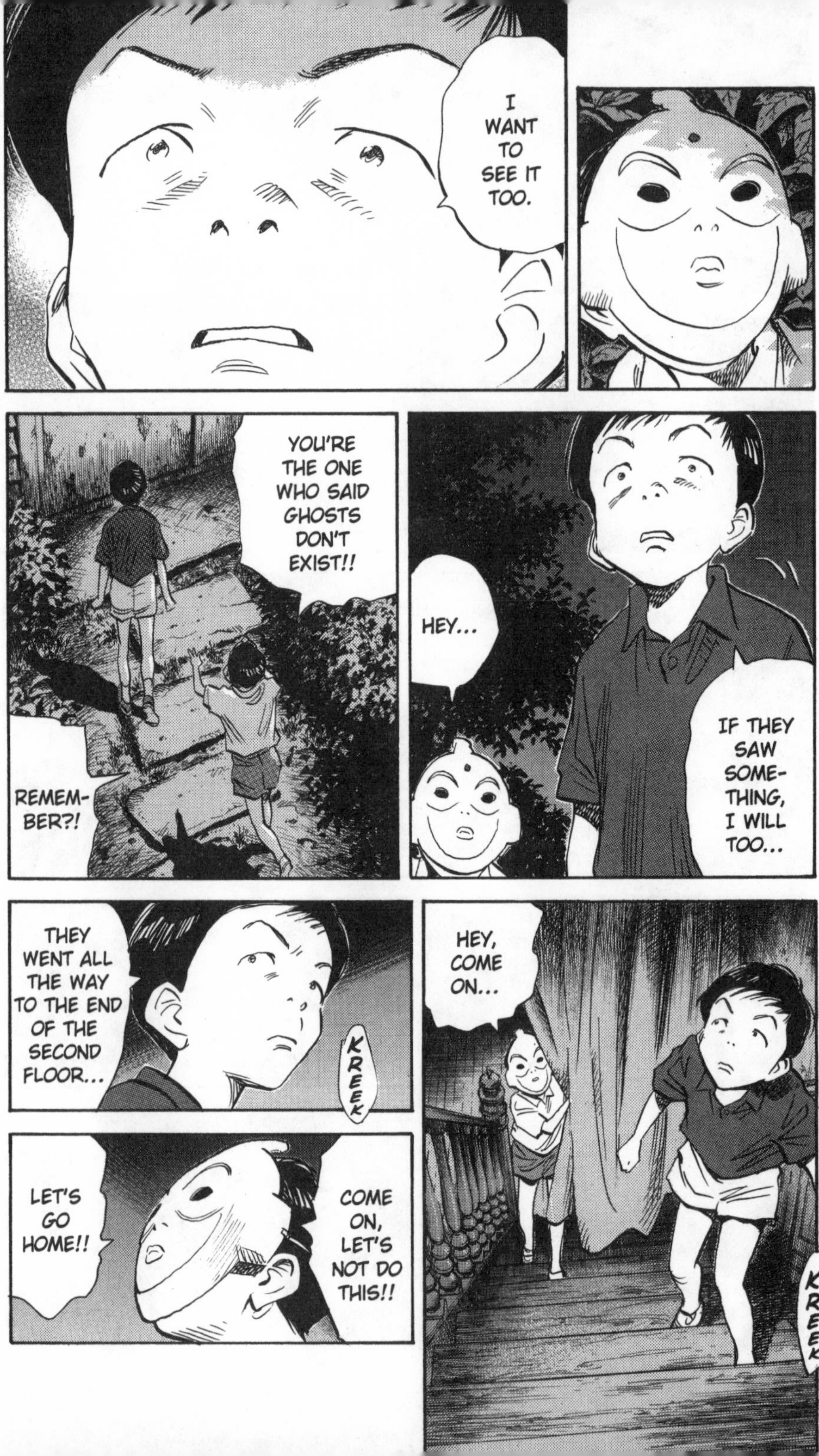
I WANT TO SEE IT TOO.
HEY...
IF THEY SAW SOMETHING, I WILL TOO...
YOU'RE THE ONE WHO SAID GHOSTS DON'T EXIST!!
REMEMBER?!
HEY, COME ON...
KREEK
THEY WENT ALL THE WAY TO THE END OF THE SECOND FLOOR...
KREEK
COME ON, LET'S NOT DO THIS!!
LET'S GO HOME!!

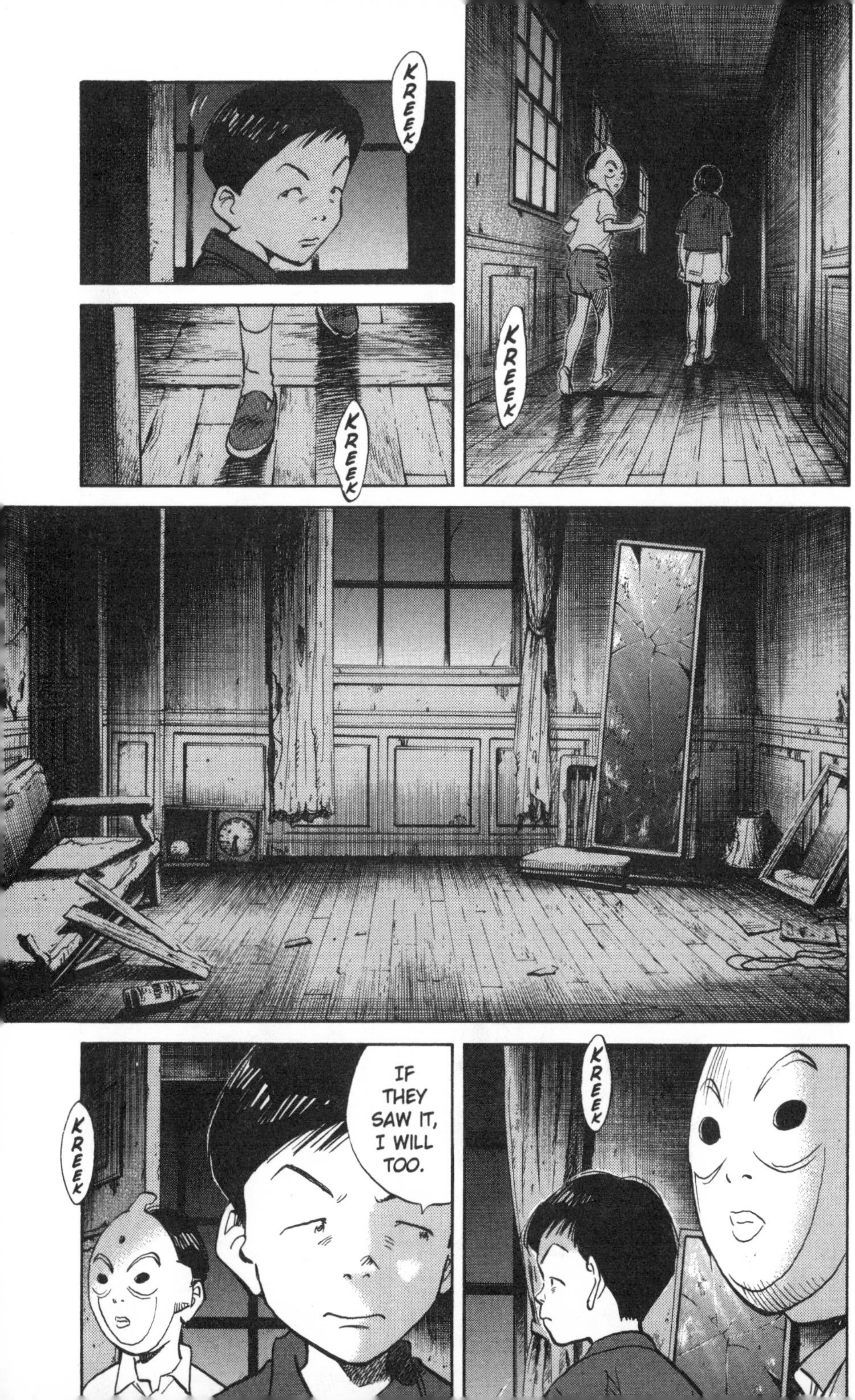

KREEK
KREEK
KREEK
KREEK
IF THEY SAW IT, I WILL TOO.
KREEK

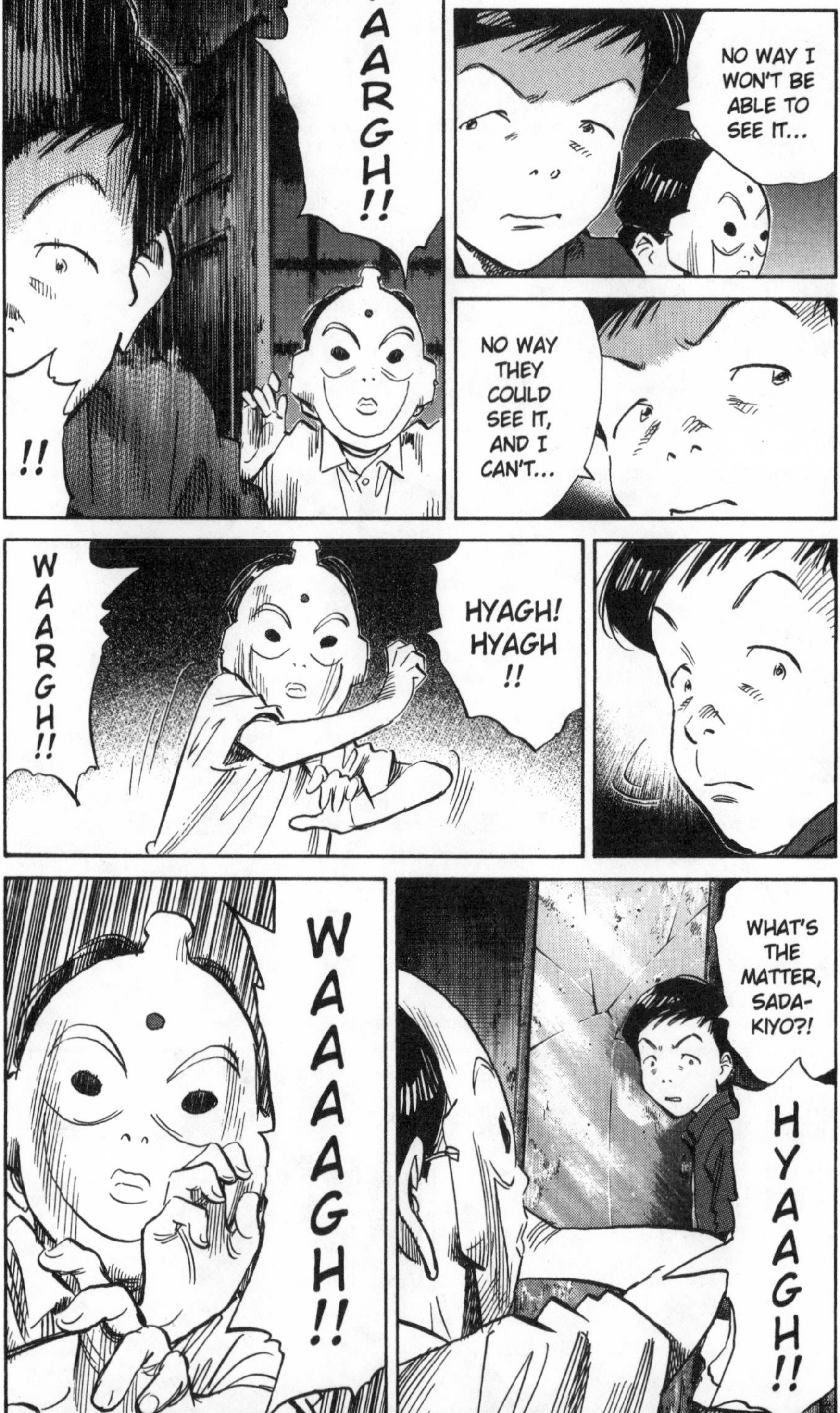
NO WAY I WON'T BE ABLE TO SEE IT...
NO WAY THEY COULD SEE IT, AND I CAN'T...
YAARGH!!
!!
HYAGH! HYAGH!!
WAARGH!!
WHAT'S THE MATTER, SADA-KIYO?!
HYAAGH!!
WAAAAAGH!!

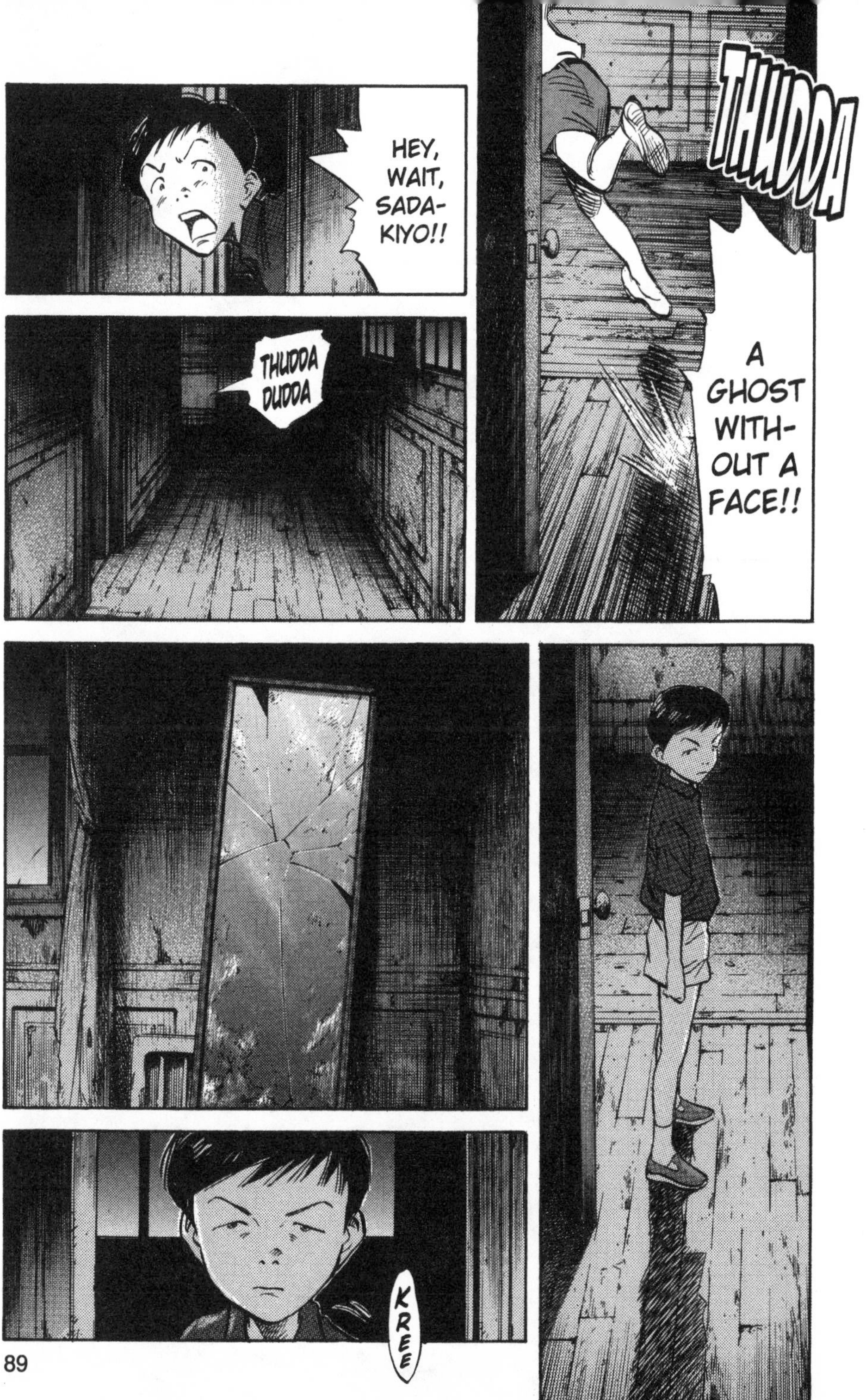
THUDDA
A GHOST WITH-OUT A FACE!!
HEY, WAIT, SADA-KIYO!!
THUDDA DUDDA
KREE

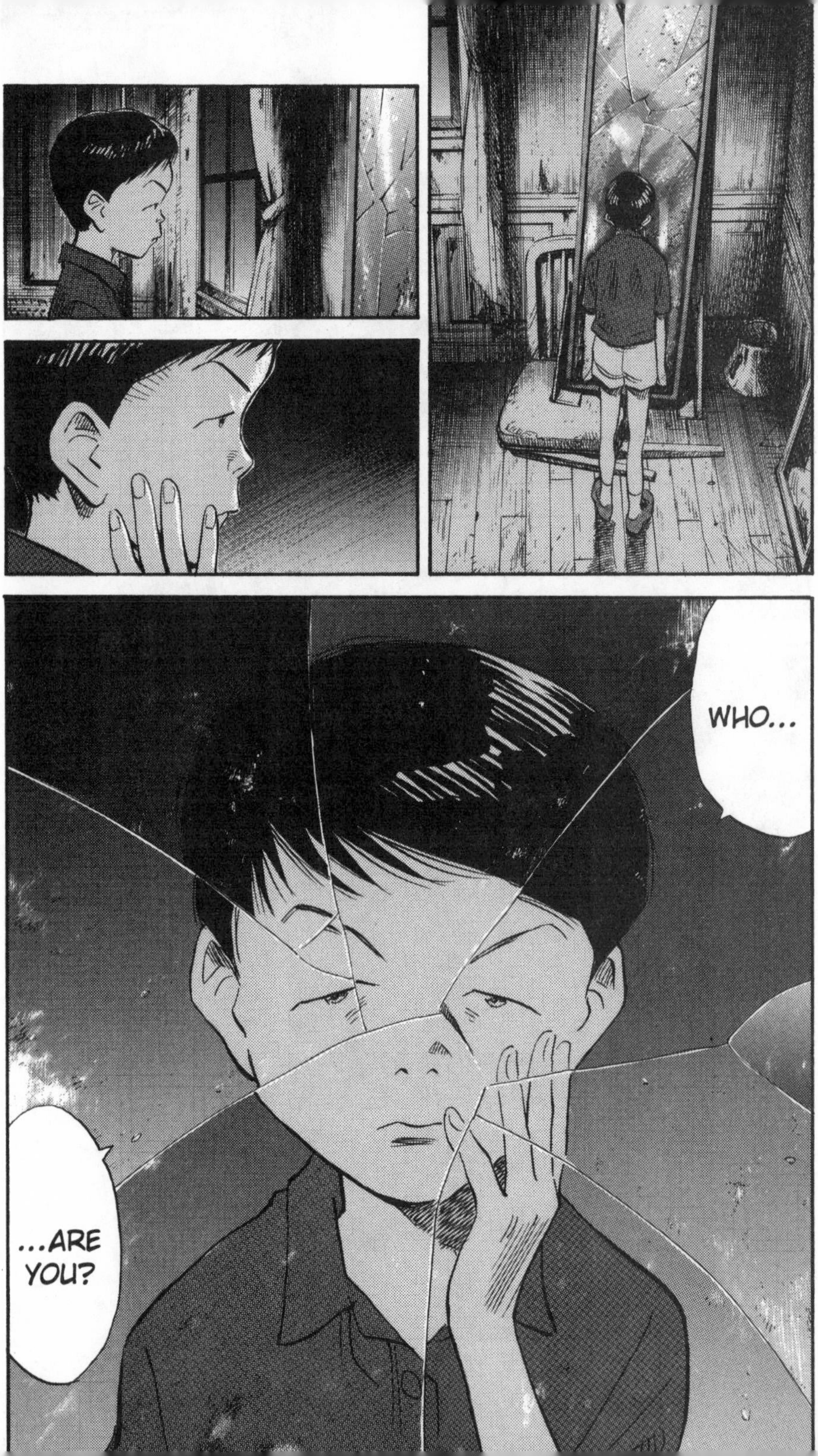
WHO...
...ARE YOU?

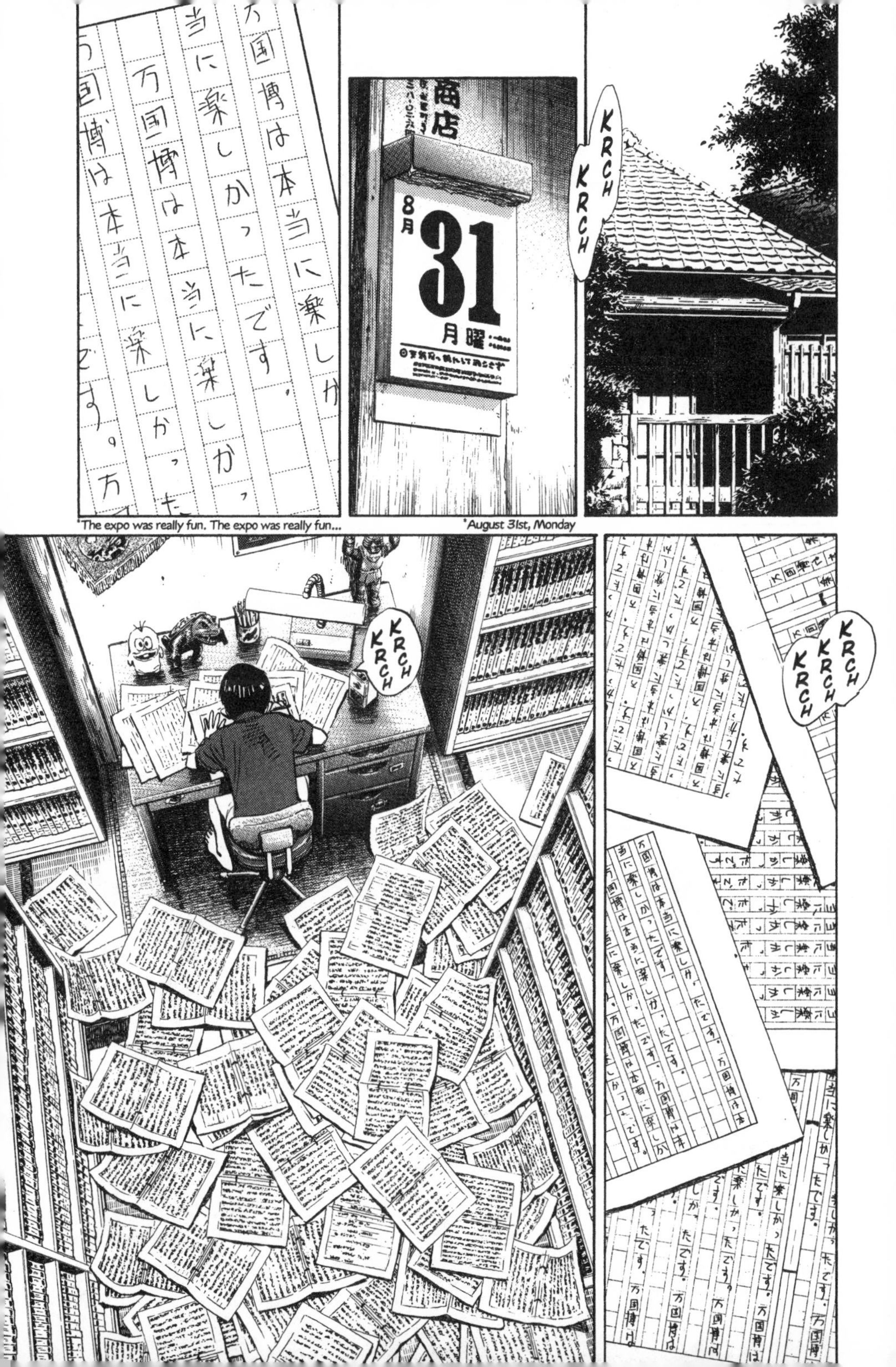
KRCH KRCH
商店
8月
31
月曜
*August 31st, Monday
万国博は本当に楽しかったです。万国博は本当に楽しかったです。万国博は本当に楽しかったです。万
*The expo was really fun. The expo was really fun...
KRCH KRCH KRCH
KRCH KRCH

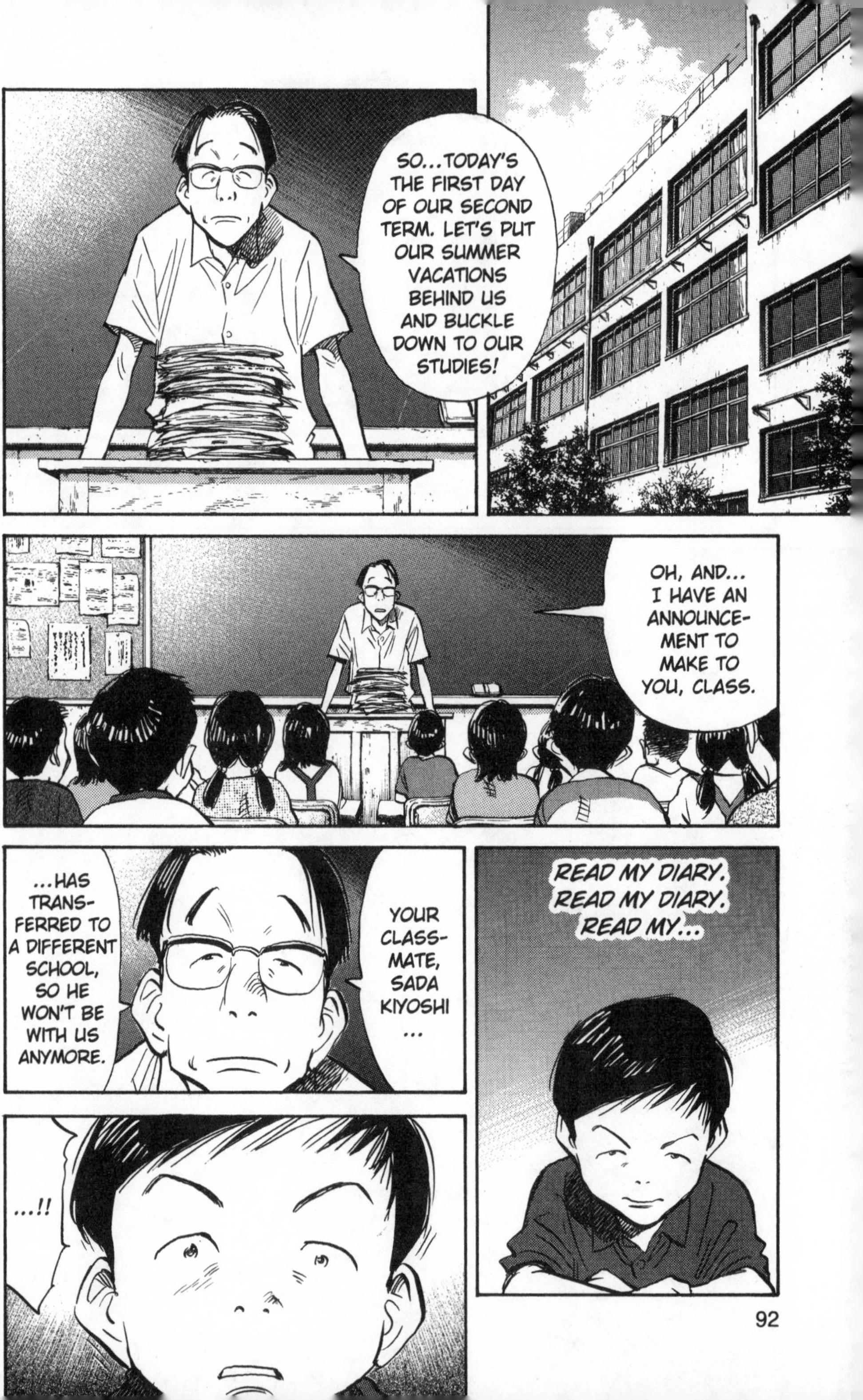
SO...TODAY'S THE FIRST DAY OF OUR SECOND TERM. LET'S PUT OUR SUMMER VACATIONS BEHIND US AND BUCKLE DOWN TO OUR STUDIES!
OH, AND... I HAVE AN ANNOUNCEMENT TO MAKE TO YOU, CLASS.
READ MY DIARY. READ MY DIARY. READ MY...
YOUR CLASSMATE, SADA KIYOSHI...
...HAS TRANSFERRED TO A DIFFERENT SCHOOL, SO HE WON'T BE WITH US ANYMORE.
...!!

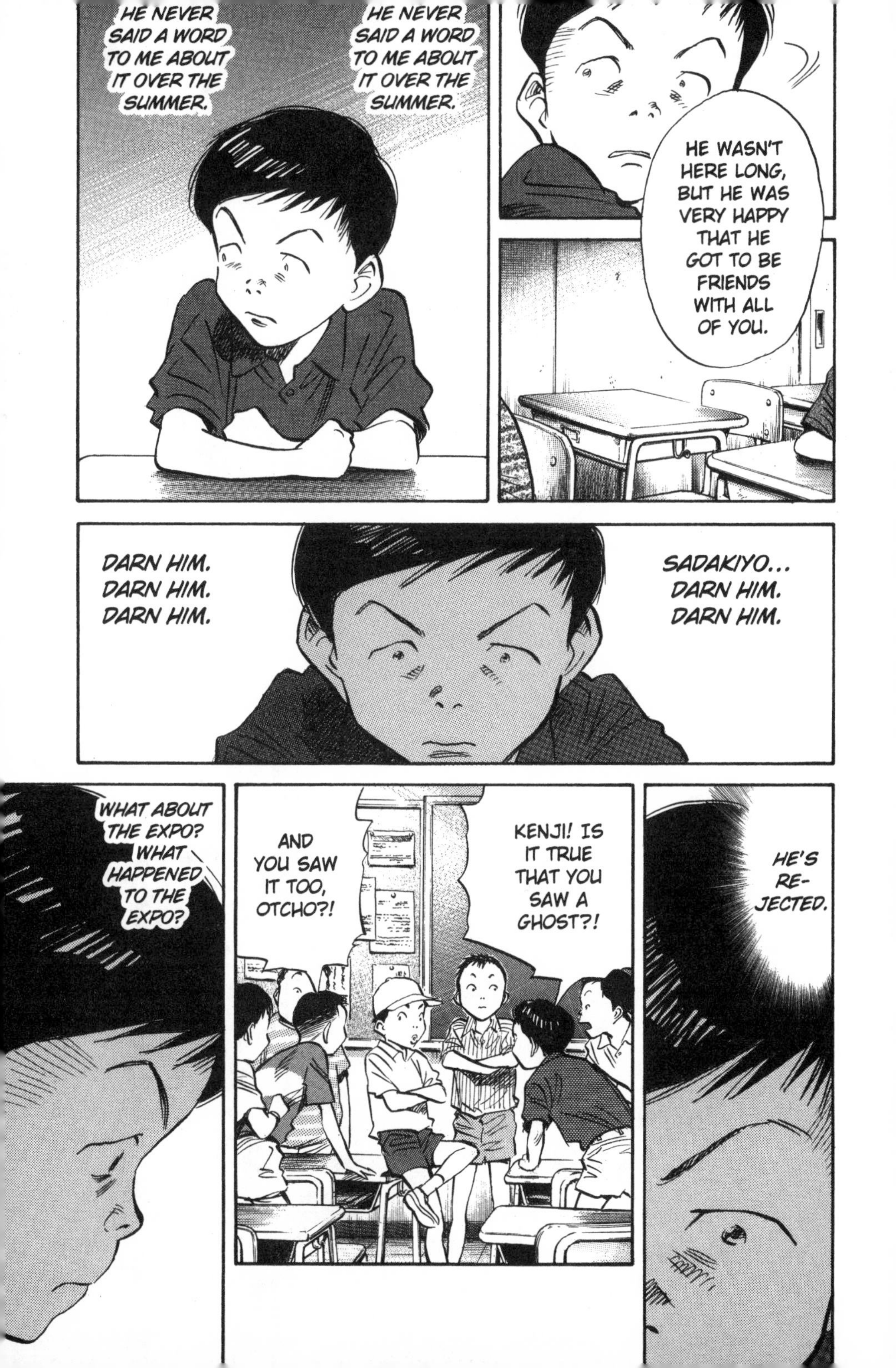
HE WASN'T HERE LONG, BUT HE WAS VERY HAPPY THAT HE GOT TO BE FRIENDS WITH ALL OF YOU.
HE NEVER SAID A WORD TO ME ABOUT IT OVER THE SUMMER.
HE NEVER SAID A WORD TO ME ABOUT IT OVER THE SUMMER.
SADAKIYO... DARN HIM. DARN HIM.
DARN HIM. DARN HIM. DARN HIM.
HE'S RE-JECTED.
KENJI! IS IT TRUE THAT YOU SAW A GHOST?!
AND YOU SAW IT TOO, OTCHO?!
WHAT ABOUT THE EXPO? WHAT HAPPENED TO THE EXPO?

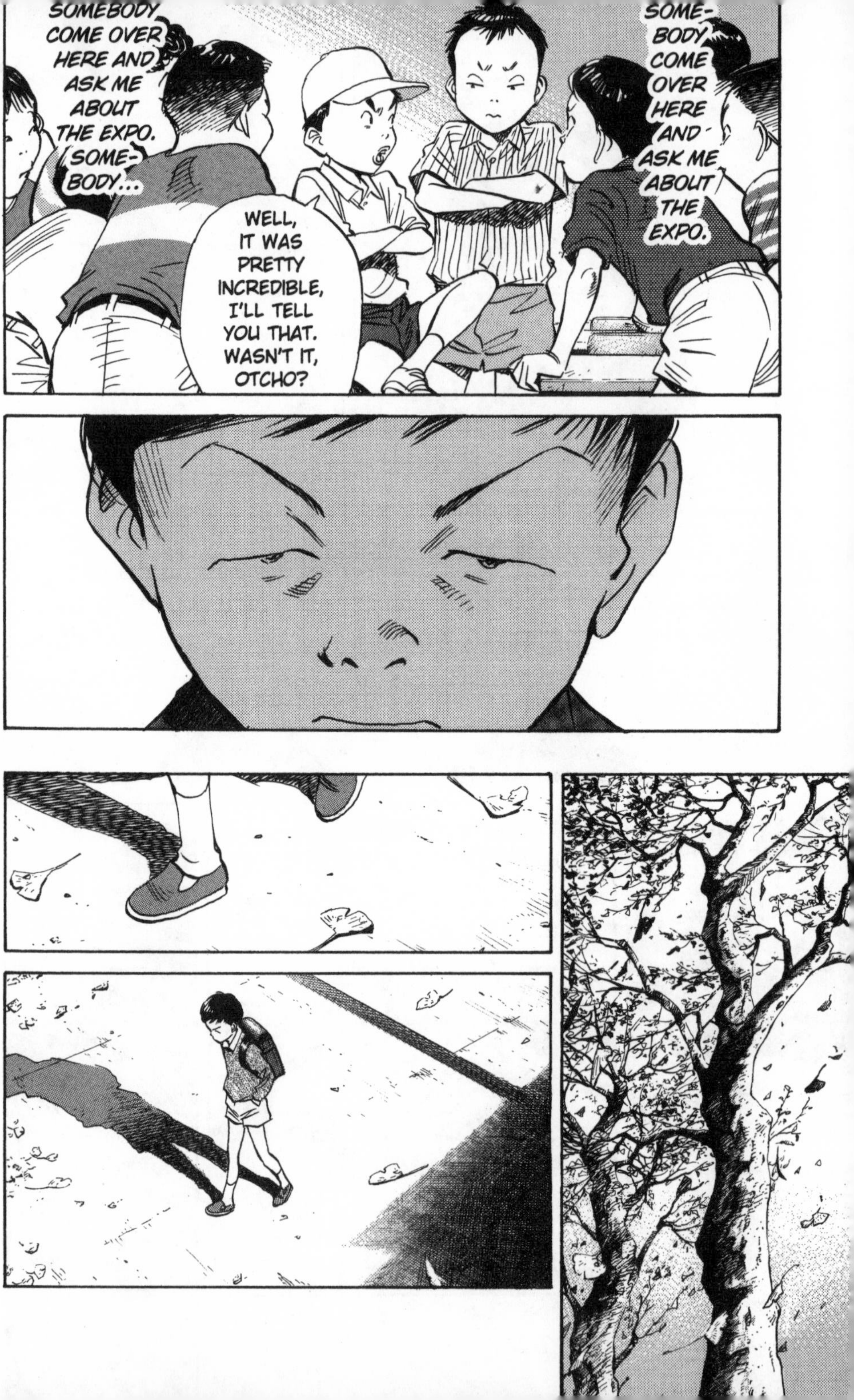
SOME-BODY COME OVER HERE AND ASK ME ABOUT THE EXPO.
SOMEBODY COME OVER HERE AND ASK ME ABOUT THE EXPO. SOME-BODY...
WELL, IT WAS PRETTY INCREDIBLE, I'LL TELL YOU THAT. WASN'T IT, OTCHO?

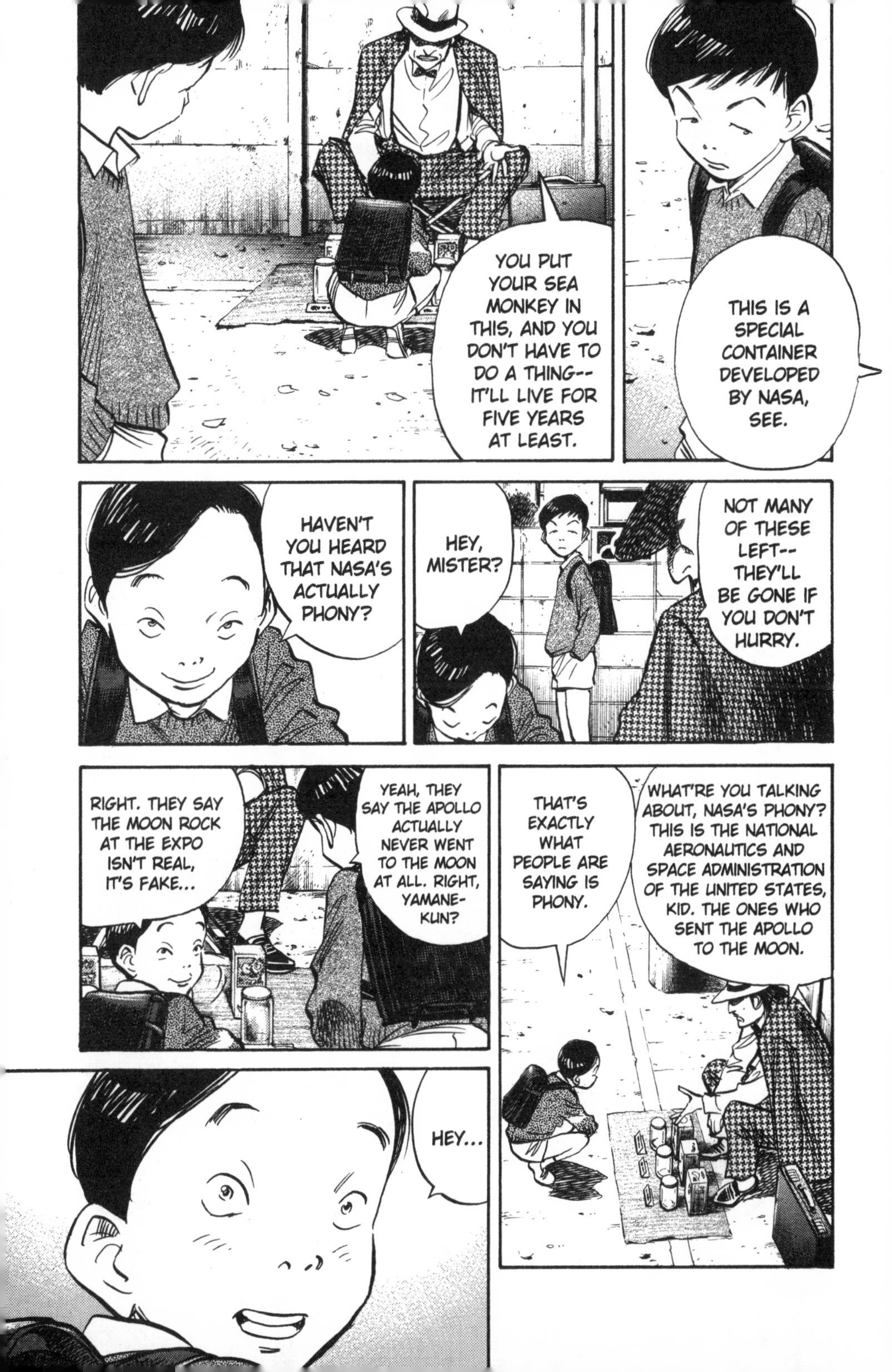
THIS IS A SPECIAL CONTAINER DEVELOPED BY NASA, SEE.
YOU PUT YOUR SEA MONKEY IN THIS, AND YOU DON'T HAVE TO DO A THING-- IT'LL LIVE FOR FIVE YEARS AT LEAST.
NOT MANY OF THESE LEFT-- THEY'LL BE GONE IF YOU DON'T HURRY.
HEY, MISTER?
HAVEN'T YOU HEARD THAT NASA'S ACTUALLY PHONY?
WHAT'RE YOU TALKING ABOUT, NASA'S PHONY? THIS IS THE NATIONAL AERONAUTICS AND SPACE ADMINISTRATION OF THE UNITED STATES, KID. THE ONES WHO SENT THE APOLLO TO THE MOON.
THAT'S EXACTLY WHAT PEOPLE ARE SAYING IS PHONY.
YEAH, THEY SAY THE APOLLO ACTUALLY NEVER WENT TO THE MOON AT ALL. RIGHT, YAMANE-KUN?
RIGHT. THEY SAY THE MOON ROCK AT THE EXPO ISN'T REAL, IT'S FAKE...
HEY...

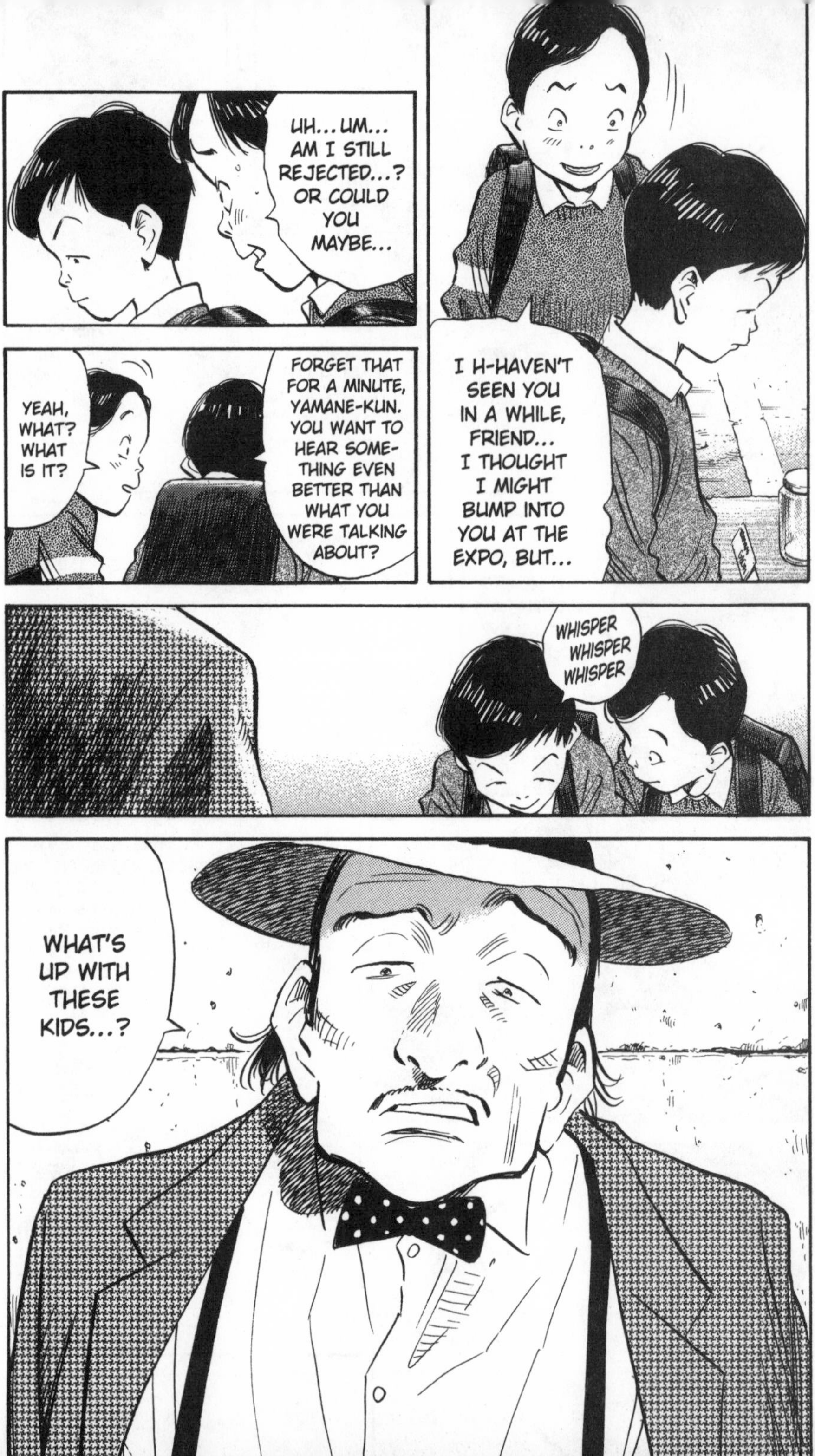
I H-HAVEN'T SEEN YOU IN A WHILE, FRIEND... I THOUGHT I MIGHT BUMP INTO YOU AT THE EXPO, BUT...
UH...UM... AM I STILL REJECTED...? OR COULD YOU MAYBE...
FORGET THAT FOR A MINUTE, YAMANE-KUN. YOU WANT TO HEAR SOMETHING EVEN BETTER THAN WHAT YOU WERE TALKING ABOUT?
YEAH, WHAT? WHAT IS IT?
WHISPER WHISPER WHISPER
WHAT'S UP WITH THESE KIDS...?

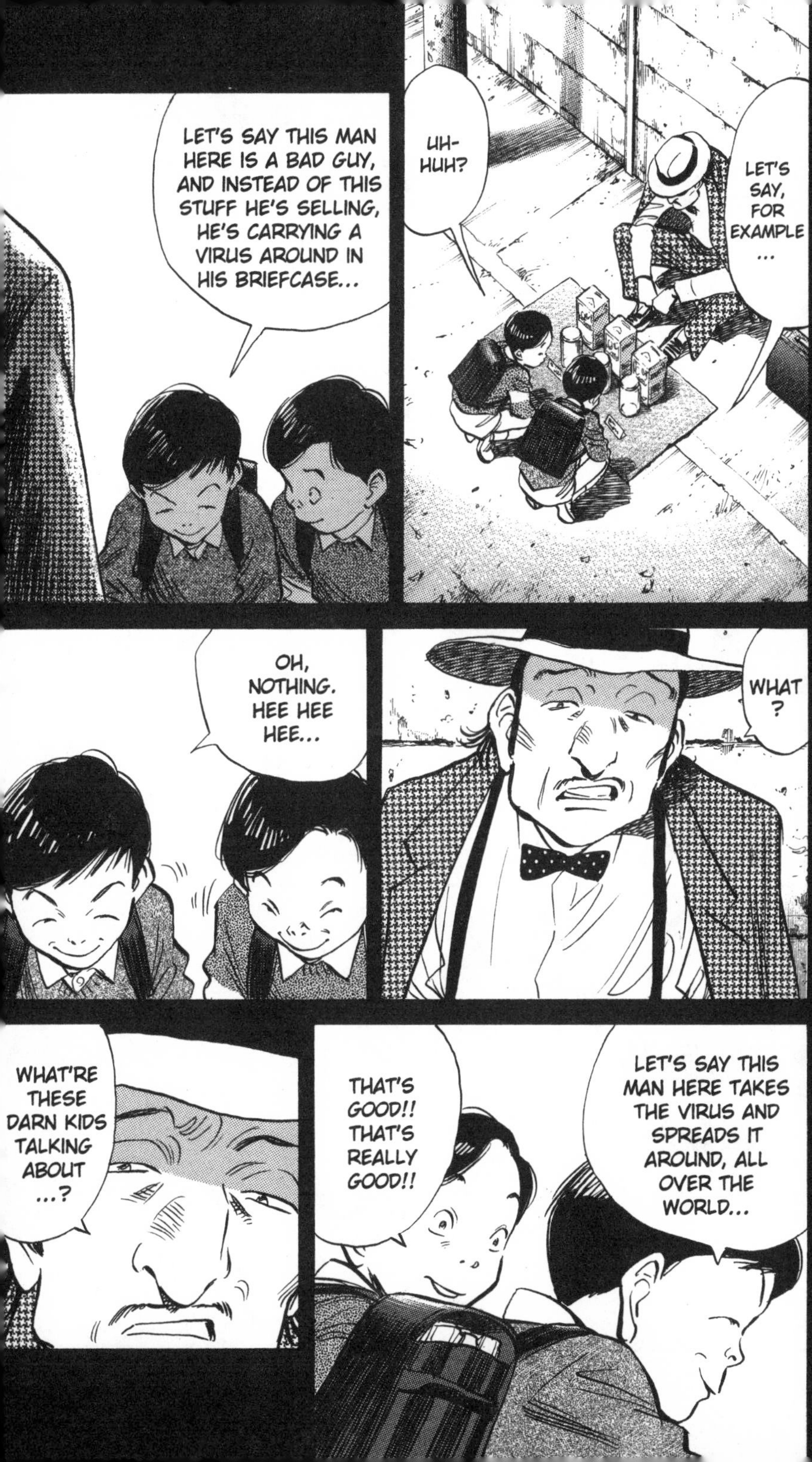
LET'S SAY, FOR EXAMPLE...
UH-HUH?
LET'S SAY THIS MAN HERE IS A BAD GUY, AND INSTEAD OF THIS STUFF HE'S SELLING, HE'S CARRYING A VIRUS AROUND IN HIS BRIEFCASE...
WHAT?
OH, NOTHING. HEE HEE HEE...
LET'S SAY THIS MAN HERE TAKES THE VIRUS AND SPREADS IT AROUND, ALL OVER THE WORLD...
THAT'S GOOD!! THAT'S REALLY GOOD!!
WHAT'RE THESE DARN KIDS TALKING ABOUT...?

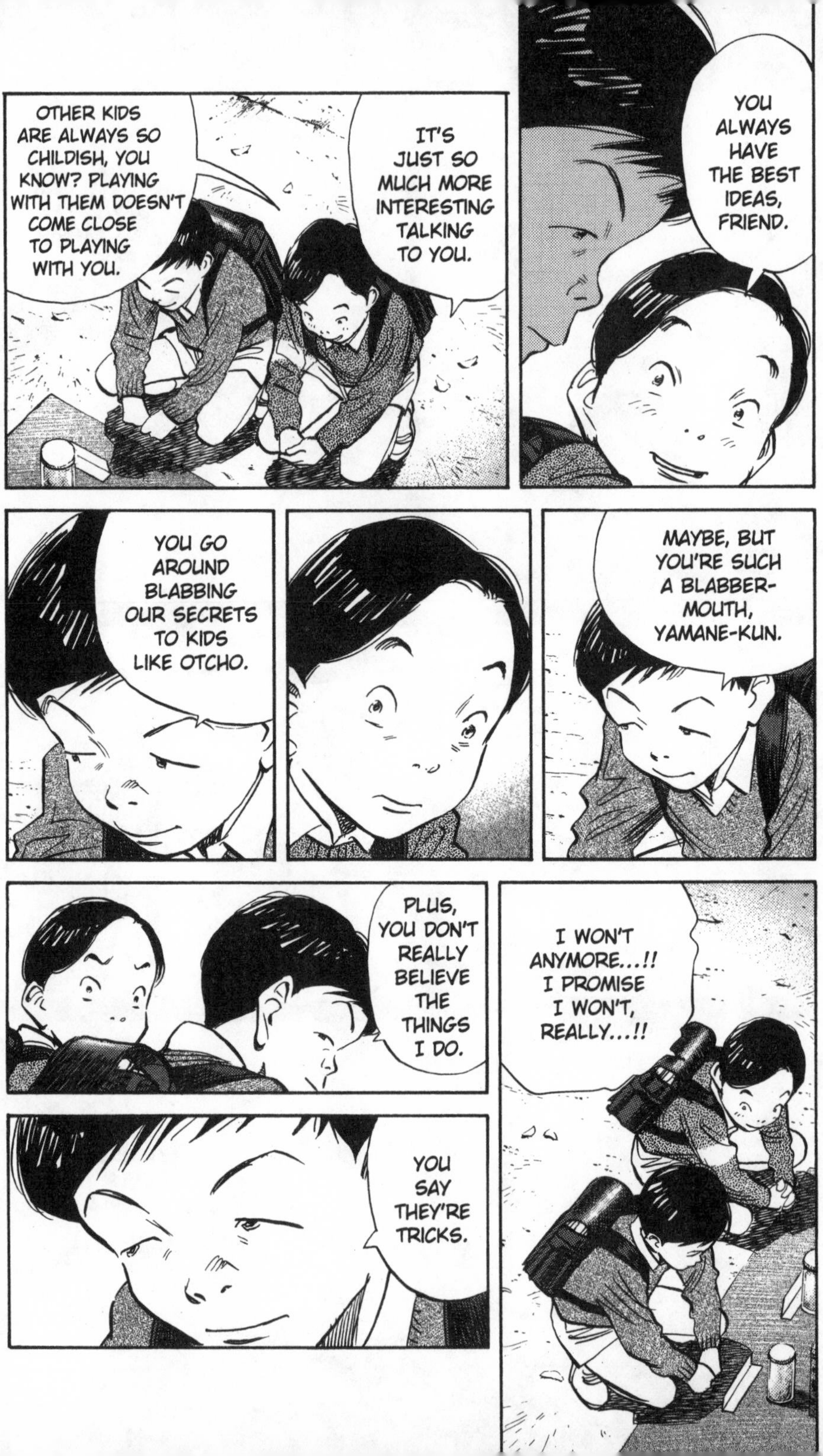
YOU ALWAYS HAVE THE BEST IDEAS, FRIEND.
OTHER KIDS ARE ALWAYS SO CHILDISH, YOU KNOW? PLAYING WITH THEM DOESN'T COME CLOSE TO PLAYING WITH YOU.
IT'S JUST SO MUCH MORE INTERESTING TALKING TO YOU.
MAYBE, BUT YOU'RE SUCH A BLABBER-MOUTH, YAMANE-KUN.
YOU GO AROUND BLABBING OUR SECRETS TO KIDS LIKE OTCHO.
I WON'T ANYMORE...!! I PROMISE I WON'T, REALLY...!!
PLUS, YOU DON'T REALLY BELIEVE THE THINGS I DO.
YOU SAY THEY'RE TRICKS.

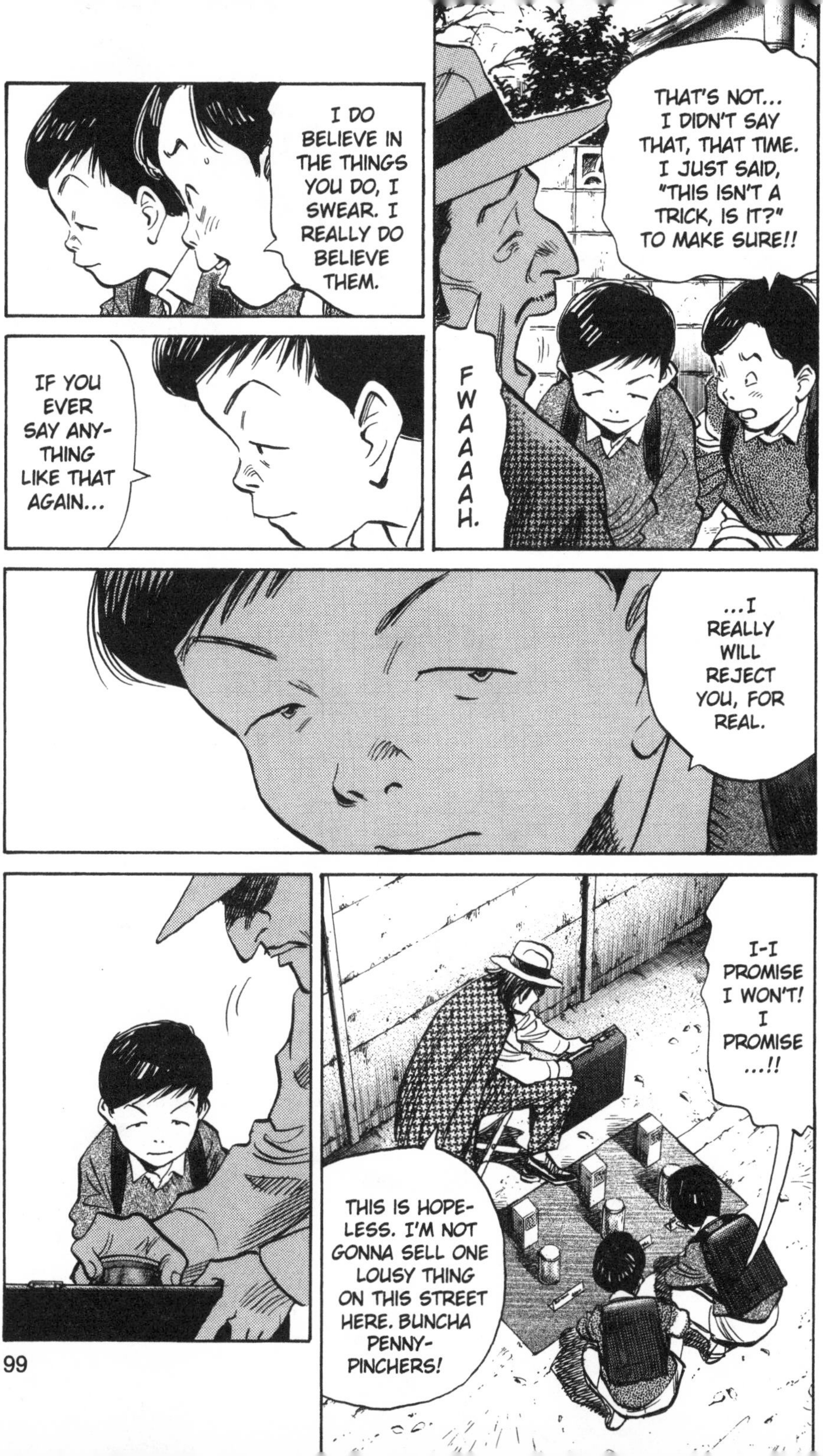
THAT'S NOT... I DIDN'T SAY THAT, THAT TIME. I JUST SAID, "THIS ISN'T A TRICK, IS IT?" TO MAKE SURE!!
FWAAAAAH.
I DO BELIEVE IN THE THINGS YOU DO, I SWEAR. I REALLY DO BELIEVE THEM.
IF YOU EVER SAY ANY-THING LIKE THAT AGAIN...
...I REALLY WILL REJECT YOU, FOR REAL.
I-I PROMISE I WON'T! I PROMISE ...!!
THIS IS HOPE-LESS. I'M NOT GONNA SELL ONE LOUSY THING ON THIS STREET HERE. BUNCHA PENNY-PINCHERS!

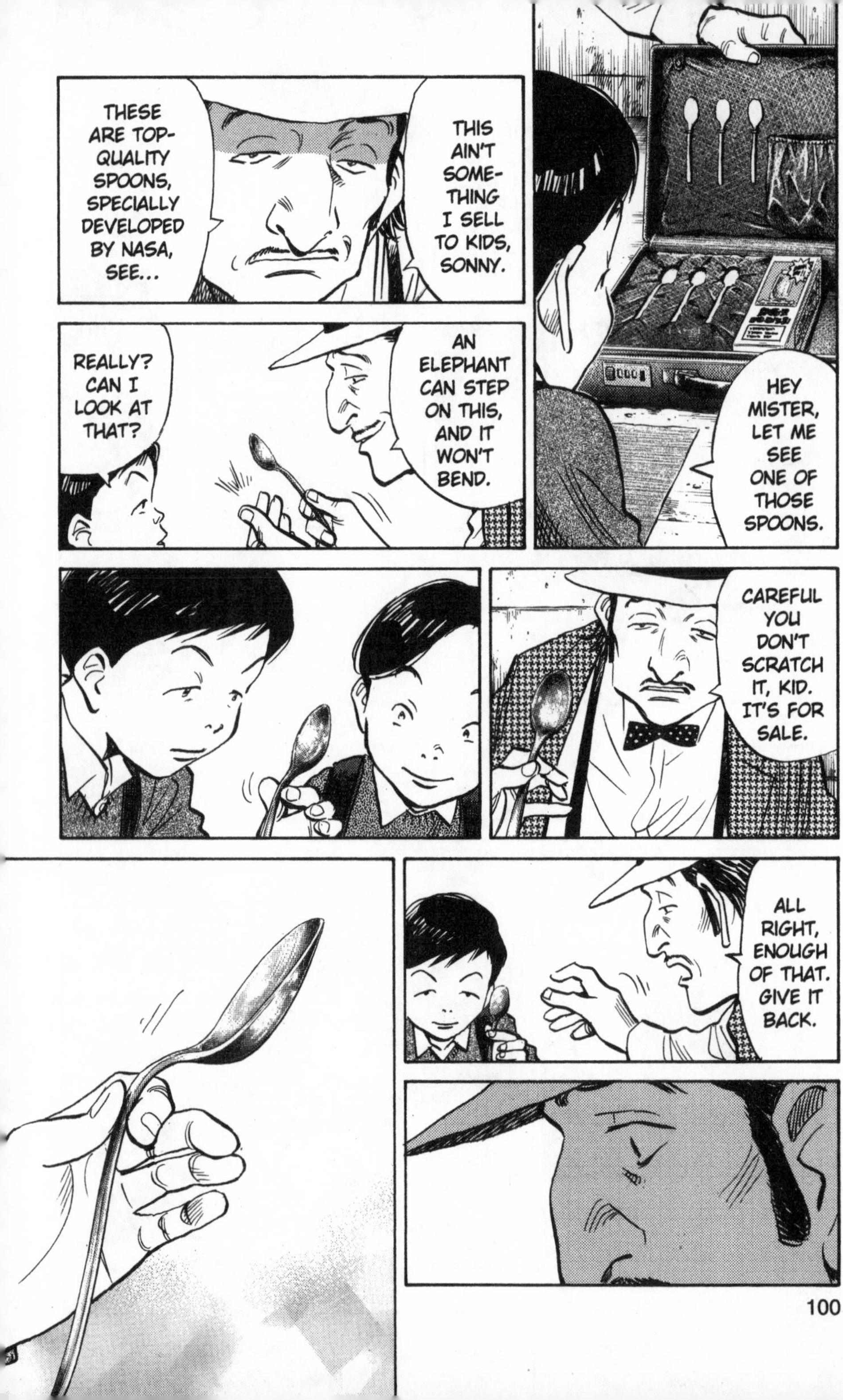
HEY MISTER, LET ME SEE ONE OF THOSE SPOONS.
THIS AIN'T SOME-THING I SELL TO KIDS, SONNY.
THESE ARE TOP-QUALITY SPOONS, SPECIALLY DEVELOPED BY NASA, SEE...
AN ELEPHANT CAN STEP ON THIS, AND IT WON'T BEND.
REALLY? CAN I LOOK AT THAT?
CAREFUL YOU DON'T SCRATCH IT, KID. IT'S FOR SALE.
ALL RIGHT, ENOUGH OF THAT. GIVE IT BACK.

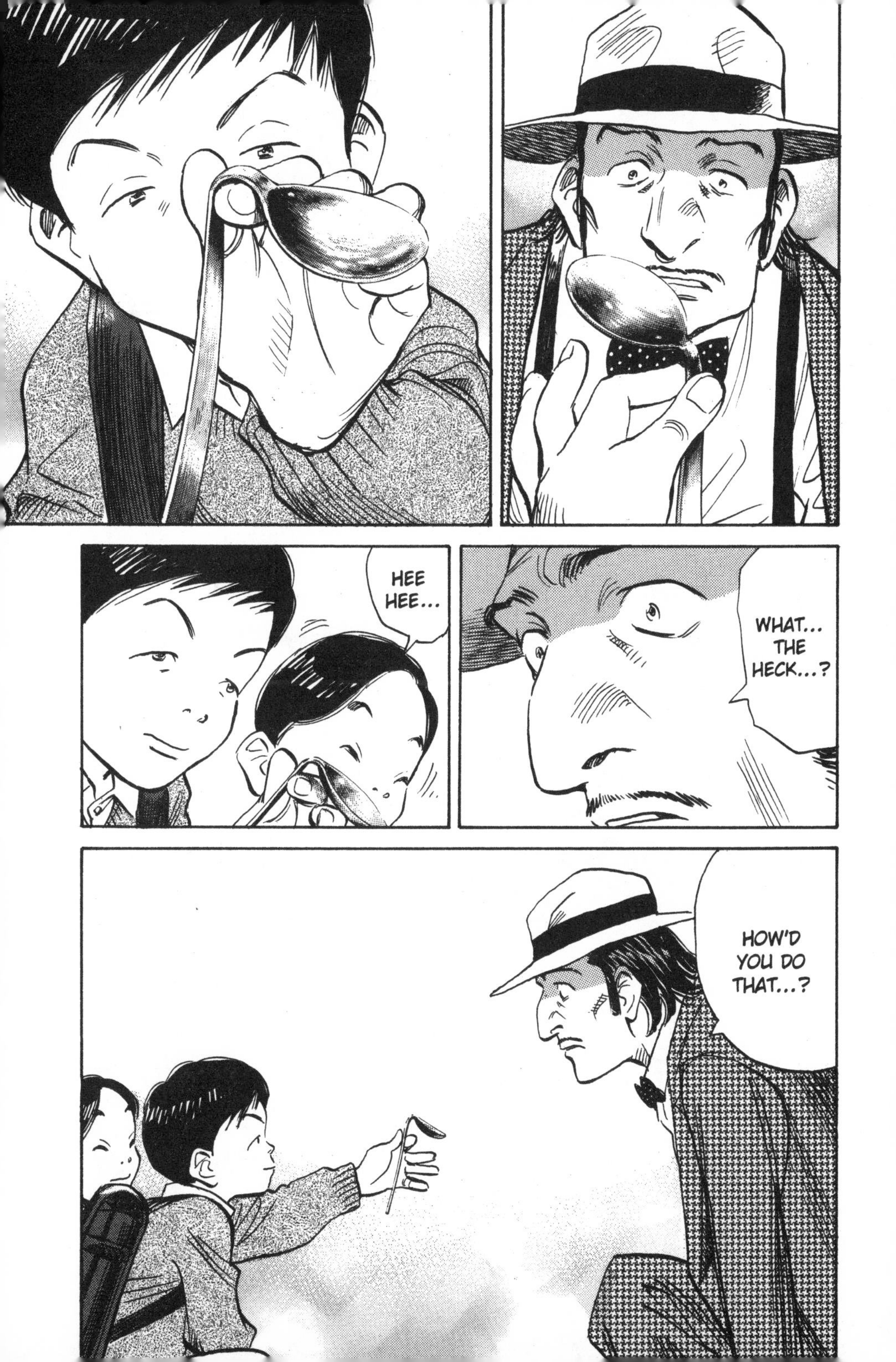
WHAT... THE HECK...?
HEE HEE...
HOW'D YOU DO THAT...?

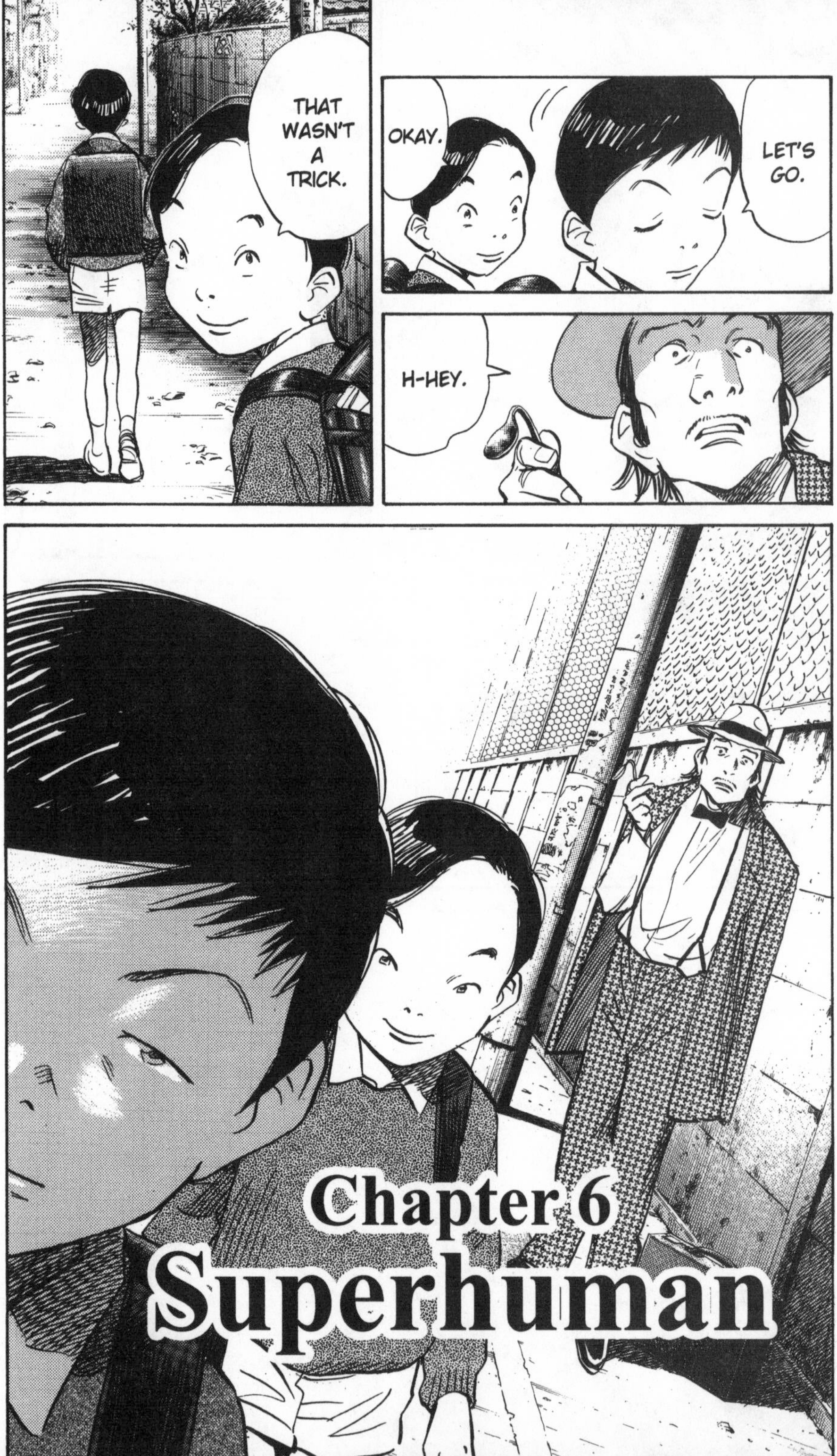
LET'S GO.
OKAY.
H-HEY.
THAT WASN'T A TRICK.
Chapter 6
Superhuman

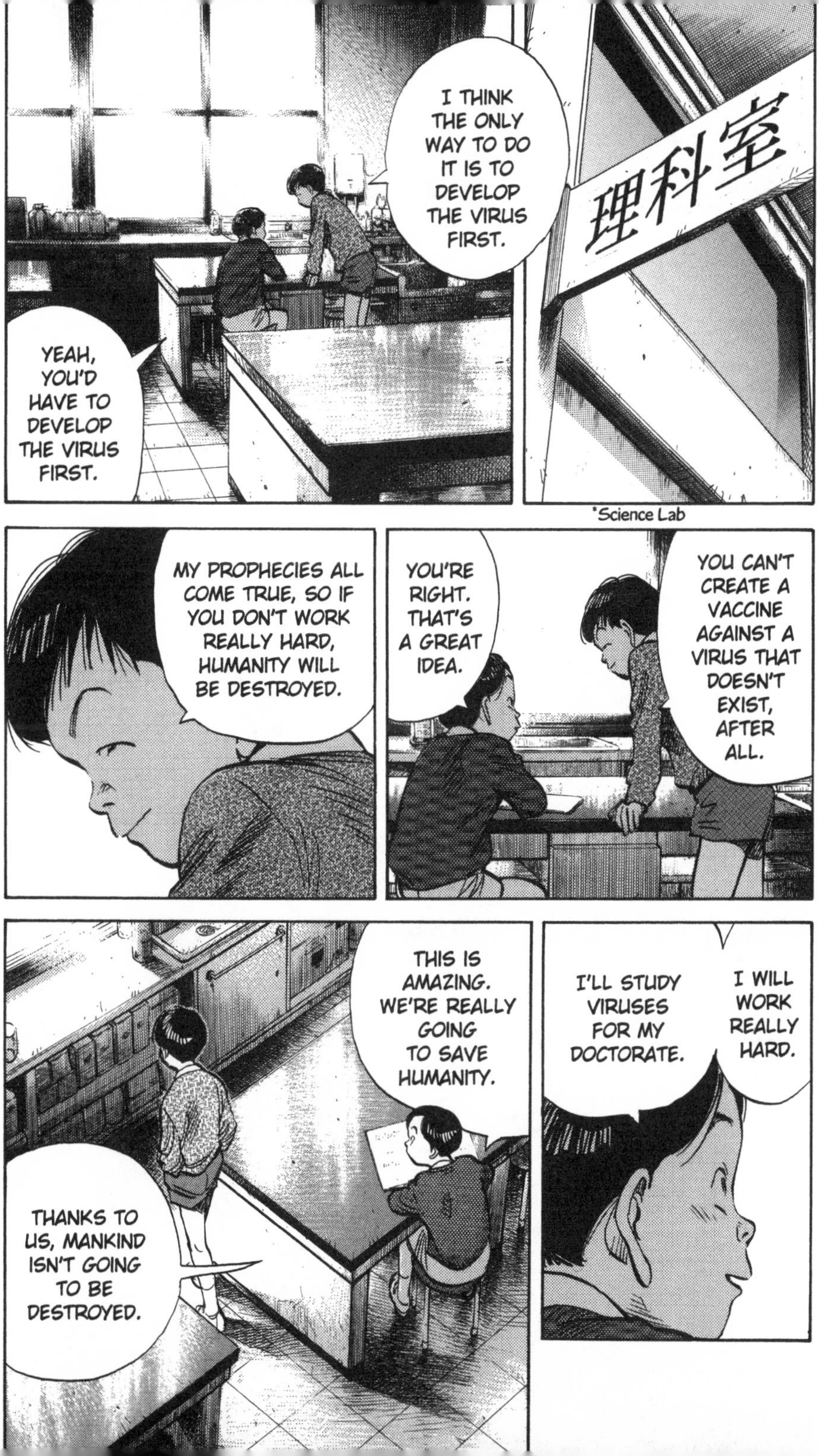
理科室
*Science Lab
I THINK THE ONLY WAY TO DO IT IS TO DEVELOP THE VIRUS FIRST.
YEAH, YOU'D HAVE TO DEVELOP THE VIRUS FIRST.
YOU CAN'T CREATE A VACCINE AGAINST A VIRUS THAT DOESN'T EXIST, AFTER ALL.
YOU'RE RIGHT. THAT'S A GREAT IDEA.
MY PROPHECIES ALL COME TRUE, SO IF YOU DON'T WORK REALLY HARD, HUMANITY WILL BE DESTROYED.
I WILL WORK REALLY HARD.
I'LL STUDY VIRUSES FOR MY DOCTORATE.
THIS IS AMAZING. WE'RE REALLY GOING TO SAVE HUMANITY.
THANKS TO US, MANKIND ISN'T GOING TO BE DESTROYED.

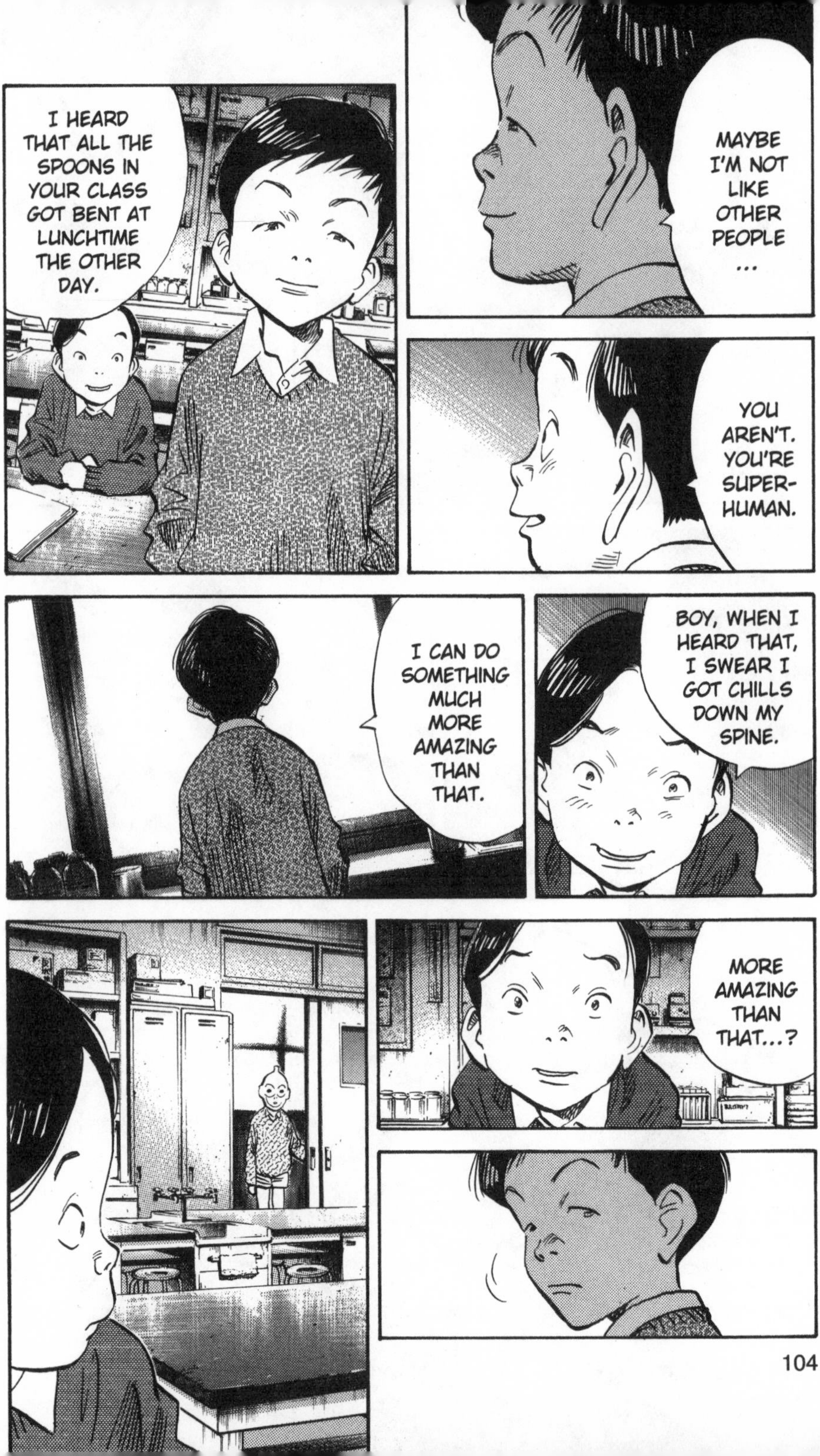
MAYBE I'M NOT LIKE OTHER PEOPLE ...
YOU AREN'T. YOU'RE SUPER-HUMAN.
I HEARD THAT ALL THE SPOONS IN YOUR CLASS GOT BENT AT LUNCHTIME THE OTHER DAY.
BOY, WHEN I HEARD THAT, I SWEAR I GOT CHILLS DOWN MY SPINE.
I CAN DO SOMETHING MUCH MORE AMAZING THAN THAT.
MORE AMAZING THAN THAT...?

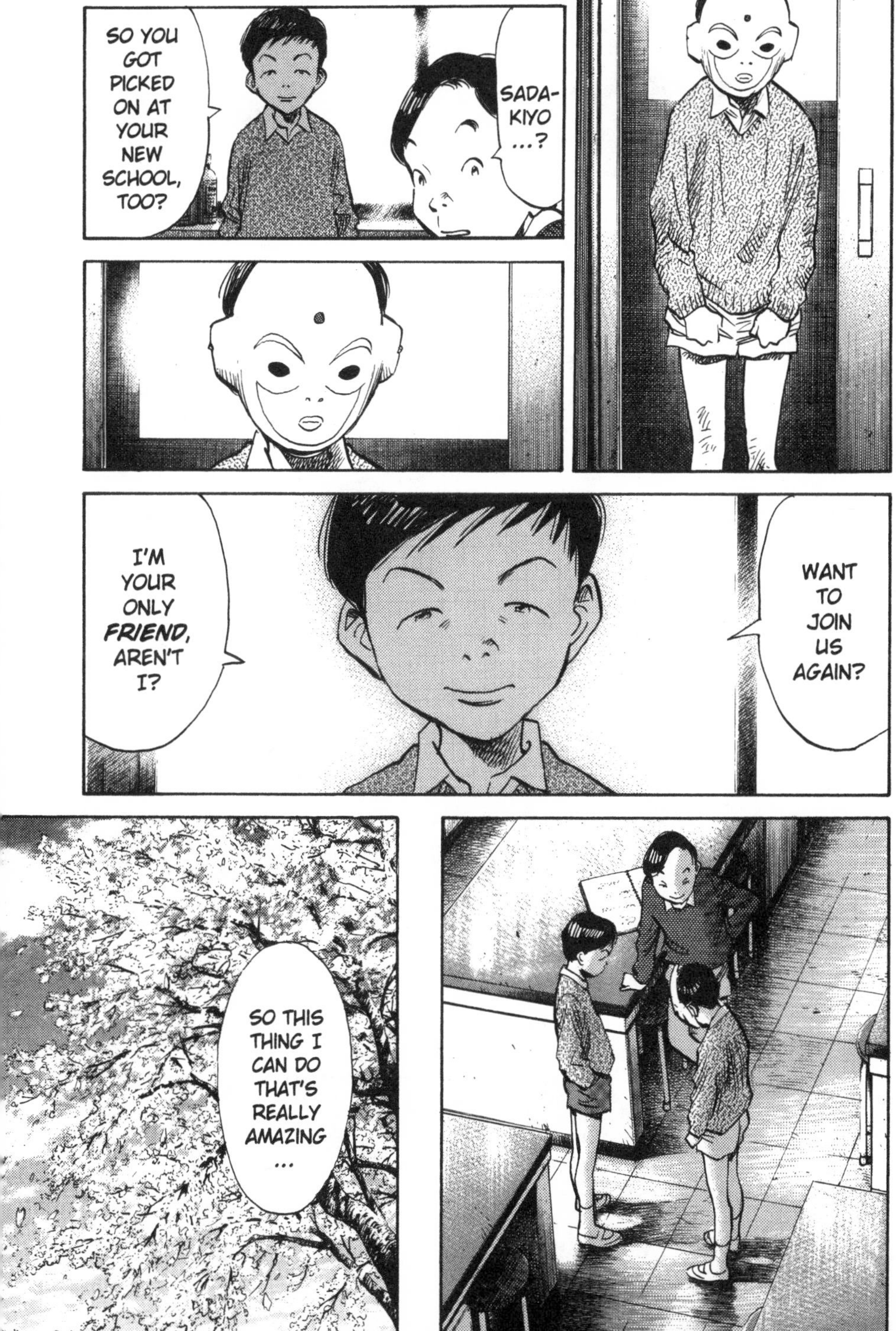
SADA-KIYO ...?
SO YOU GOT PICKED ON AT YOUR NEW SCHOOL, TOO?
WANT TO JOIN US AGAIN?
I'M YOUR ONLY *FRIEND*, AREN'T I?
SO THIS THING I CAN DO THAT'S REALLY AMAZING ...

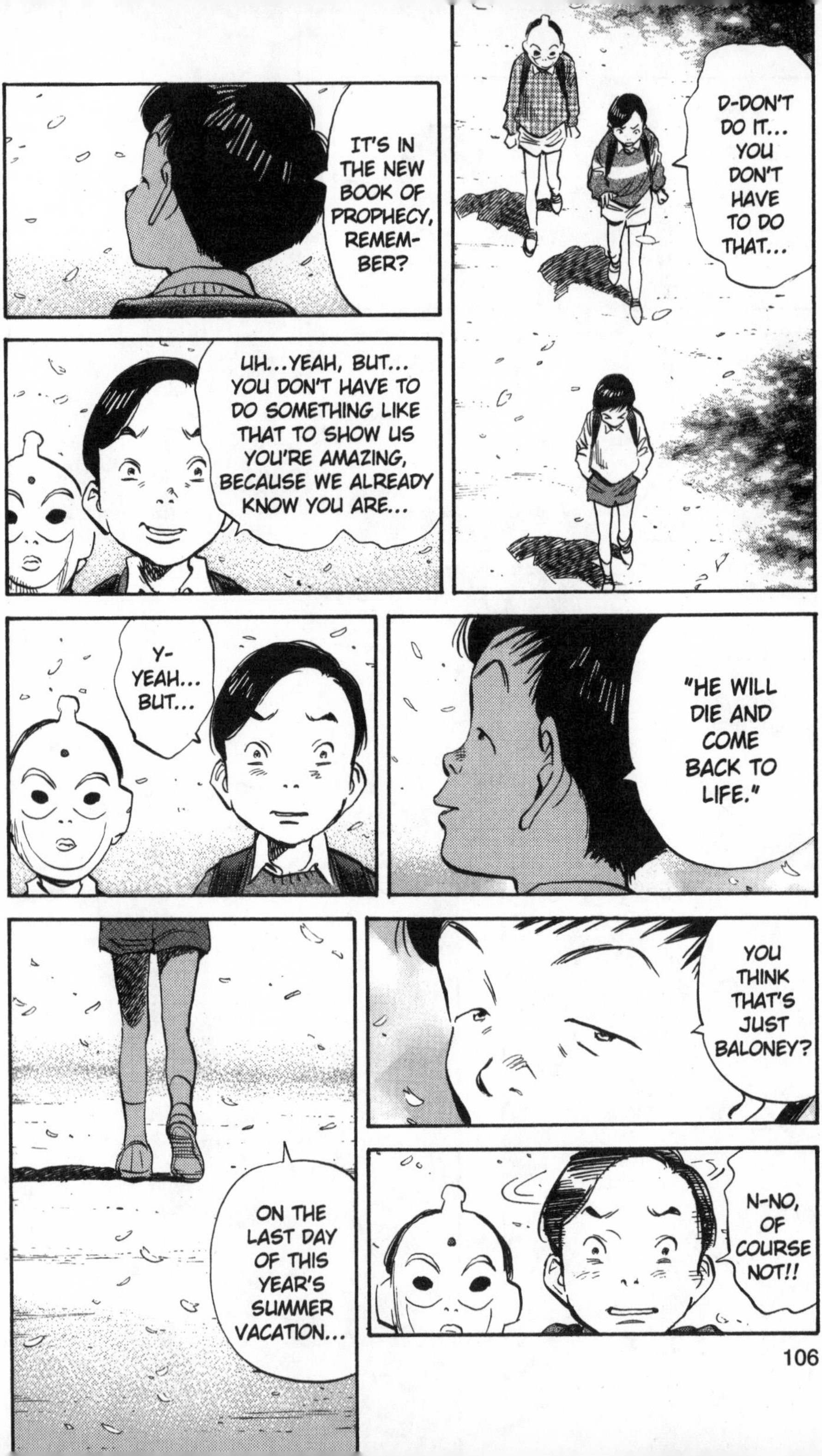
D-DON'T DO IT... YOU DON'T HAVE TO DO THAT...
IT'S IN THE NEW BOOK OF PROPHECY, REMEMBER?
UH...YEAH, BUT... YOU DON'T HAVE TO DO SOMETHING LIKE THAT TO SHOW US YOU'RE AMAZING, BECAUSE WE ALREADY KNOW YOU ARE...
"HE WILL DIE AND COME BACK TO LIFE."
Y-YEAH... BUT...
YOU THINK THAT'S JUST BALONEY?
N-NO, OF COURSE NOT!!
ON THE LAST DAY OF THIS YEAR'S SUMMER VACATION...

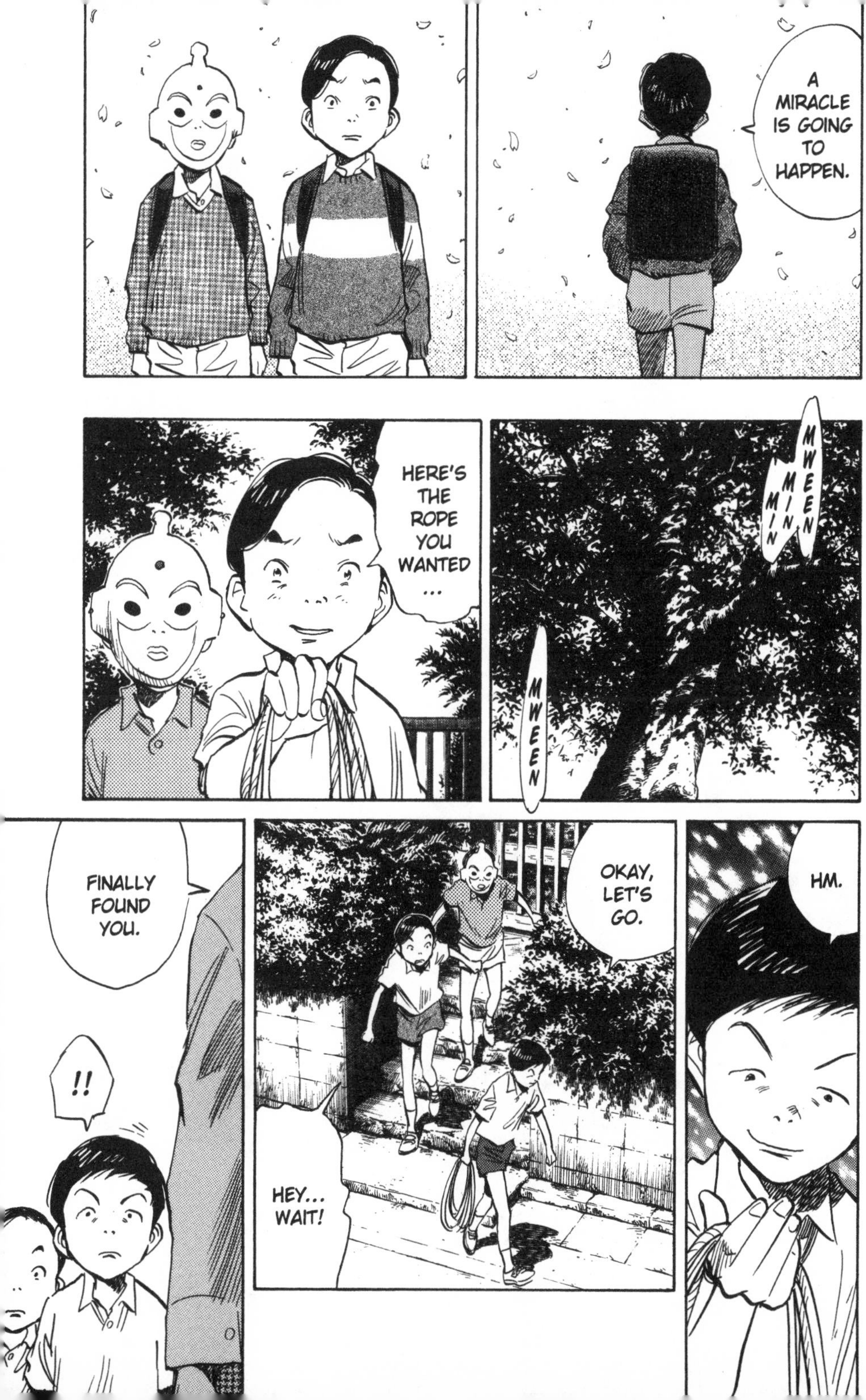
A MIRACLE IS GOING TO HAPPEN.
MWEEN
MIN MIN
MWEEN
HERE'S THE ROPE YOU WANTED ...
HM.
OKAY, LET'S GO.
HEY... WAIT!
FINALLY FOUND YOU.
!!

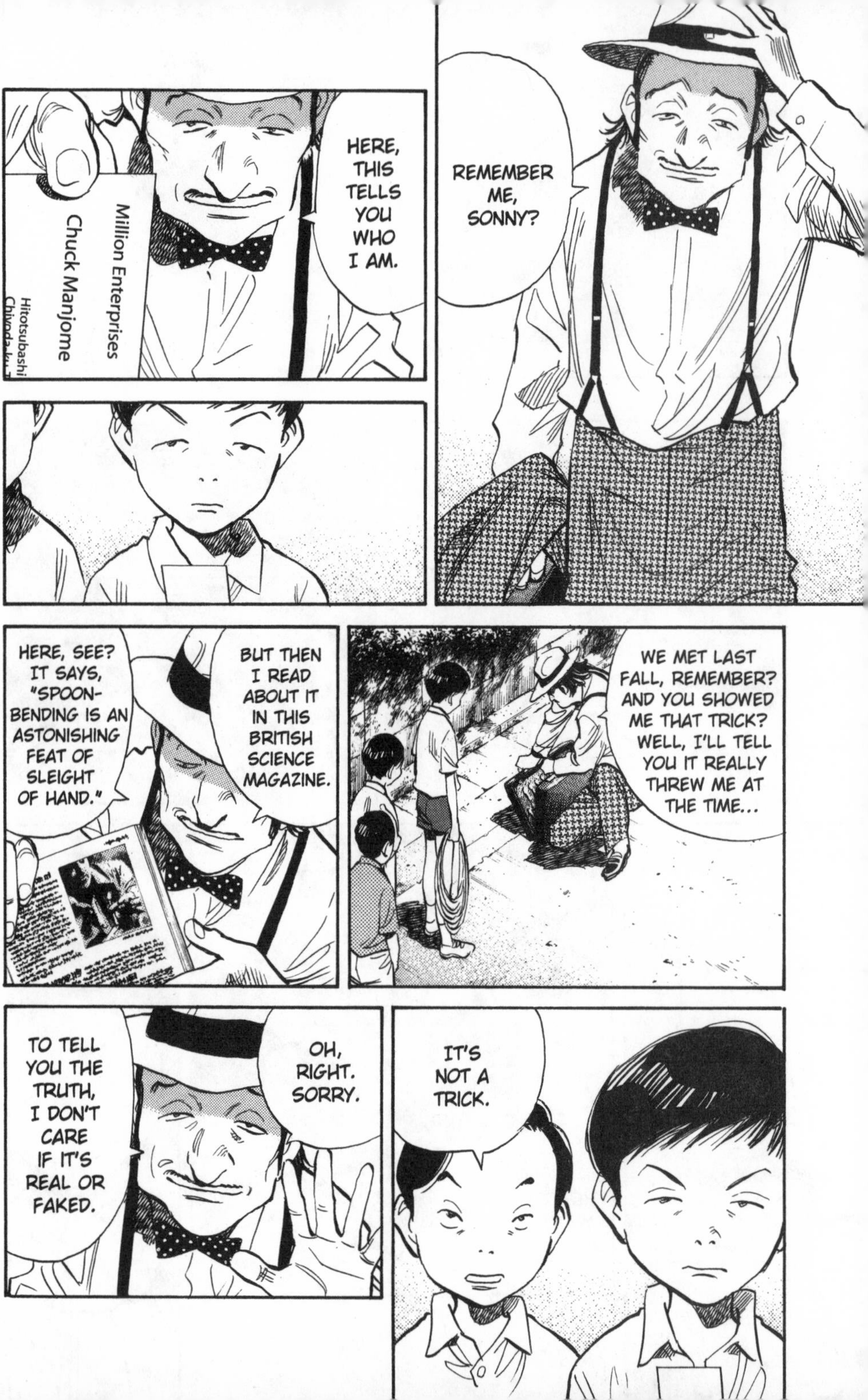
REMEMBER ME, SONNY?
HERE, THIS TELLS YOU WHO I AM.
Million Enterprises
Chuck Manjome
Hitotsubashi
WE MET LAST FALL, REMEMBER? AND YOU SHOWED ME THAT TRICK? WELL, I'LL TELL YOU IT REALLY THREW ME AT THE TIME...
BUT THEN I READ ABOUT IT IN THIS BRITISH SCIENCE MAGAZINE.
HERE, SEE? IT SAYS, "SPOON-BENDING IS AN ASTONISHING FEAT OF SLEIGHT OF HAND."
IT'S NOT A TRICK.
OH, RIGHT. SORRY.
TO TELL YOU THE TRUTH, I DON'T CARE IF IT'S REAL OR FAKED.

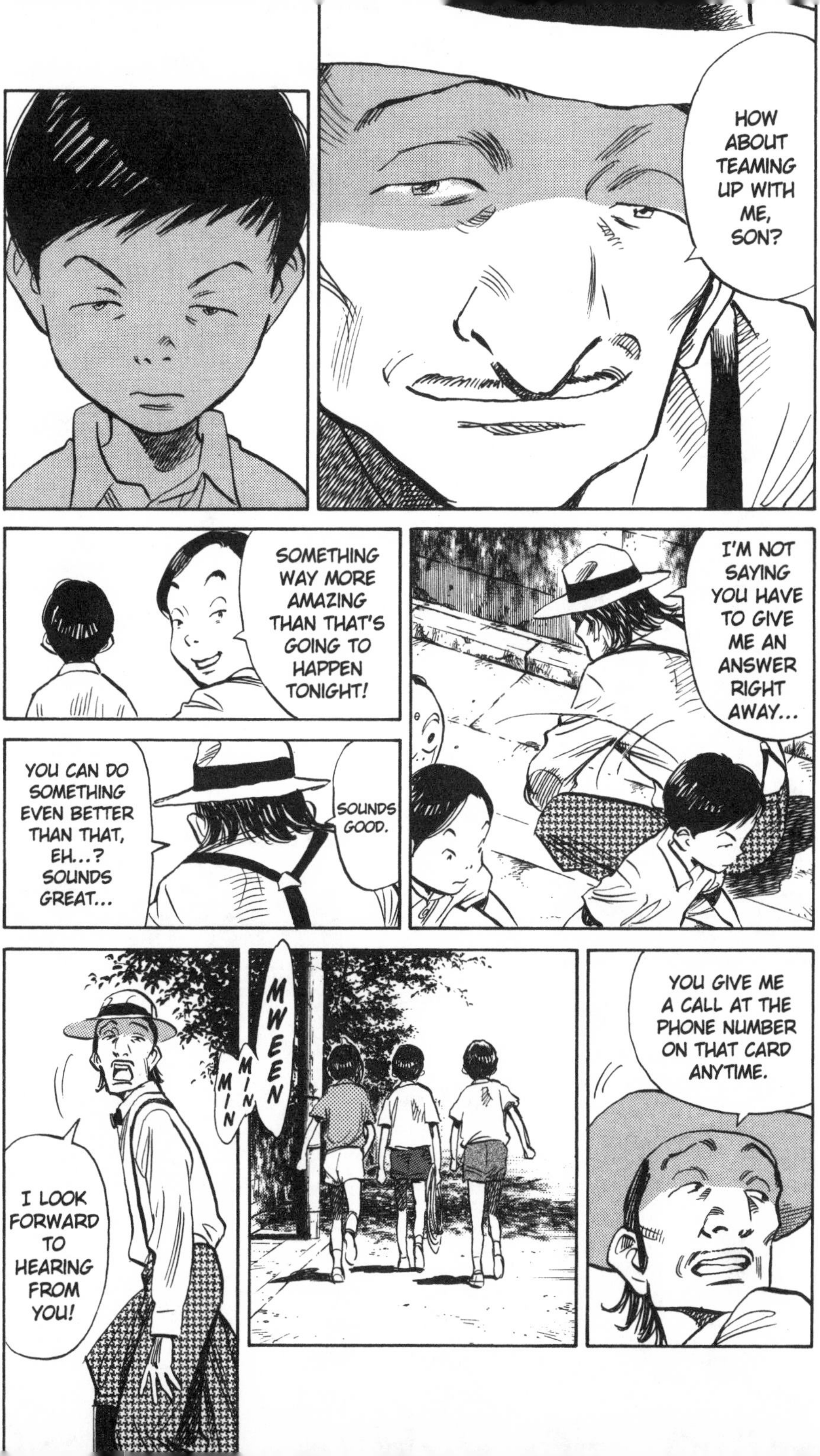
HOW ABOUT TEAMING UP WITH ME, SON?
I'M NOT SAYING YOU HAVE TO GIVE ME AN ANSWER RIGHT AWAY...
SOMETHING WAY MORE AMAZING THAN THAT'S GOING TO HAPPEN TONIGHT!
SOUNDS GOOD.
YOU CAN DO SOMETHING EVEN BETTER THAN THAT, EH...? SOUNDS GREAT...
YOU GIVE ME A CALL AT THE PHONE NUMBER ON THAT CARD ANYTIME.
MWEEN
MIN MIN
I LOOK FORWARD TO HEARING FROM YOU!

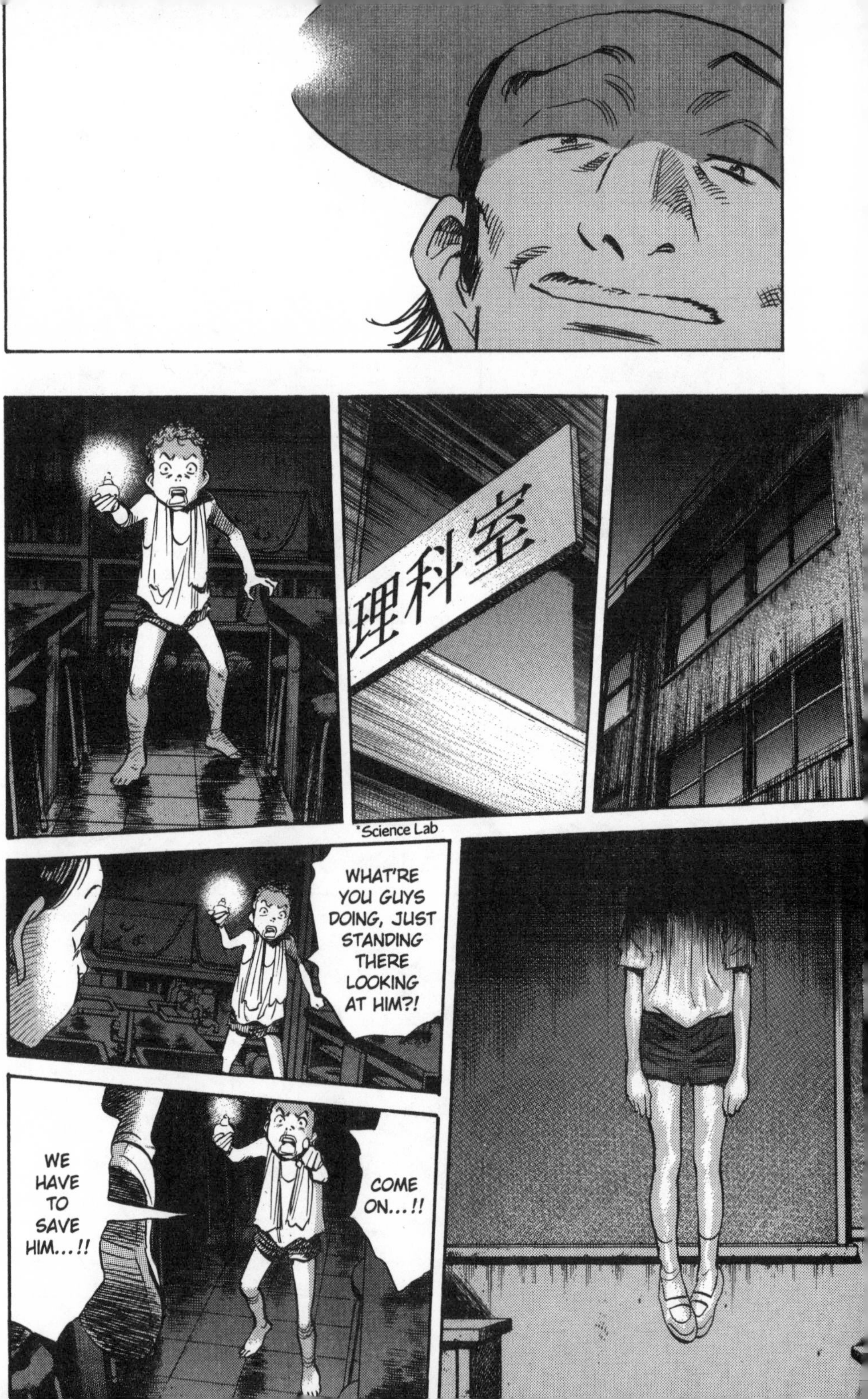
理科室
*Science Lab
WHAT'RE YOU GUYS DOING, JUST STANDING THERE LOOKING AT HIM?!
COME ON...!!
WE HAVE TO SAVE HIM...!!

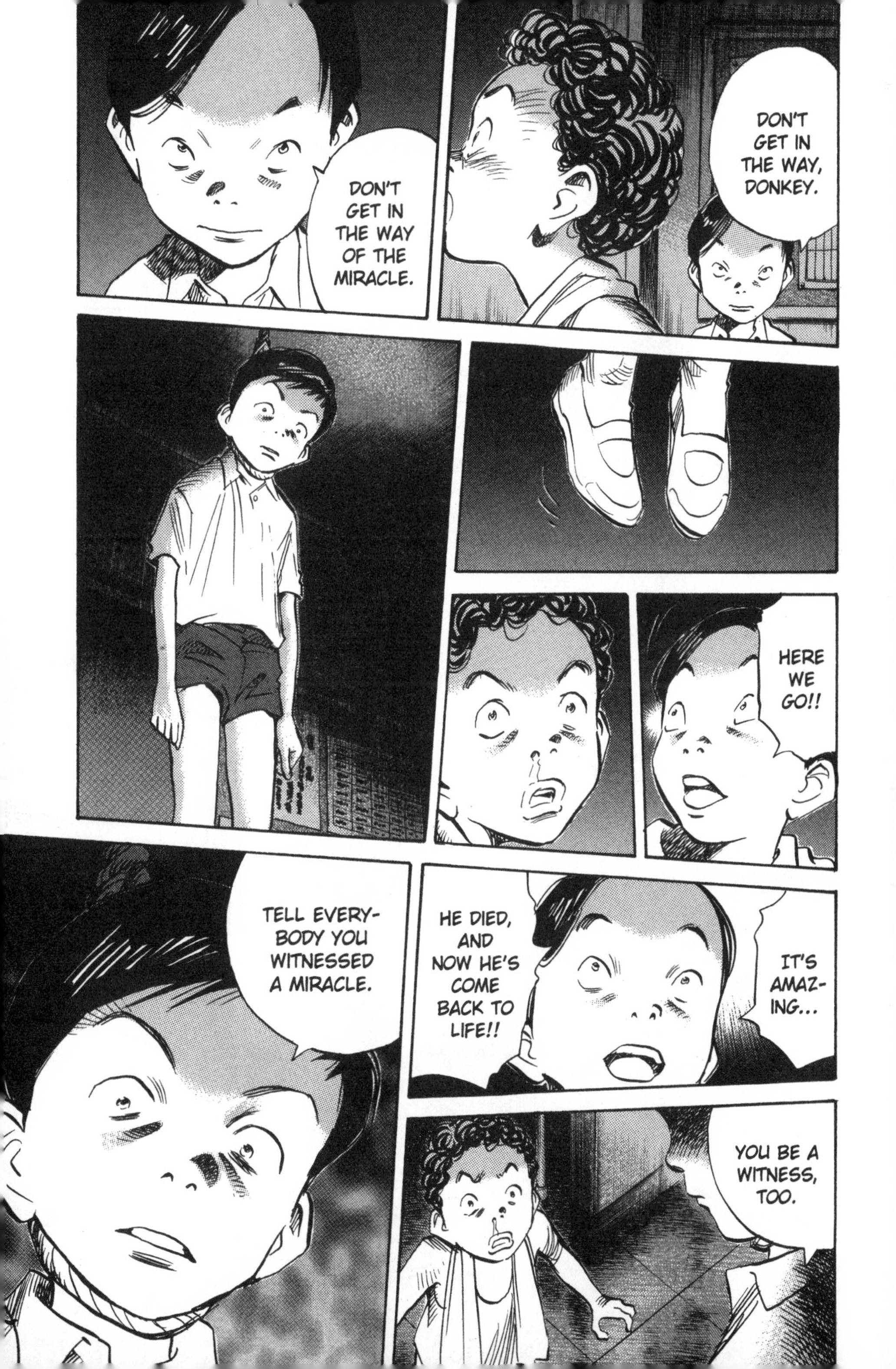
DON'T GET IN THE WAY, DONKEY.
DON'T GET IN THE WAY OF THE MIRACLE.
HERE WE GO!!
IT'S AMAZ-ING...
HE DIED, AND NOW HE'S COME BACK TO LIFE!!
YOU BE A WITNESS, TOO.
TELL EVERY-BODY YOU WITNESSED A MIRACLE.

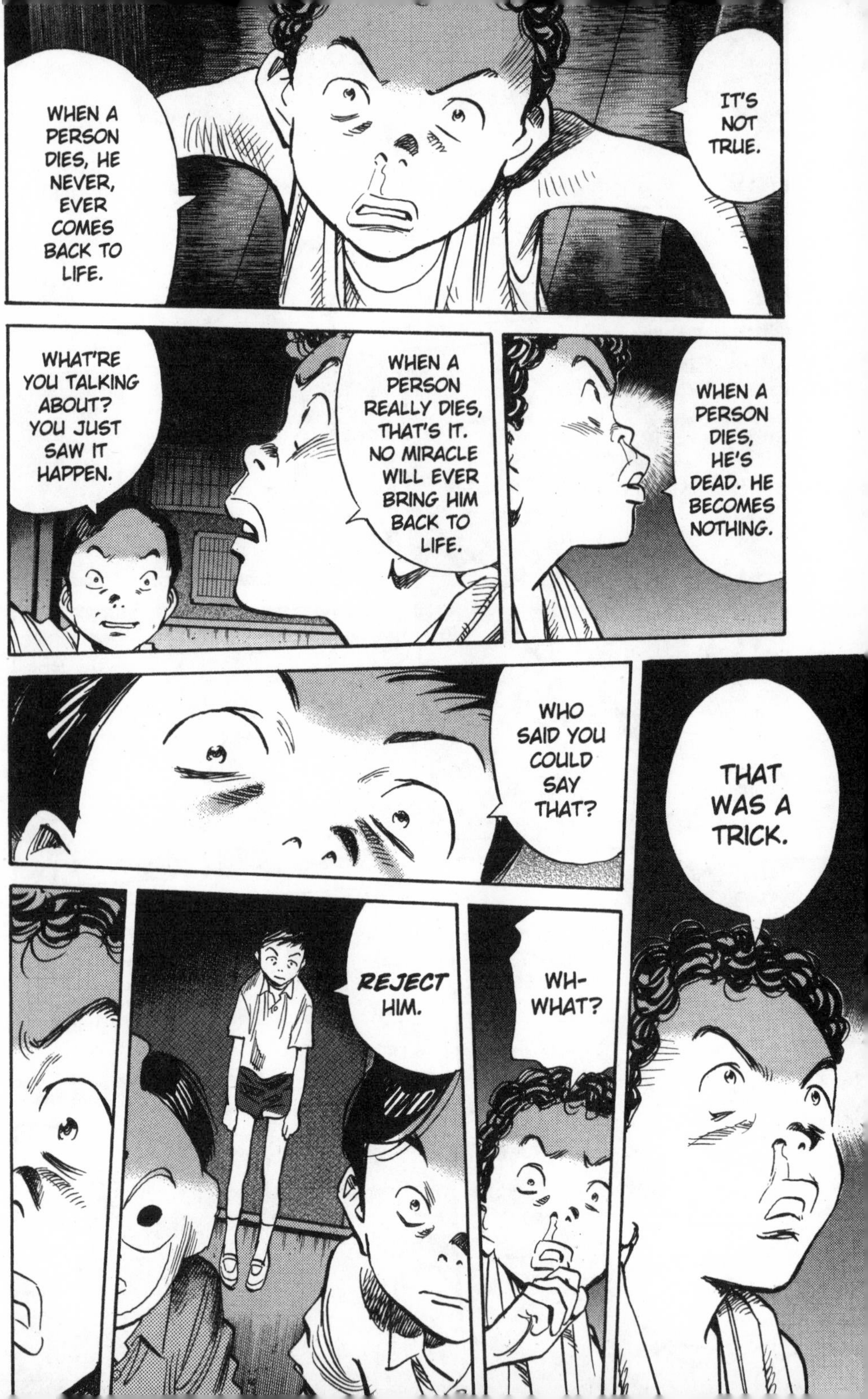
IT'S NOT TRUE.
WHEN A PERSON DIES, HE NEVER, EVER COMES BACK TO LIFE.
WHEN A PERSON DIES, HE'S DEAD. HE BECOMES NOTHING.
WHEN A PERSON REALLY DIES, THAT'S IT. NO MIRACLE WILL EVER BRING HIM BACK TO LIFE.
WHAT'RE YOU TALKING ABOUT? YOU JUST SAW IT HAPPEN.
THAT WAS A TRICK.
WHO SAID YOU COULD SAY THAT?
WH- WHAT?
REJECT HIM.

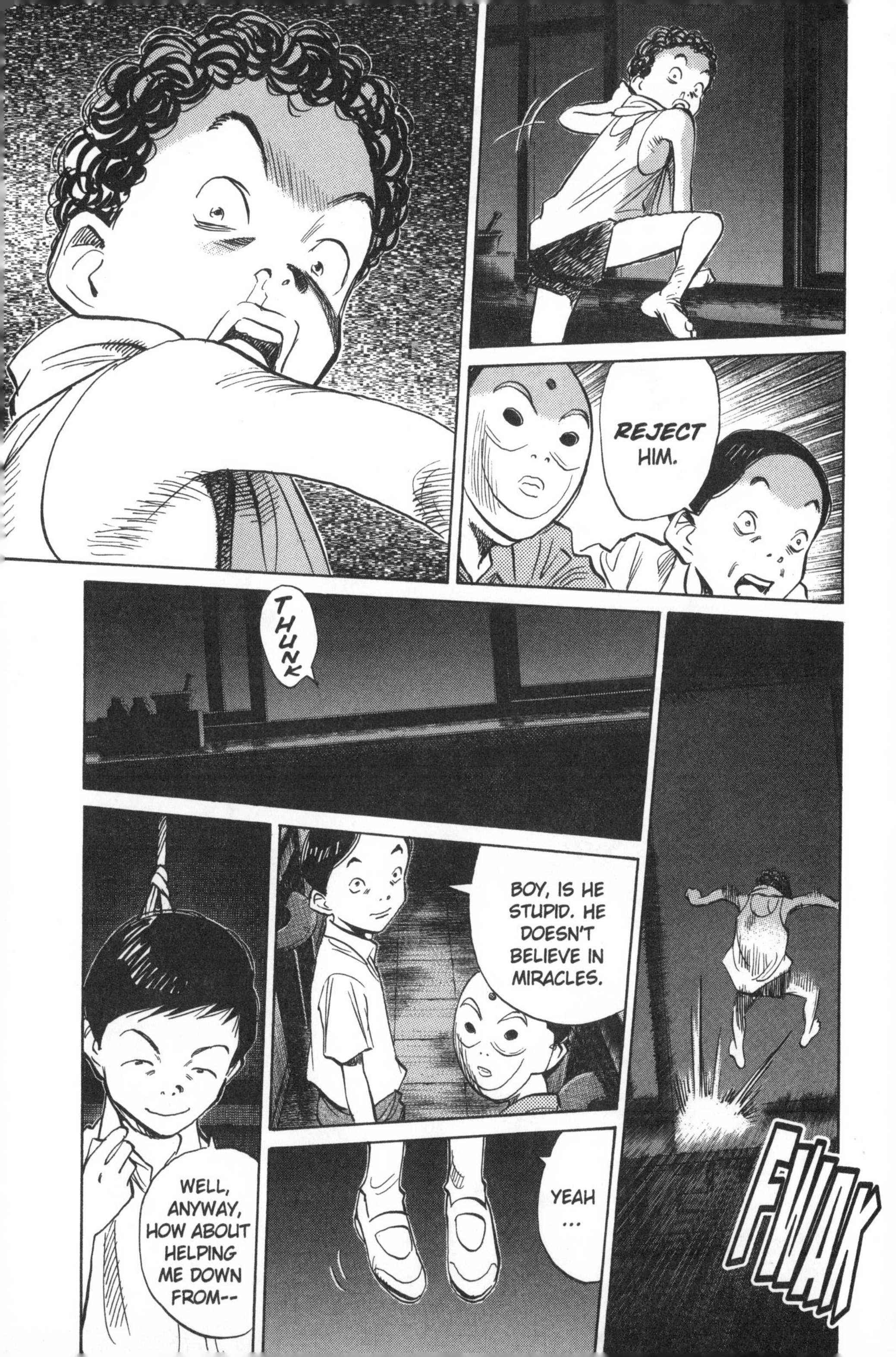
REJECT HIM.
FWAK
THUNK
BOY, IS HE STUPID. HE DOESN'T BELIEVE IN MIRACLES.
YEAH ...
WELL, ANYWAY, HOW ABOUT HELPING ME DOWN FROM--

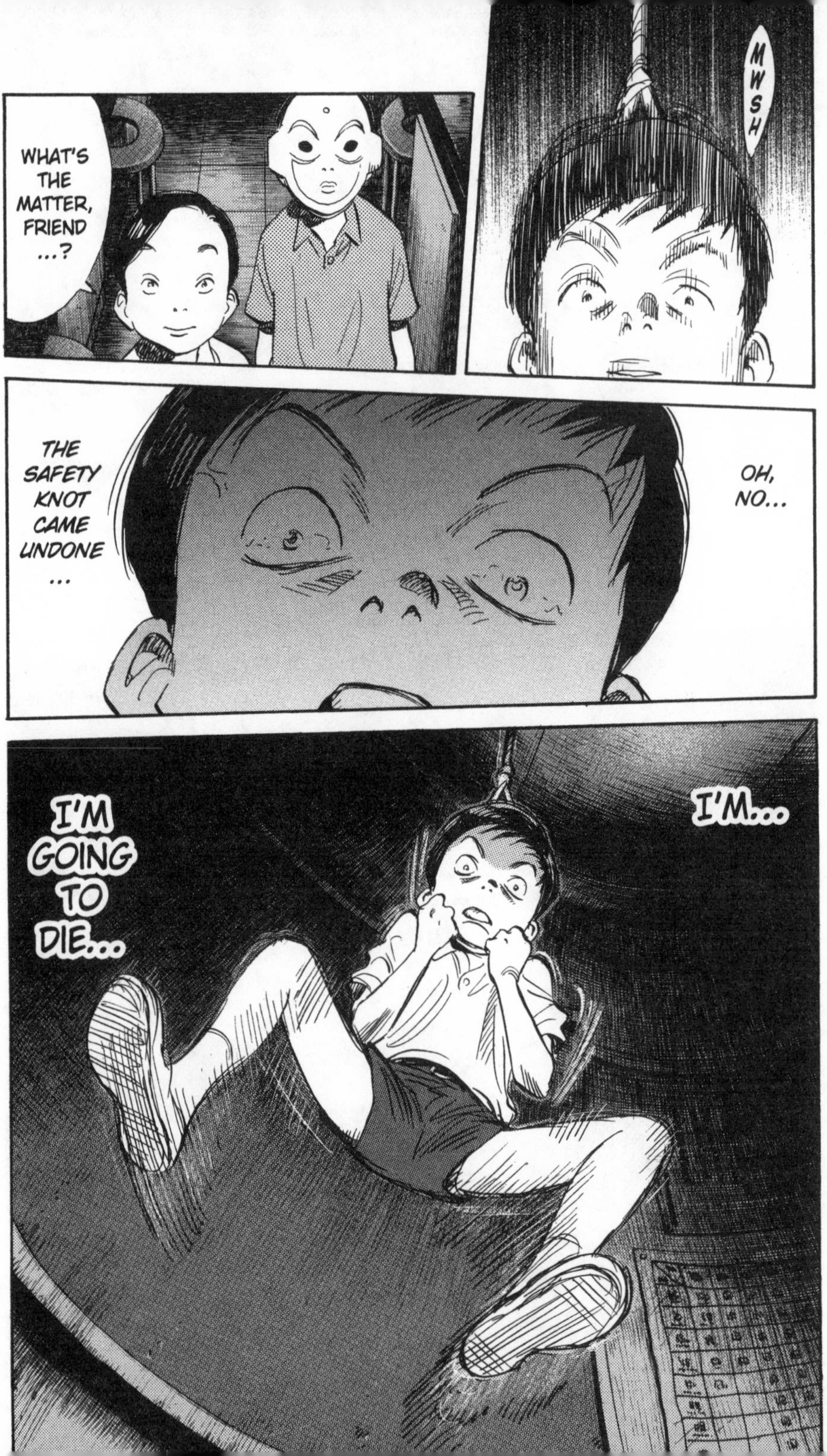
MWSH
WHAT'S THE MATTER, FRIEND ...?
OH, NO...
THE SAFETY KNOT CAME UNDONE ...
I'M...
I'M GOING TO DIE...

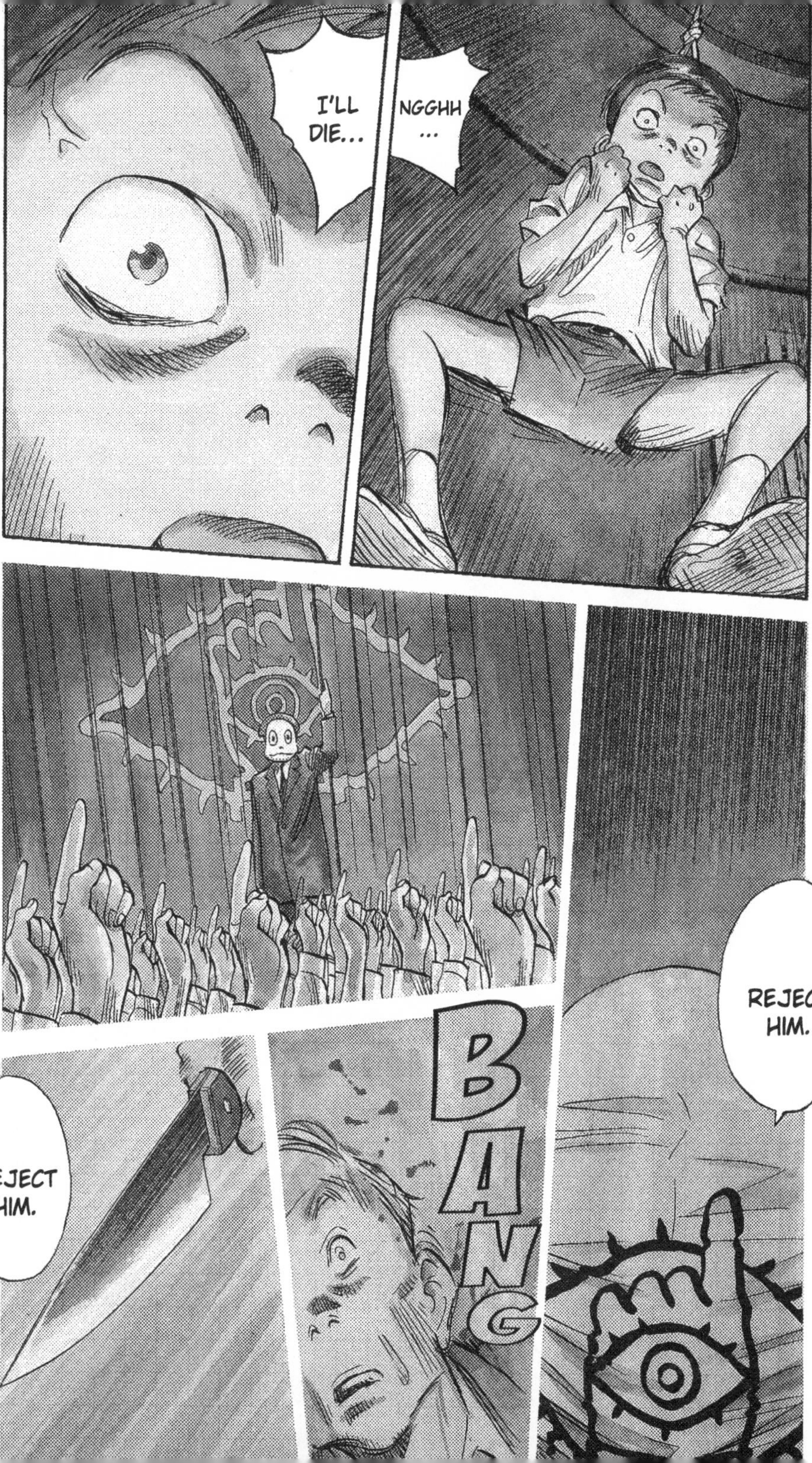
NGGHH ...
I'LL DIE...
REJECT HIM.
BANG
REJECT HIM.

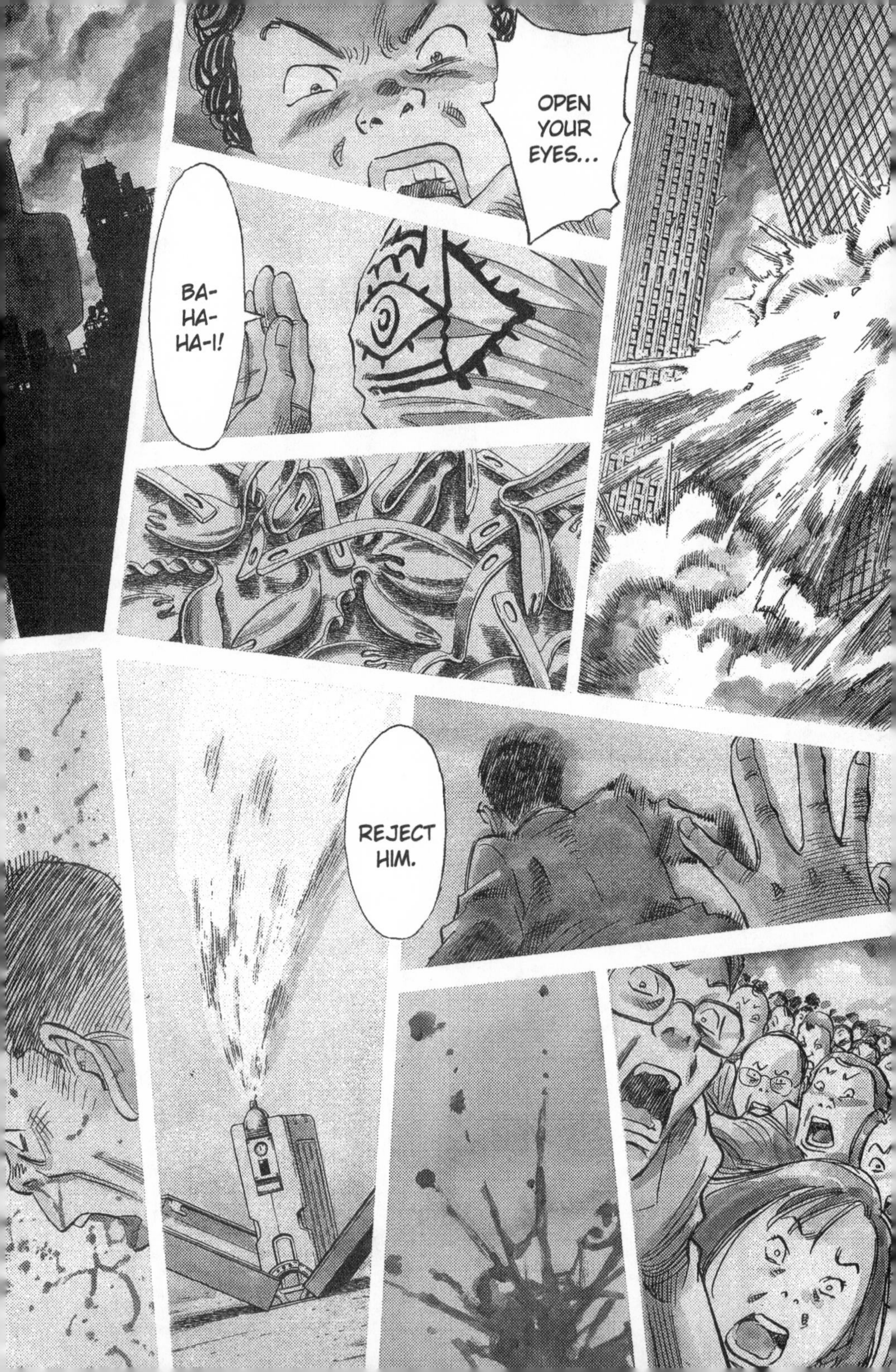
OPEN YOUR EYES...
BA-HA-HA-!!
REJECT HIM.

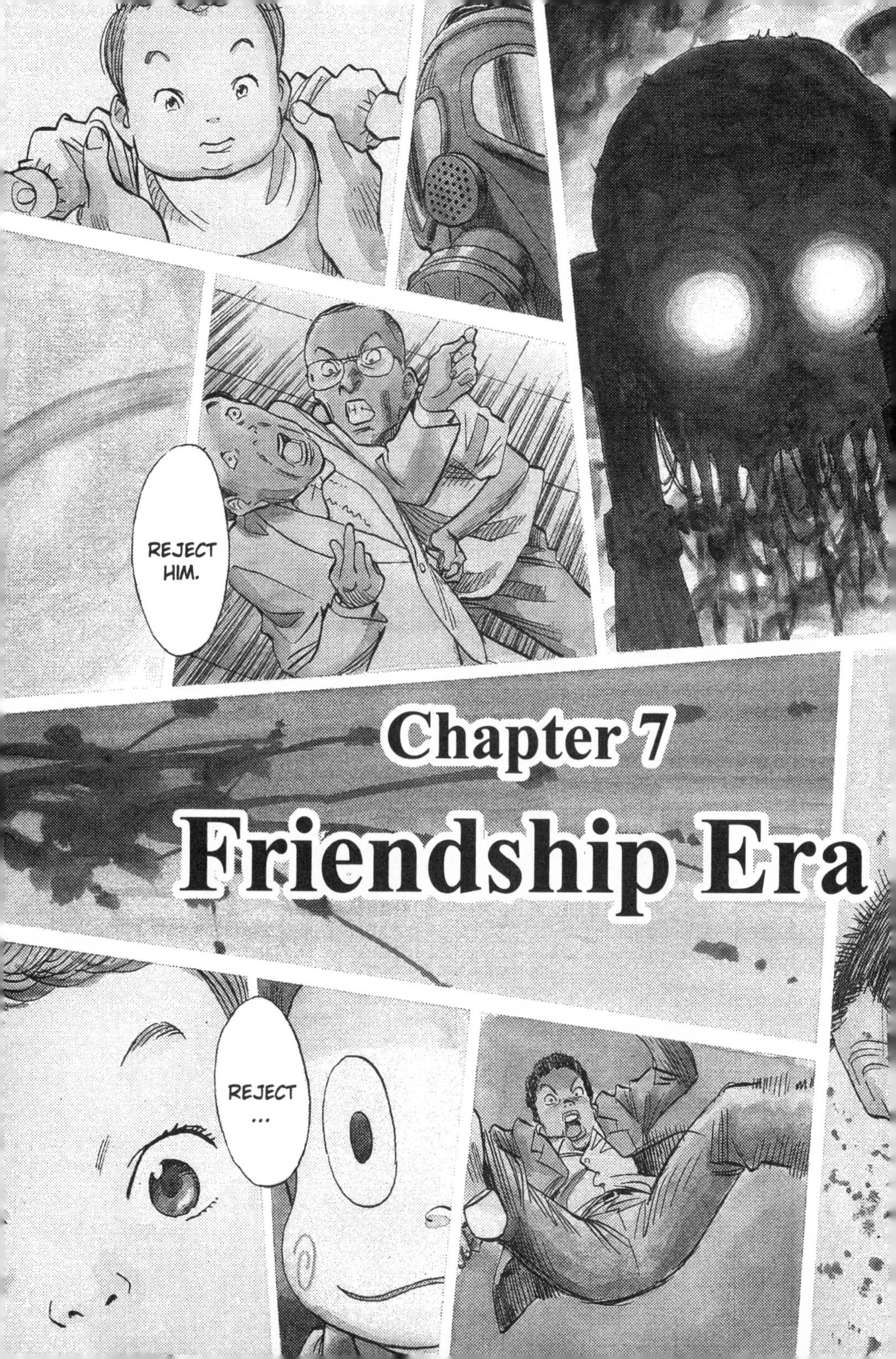
REJECT HIM.
Chapter 7
Friendship Era
REJECT ...

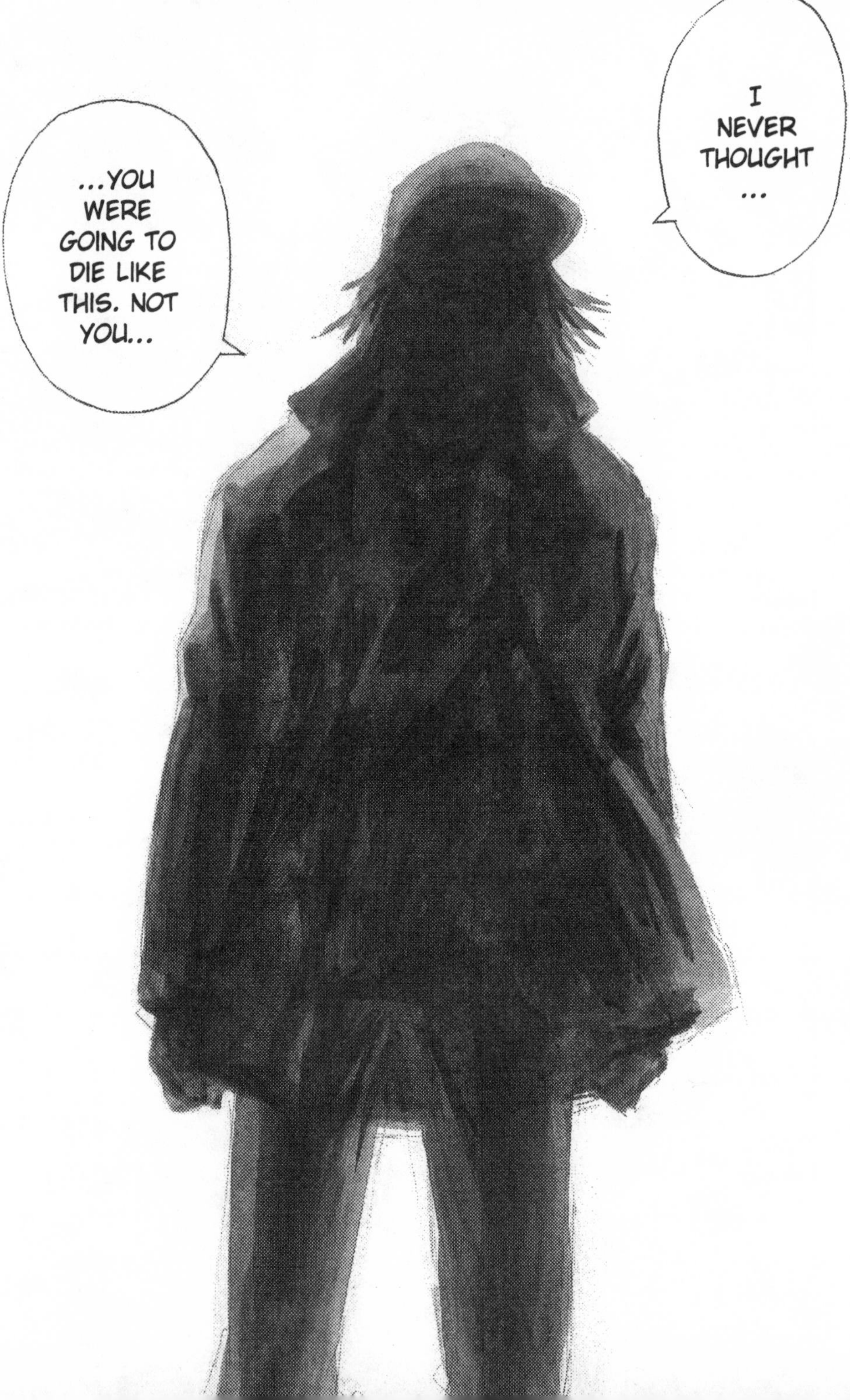
I NEVER THOUGHT ...
...YOU WERE GOING TO DIE LIKE THIS. NOT YOU...

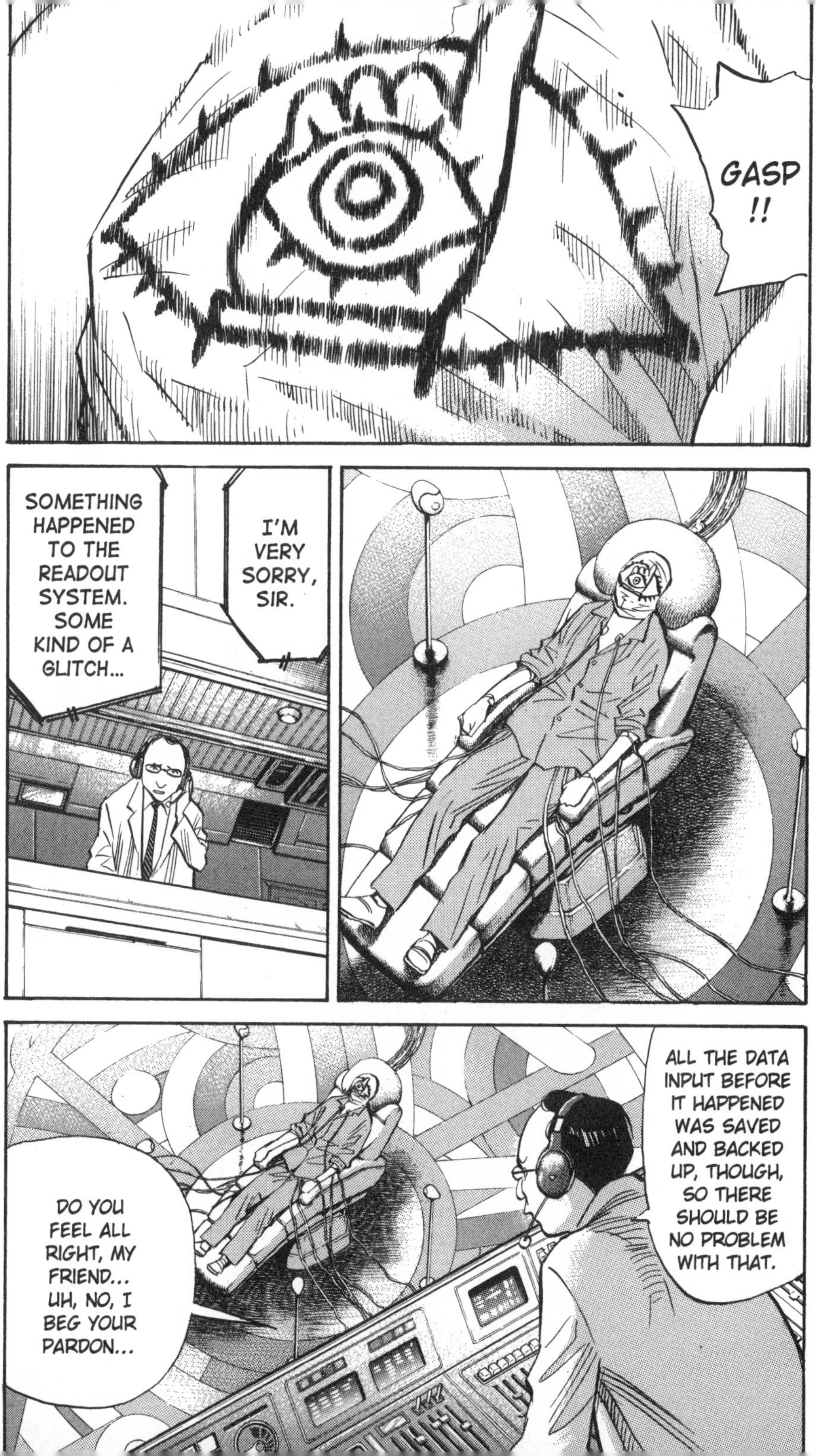
GASP !!
I'M VERY SORRY, SIR.
SOMETHING HAPPENED TO THE READOUT SYSTEM. SOME KIND OF A GLITCH...
ALL THE DATA INPUT BEFORE IT HAPPENED WAS SAVED AND BACKED UP, THOUGH, SO THERE SHOULD BE NO PROBLEM WITH THAT.
DO YOU FEEL ALL RIGHT, MY FRIEND... UH, NO, I BEG YOUR PARDON...

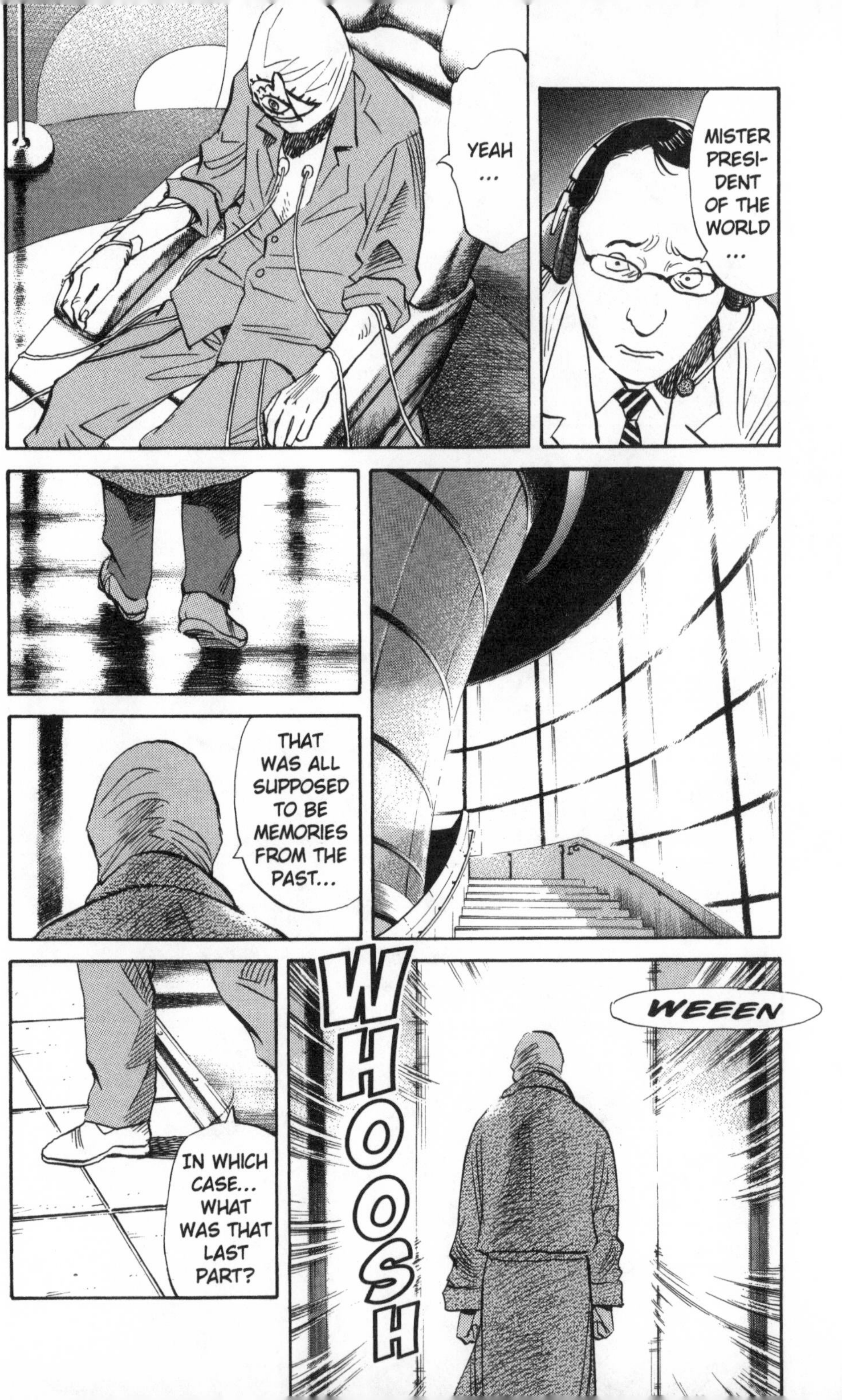
MISTER PRESIDENT OF THE WORLD ...
YEAH ...
THAT WAS ALL SUPPOSED TO BE MEMORIES FROM THE PAST...
WEEEN
WHOOSH
IN WHICH CASE... WHAT WAS THAT LAST PART?

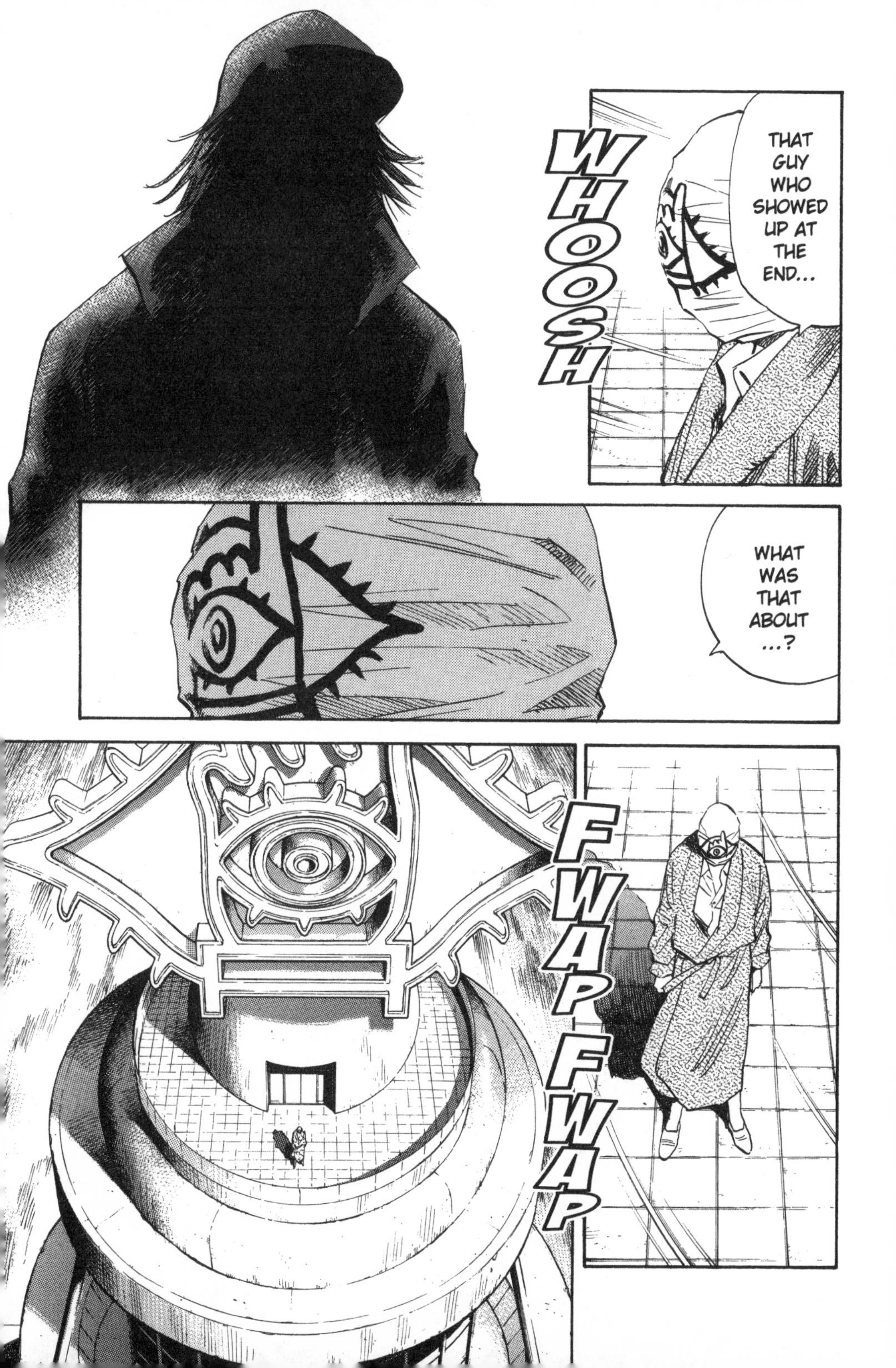
THAT GUY WHO SHOWED UP AT THE END...
WHOOSH
WHAT WAS THAT ABOUT ...?
FWAP FWAP

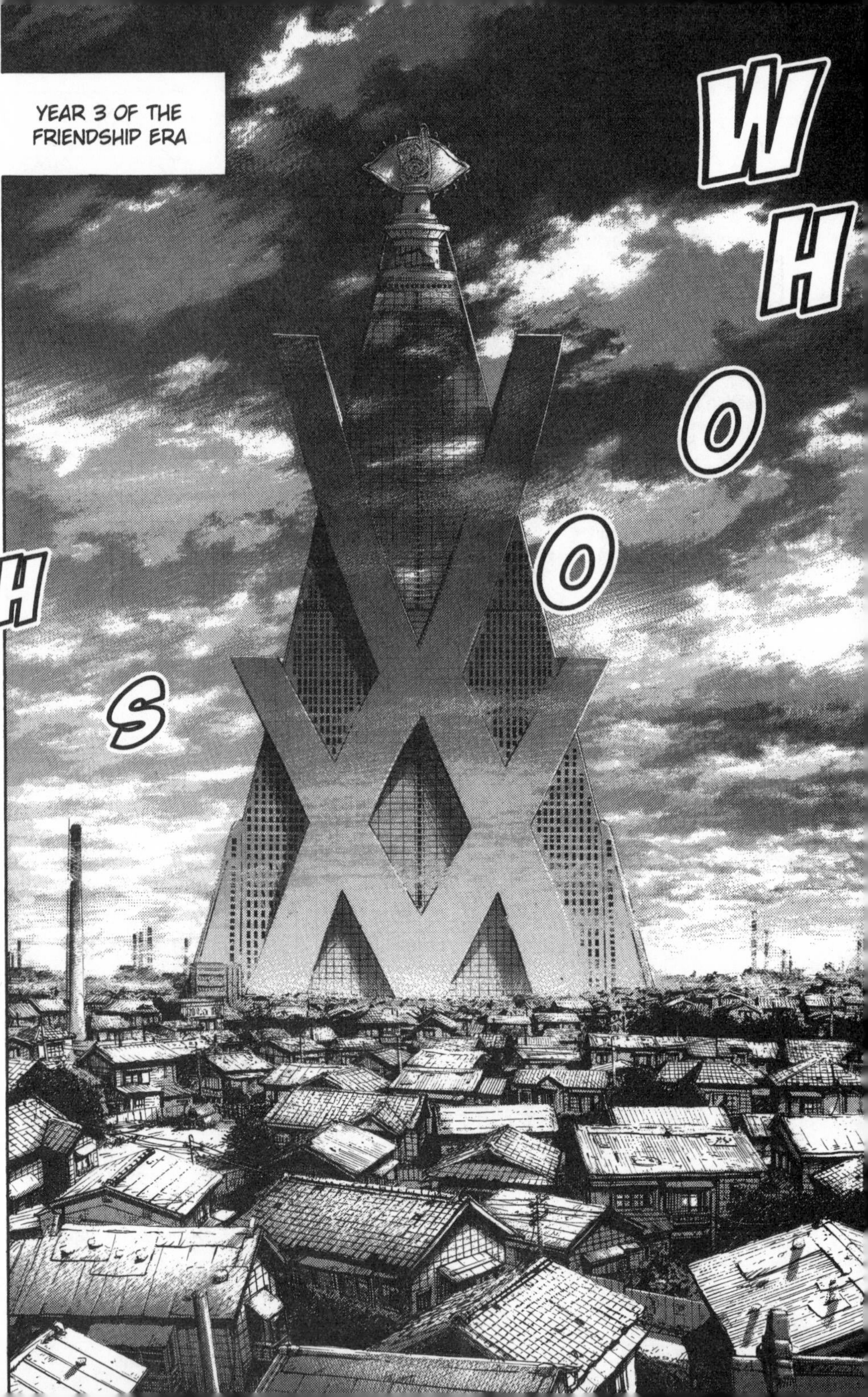
YEAR 3 OF THE FRIENDSHIP ERA
WHOOSH

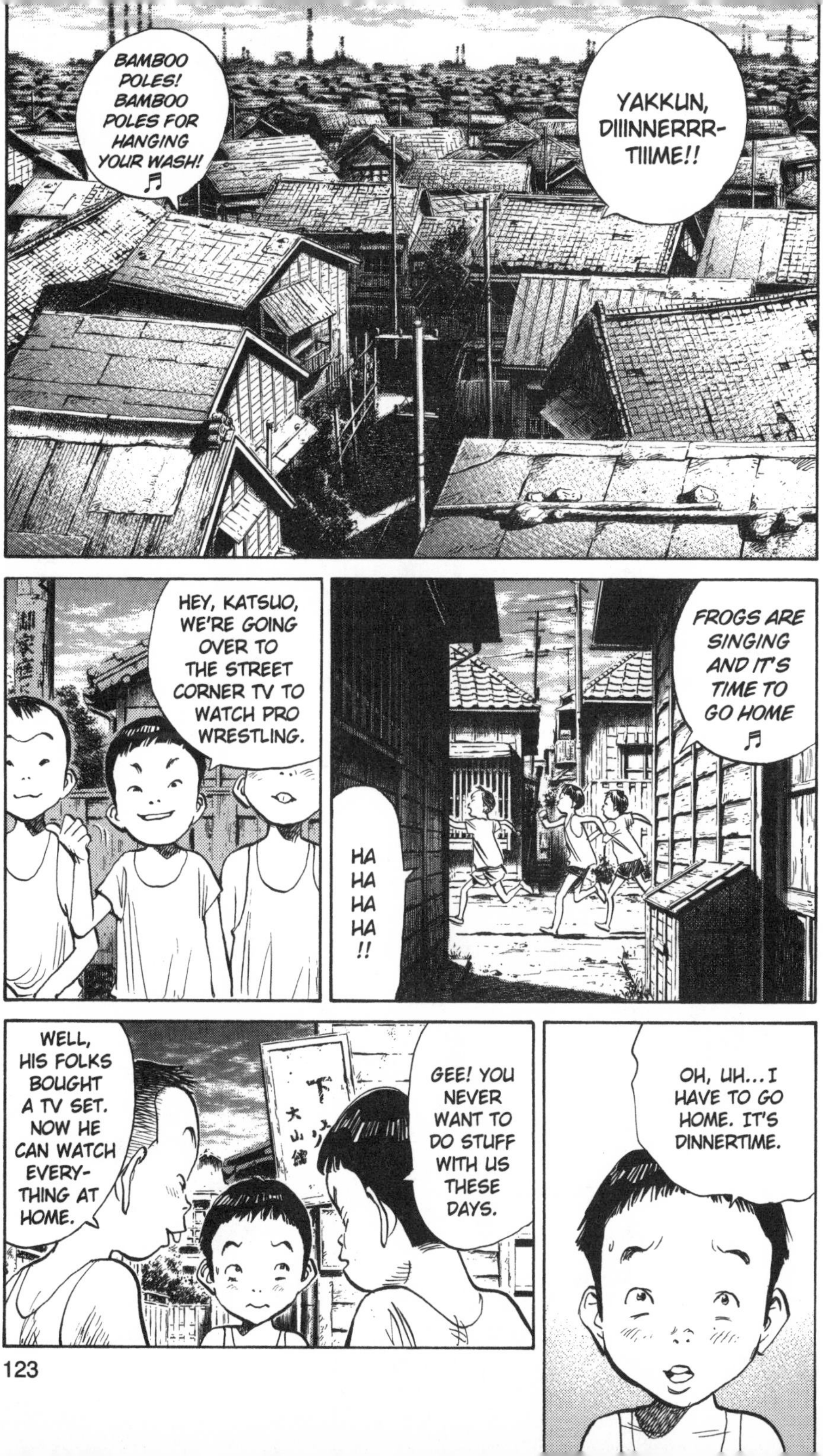

YAKKUN, DIIINNERRR-TIIIME!!
BAMBOO POLES! BAMBOO POLES FOR HANGING YOUR WASH! ♬
FROGS ARE SINGING AND IT'S TIME TO GO HOME ♬
HA HA HA HA!!
HEY, KATSUO, WE'RE GOING OVER TO THE STREET CORNER TV TO WATCH PRO WRESTLING.
OH, UH... I HAVE TO GO HOME. IT'S DINNERTIME.
GEE! YOU NEVER WANT TO DO STUFF WITH US THESE DAYS.
WELL, HIS FOLKS BOUGHT A TV SET. NOW HE CAN WATCH EVERY-THING AT HOME.

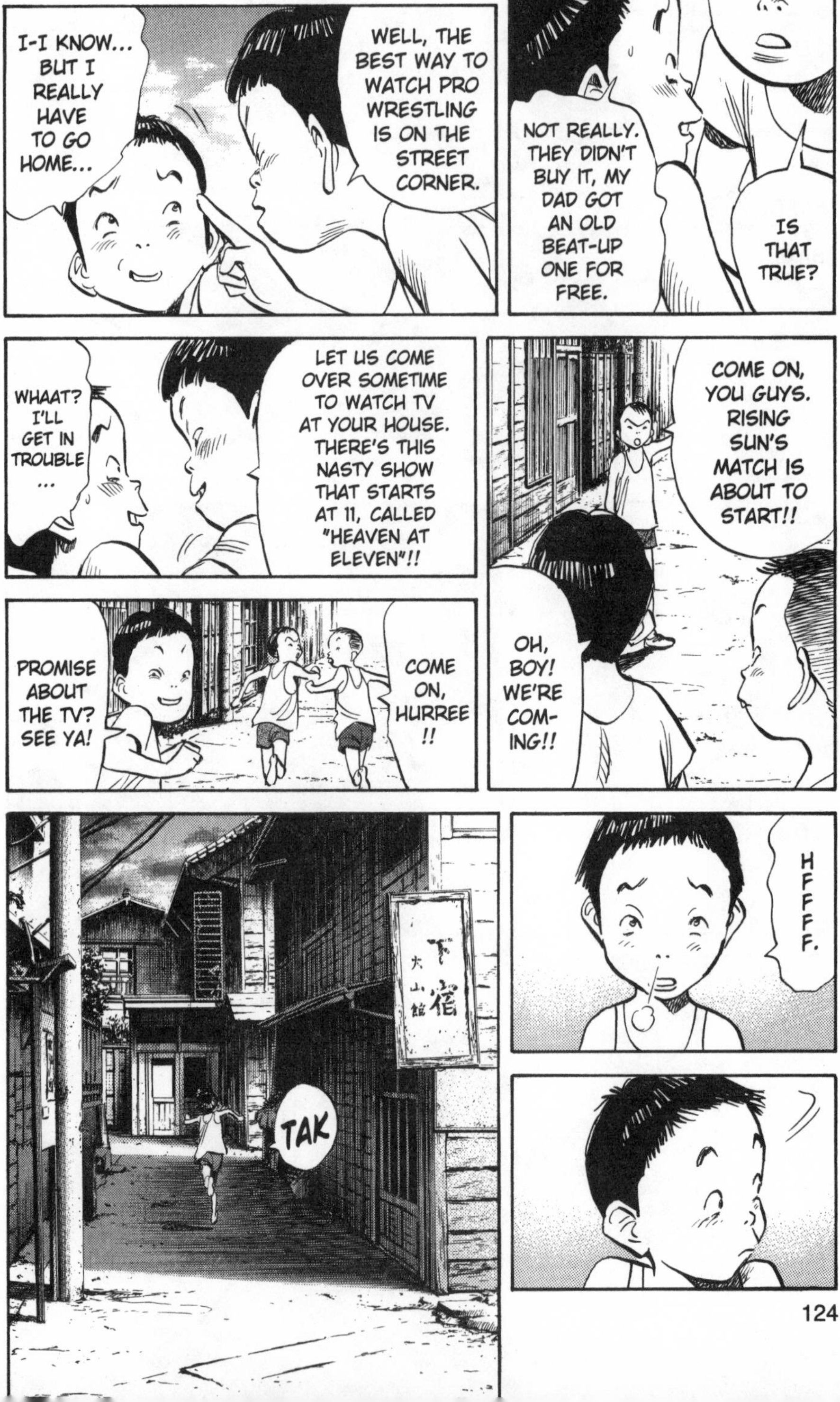
IS THAT TRUE?
NOT REALLY. THEY DIDN'T BUY IT, MY DAD GOT AN OLD BEAT-UP ONE FOR FREE.
WELL, THE BEST WAY TO WATCH PRO WRESTLING IS ON THE STREET CORNER.
I-I KNOW... BUT I REALLY HAVE TO GO HOME...
COME ON, YOU GUYS. RISING SUN'S MATCH IS ABOUT TO START!!
LET US COME OVER SOMETIME TO WATCH TV AT YOUR HOUSE. THERE'S THIS NASTY SHOW THAT STARTS AT 11, CALLED "HEAVEN AT ELEVEN"!!
WHAAT? I'LL GET IN TROUBLE...
OH, BOY! WE'RE COM-ING!!
COME ON, HURREE!!
PROMISE ABOUT THE TV? SEE YA!
HFFFF.
下宿
大山館
TAK

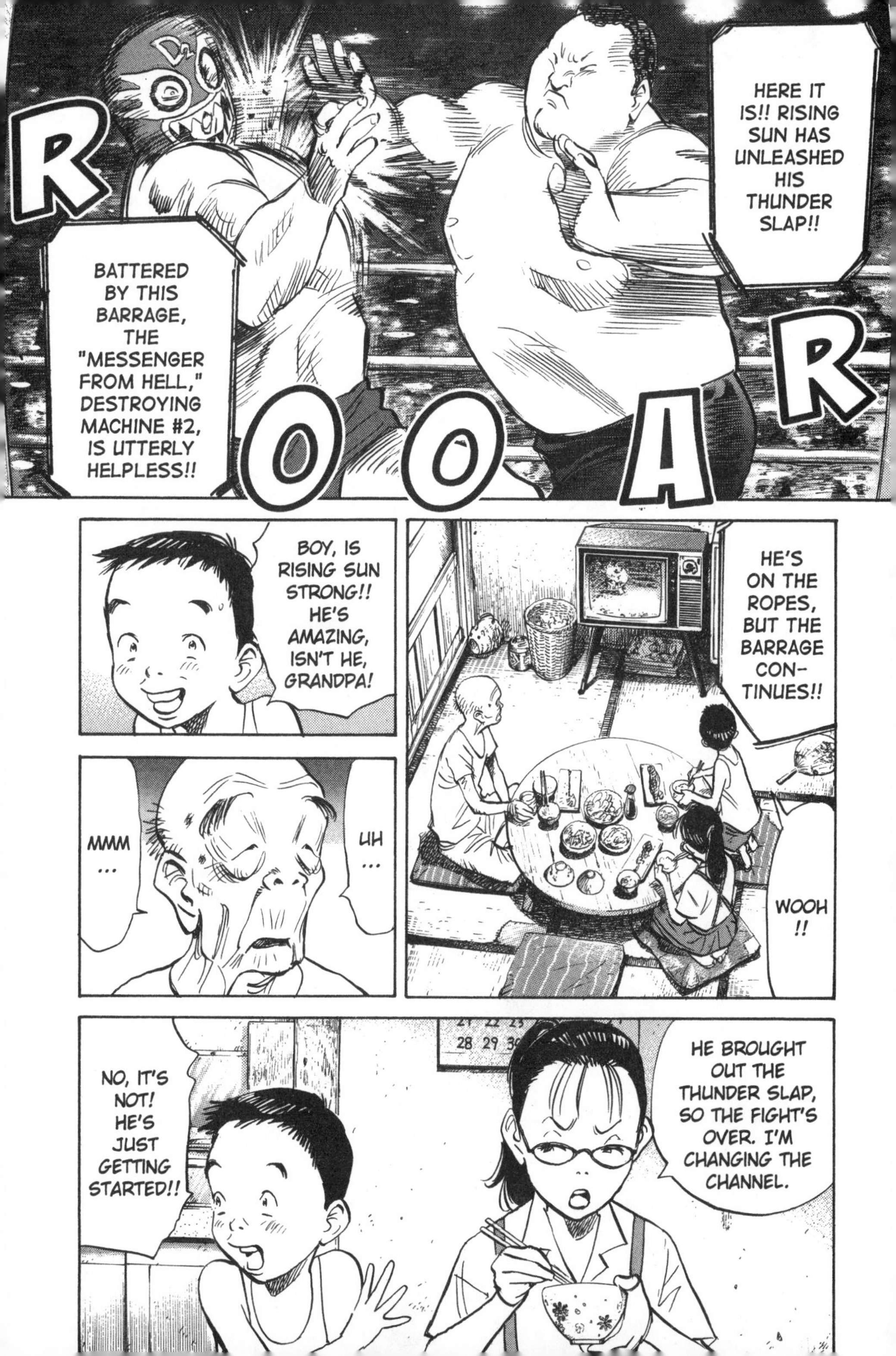
HERE IT IS!! RISING SUN HAS UNLEASHED HIS THUNDER SLAP!!
BATTERED BY THIS BARRAGE, THE "MESSENGER FROM HELL," DESTROYING MACHINE #2, IS UTTERLY HELPLESS!!
ROOAR
HE'S ON THE ROPES, BUT THE BARRAGE CON-TINUES!!
WOOH !!
BOY, IS RISING SUN STRONG!! HE'S AMAZING, ISN'T HE, GRANDPA!
UH ...
MMM ...
HE BROUGHT OUT THE THUNDER SLAP, SO THE FIGHT'S OVER. I'M CHANGING THE CHANNEL.
NO, IT'S NOT! HE'S JUST GETTING STARTED!!

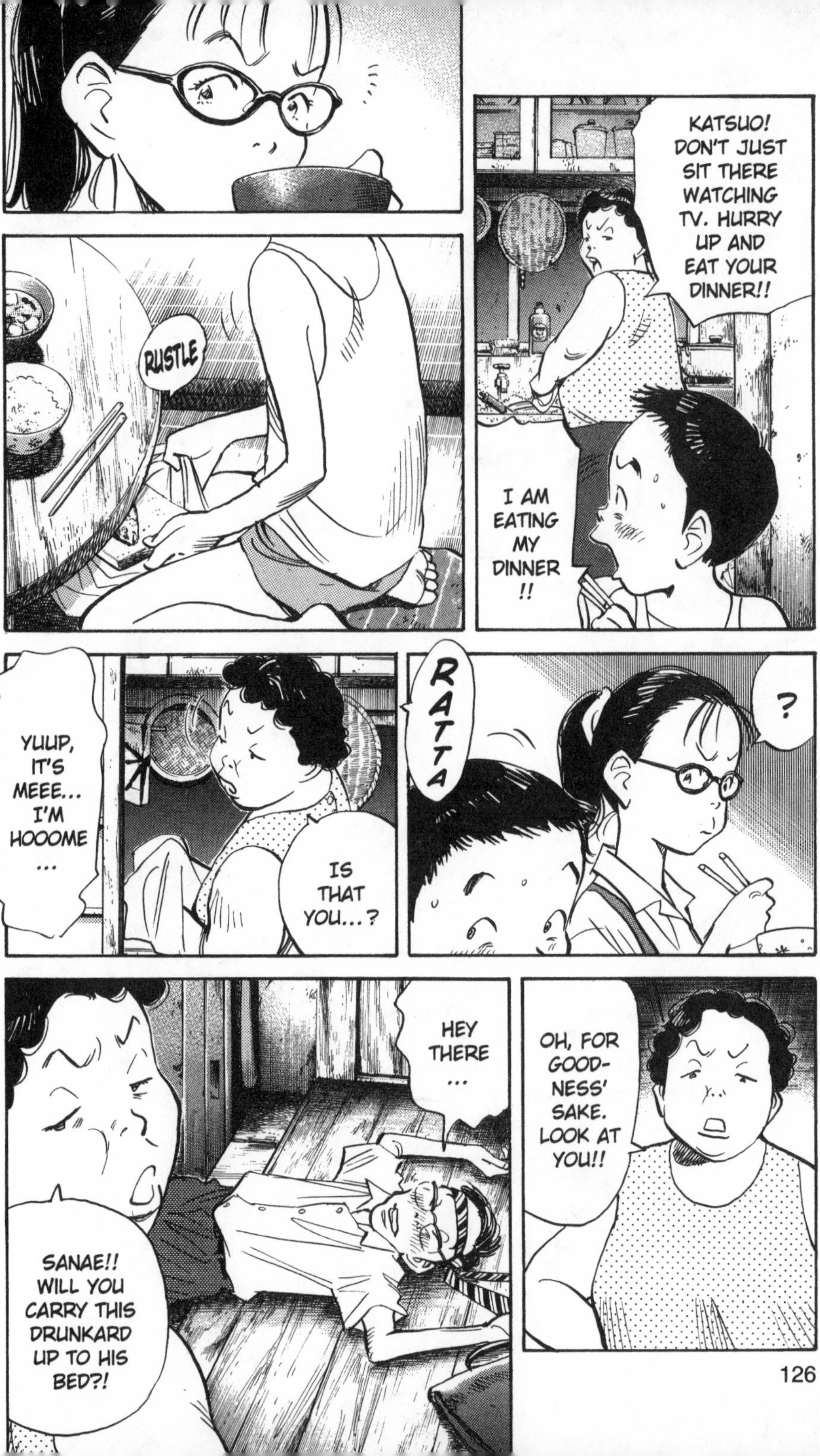
KATSUO! DON'T JUST SIT THERE WATCHING TV. HURRY UP AND EAT YOUR DINNER!!
I AM EATING MY DINNER !!
RUSTLE
?
RATTA
IS THAT YOU...?
YUUP, IT'S MEEE... I'M HOOOME ...
OH, FOR GOODNESS' SAKE. LOOK AT YOU!!
HEY THERE ...
SANAE!! WILL YOU CARRY THIS DRUNKARD UP TO HIS BED?!

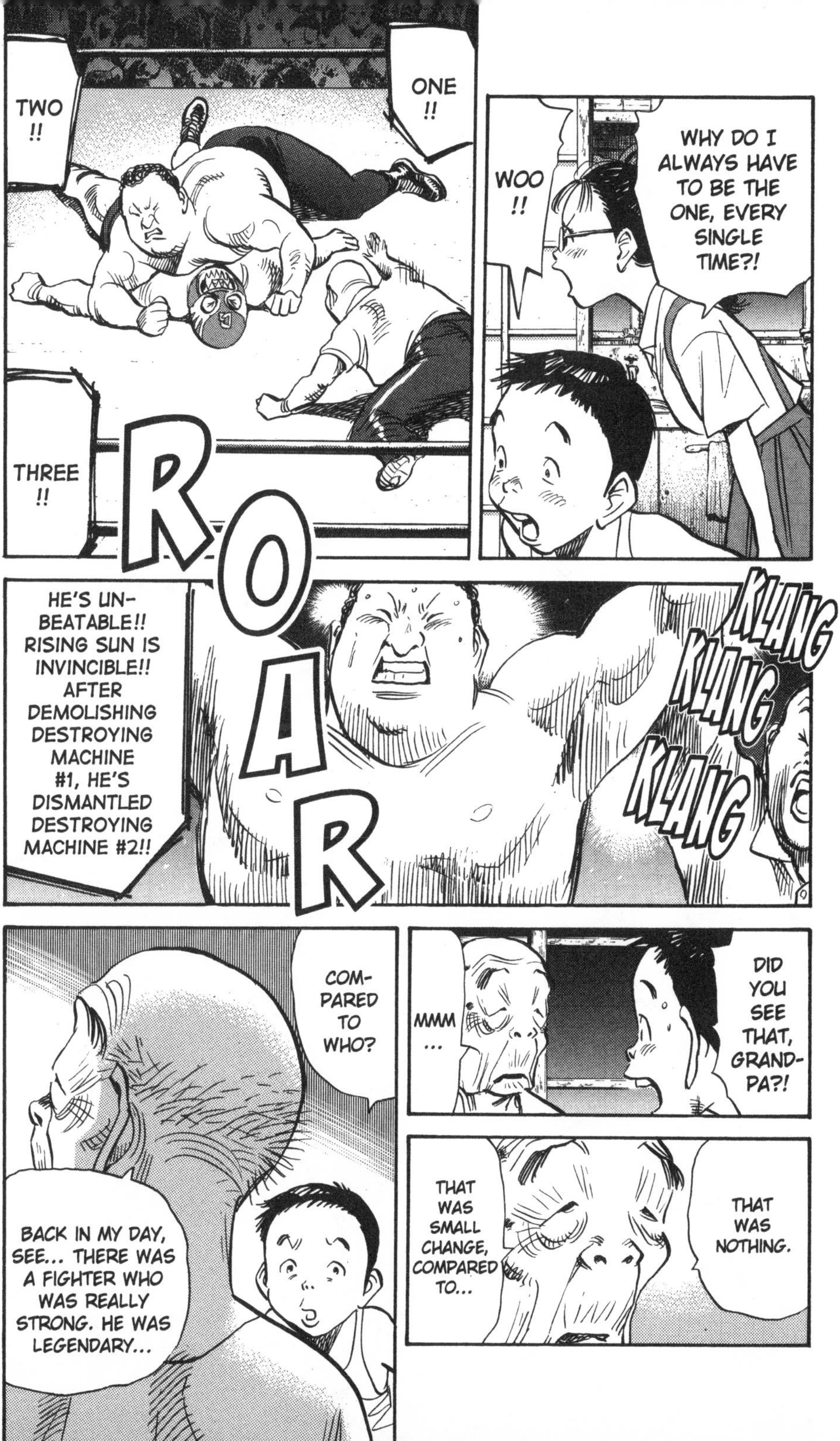

WHY DO I ALWAYS HAVE TO BE THE ONE, EVERY SINGLE TIME?!
WOO!!
ONE!!
TWO!!
THREE!!
ROAR
KLANG KLANG KLANG
HE'S UNBEATABLE!! RISING SUN IS INVINCIBLE!! AFTER DEMOLISHING DESTROYING MACHINE #1, HE'S DISMANTLED DESTROYING MACHINE #2!!
DID YOU SEE THAT, GRANDPA?!
MMM...
THAT WAS NOTHING.
THAT WAS SMALL CHANGE, COMPARED TO...
COMPARED TO WHO?
BACK IN MY DAY, SEE... THERE WAS A FIGHTER WHO WAS REALLY STRONG. HE WAS LEGENDARY...

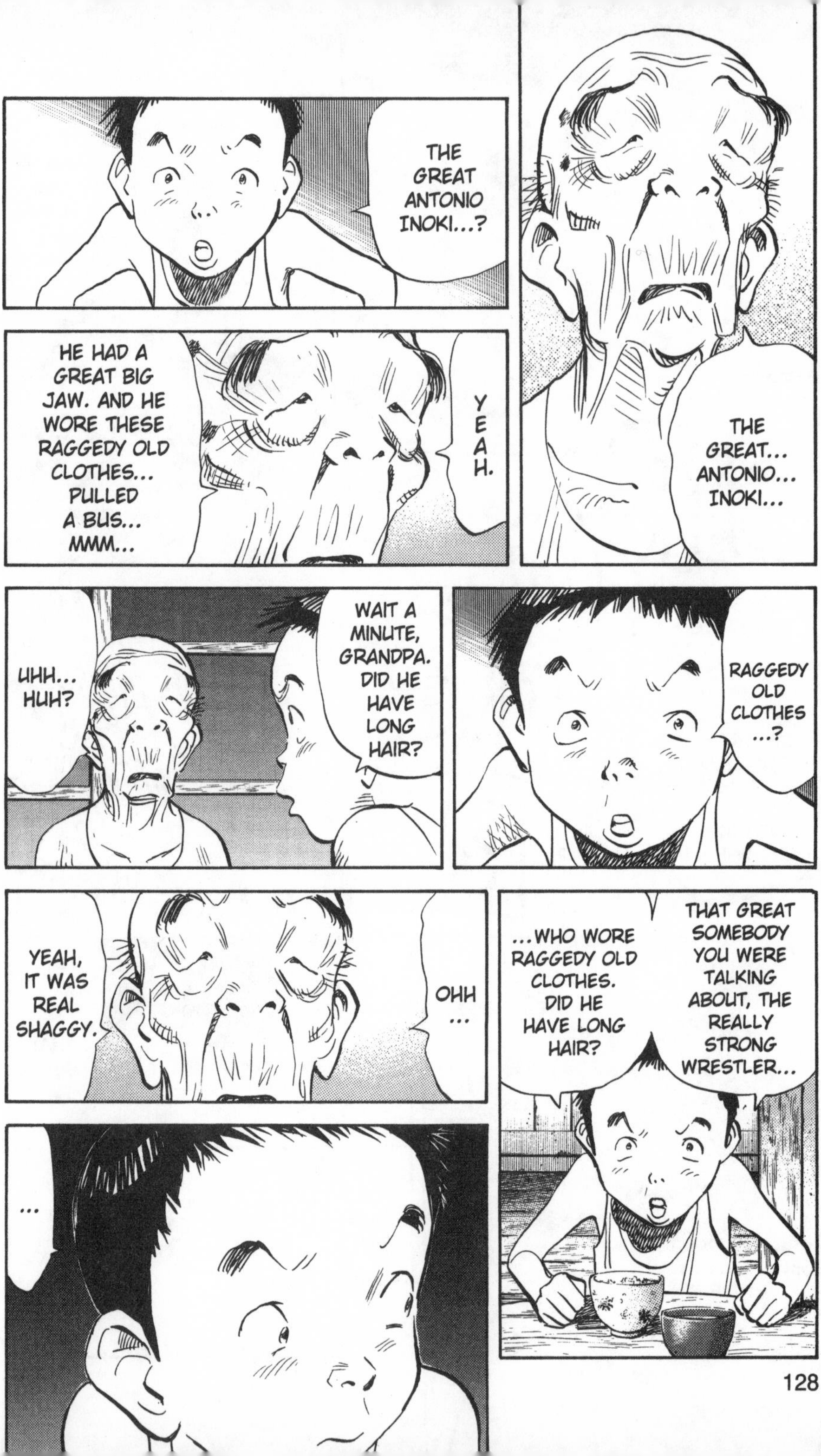
THE GREAT... ANTONIO... INOKI...
THE GREAT ANTONIO INOKI...?
YEAH.
HE HAD A GREAT BIG JAW. AND HE WORE THESE RAGGEDY OLD CLOTHES... PULLED A BUS... MMM...
RAGGEDY OLD CLOTHES ...?
WAIT A MINUTE, GRANDPA. DID HE HAVE LONG HAIR?
UHH... HUH?
THAT GREAT SOMEBODY YOU WERE TALKING ABOUT, THE REALLY STRONG WRESTLER...
...WHO WORE RAGGEDY OLD CLOTHES. DID HE HAVE LONG HAIR?
OHH ...
YEAH, IT WAS REAL SHAGGY.
...

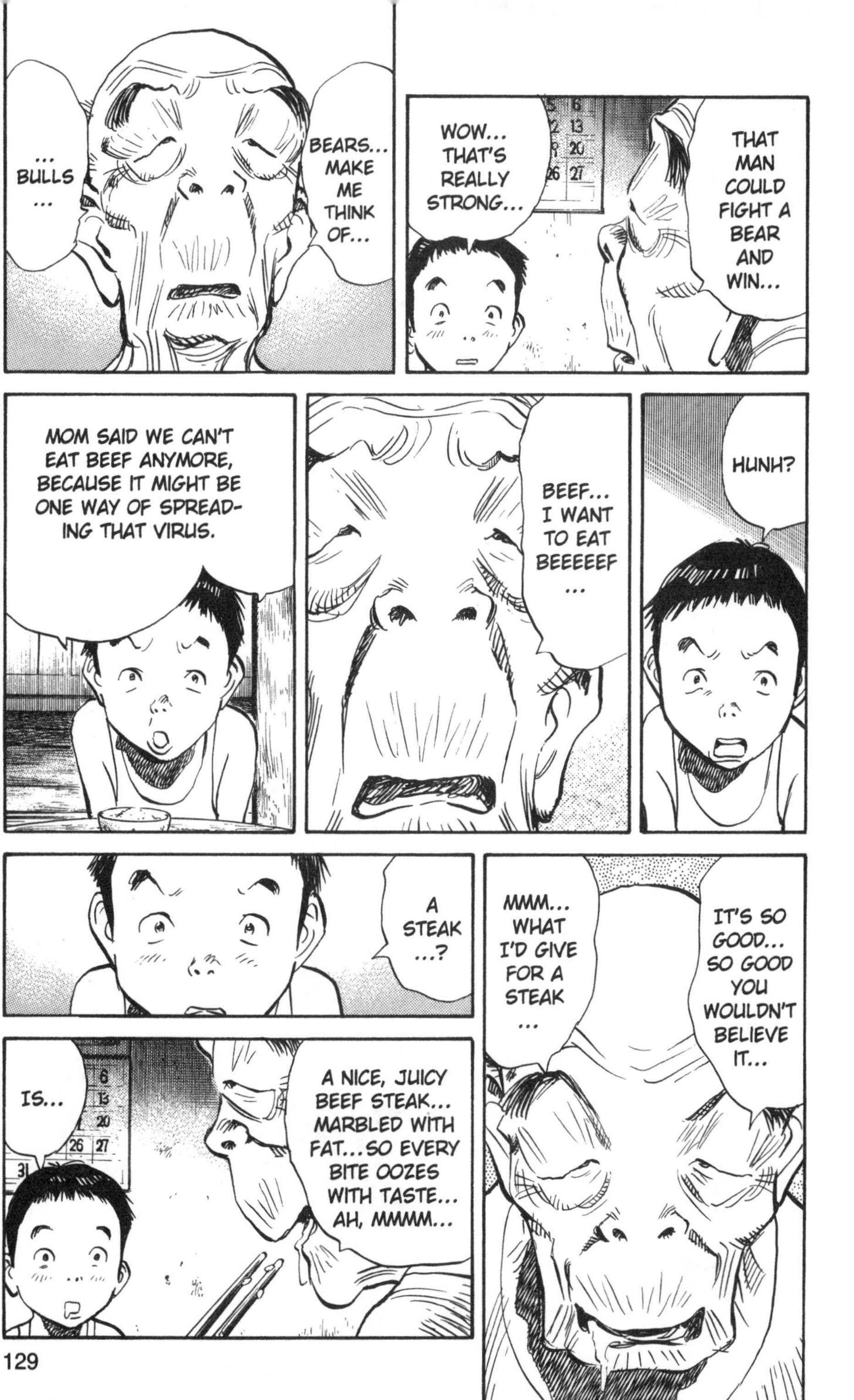
THAT MAN COULD FIGHT A BEAR AND WIN...
WOW... THAT'S REALLY STRONG...
BEARS... MAKE ME THINK OF...
... BULLS ...
HUNH?
BEEF... I WANT TO EAT BEEEEEF ...
MOM SAID WE CAN'T EAT BEEF ANYMORE, BECAUSE IT MIGHT BE ONE WAY OF SPREAD-ING THAT VIRUS.
IT'S SO GOOD... SO GOOD YOU WOULDN'T BELIEVE IT...
MMM... WHAT I'D GIVE FOR A STEAK ...
A STEAK ...?
A NICE, JUICY BEEF STEAK... MARBLED WITH FAT...SO EVERY BITE OOZES WITH TASTE... AH, MMMM...
IS...

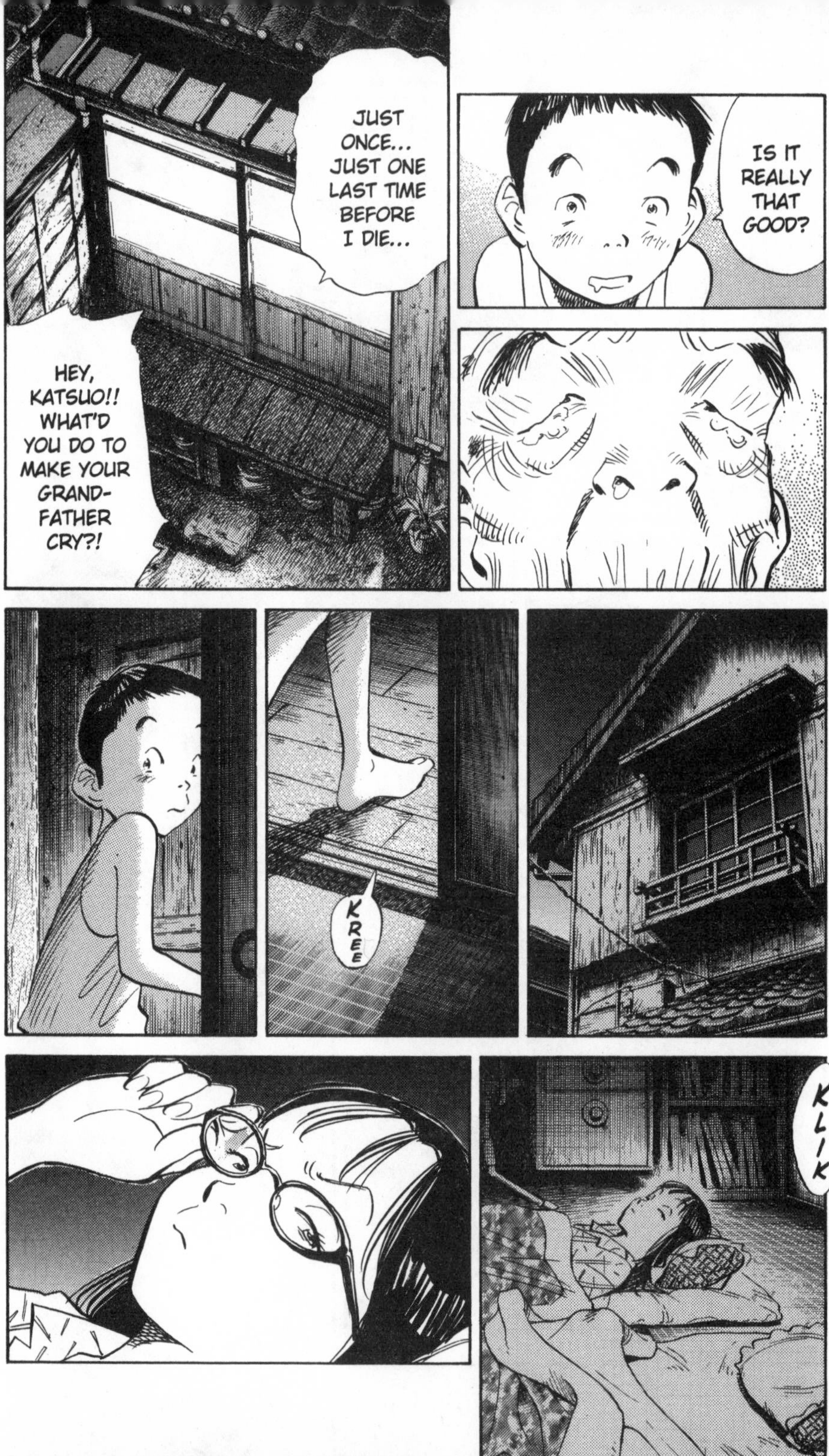
IS IT REALLY THAT GOOD?
JUST ONCE... JUST ONE LAST TIME BEFORE I DIE...
HEY, KATSUO!! WHAT'D YOU DO TO MAKE YOUR GRAND-FATHER CRY?!
KREE
KLIK

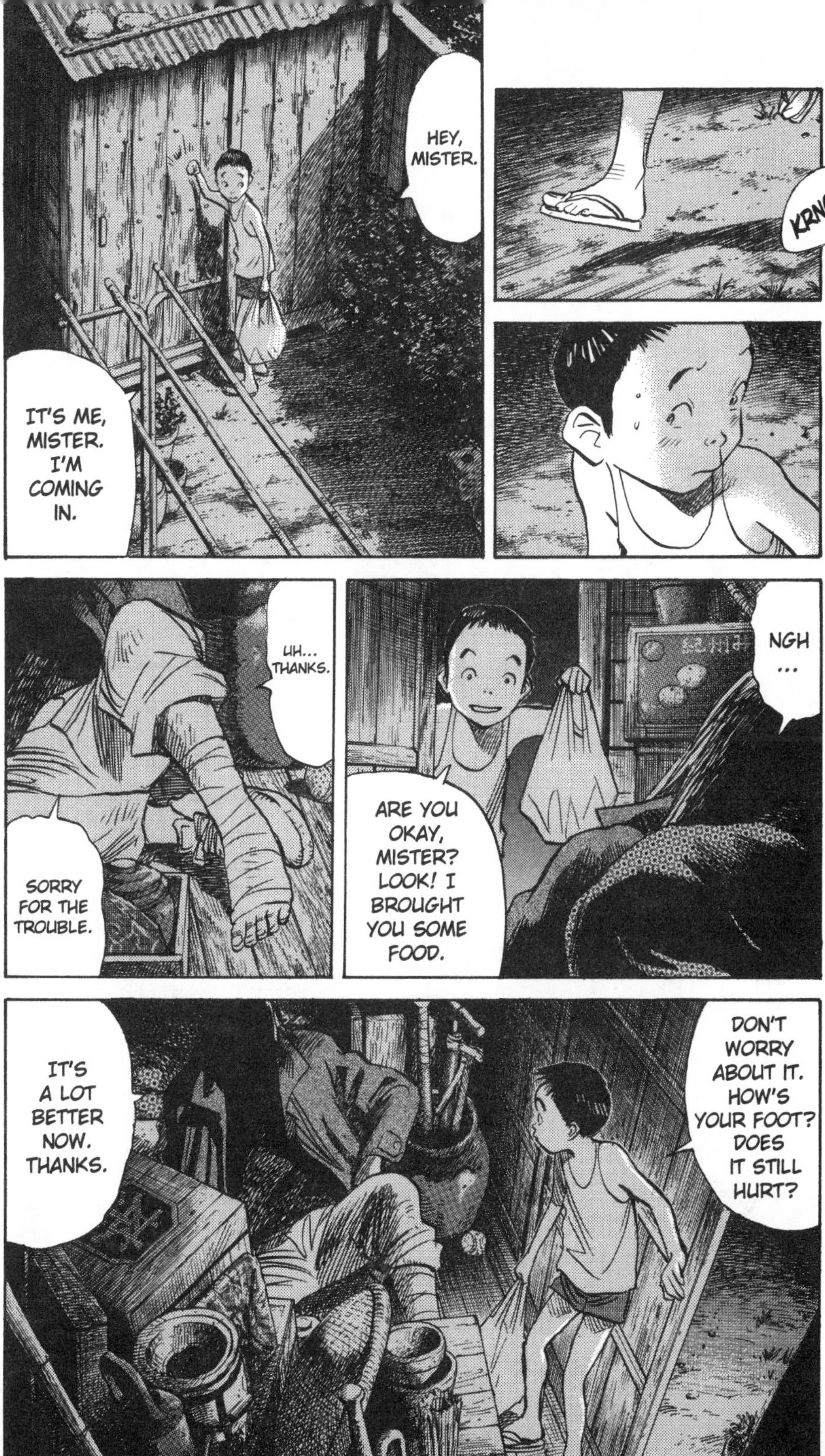
KRNCH
HEY, MISTER.
IT'S ME, MISTER. I'M COMING IN.
NGH ...
ARE YOU OKAY, MISTER? LOOK! I BROUGHT YOU SOME FOOD.
UH... THANKS.
SORRY FOR THE TROUBLE.
DON'T WORRY ABOUT IT. HOW'S YOUR FOOT? DOES IT STILL HURT?
IT'S A LOT BETTER NOW. THANKS.

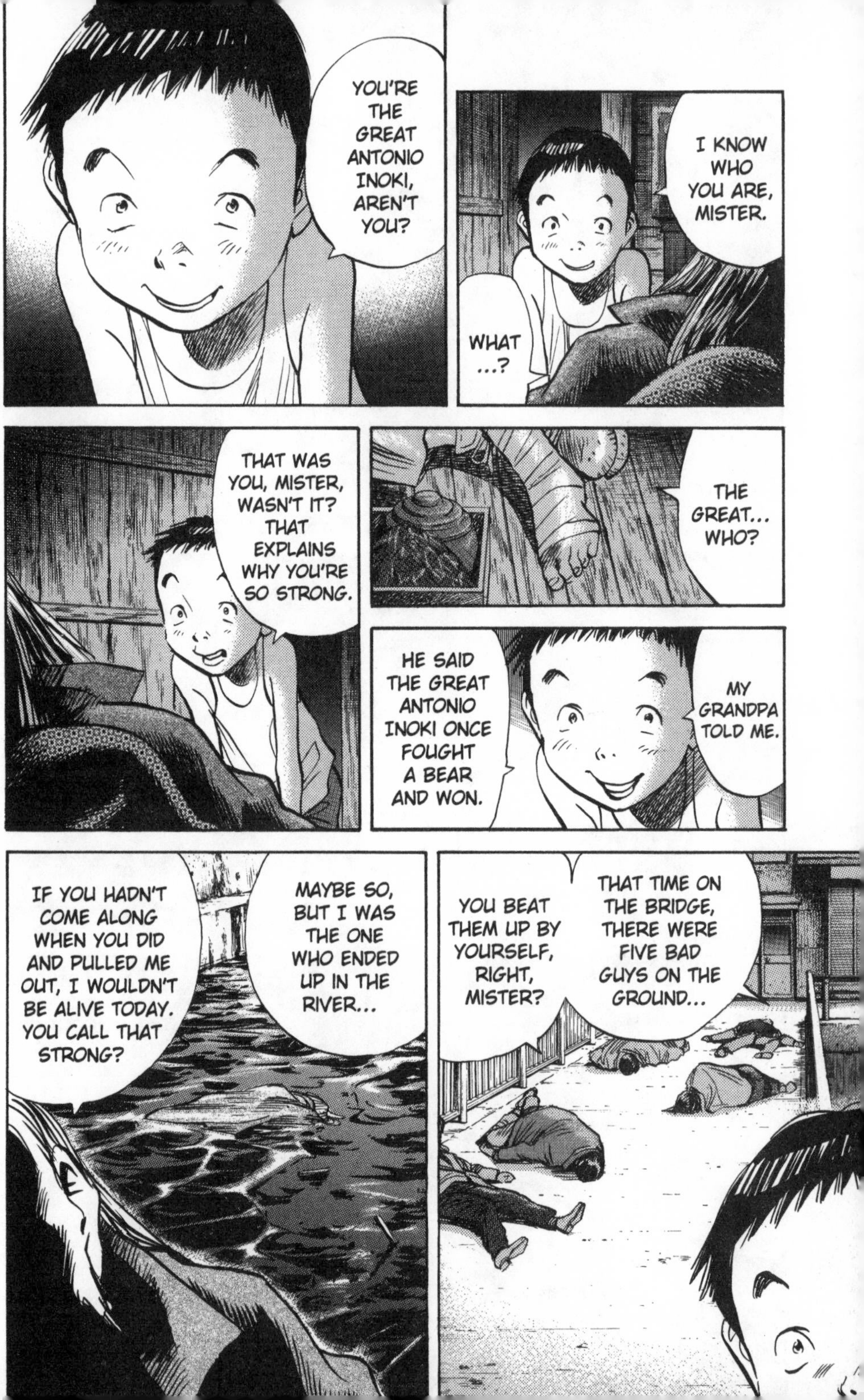

I KNOW WHO YOU ARE, MISTER.
WHAT ...?
YOU'RE THE GREAT ANTONIO INOKI, AREN'T YOU?
THE GREAT... WHO?
MY GRANDPA TOLD ME.
HE SAID THE GREAT ANTONIO INOKI ONCE FOUGHT A BEAR AND WON.
THAT WAS YOU, MISTER, WASN'T IT? THAT EXPLAINS WHY YOU'RE SO STRONG.
THAT TIME ON THE BRIDGE, THERE WERE FIVE BAD GUYS ON THE GROUND...
YOU BEAT THEM UP BY YOURSELF, RIGHT, MISTER?
MAYBE SO, BUT I WAS THE ONE WHO ENDED UP IN THE RIVER...
IF YOU HADN'T COME ALONG WHEN YOU DID AND PULLED ME OUT, I WOULDN'T BE ALIVE TODAY. YOU CALL THAT STRONG?

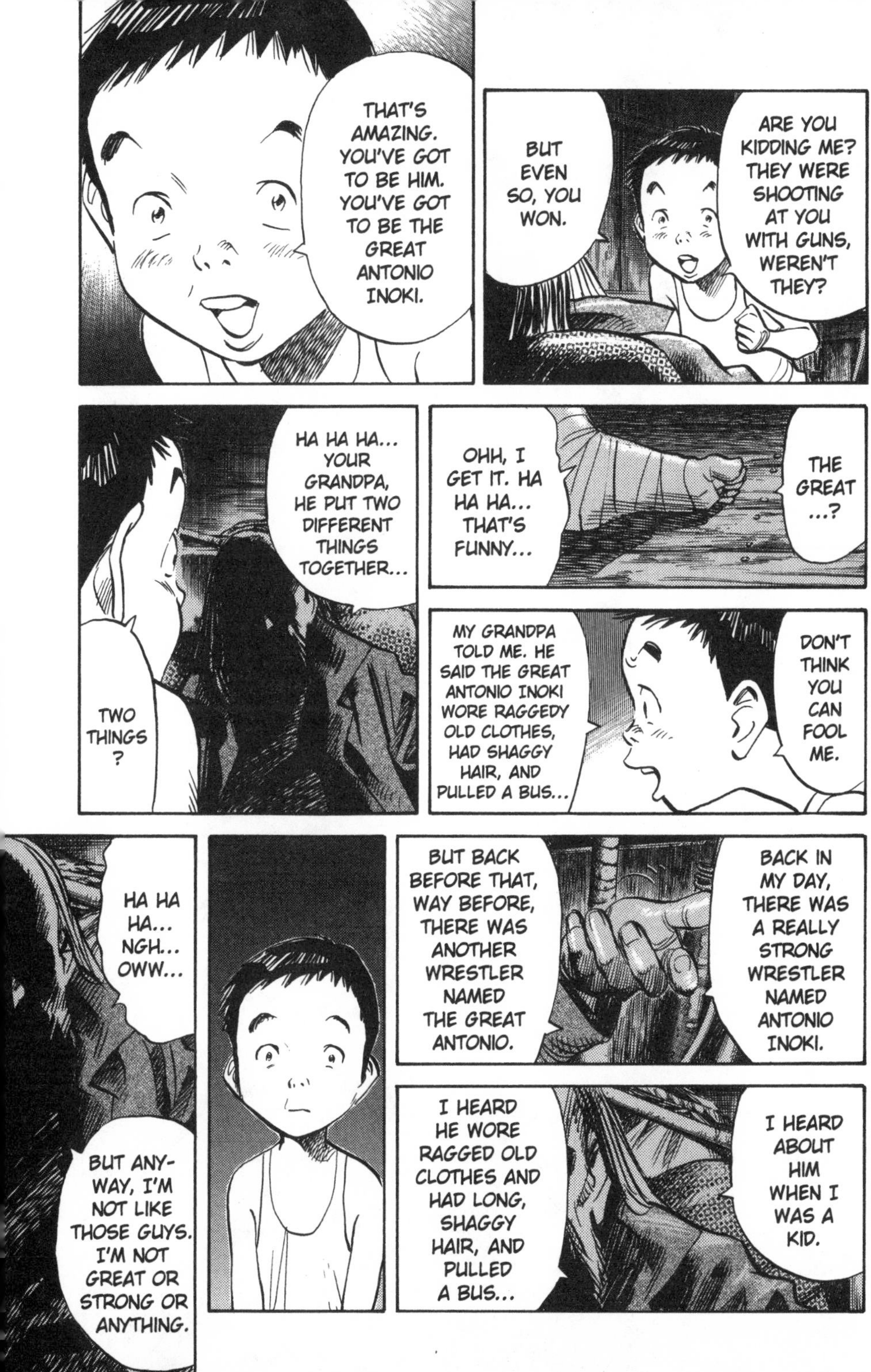
ARE YOU KIDDING ME? THEY WERE SHOOTING AT YOU WITH GUNS, WEREN'T THEY?
BUT EVEN SO, YOU WON.
THAT'S AMAZING. YOU'VE GOT TO BE HIM. YOU'VE GOT TO BE THE GREAT ANTONIO INOKI.
THE GREAT ...?
OHH, I GET IT. HA HA HA... THAT'S FUNNY...
DON'T THINK YOU CAN FOOL ME.
MY GRANDPA TOLD ME. HE SAID THE GREAT ANTONIO INOKI WORE RAGGEDY OLD CLOTHES, HAD SHAGGY HAIR, AND PULLED A BUS...
HA HA HA... YOUR GRANDPA, HE PUT TWO DIFFERENT THINGS TOGETHER...
TWO THINGS ?
BACK IN MY DAY, THERE WAS A REALLY STRONG WRESTLER NAMED ANTONIO INOKI.
BUT BACK BEFORE THAT, WAY BEFORE, THERE WAS ANOTHER WRESTLER NAMED THE GREAT ANTONIO.
I HEARD ABOUT HIM WHEN I WAS A KID.
I HEARD HE WORE RAGGED OLD CLOTHES AND HAD LONG, SHAGGY HAIR, AND PULLED A BUS...
HA HA HA... NGH... OWW...
BUT ANY-WAY, I'M NOT LIKE THOSE GUYS. I'M NOT GREAT OR STRONG OR ANYTHING.

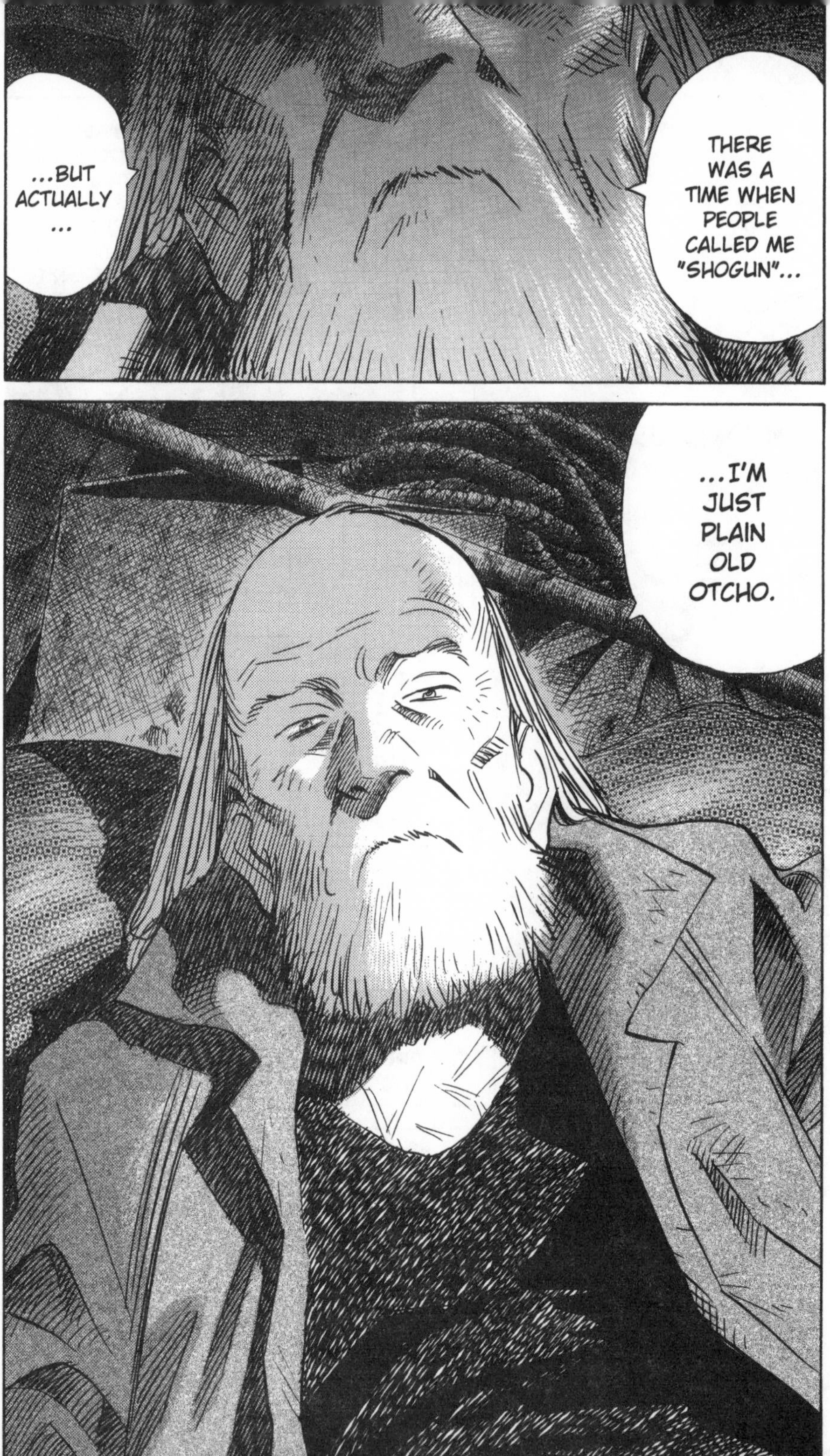
THERE WAS A TIME WHEN PEOPLE CALLED ME "SHOGUN"...
...BUT ACTUALLY ...
...I'M JUST PLAIN OLD OTCHO.

Chapter 8 Pole Vaulter

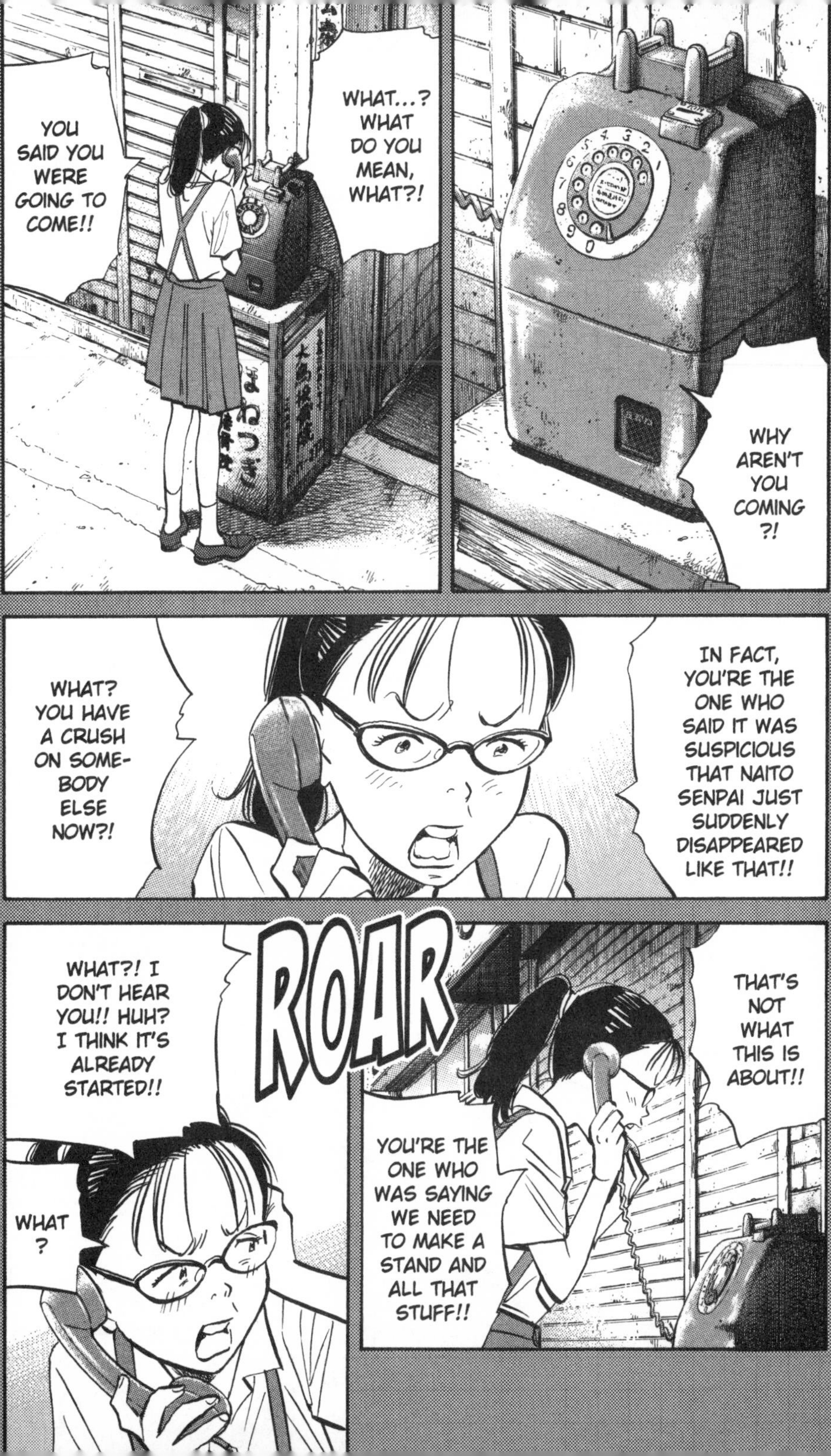

WHY AREN'T YOU COMING ?!
WHAT...? WHAT DO YOU MEAN, WHAT?!
YOU SAID YOU WERE GOING TO COME!!
IN FACT, YOU'RE THE ONE WHO SAID IT WAS SUSPICIOUS THAT NAITO SENPAI JUST SUDDENLY DISAPPEARED LIKE THAT!!
WHAT? YOU HAVE A CRUSH ON SOME-BODY ELSE NOW?!
THAT'S NOT WHAT THIS IS ABOUT!!
YOU'RE THE ONE WHO WAS SAYING WE NEED TO MAKE A STAND AND ALL THAT STUFF!!
ROAR
WHAT?! I DON'T HEAR YOU!! HUH? I THINK IT'S ALREADY STARTED!!
WHAT ?

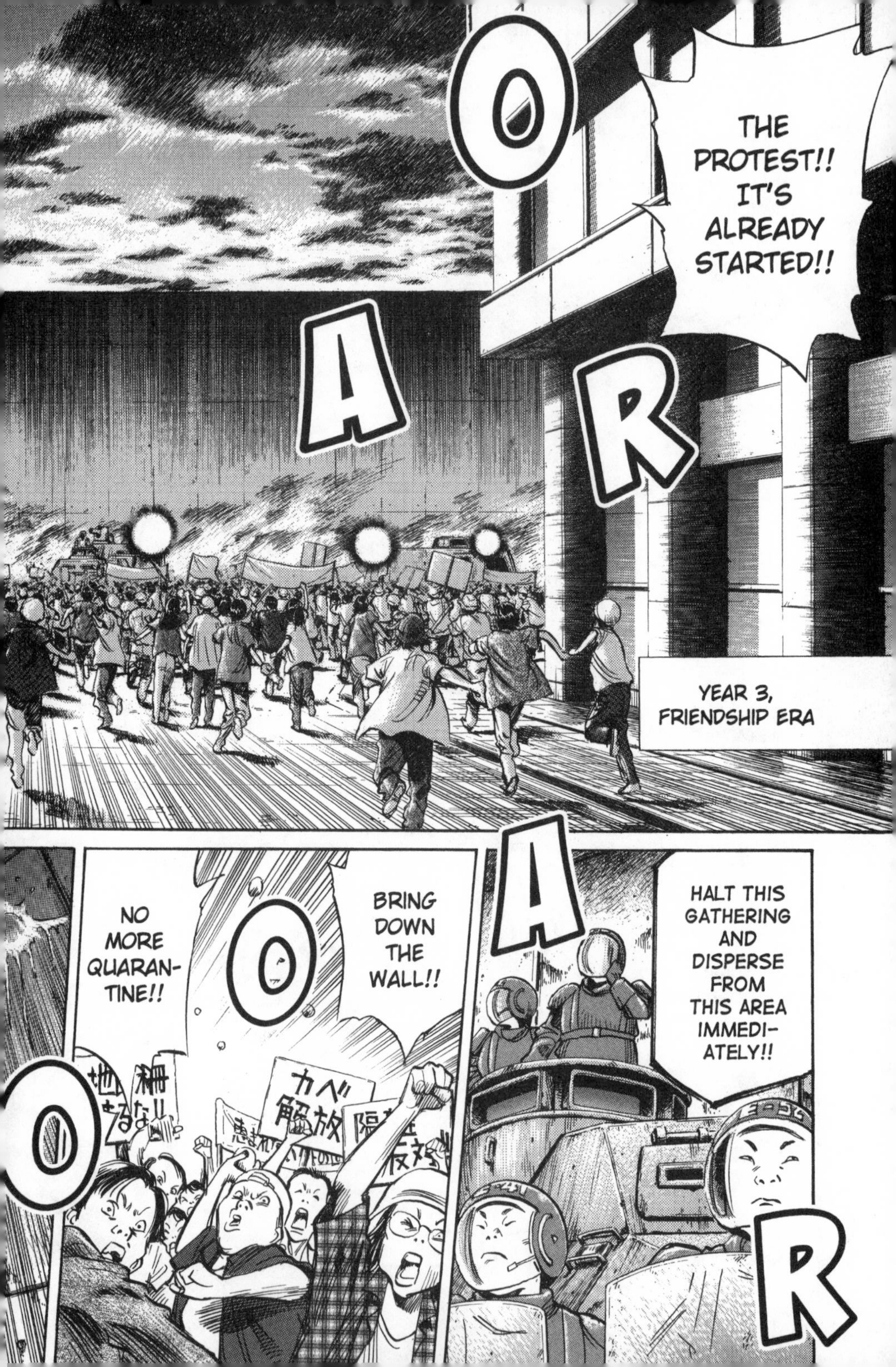
O
A
R
THE PROTEST!! IT'S ALREADY STARTED!!
YEAR 3, FRIENDSHIP ERA
HALT THIS GATHERING AND DISPERSE FROM THIS AREA IMMEDI-ATELY!!
A
R
BRING DOWN THE WALL!!
NO MORE QUARAN-TINE!!
O
O
カベ解放

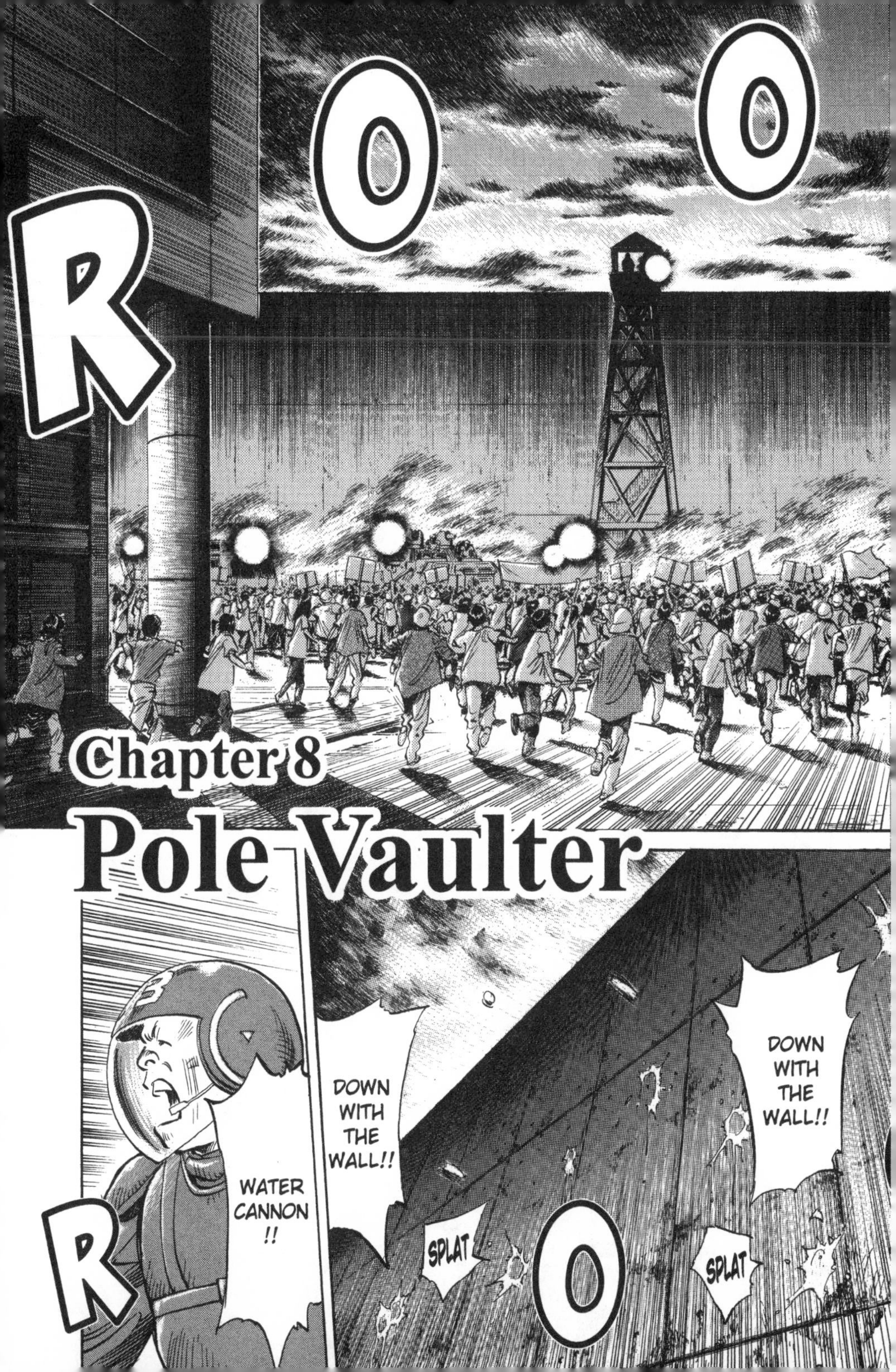
ROOO
Chapter 8
Pole Vaulter
DOWN WITH THE WALL!!
DOWN WITH THE WALL!!
SPLAT
SPLAT
WATER CANNON!!
RO

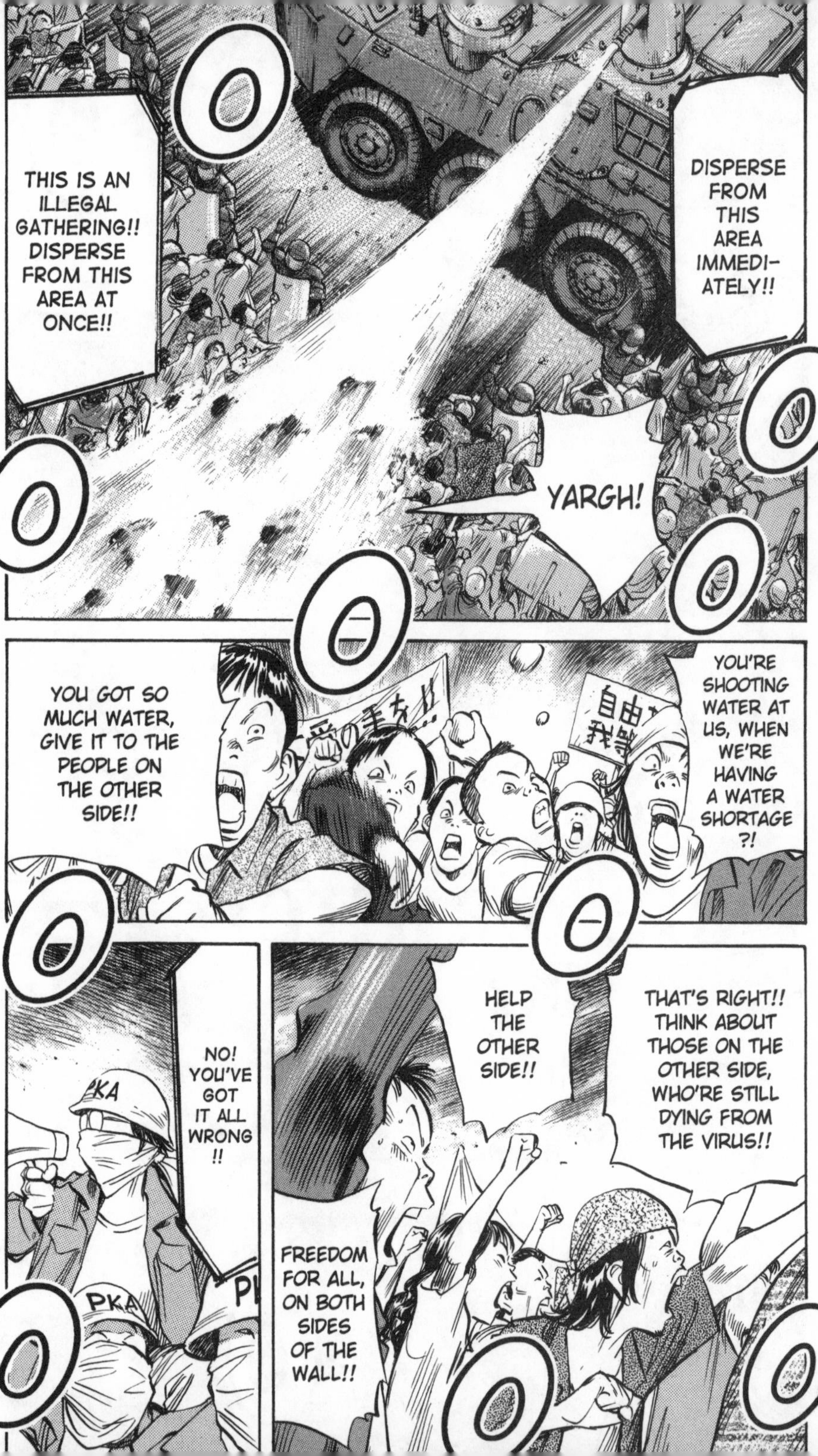
DISPERSE FROM THIS AREA IMMEDIATELY!!
THIS IS AN ILLEGAL GATHERING!! DISPERSE FROM THIS AREA AT ONCE!!
YARGH!
YOU'RE SHOOTING WATER AT US, WHEN WE'RE HAVING A WATER SHORTAGE ?!
YOU GOT SO MUCH WATER, GIVE IT TO THE PEOPLE ON THE OTHER SIDE!!
THAT'S RIGHT!! THINK ABOUT THOSE ON THE OTHER SIDE, WHO'RE STILL DYING FROM THE VIRUS!!
HELP THE OTHER SIDE!!
FREEDOM FOR ALL, ON BOTH SIDES OF THE WALL!!
NO! YOU'VE GOT IT ALL WRONG!!
PKA
PKA

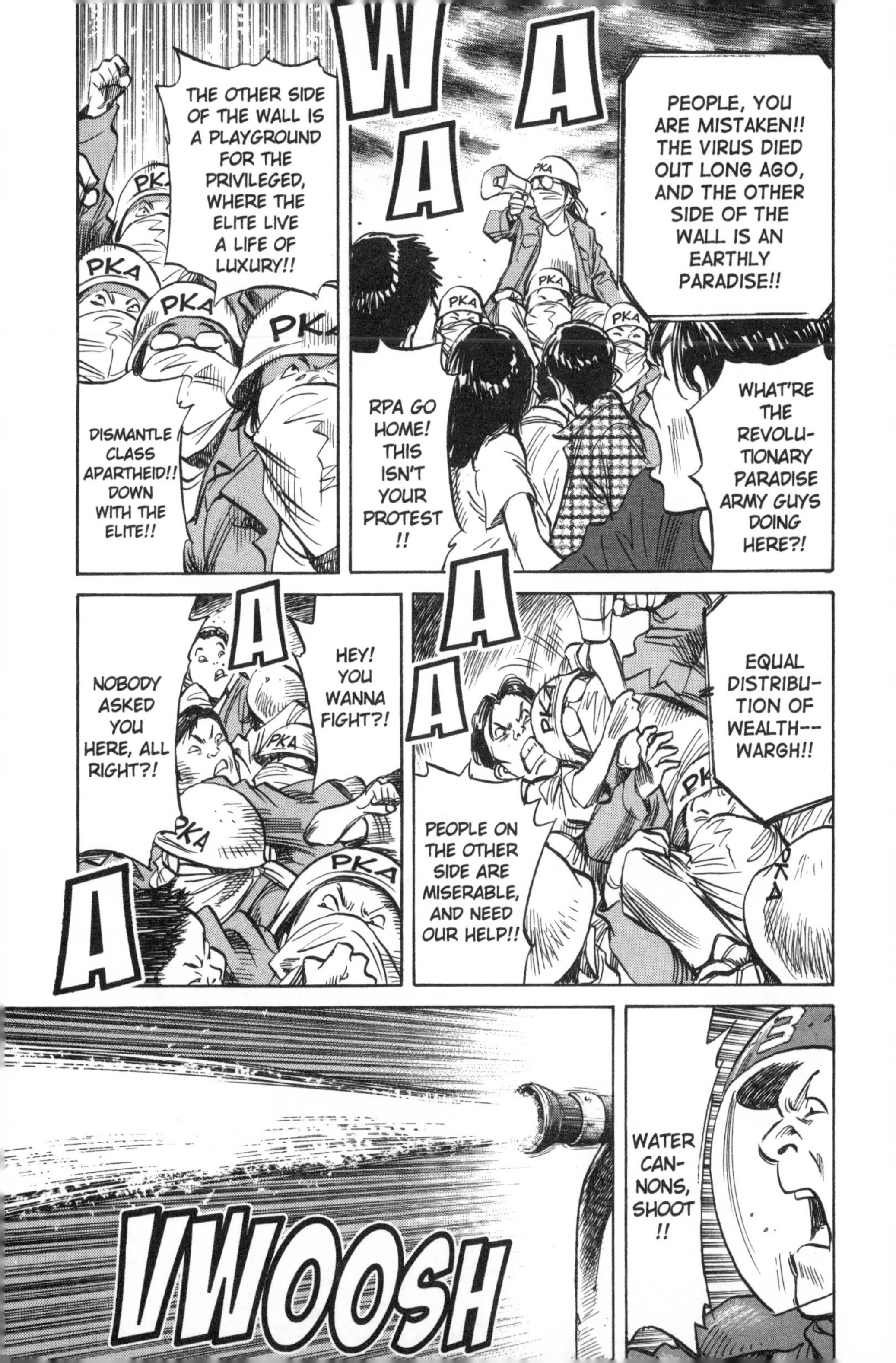
WAAA
PEOPLE, YOU ARE MISTAKEN!! THE VIRUS DIED OUT LONG AGO, AND THE OTHER SIDE OF THE WALL IS AN EARTHLY PARADISE!!
WHAT'RE THE REVOLUTIONARY PARADISE ARMY GUYS DOING HERE?!
RPA GO HOME! THIS ISN'T YOUR PROTEST!!
THE OTHER SIDE OF THE WALL IS A PLAYGROUND FOR THE PRIVILEGED, WHERE THE ELITE LIVE A LIFE OF LUXURY!!
DISMANTLE CLASS APARTHEID!! DOWN WITH THE ELITE!!
AA
EQUAL DISTRIBUTION OF WEALTH-- WARGH!!
PEOPLE ON THE OTHER SIDE ARE MISERABLE, AND NEED OUR HELP!!
A
HEY! YOU WANNA FIGHT?!
NOBODY ASKED YOU HERE, ALL RIGHT?!
A
WATER CANNONS, SHOOT!!
VWOOSH

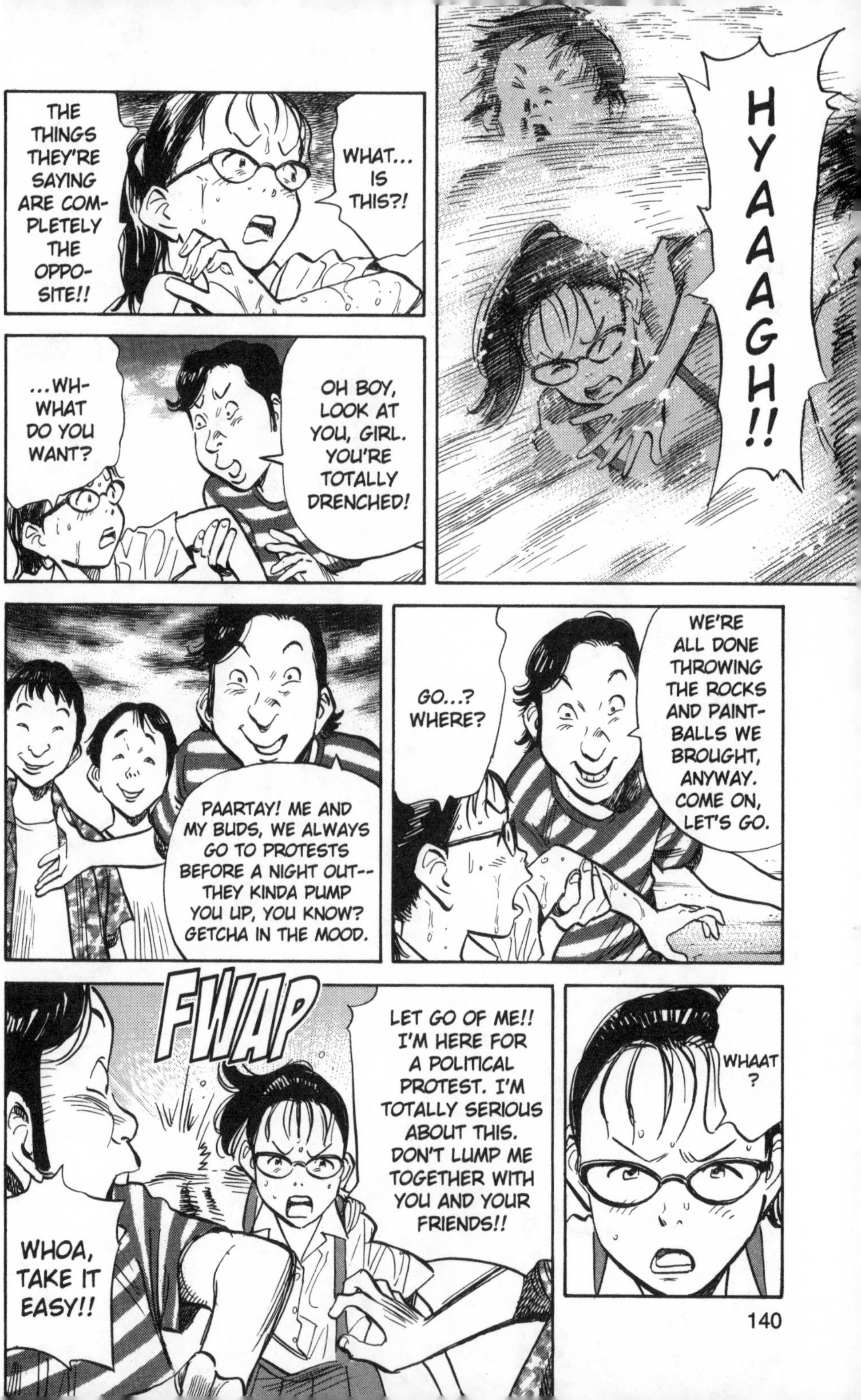
HYAAAGH!!
WHAT... IS THIS?!
THE THINGS THEY'RE SAYING ARE COMPLETELY THE OPPOSITE!!
OH BOY, LOOK AT YOU, GIRL. YOU'RE TOTALLY DRENCHED!
...WH-WHAT DO YOU WANT?
WE'RE ALL DONE THROWING THE ROCKS AND PAINTBALLS WE BROUGHT, ANYWAY. COME ON, LET'S GO.
GO...? WHERE?
PAARTAY! ME AND MY BUDS, WE ALWAYS GO TO PROTESTS BEFORE A NIGHT OUT-- THEY KINDA PUMP YOU UP, YOU KNOW? GETCHA IN THE MOOD.
WHAAT?
LET GO OF ME!! I'M HERE FOR A POLITICAL PROTEST. I'M TOTALLY SERIOUS ABOUT THIS. DON'T LUMP ME TOGETHER WITH YOU AND YOUR FRIENDS!!
FWAP
WHOA, TAKE IT EASY!!

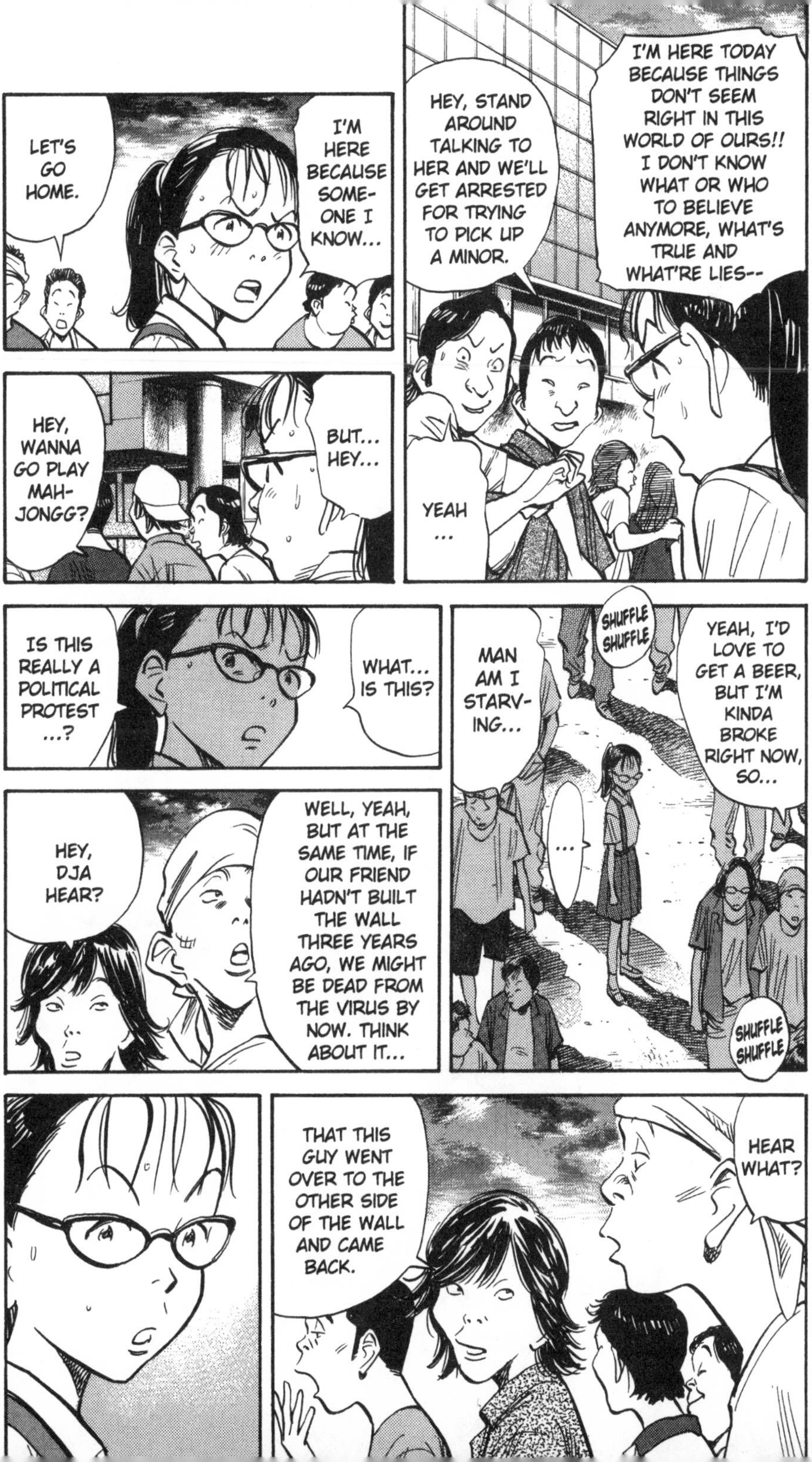
I'M HERE TODAY BECAUSE THINGS DON'T SEEM RIGHT IN THIS WORLD OF OURS!! I DON'T KNOW WHAT OR WHO TO BELIEVE ANYMORE, WHAT'S TRUE AND WHAT'RE LIES--
HEY, STAND AROUND TALKING TO HER AND WE'LL GET ARRESTED FOR TRYING TO PICK UP A MINOR.
YEAH ...
I'M HERE BECAUSE SOME-ONE I KNOW...
LET'S GO HOME.
BUT... HEY...
HEY, WANNA GO PLAY MAH-JONGG?
YEAH, I'D LOVE TO GET A BEER, BUT I'M KINDA BROKE RIGHT NOW, SO...
SHUFFLE SHUFFLE
MAN AM I STARV-ING...
...
SHUFFLE SHUFFLE
WHAT... IS THIS?
IS THIS REALLY A POLITICAL PROTEST ...?
WELL, YEAH, BUT AT THE SAME TIME, IF OUR FRIEND HADN'T BUILT THE WALL THREE YEARS AGO, WE MIGHT BE DEAD FROM THE VIRUS BY NOW. THINK ABOUT IT...
HEY, DJA HEAR?
HEAR WHAT?
THAT THIS GUY WENT OVER TO THE OTHER SIDE OF THE WALL AND CAME BACK.

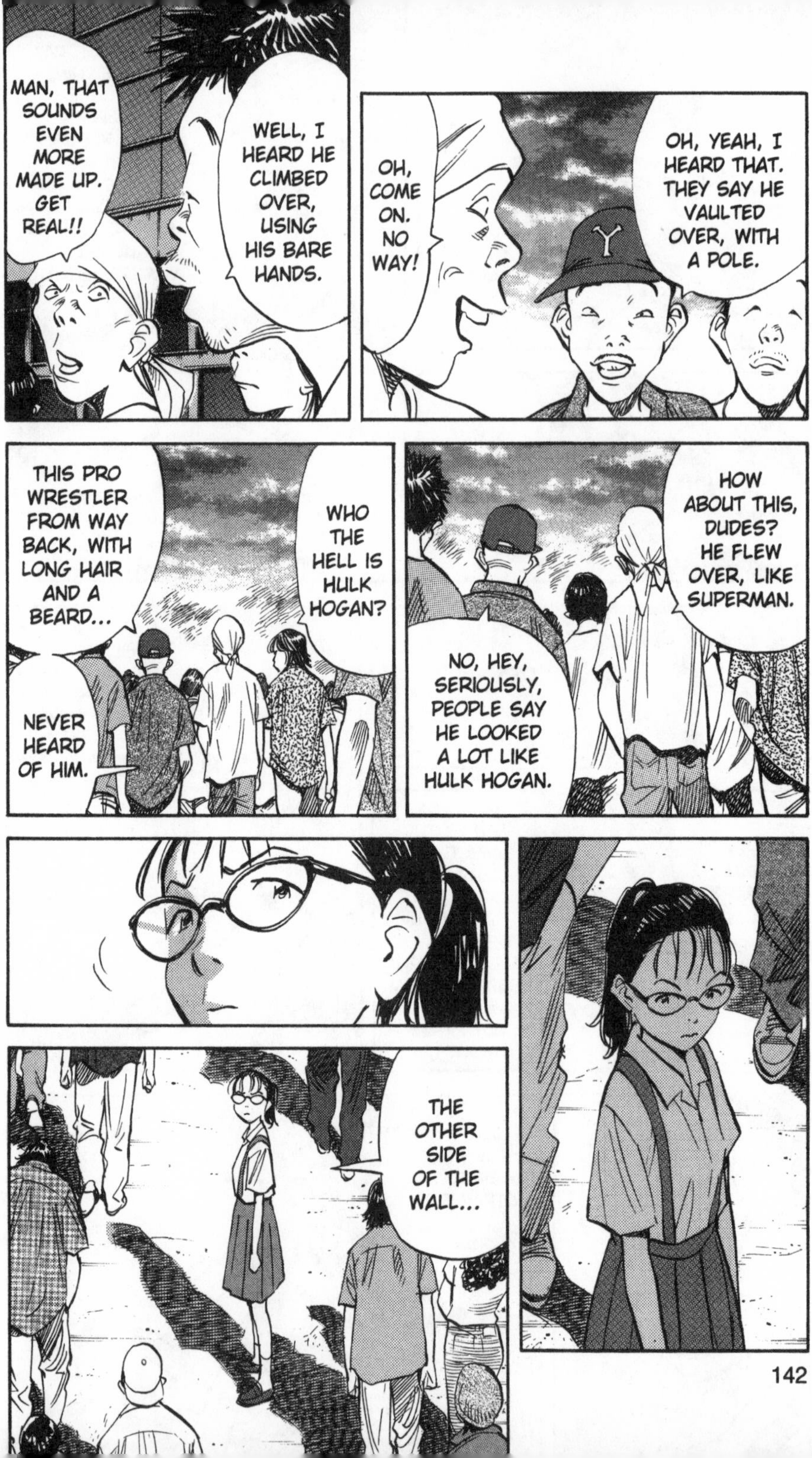
OH, YEAH, I HEARD THAT. THEY SAY HE VAULTED OVER, WITH A POLE.
OH, COME ON. NO WAY!
WELL, I HEARD HE CLIMBED OVER, USING HIS BARE HANDS.
MAN, THAT SOUNDS EVEN MORE MADE UP. GET REAL!!
HOW ABOUT THIS, DUDES? HE FLEW OVER, LIKE SUPERMAN.
NO, HEY, SERIOUSLY, PEOPLE SAY HE LOOKED A LOT LIKE HULK HOGAN.
WHO THE HELL IS HULK HOGAN?
THIS PRO WRESTLER FROM WAY BACK, WITH LONG HAIR AND A BEARD...
NEVER HEARD OF HIM.
THE OTHER SIDE OF THE WALL...

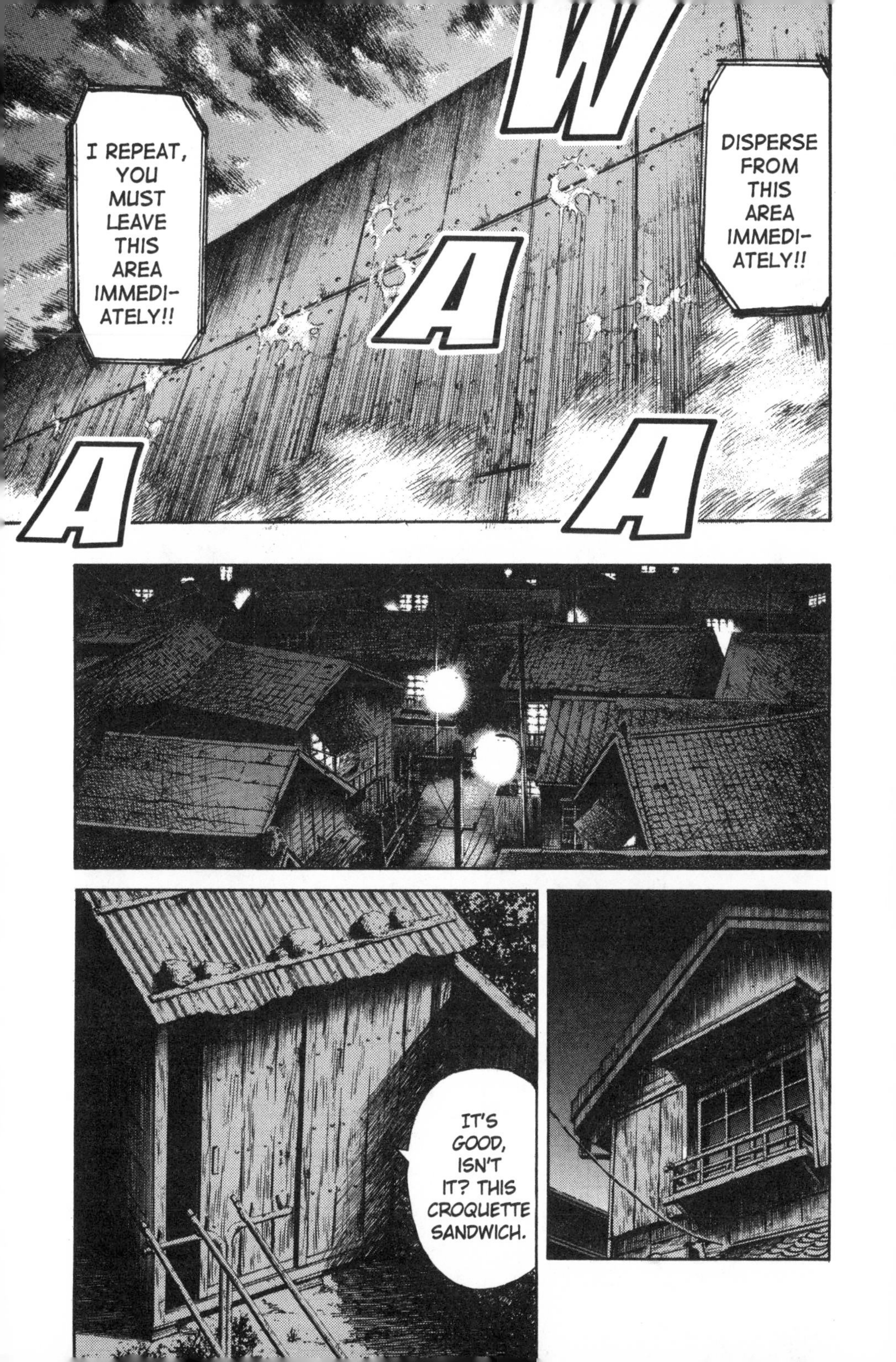
DISPERSE FROM THIS AREA IMMEDIATELY!!
I REPEAT, YOU MUST LEAVE THIS AREA IMMEDIATELY!!
WAAAA
IT'S GOOD, ISN'T IT? THIS CROQUETTE SANDWICH.

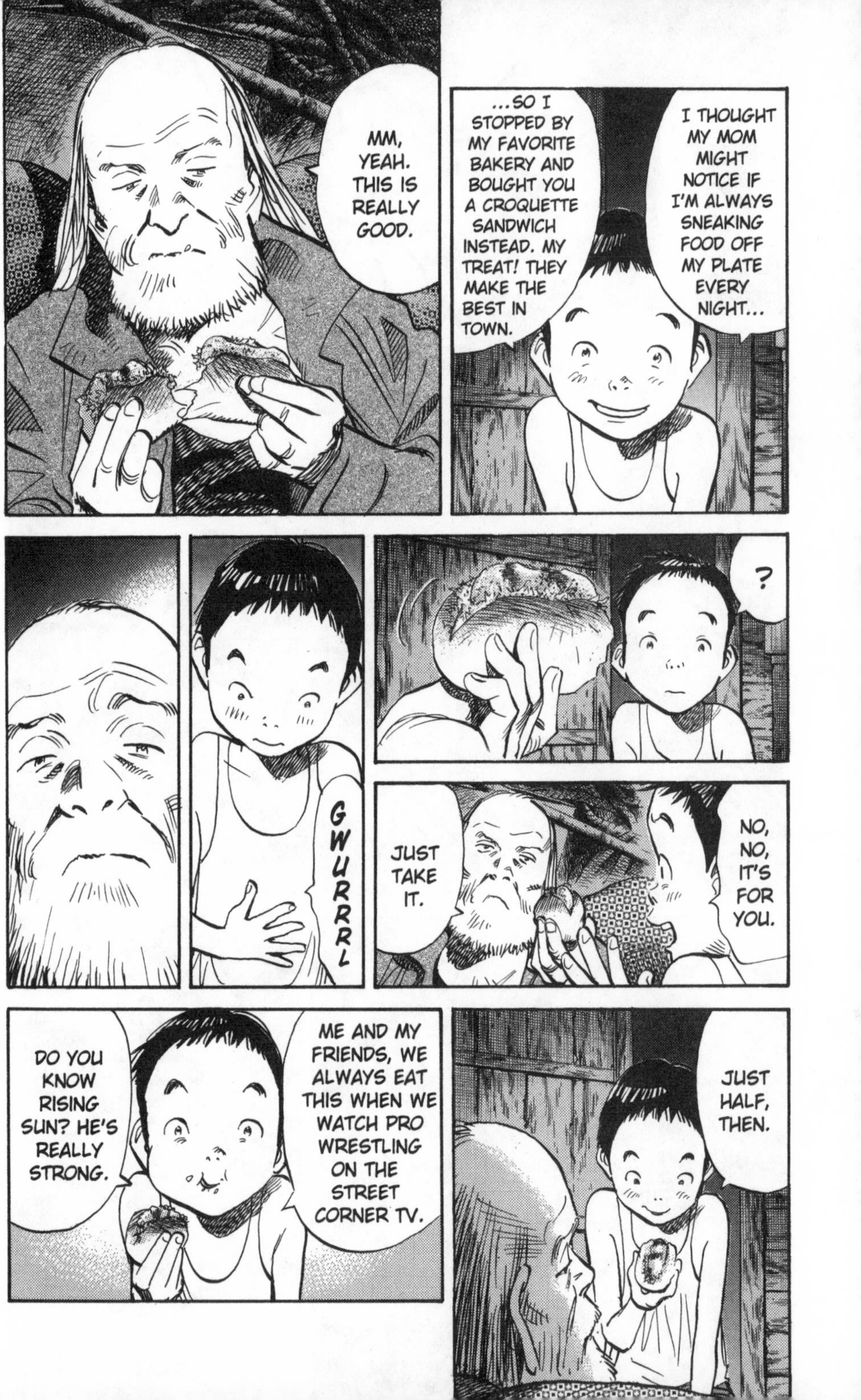
I THOUGHT MY MOM MIGHT NOTICE IF I'M ALWAYS SNEAKING FOOD OFF MY PLATE EVERY NIGHT...
...SO I STOPPED BY MY FAVORITE BAKERY AND BOUGHT YOU A CROQUETTE SANDWICH INSTEAD. MY TREAT! THEY MAKE THE BEST IN TOWN.
MM, YEAH. THIS IS REALLY GOOD.
?
NO, NO, IT'S FOR YOU.
JUST TAKE IT.
GWURRRL
JUST HALF, THEN.
ME AND MY FRIENDS, WE ALWAYS EAT THIS WHEN WE WATCH PRO WRESTLING ON THE STREET CORNER TV.
DO YOU KNOW RISING SUN? HE'S REALLY STRONG.

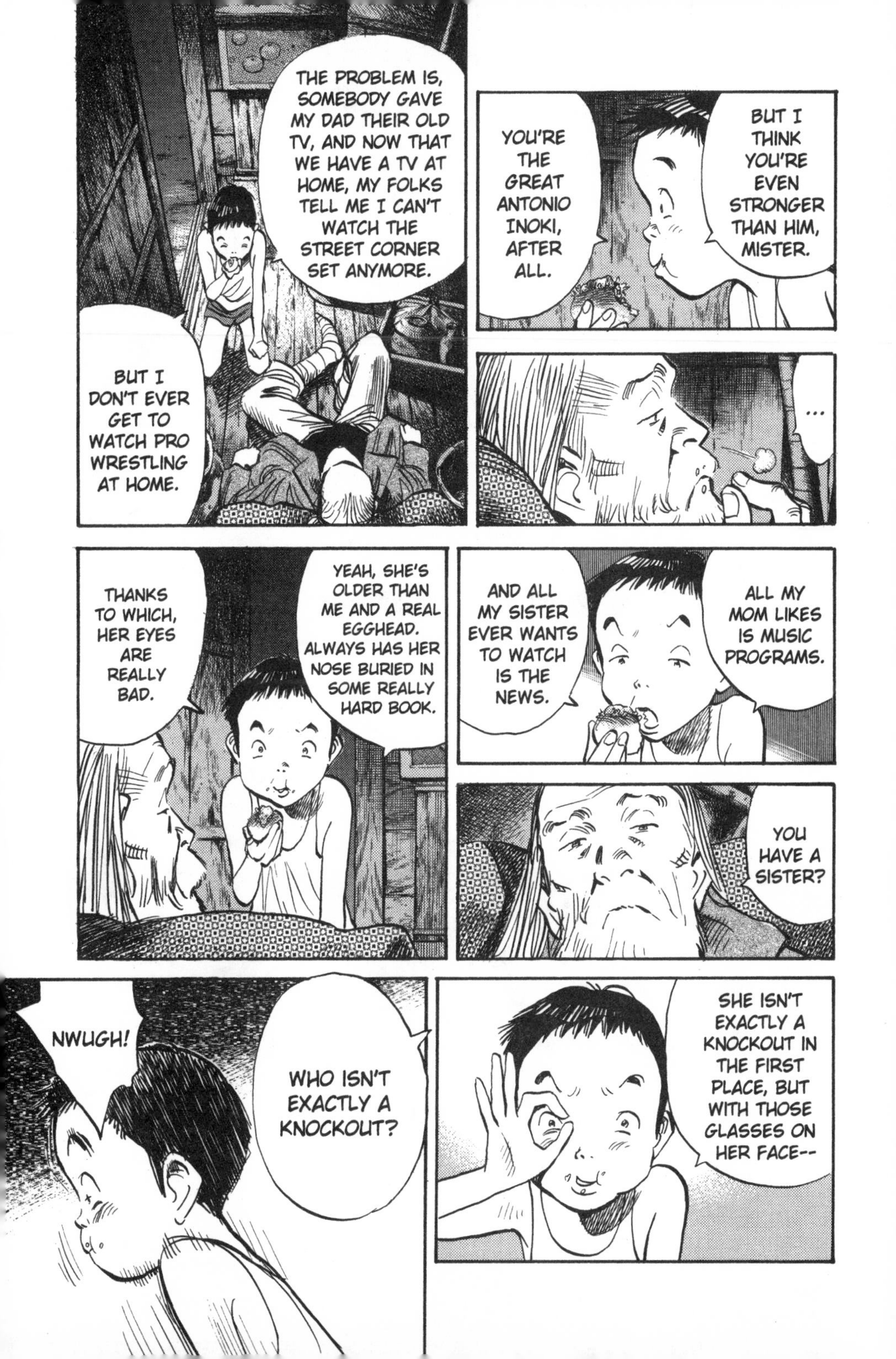
BUT I THINK YOU'RE EVEN STRONGER THAN HIM, MISTER.
YOU'RE THE GREAT ANTONIO INOKI, AFTER ALL.
...
THE PROBLEM IS, SOMEBODY GAVE MY DAD THEIR OLD TV, AND NOW THAT WE HAVE A TV AT HOME, MY FOLKS TELL ME I CAN'T WATCH THE STREET CORNER SET ANYMORE.
BUT I DON'T EVER GET TO WATCH PRO WRESTLING AT HOME.
ALL MY MOM LIKES IS MUSIC PROGRAMS.
AND ALL MY SISTER EVER WANTS TO WATCH IS THE NEWS.
YOU HAVE A SISTER?
YEAH, SHE'S OLDER THAN ME AND A REAL EGGHEAD. ALWAYS HAS HER NOSE BURIED IN SOME REALLY HARD BOOK.
THANKS TO WHICH, HER EYES ARE REALLY BAD.
SHE ISN'T EXACTLY A KNOCKOUT IN THE FIRST PLACE, BUT WITH THOSE GLASSES ON HER FACE--
WHO ISN'T EXACTLY A KNOCKOUT?
NWUGH!

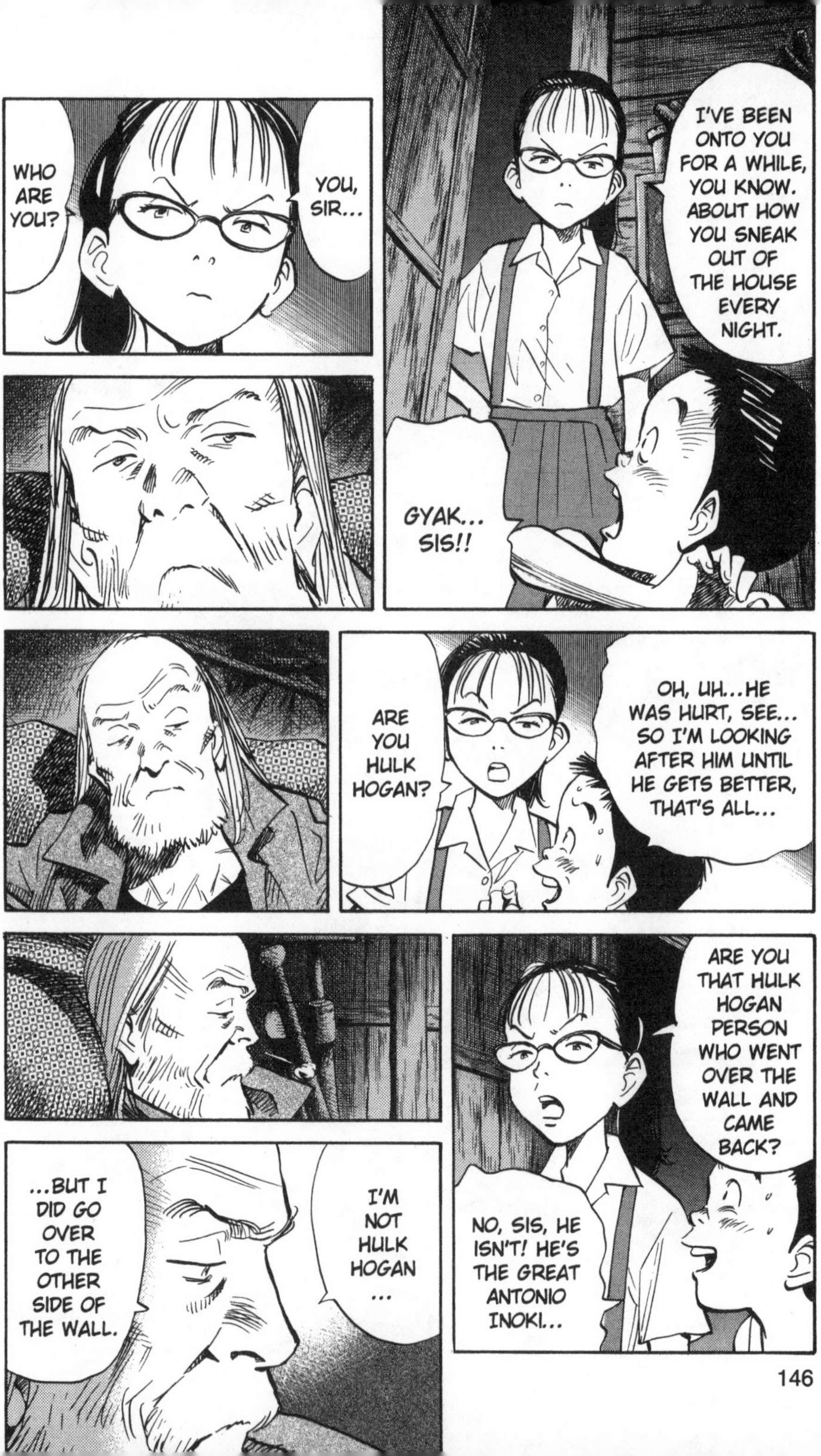
I'VE BEEN ONTO YOU FOR A WHILE, YOU KNOW. ABOUT HOW YOU SNEAK OUT OF THE HOUSE EVERY NIGHT.
GYAK... SIS!!
YOU, SIR...
WHO ARE YOU?
OH, UH...HE WAS HURT, SEE... SO I'M LOOKING AFTER HIM UNTIL HE GETS BETTER, THAT'S ALL...
ARE YOU HULK HOGAN?
ARE YOU THAT HULK HOGAN PERSON WHO WENT OVER THE WALL AND CAME BACK?
NO, SIS, HE ISN'T! HE'S THE GREAT ANTONIO INOKI...
I'M NOT HULK HOGAN ...
...BUT I DID GO OVER TO THE OTHER SIDE OF THE WALL.

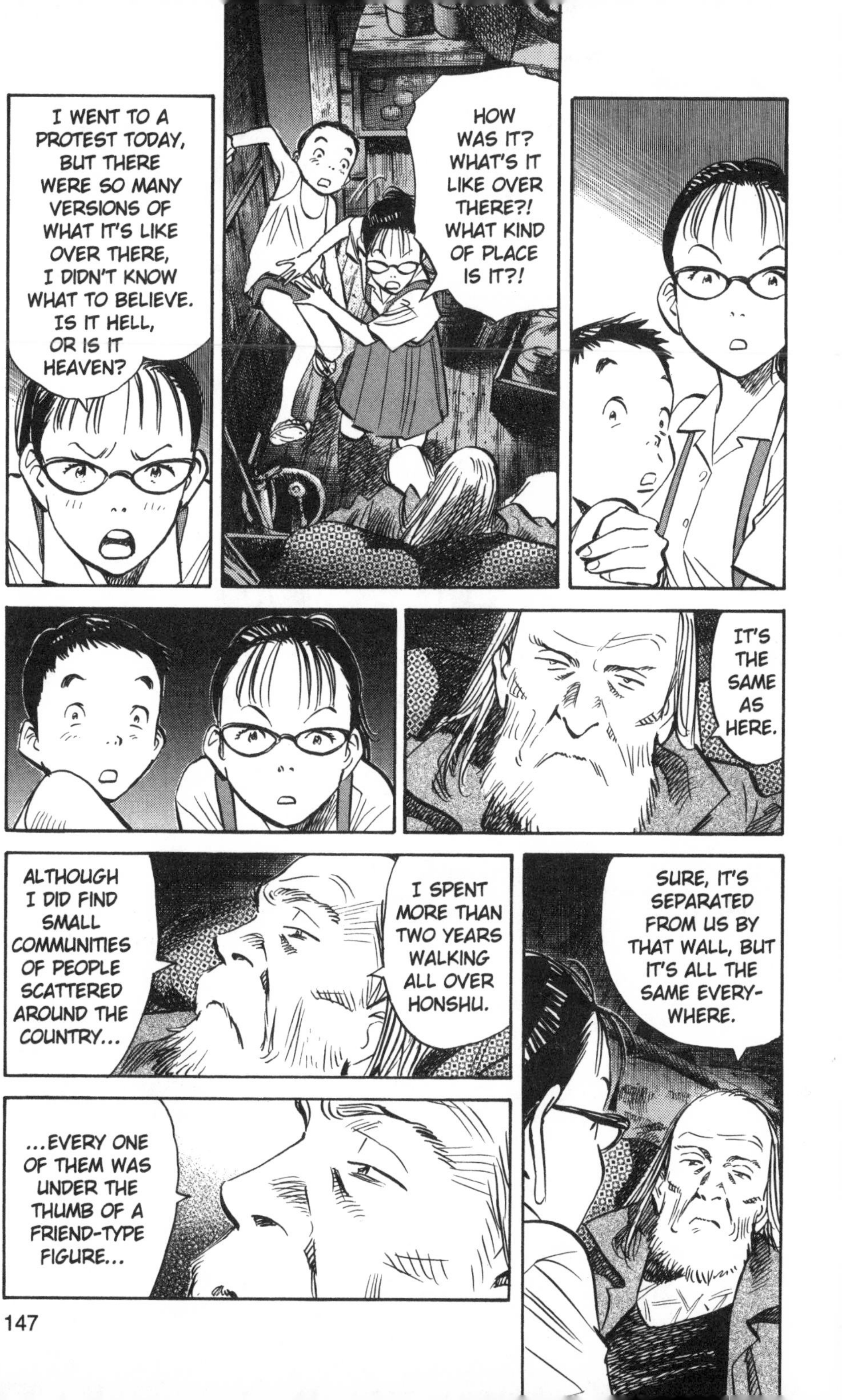
HOW WAS IT? WHAT'S IT LIKE OVER THERE?! WHAT KIND OF PLACE IS IT?!
I WENT TO A PROTEST TODAY, BUT THERE WERE SO MANY VERSIONS OF WHAT IT'S LIKE OVER THERE, I DIDN'T KNOW WHAT TO BELIEVE. IS IT HELL, OR IS IT HEAVEN?
IT'S THE SAME AS HERE.
SURE, IT'S SEPARATED FROM US BY THAT WALL, BUT IT'S ALL THE SAME EVERY-WHERE.
I SPENT MORE THAN TWO YEARS WALKING ALL OVER HONSHU.
ALTHOUGH I DID FIND SMALL COMMUNITIES OF PEOPLE SCATTERED AROUND THE COUNTRY...
...EVERY ONE OF THEM WAS UNDER THE THUMB OF A FRIEND-TYPE FIGURE...

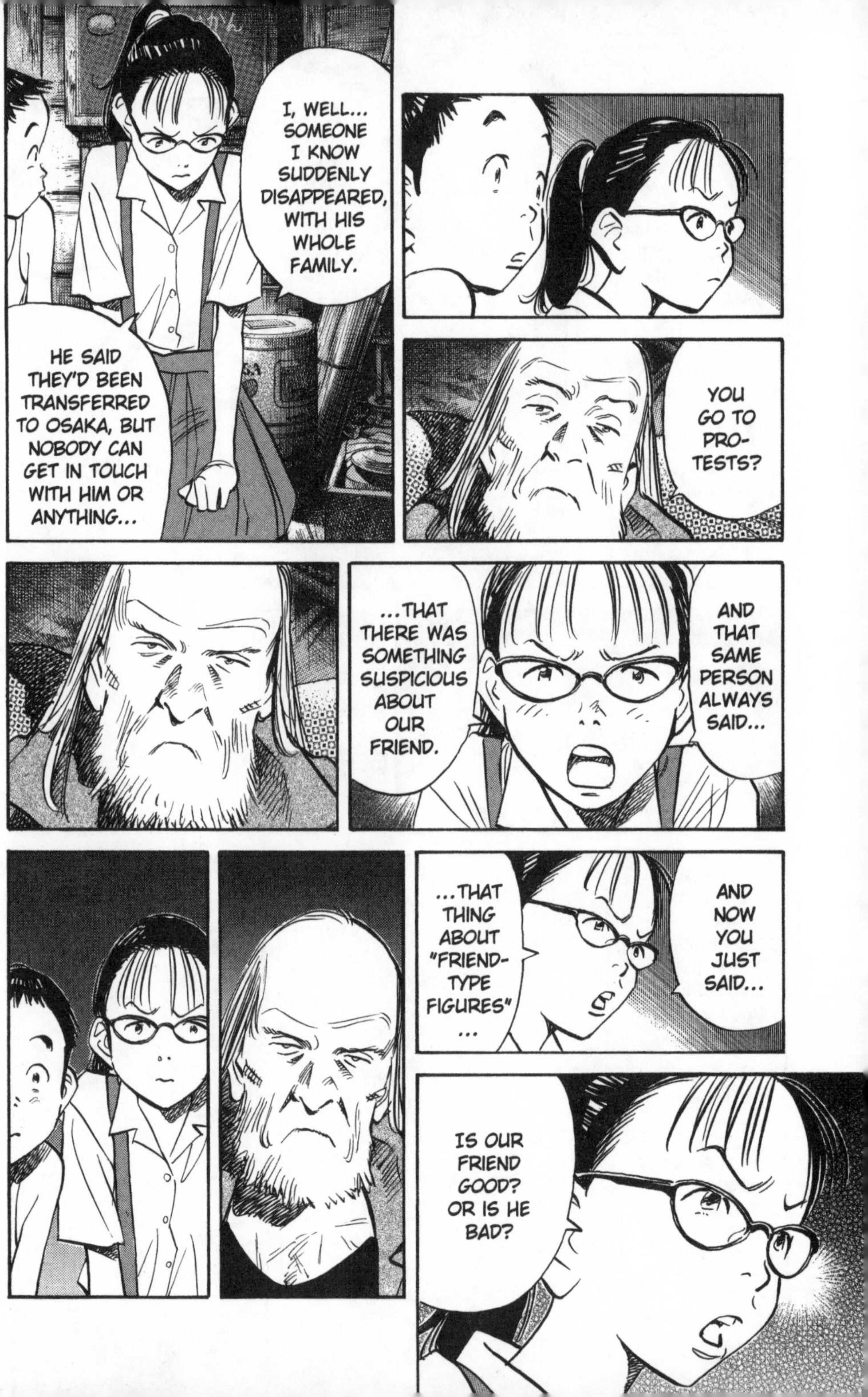
YOU GO TO PRO-TESTS?
I, WELL... SOMEONE I KNOW SUDDENLY DISAPPEARED, WITH HIS WHOLE FAMILY.
HE SAID THEY'D BEEN TRANSFERRED TO OSAKA, BUT NOBODY CAN GET IN TOUCH WITH HIM OR ANYTHING...
AND THAT SAME PERSON ALWAYS SAID...
...THAT THERE WAS SOMETHING SUSPICIOUS ABOUT OUR FRIEND.
AND NOW YOU JUST SAID...
...THAT THING ABOUT "FRIEND-TYPE FIGURES" ...
IS OUR FRIEND GOOD? OR IS HE BAD?

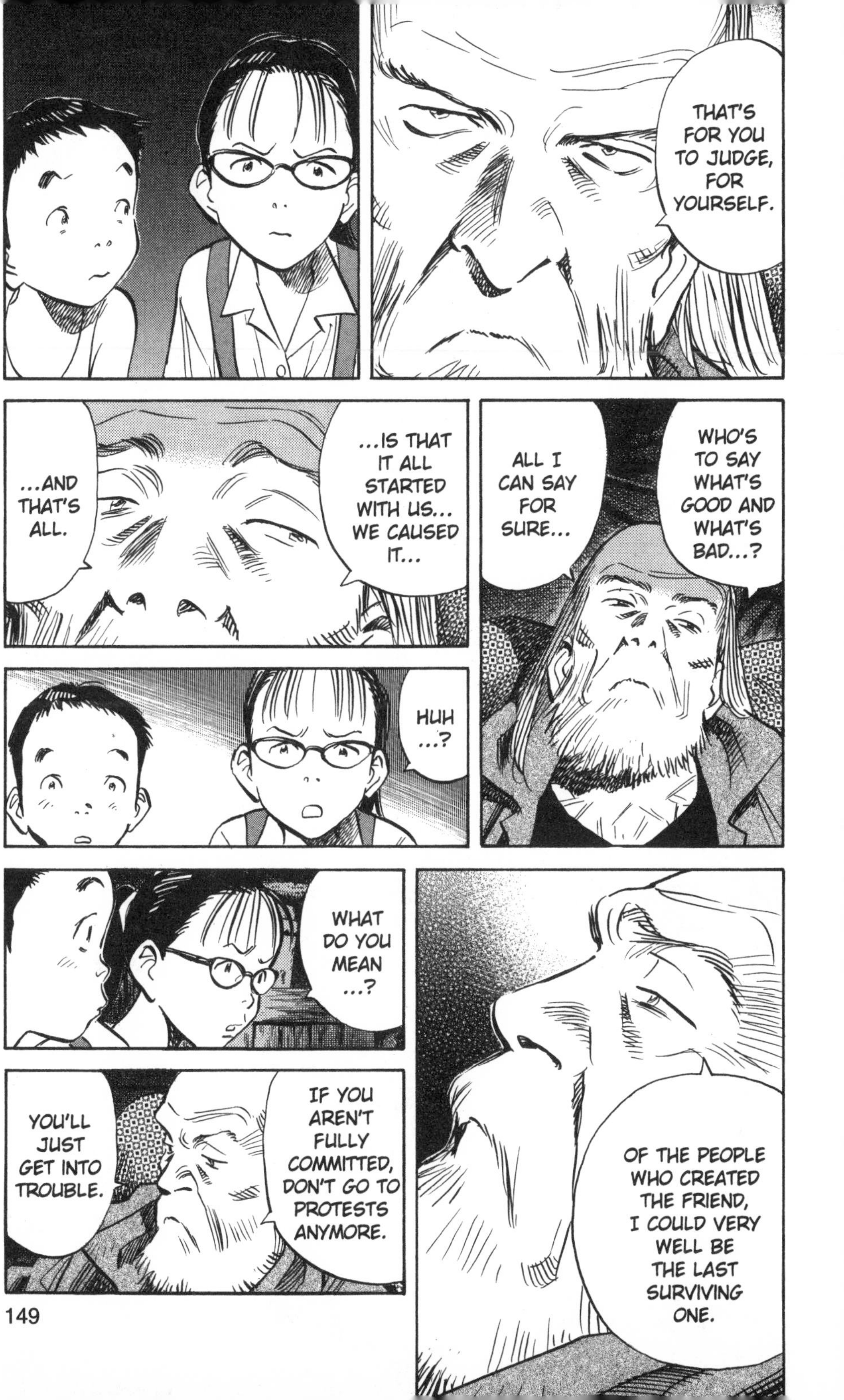
THAT'S FOR YOU TO JUDGE, FOR YOURSELF.
WHO'S TO SAY WHAT'S GOOD AND WHAT'S BAD...?
ALL I CAN SAY FOR SURE...
...IS THAT IT ALL STARTED WITH US... WE CAUSED IT...
...AND THAT'S ALL.
HUH ...?
OF THE PEOPLE WHO CREATED THE FRIEND, I COULD VERY WELL BE THE LAST SURVIVING ONE.
WHAT DO YOU MEAN ...?
IF YOU AREN'T FULLY COMMITTED, DON'T GO TO PROTESTS ANYMORE.
YOU'LL JUST GET INTO TROUBLE.

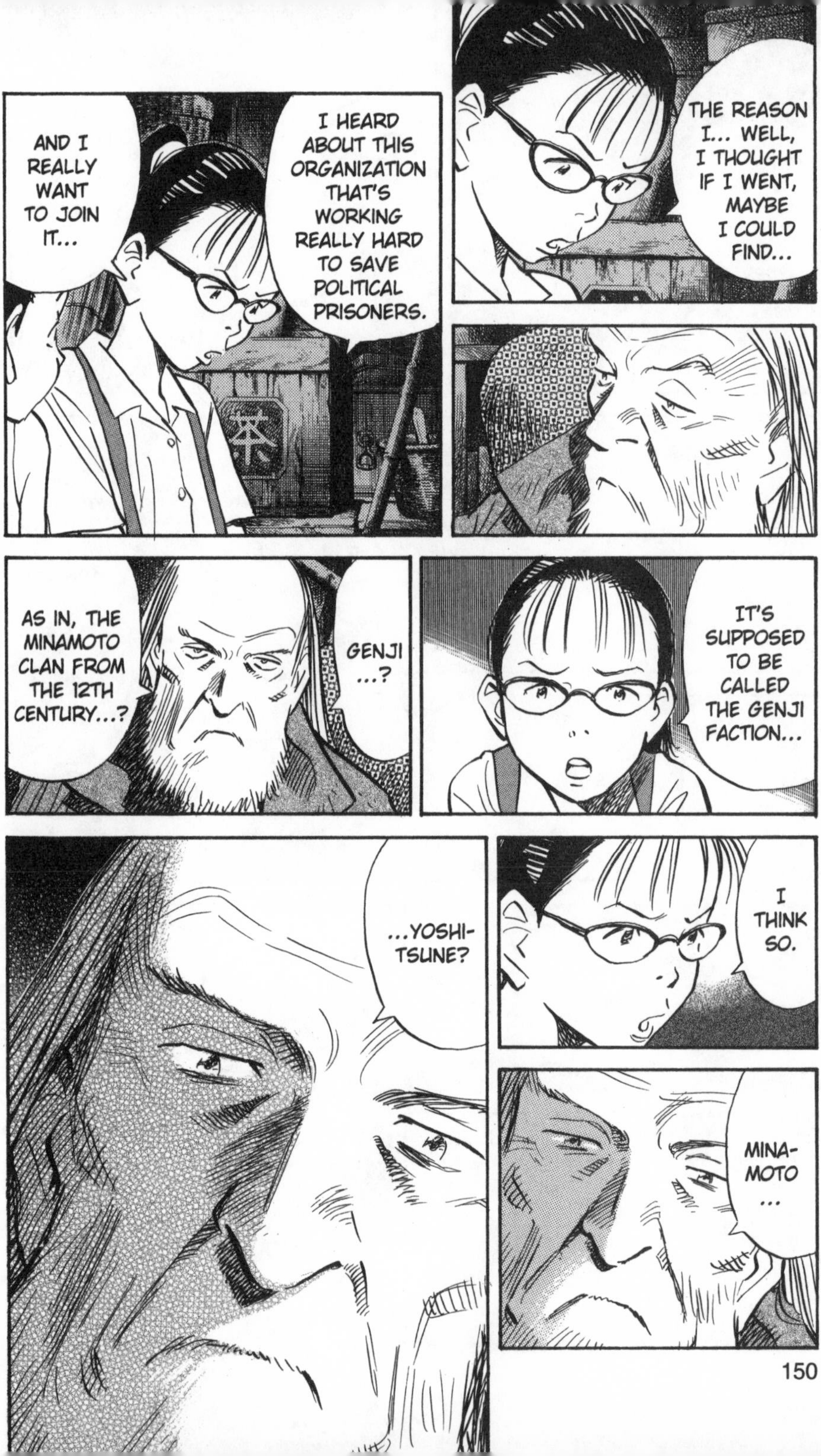
THE REASON I... WELL, I THOUGHT IF I WENT, MAYBE I COULD FIND...
I HEARD ABOUT THIS ORGANIZATION THAT'S WORKING REALLY HARD TO SAVE POLITICAL PRISONERS.
AND I REALLY WANT TO JOIN IT...
IT'S SUPPOSED TO BE CALLED THE GENJI FACTION...
GENJI ...?
AS IN, THE MINAMOTO CLAN FROM THE 12TH CENTURY...?
I THINK SO.
MINA-MOTO ...
...YOSHI-TSUNE?

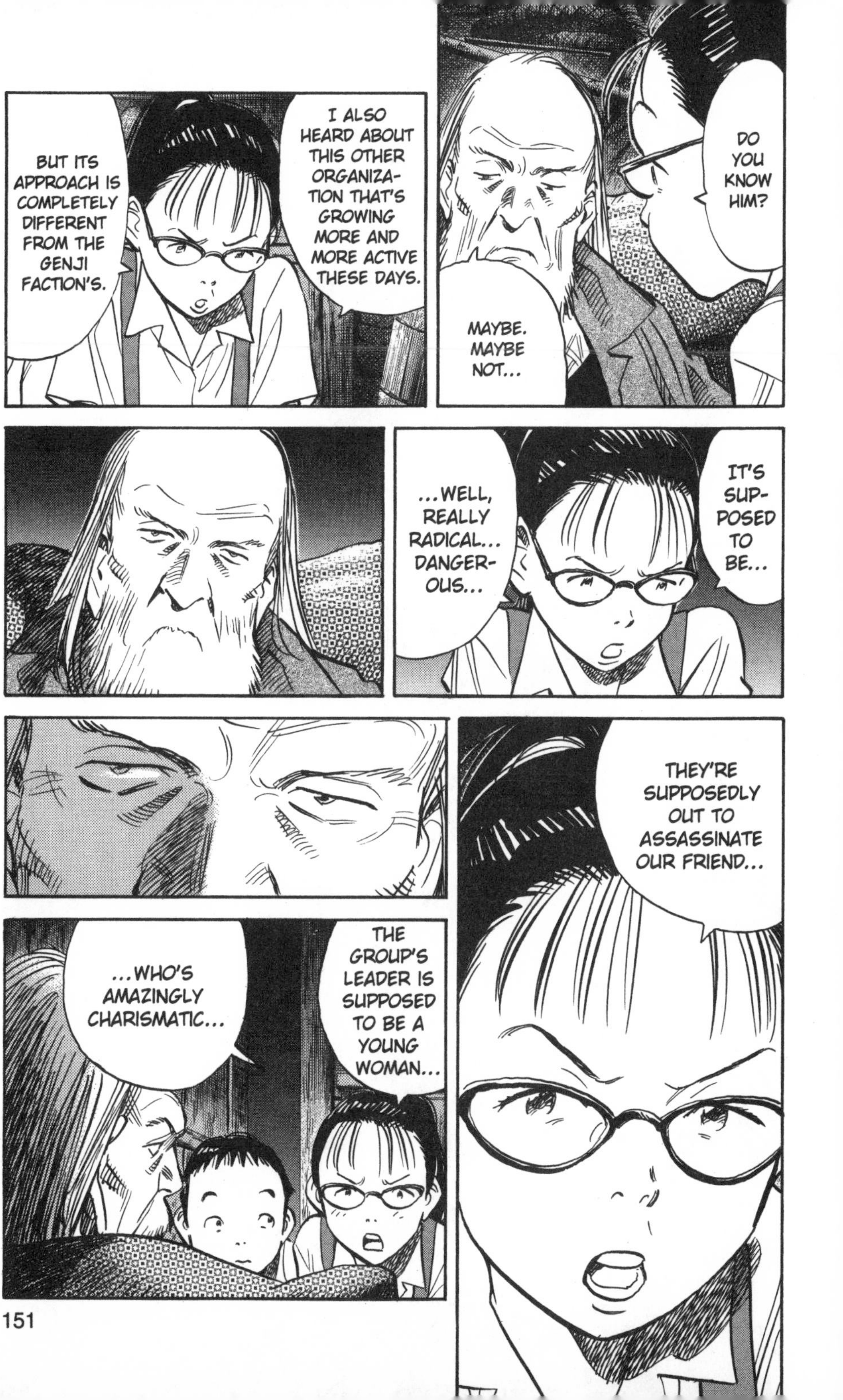
DO YOU KNOW HIM?
MAYBE. MAYBE NOT...
I ALSO HEARD ABOUT THIS OTHER ORGANIZATION THAT'S GROWING MORE AND MORE ACTIVE THESE DAYS.
BUT ITS APPROACH IS COMPLETELY DIFFERENT FROM THE GENJI FACTION'S.
IT'S SUPPOSED TO BE...
...WELL, REALLY RADICAL... DANGEROUS...
THEY'RE SUPPOSEDLY OUT TO ASSASSINATE OUR FRIEND...
THE GROUP'S LEADER IS SUPPOSED TO BE A YOUNG WOMAN...
...WHO'S AMAZINGLY CHARISMATIC...

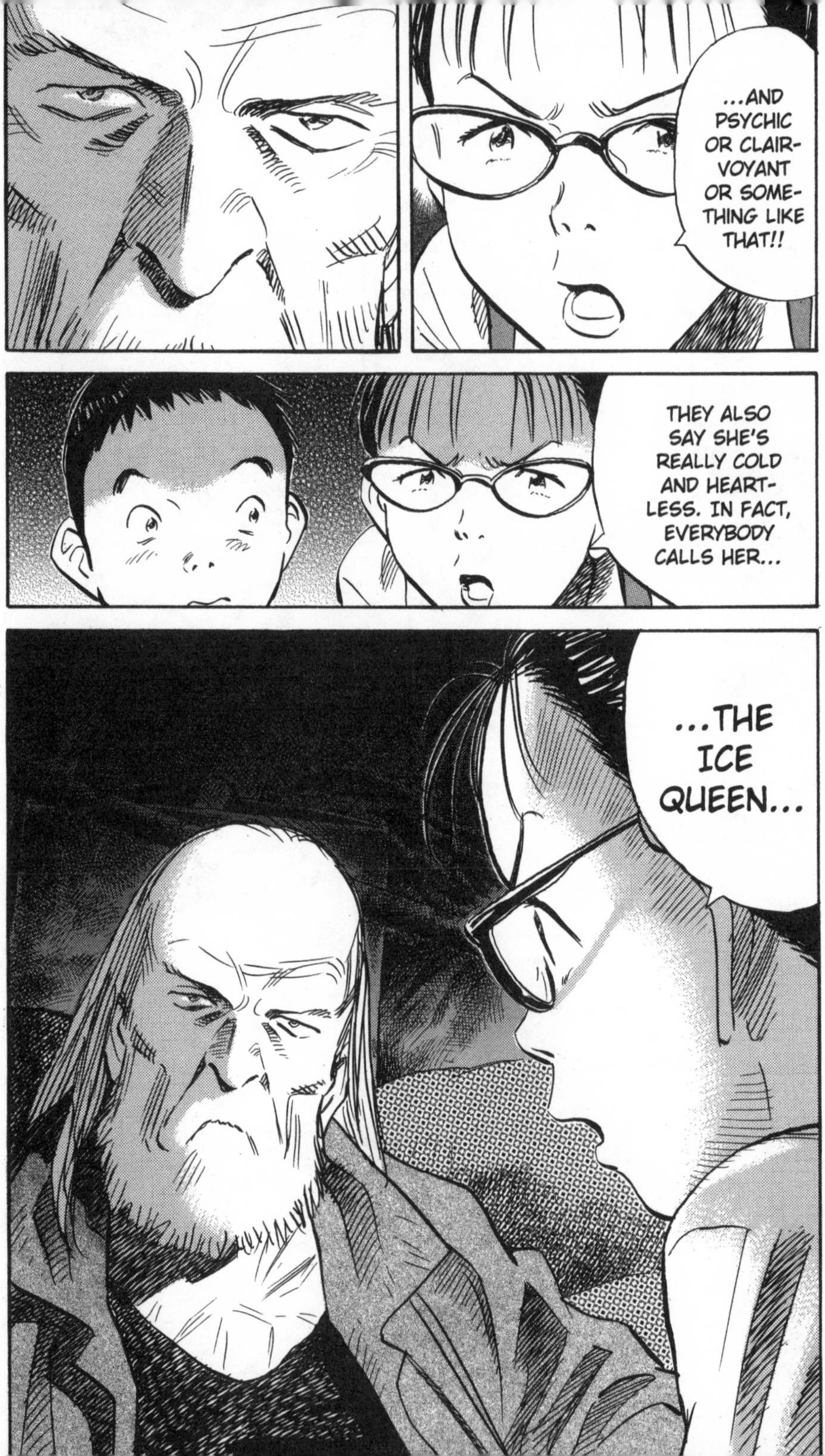
...AND PSYCHIC OR CLAIR-VOYANT OR SOME-THING LIKE THAT!!
THEY ALSO SAY SHE'S REALLY COLD AND HEART-LESS. IN FACT, EVERYBODY CALLS HER...
...THE ICE QUEEN...

Chapter 9 Modern History

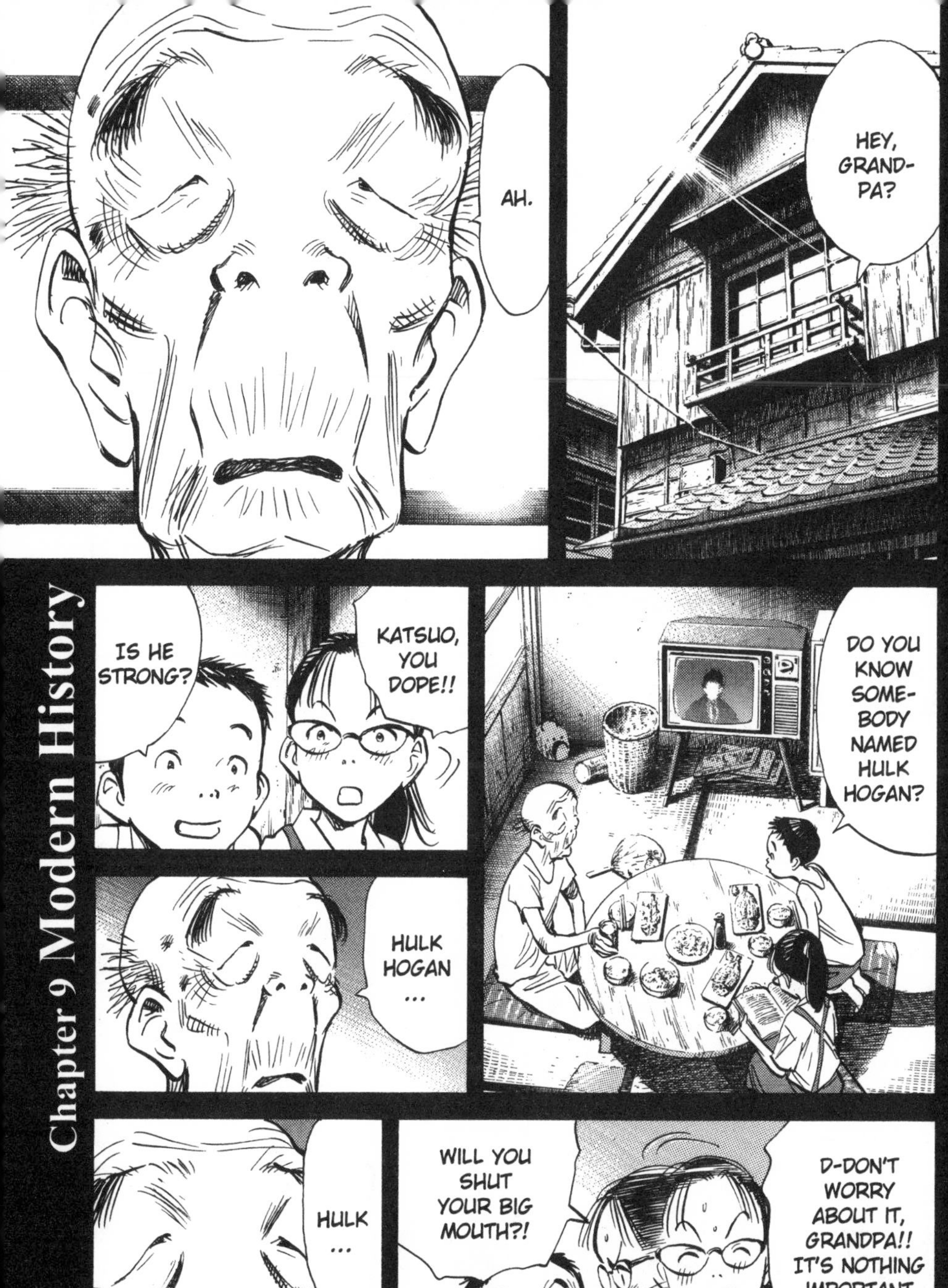
HEY, GRANDPA?
AH.
DO YOU KNOW SOMEBODY NAMED HULK HOGAN?
KATSUO, YOU DOPE!!
IS HE STRONG?
HULK HOGAN ...
D-DON'T WORRY ABOUT IT, GRANDPA!! IT'S NOTHING IMPORTANT ANYWAY...!!
WILL YOU SHUT YOUR BIG MOUTH?!
HULK ...

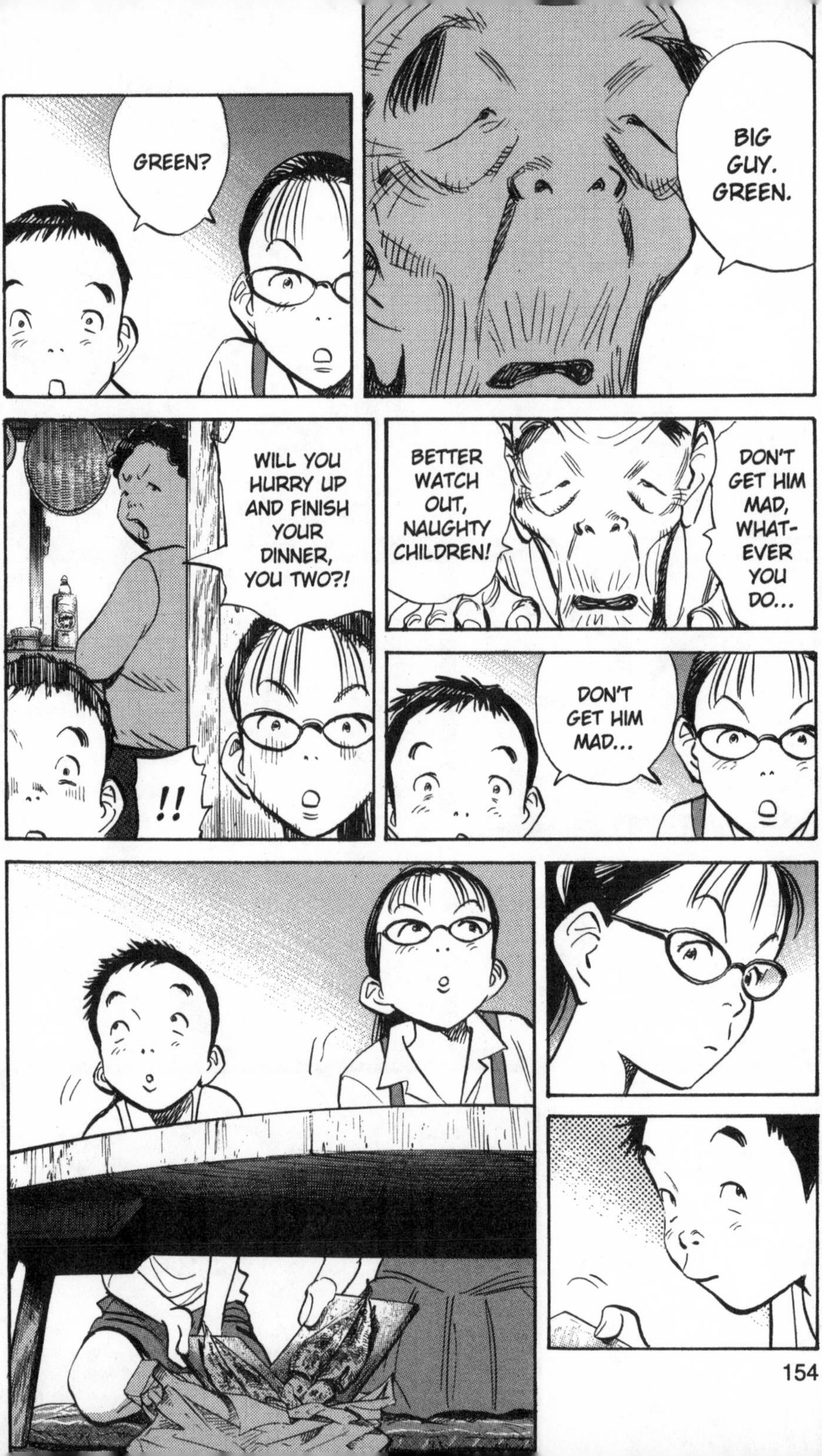
BIG GUY. GREEN.
GREEN?
DON'T GET HIM MAD, WHAT-EVER YOU DO...
BETTER WATCH OUT, NAUGHTY CHILDREN!
DON'T GET HIM MAD...
WILL YOU HURRY UP AND FINISH YOUR DINNER, YOU TWO?!
!!

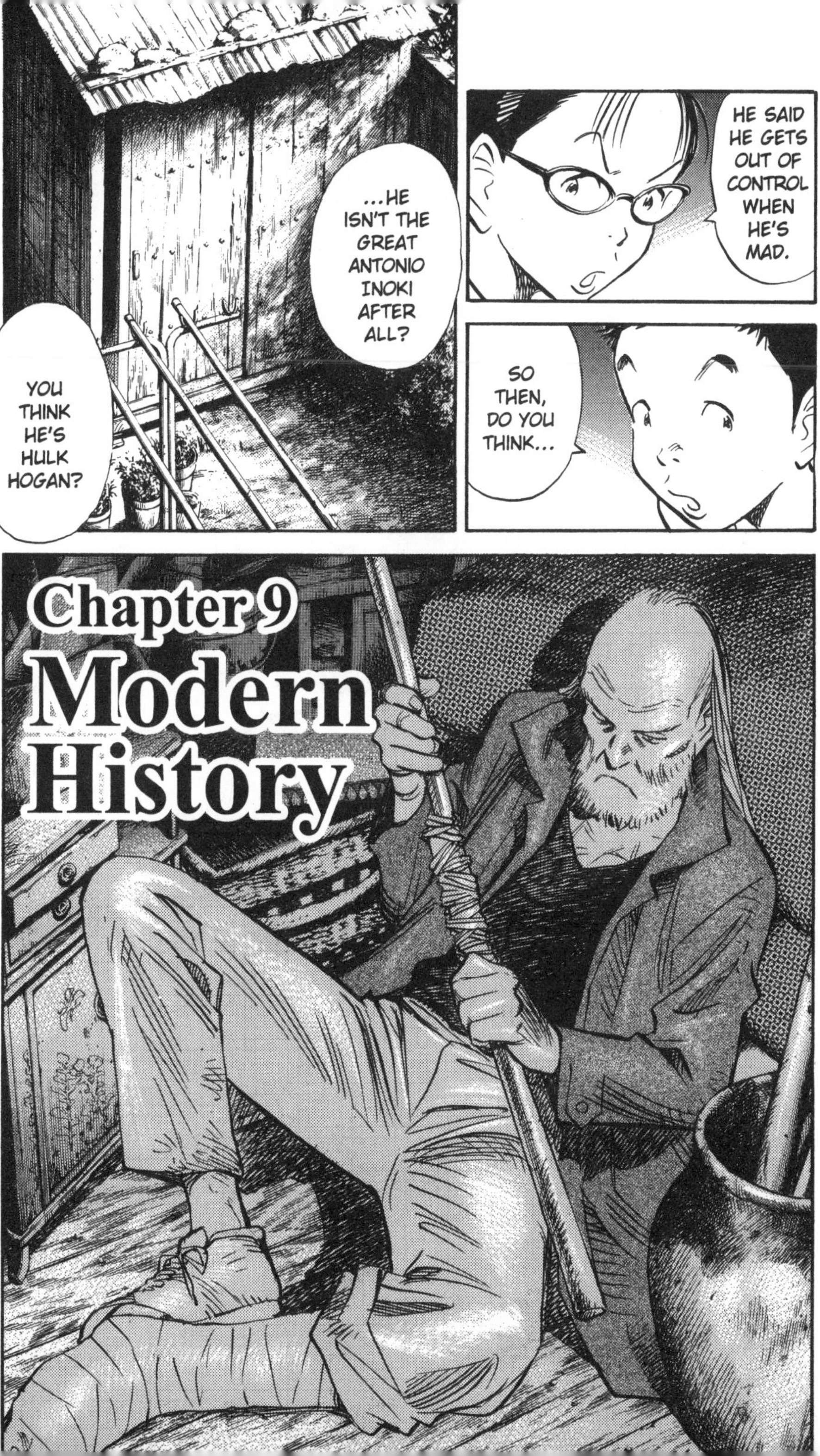
HE SAID HE GETS OUT OF CONTROL WHEN HE'S MAD.
SO THEN, DO YOU THINK...
...HE ISN'T THE GREAT ANTONIO INOKI AFTER ALL?
YOU THINK HE'S HULK HOGAN?
Chapter 9
Modern History

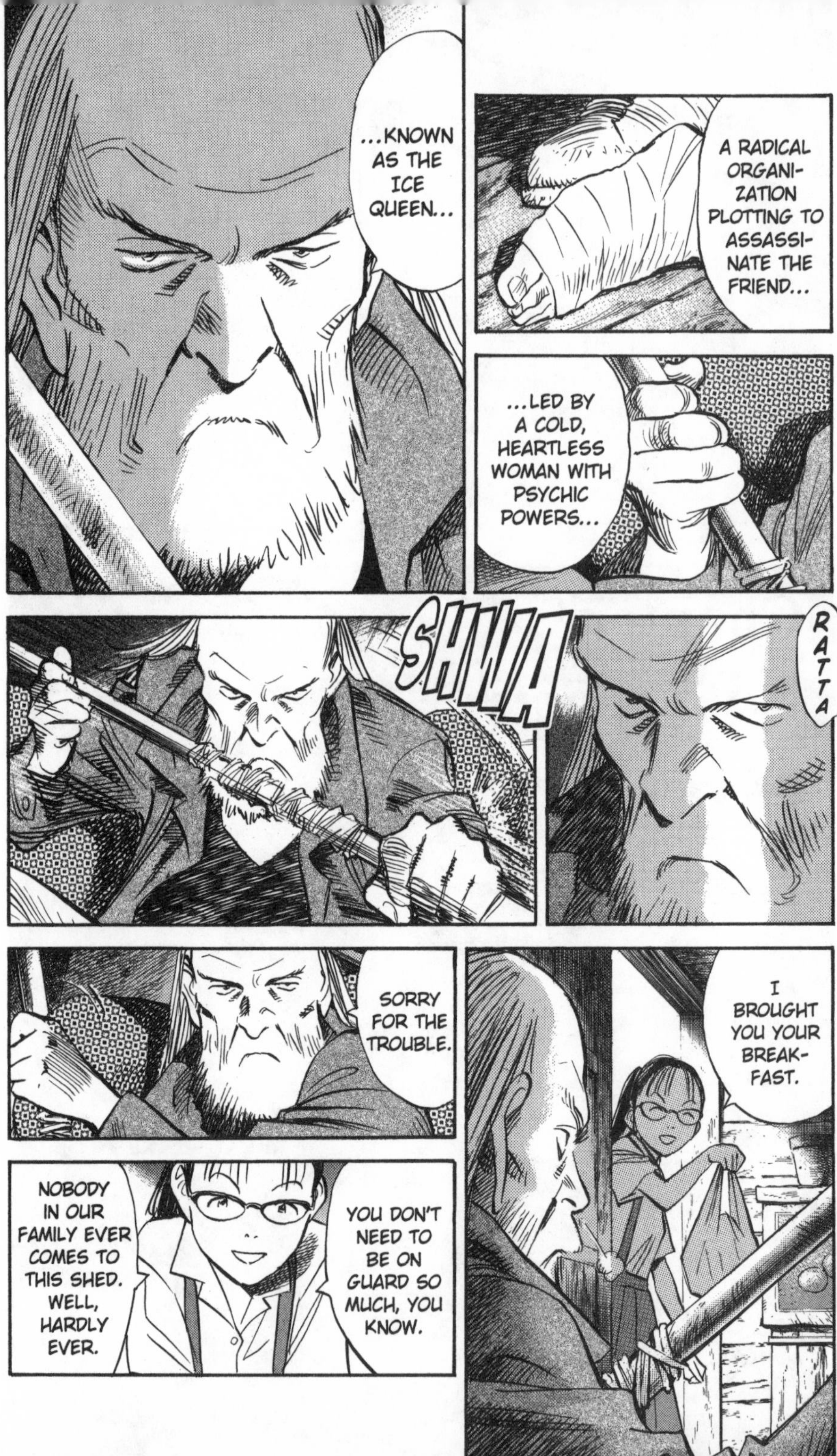
A RADICAL ORGANIZATION PLOTTING TO ASSASSINATE THE FRIEND...
...LED BY A COLD, HEARTLESS WOMAN WITH PSYCHIC POWERS...
...KNOWN AS THE ICE QUEEN...
RATTA
SHWA
I BROUGHT YOU YOUR BREAKFAST.
SORRY FOR THE TROUBLE.
YOU DON'T NEED TO BE ON GUARD SO MUCH, YOU KNOW.
NOBODY IN OUR FAMILY EVER COMES TO THIS SHED. WELL, HARDLY EVER.

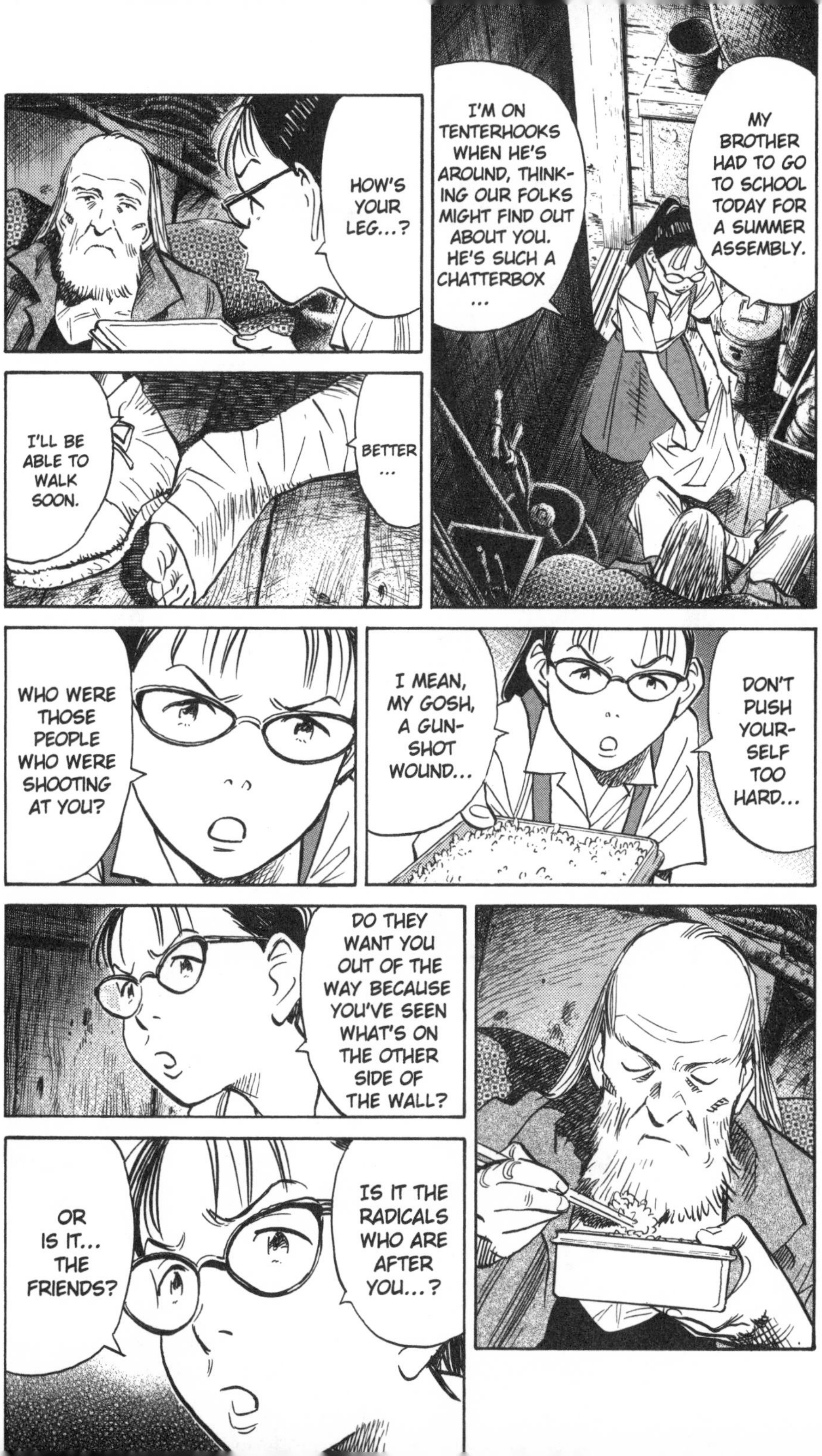
MY BROTHER HAD TO GO TO SCHOOL TODAY FOR A SUMMER ASSEMBLY.
I'M ON TENTERHOOKS WHEN HE'S AROUND, THINKING OUR FOLKS MIGHT FIND OUT ABOUT YOU. HE'S SUCH A CHATTERBOX...
HOW'S YOUR LEG...?
BETTER...
I'LL BE ABLE TO WALK SOON.
DON'T PUSH YOURSELF TOO HARD...
I MEAN, MY GOSH, A GUNSHOT WOUND...
WHO WERE THOSE PEOPLE WHO WERE SHOOTING AT YOU?
DO THEY WANT YOU OUT OF THE WAY BECAUSE YOU'VE SEEN WHAT'S ON THE OTHER SIDE OF THE WALL?
IS IT THE RADICALS WHO ARE AFTER YOU...?
OR IS IT... THE FRIENDS?

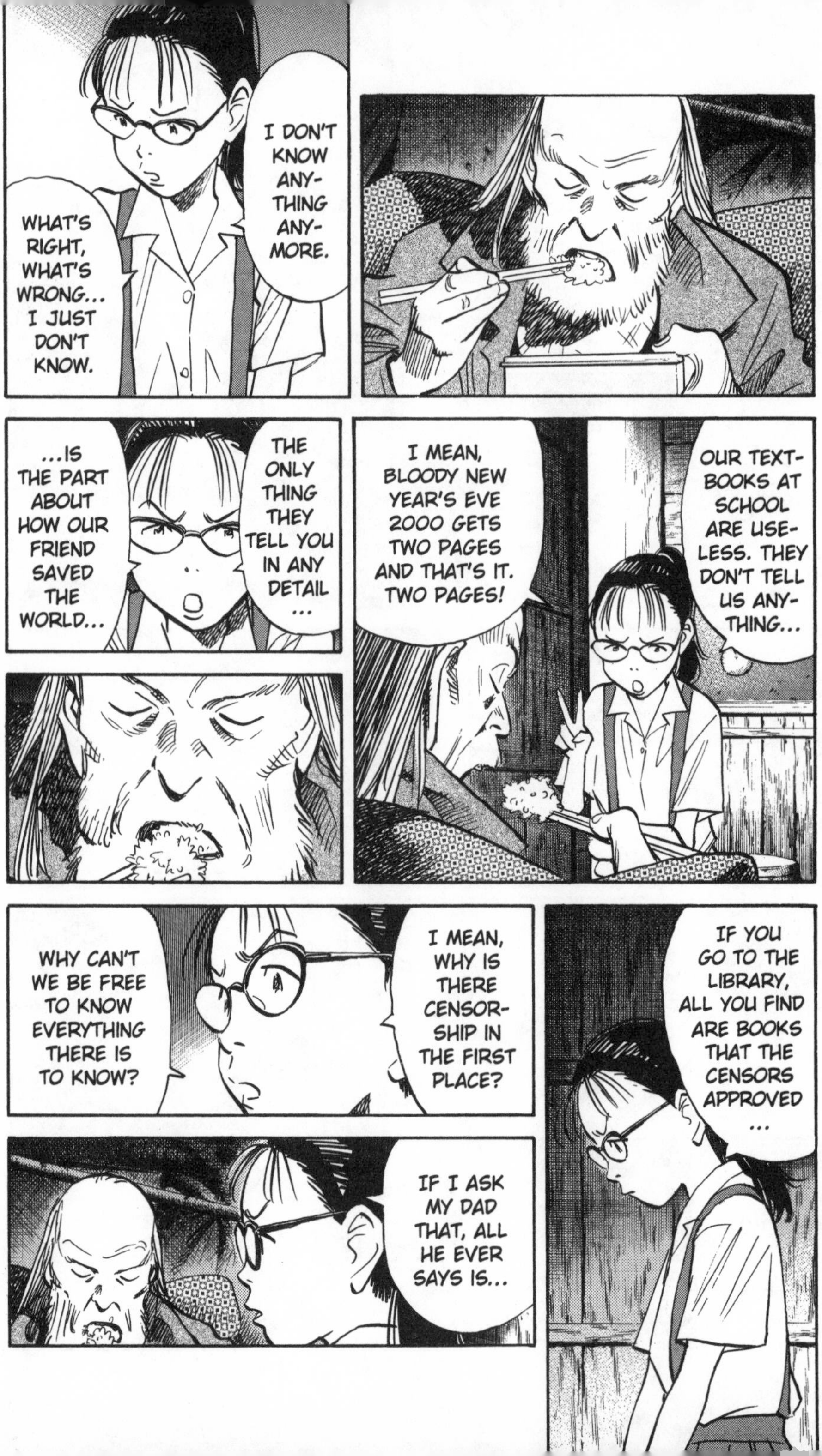
I DON'T KNOW ANYTHING ANYMORE.
WHAT'S RIGHT, WHAT'S WRONG... I JUST DON'T KNOW.
OUR TEXTBOOKS AT SCHOOL ARE USELESS. THEY DON'T TELL US ANYTHING...
I MEAN, BLOODY NEW YEAR'S EVE 2000 GETS TWO PAGES AND THAT'S IT. TWO PAGES!
THE ONLY THING THEY TELL YOU IN ANY DETAIL ...
...IS THE PART ABOUT HOW OUR FRIEND SAVED THE WORLD...
IF YOU GO TO THE LIBRARY, ALL YOU FIND ARE BOOKS THAT THE CENSORS APPROVED ...
I MEAN, WHY IS THERE CENSORSHIP IN THE FIRST PLACE?
WHY CAN'T WE BE FREE TO KNOW EVERYTHING THERE IS TO KNOW?
IF I ASK MY DAD THAT, ALL HE EVER SAYS IS...

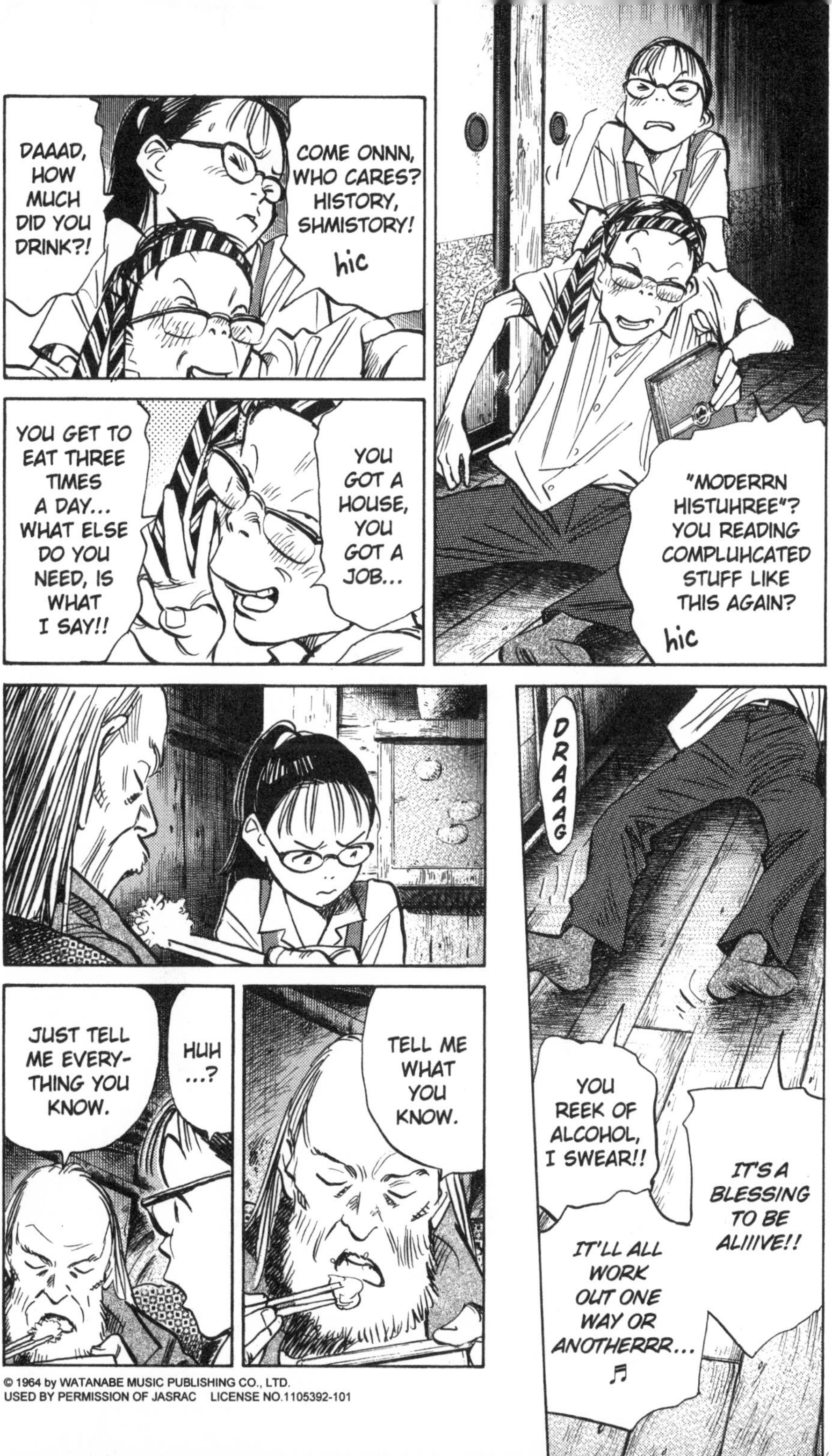
"MODERRN HISTUHREE"? YOU READING COMPLUHCATED STUFF LIKE THIS AGAIN?
hic
COME ONNN, WHO CARES? HISTORY, SHMISTORY!
hic
DAAAD, HOW MUCH DID YOU DRINK?!
YOU GOT A HOUSE, YOU GOT A JOB...
YOU GET TO EAT THREE TIMES A DAY... WHAT ELSE DO YOU NEED, IS WHAT I SAY!!
DRAAAG
YOU REEK OF ALCOHOL, I SWEAR!!
IT'S A BLESSING TO BE ALIIIVE!!
IT'LL ALL WORK OUT ONE WAY OR ANOTHERRR... ♬
TELL ME WHAT YOU KNOW.
HUH ...?
JUST TELL ME EVERY-THING YOU KNOW.

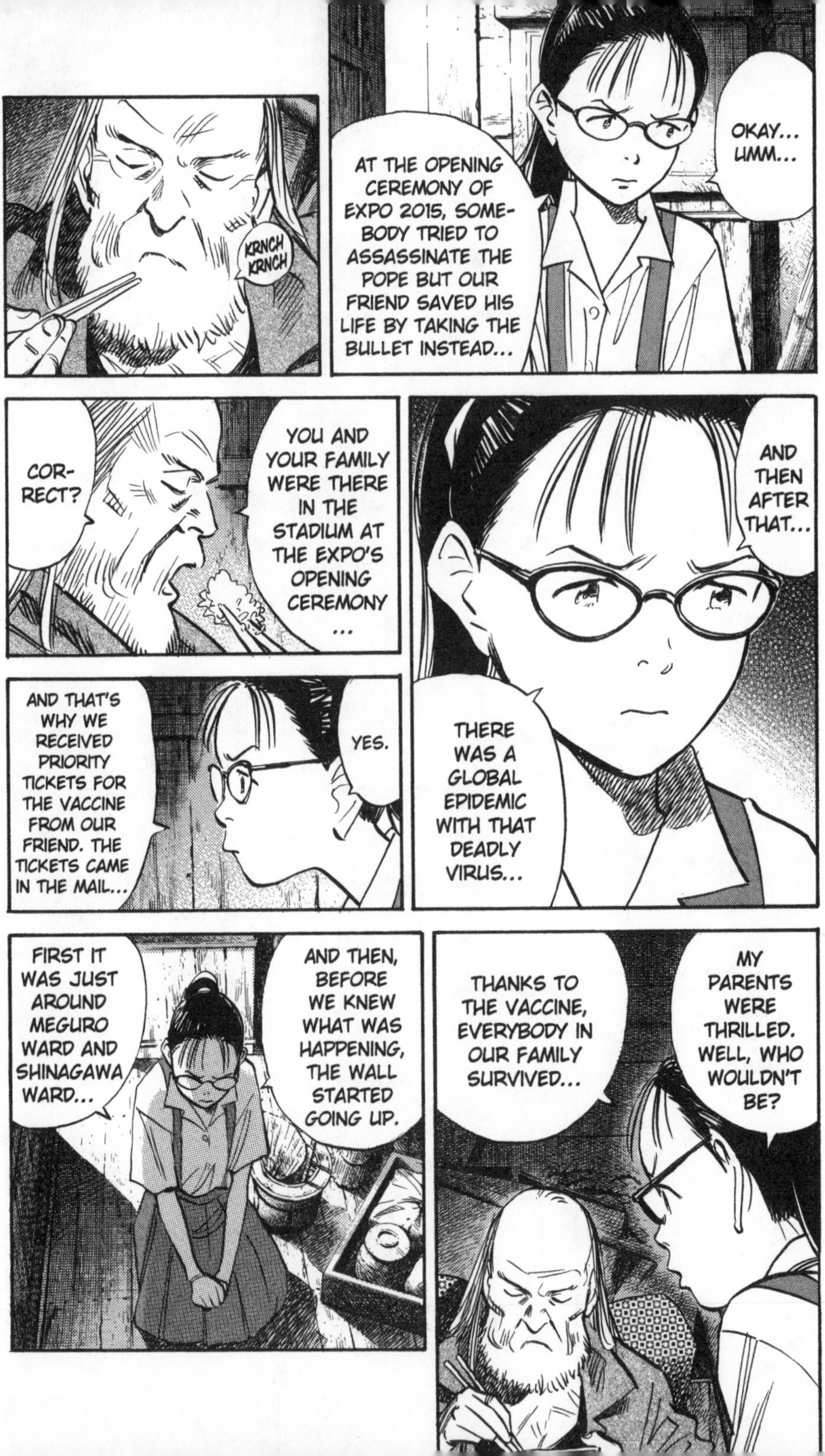
OKAY... UMM...
AT THE OPENING CEREMONY OF EXPO 2015, SOMEBODY TRIED TO ASSASSINATE THE POPE BUT OUR FRIEND SAVED HIS LIFE BY TAKING THE BULLET INSTEAD...
KRNCH KRNCH
AND THEN AFTER THAT...
THERE WAS A GLOBAL EPIDEMIC WITH THAT DEADLY VIRUS...
YOU AND YOUR FAMILY WERE THERE IN THE STADIUM AT THE EXPO'S OPENING CEREMONY...
COR-RECT?
YES.
AND THAT'S WHY WE RECEIVED PRIORITY TICKETS FOR THE VACCINE FROM OUR FRIEND. THE TICKETS CAME IN THE MAIL...
MY PARENTS WERE THRILLED. WELL, WHO WOULDN'T BE?
THANKS TO THE VACCINE, EVERYBODY IN OUR FAMILY SURVIVED...
AND THEN, BEFORE WE KNEW WHAT WAS HAPPENING, THE WALL STARTED GOING UP.
FIRST IT WAS JUST AROUND MEGURO WARD AND SHINAGAWA WARD...

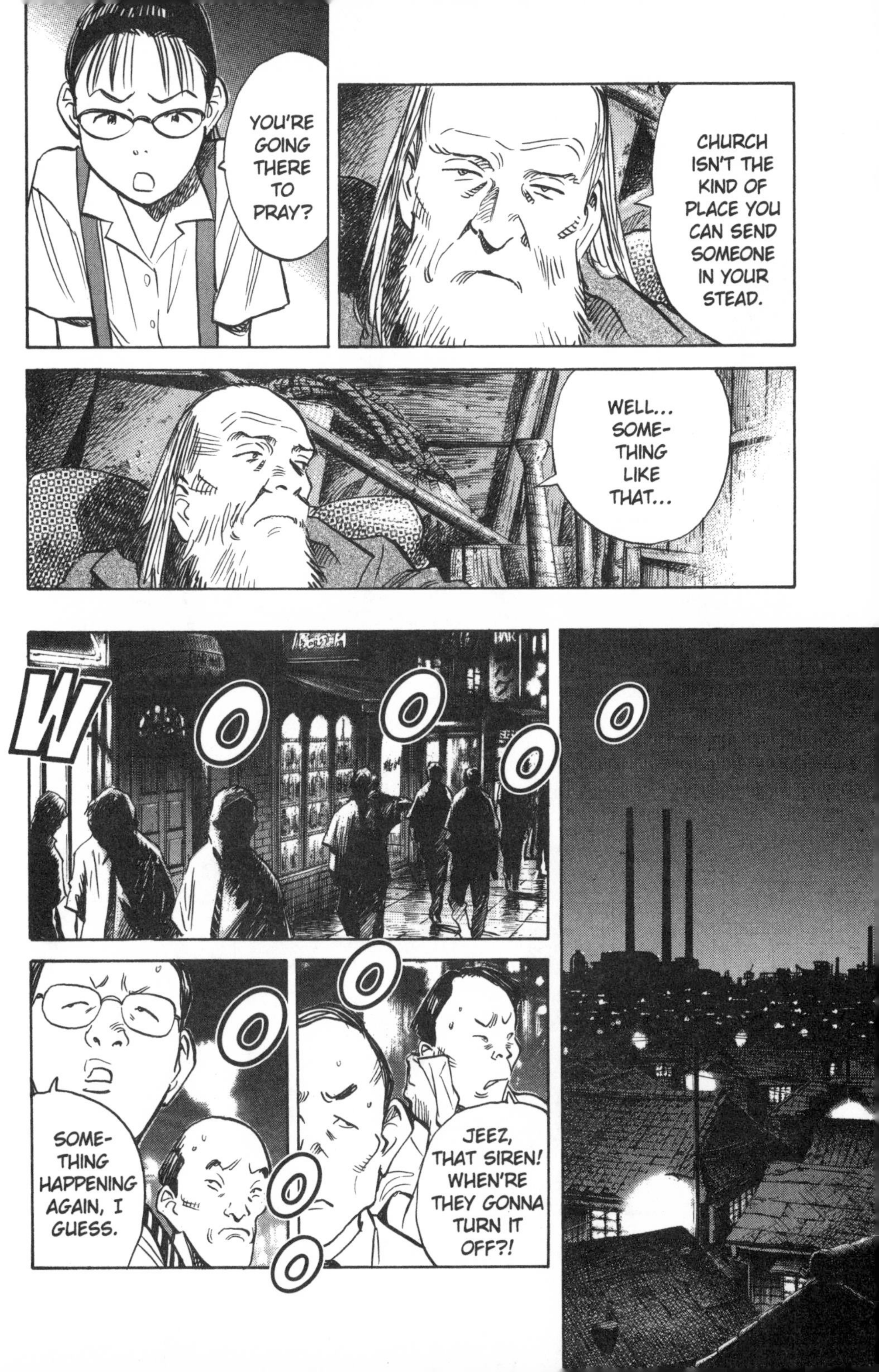
CHURCH ISN'T THE KIND OF PLACE YOU CAN SEND SOMEONE IN YOUR STEAD.
YOU'RE GOING THERE TO PRAY?
WELL... SOME-THING LIKE THAT...
WOOOO
JEEZ, THAT SIREN! WHEN'RE THEY GONNA TURN IT OFF?!
SOME-THING HAPPENING AGAIN, I GUESS.

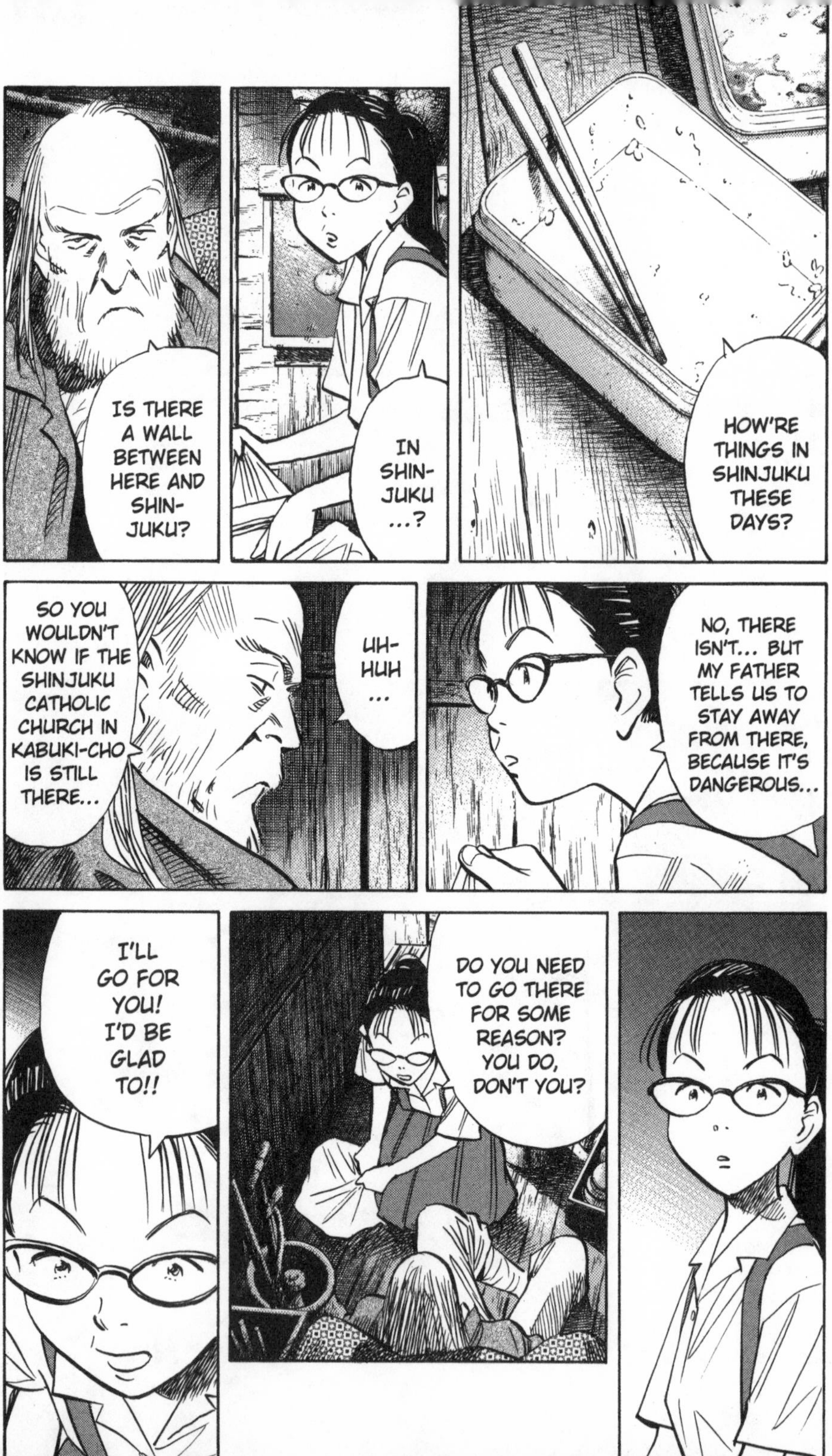
HOW'RE THINGS IN SHINJUKU THESE DAYS?
IN SHIN-JUKU...?
IS THERE A WALL BETWEEN HERE AND SHIN-JUKU?
NO, THERE ISN'T... BUT MY FATHER TELLS US TO STAY AWAY FROM THERE, BECAUSE IT'S DANGEROUS...
UH-HUH...
SO YOU WOULDN'T KNOW IF THE SHINJUKU CATHOLIC CHURCH IN KABUKI-CHO IS STILL THERE...
DO YOU NEED TO GO THERE FOR SOME REASON? YOU DO, DON'T YOU?
I'LL GO FOR YOU! I'D BE GLAD TO!!

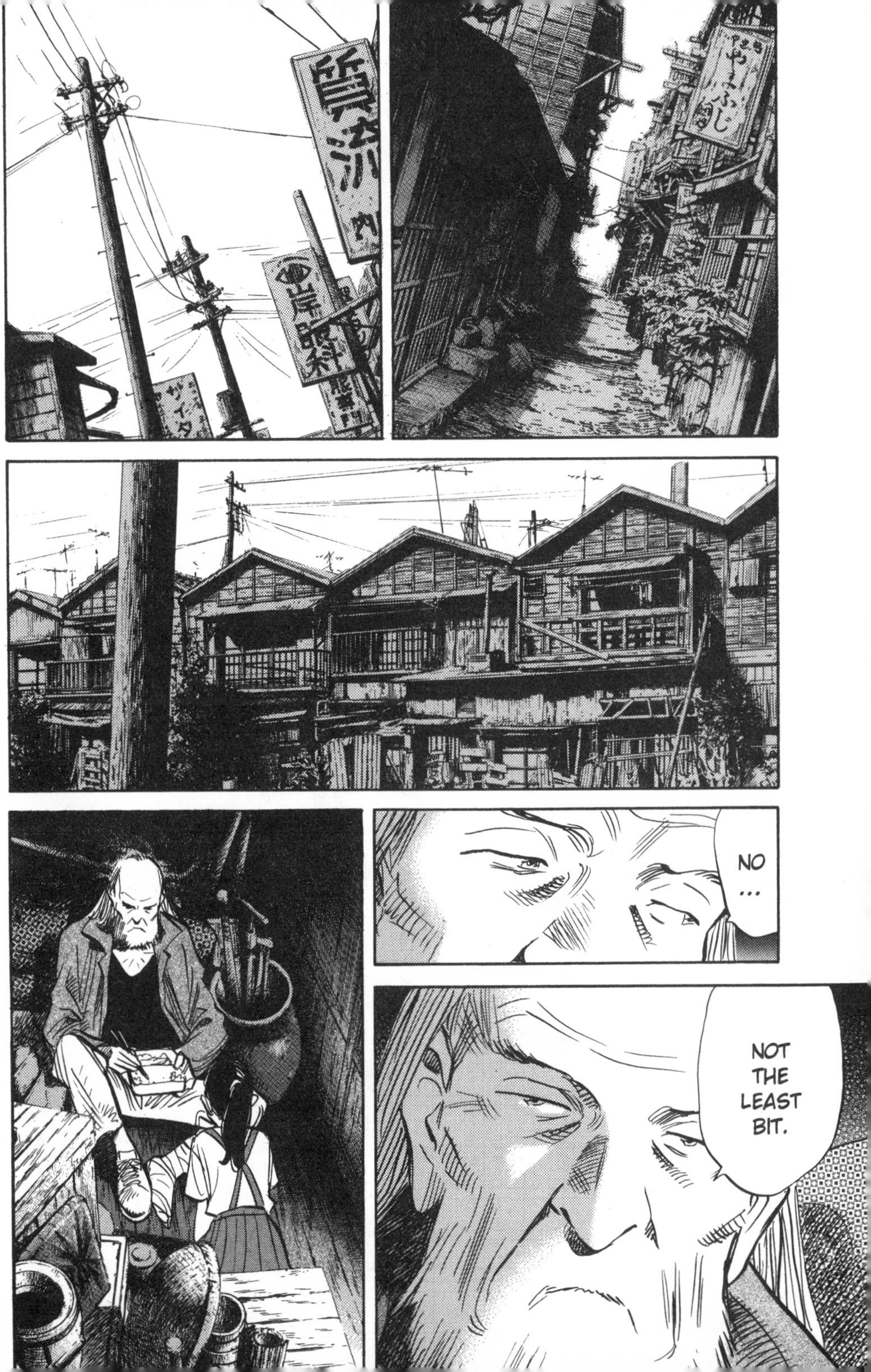
NO ...
NOT THE LEAST BIT.

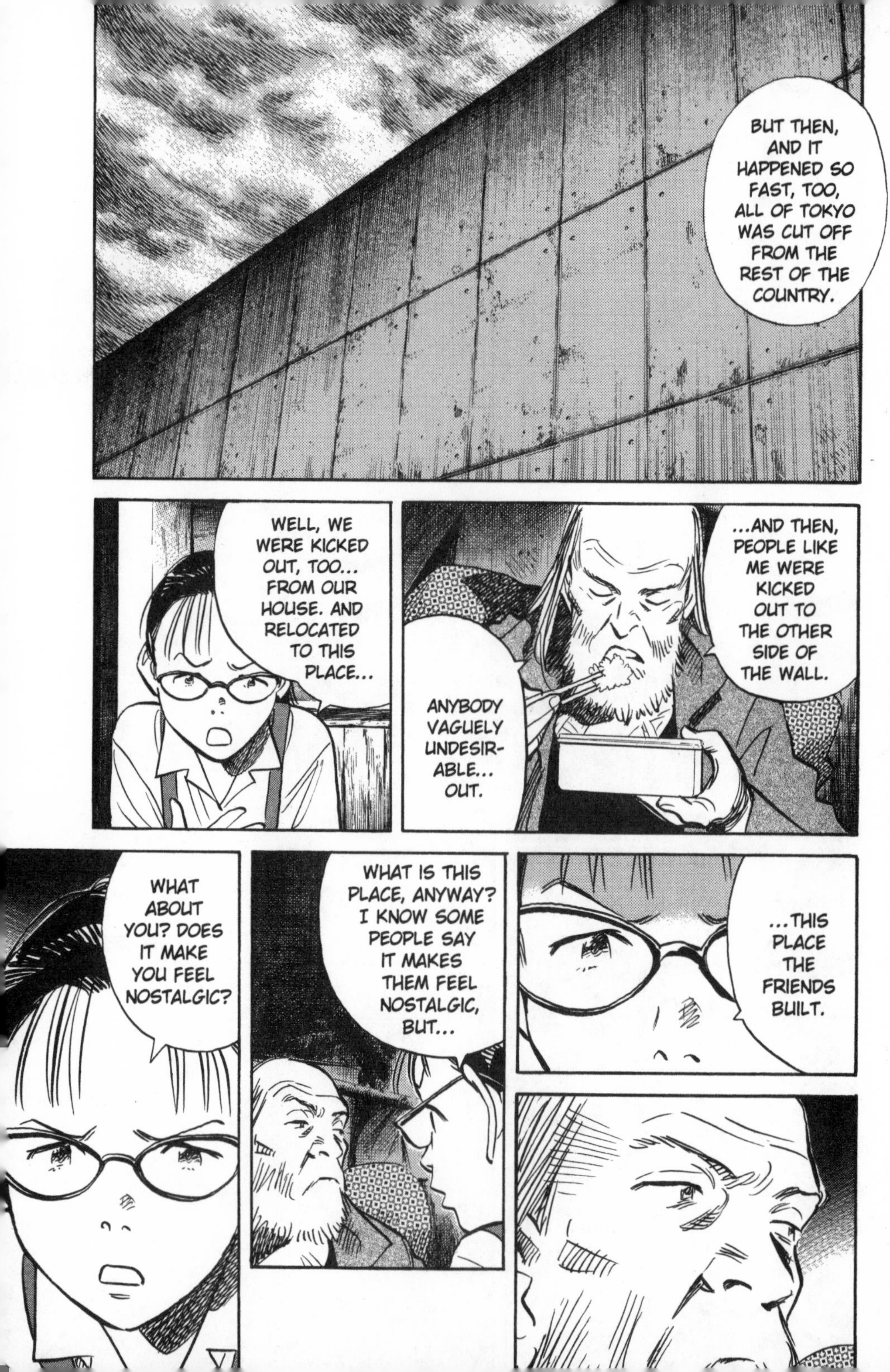
BUT THEN, AND IT HAPPENED SO FAST, TOO, ALL OF TOKYO WAS CUT OFF FROM THE REST OF THE COUNTRY.
...AND THEN, PEOPLE LIKE ME WERE KICKED OUT TO THE OTHER SIDE OF THE WALL.
ANYBODY VAGUELY UNDESIRABLE... OUT.
WELL, WE WERE KICKED OUT, TOO... FROM OUR HOUSE. AND RELOCATED TO THIS PLACE...
...THIS PLACE THE FRIENDS BUILT.
WHAT IS THIS PLACE, ANYWAY? I KNOW SOME PEOPLE SAY IT MAKES THEM FEEL NOSTALGIC, BUT...
WHAT ABOUT YOU? DOES IT MAKE YOU FEEL NOSTALGIC?

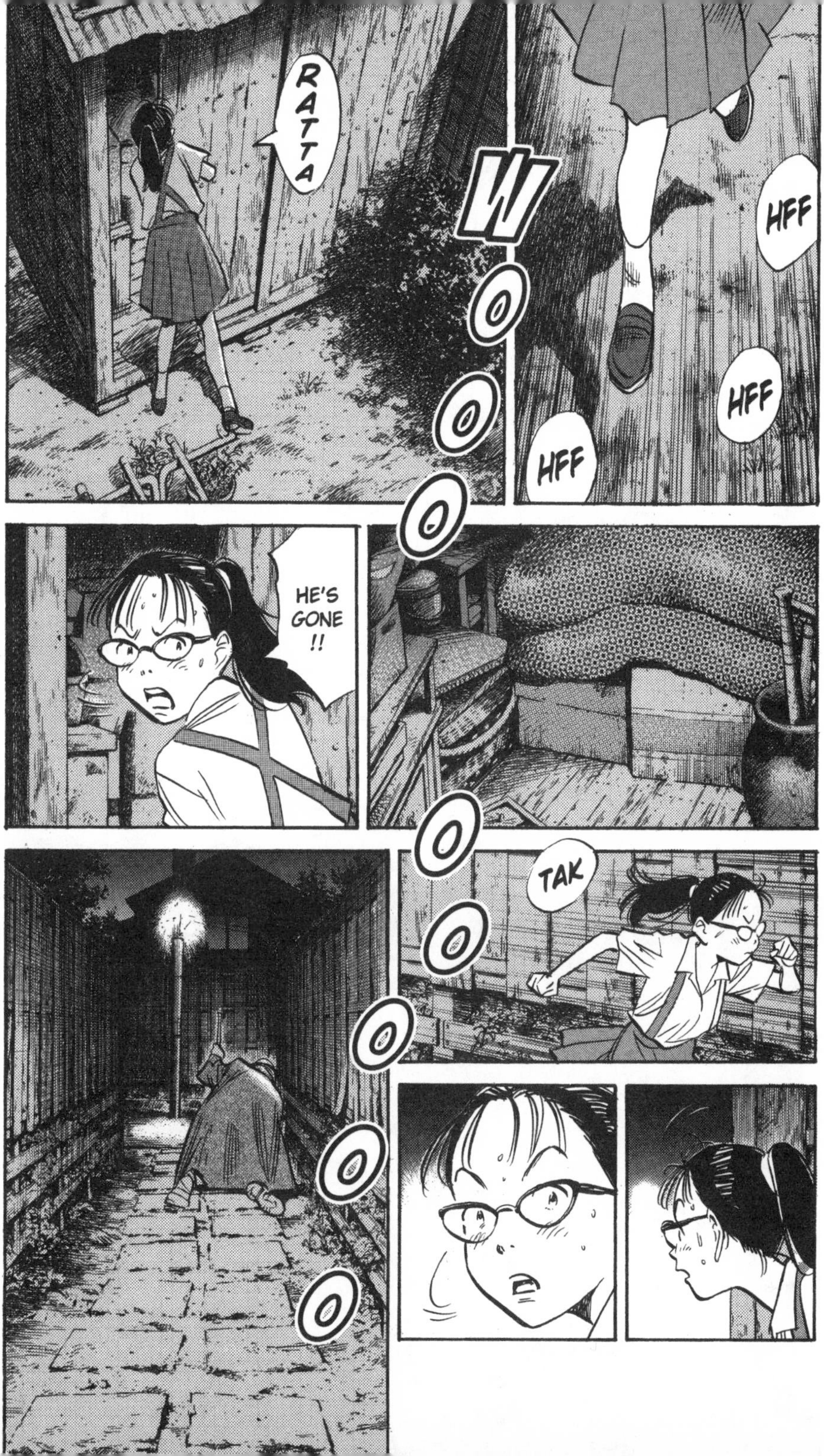

HFF
HFF
HFF
RATTA
WOOOOOOOO
HE'S GONE !!
TAK

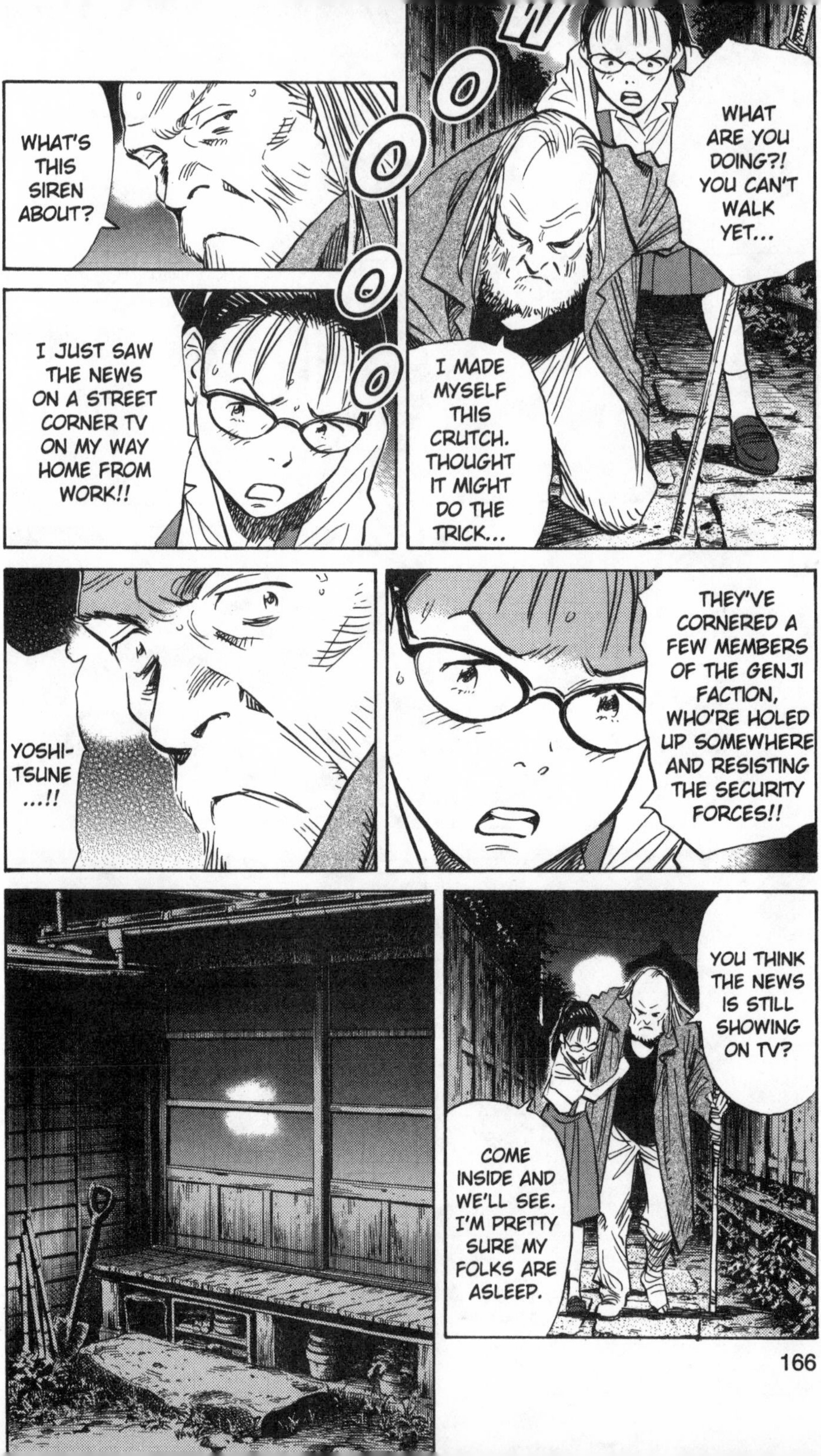
WOOOOO
WHAT ARE YOU DOING?! YOU CAN'T WALK YET...
I MADE MYSELF THIS CRUTCH. THOUGHT IT MIGHT DO THE TRICK...
WHAT'S THIS SIREN ABOUT?
I JUST SAW THE NEWS ON A STREET CORNER TV ON MY WAY HOME FROM WORK!!
THEY'VE CORNERED A FEW MEMBERS OF THE GENJI FACTION, WHO'RE HOLED UP SOMEWHERE AND RESISTING THE SECURITY FORCES!!
YOSHI-TSUNE ...!!
YOU THINK THE NEWS IS STILL SHOWING ON TV?
COME INSIDE AND WE'LL SEE. I'M PRETTY SURE MY FOLKS ARE ASLEEP.

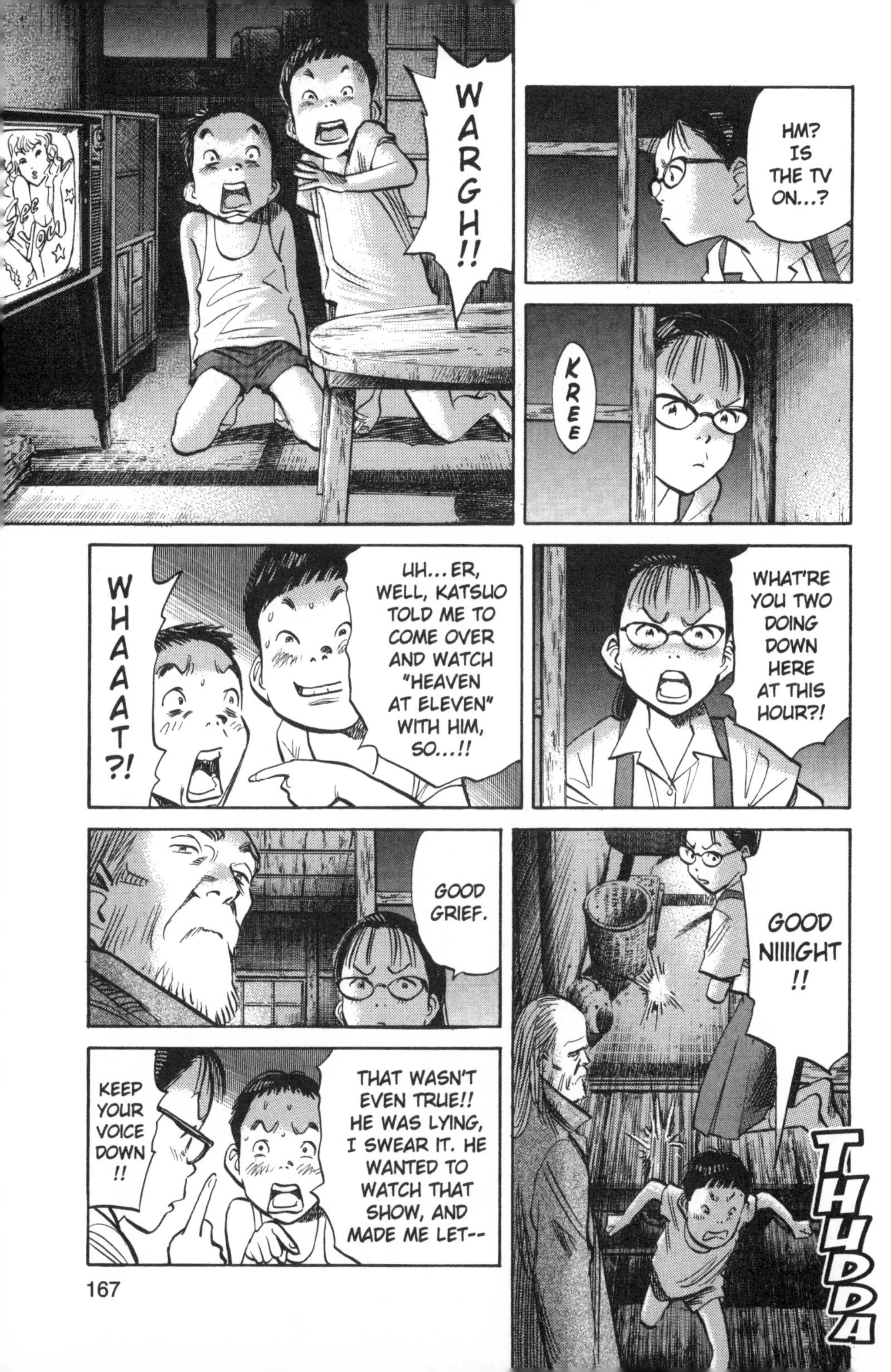
HM? IS THE TV ON...?
KREE
WARGH!!
See You
WHAT'RE YOU TWO DOING DOWN HERE AT THIS HOUR?!
UH...ER, WELL, KATSUO TOLD ME TO COME OVER AND WATCH "HEAVEN AT ELEVEN" WITH HIM, SO...!!
WHAAAAT?!
GOOD NIIIIGHT!!
THUDDA
GOOD GRIEF.
THAT WASN'T EVEN TRUE!! HE WAS LYING, I SWEAR IT. HE WANTED TO WATCH THAT SHOW, AND MADE ME LET--
KEEP YOUR VOICE DOWN!!

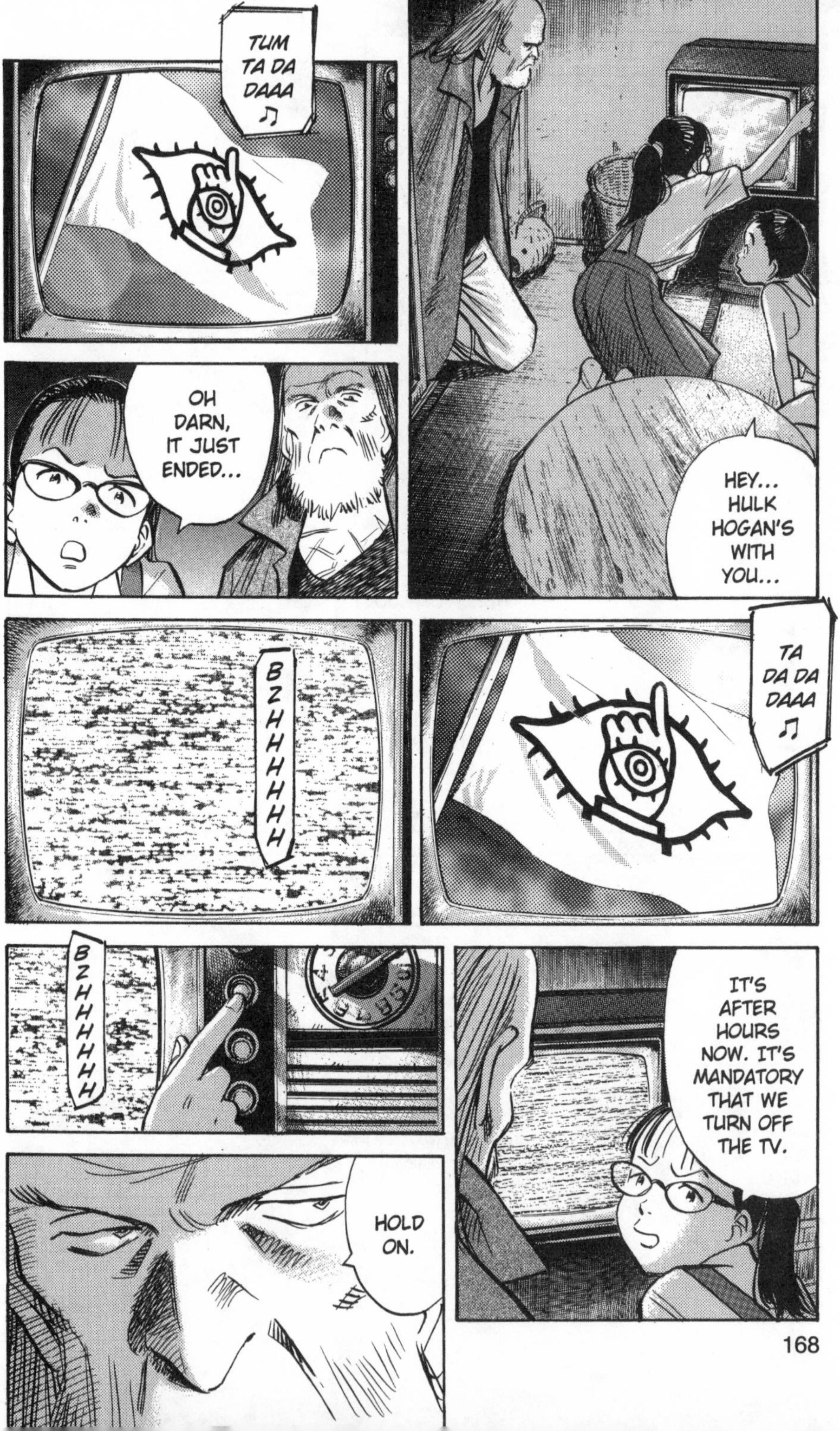
HEY... HULK HOGAN'S WITH YOU...
TUM TA DA DAAA ♫
OH DARN, IT JUST ENDED...
TA DA DA DAAA ♫
BZHHHHHHHH
IT'S AFTER HOURS NOW. IT'S MANDATORY THAT WE TURN OFF THE TV.
BZHHHHHHHH
HOLD ON.

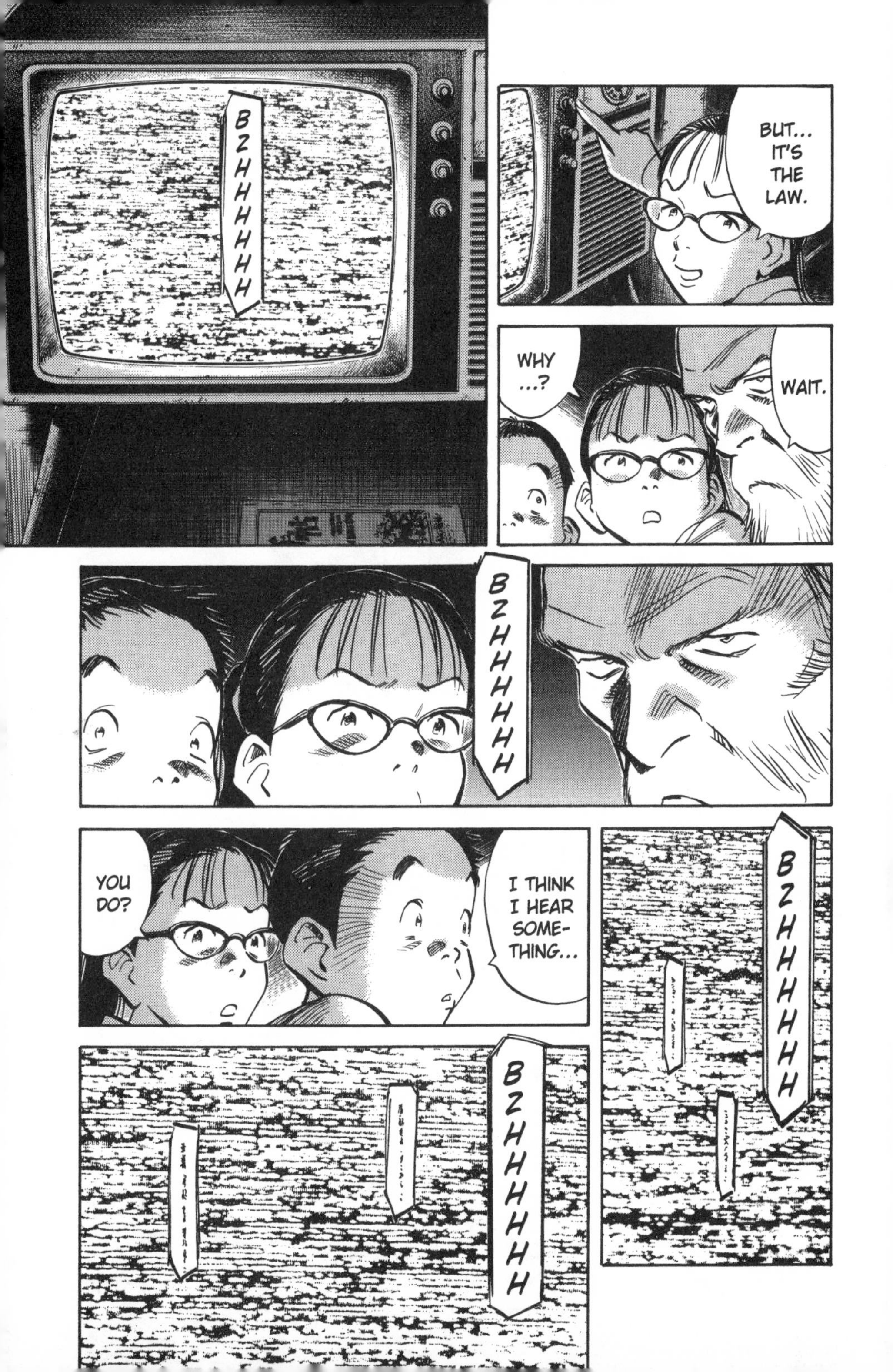
BUT... IT'S THE LAW.
WAIT.
WHY ...?
BZHHHHHHH
BZHHHHHHHH
BZHHHHHHHH
I THINK I HEAR SOME-THING...
YOU DO?
BZHHHHHHHH

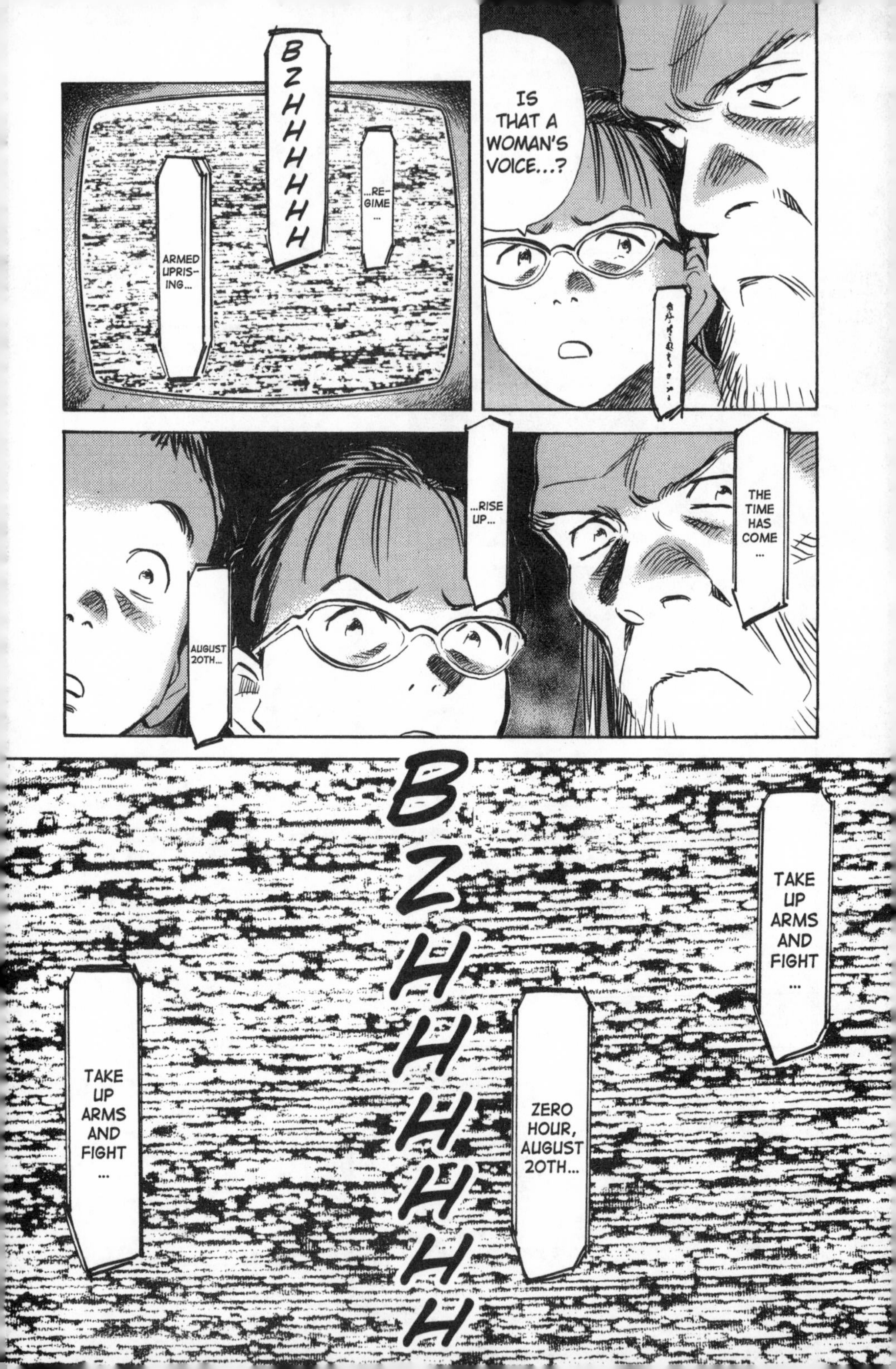
IS THAT A WOMAN'S VOICE...?
BZHHHHHH
...RE-GIME...
ARMED UPRIS-ING...
THE TIME HAS COME...
...RISE UP...
AUGUST 20TH...
TAKE UP ARMS AND FIGHT...
BZHHHHHHH
ZERO HOUR, AUGUST 20TH...
TAKE UP ARMS AND FIGHT...

Chapter 10 Kids' Talk

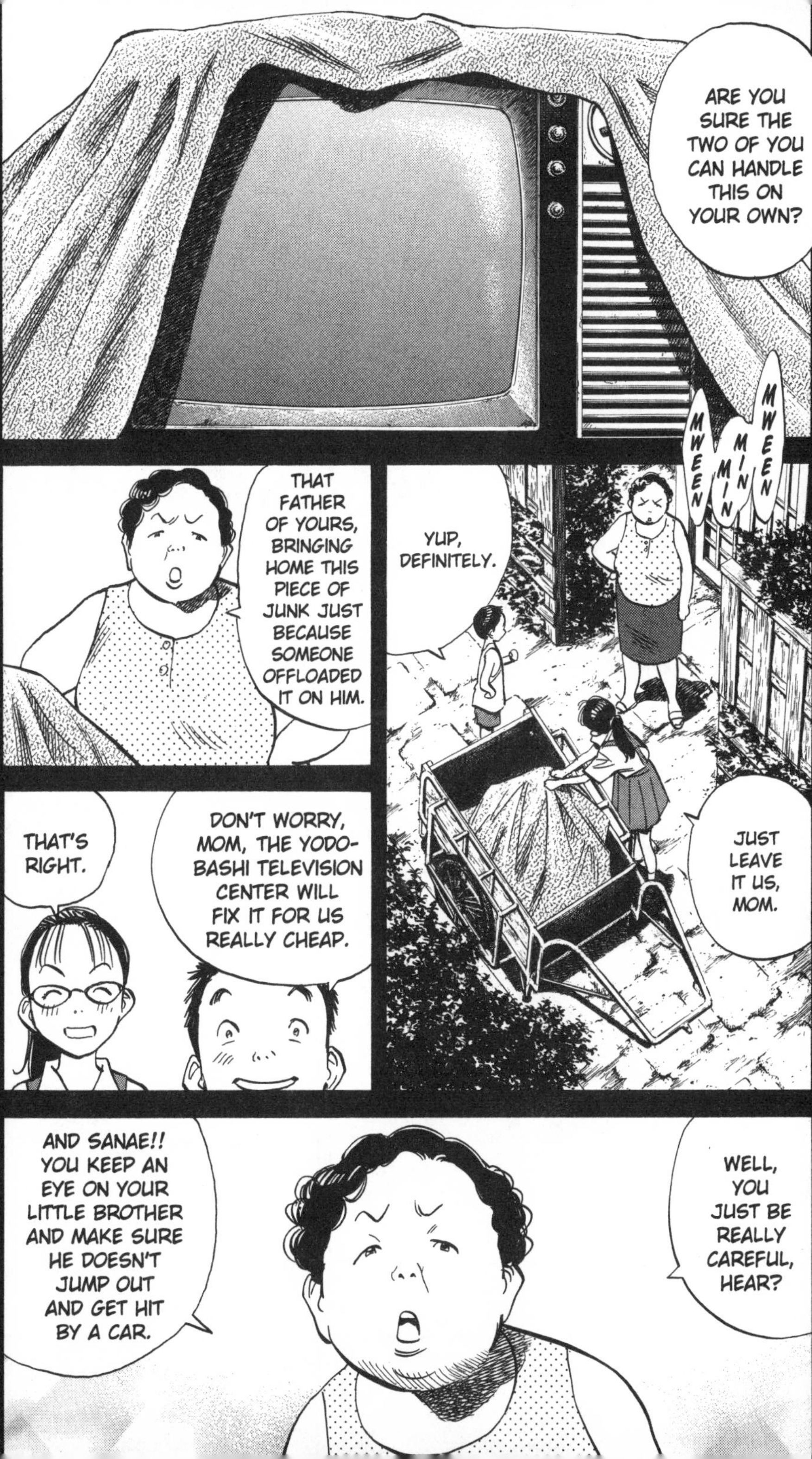
ARE YOU SURE THE TWO OF YOU CAN HANDLE THIS ON YOUR OWN?
MWEEN MIN MIN MWEEN
YUP, DEFINITELY.
JUST LEAVE IT US, MOM.
THAT FATHER OF YOURS, BRINGING HOME THIS PIECE OF JUNK JUST BECAUSE SOMEONE OFFLOADED IT ON HIM.
DON'T WORRY, MOM, THE YODO-BASHI TELEVISION CENTER WILL FIX IT FOR US REALLY CHEAP.
THAT'S RIGHT.
WELL, YOU JUST BE REALLY CAREFUL, HEAR?
AND SANAE!! YOU KEEP AN EYE ON YOUR LITTLE BROTHER AND MAKE SURE HE DOESN'T JUMP OUT AND GET HIT BY A CAR.

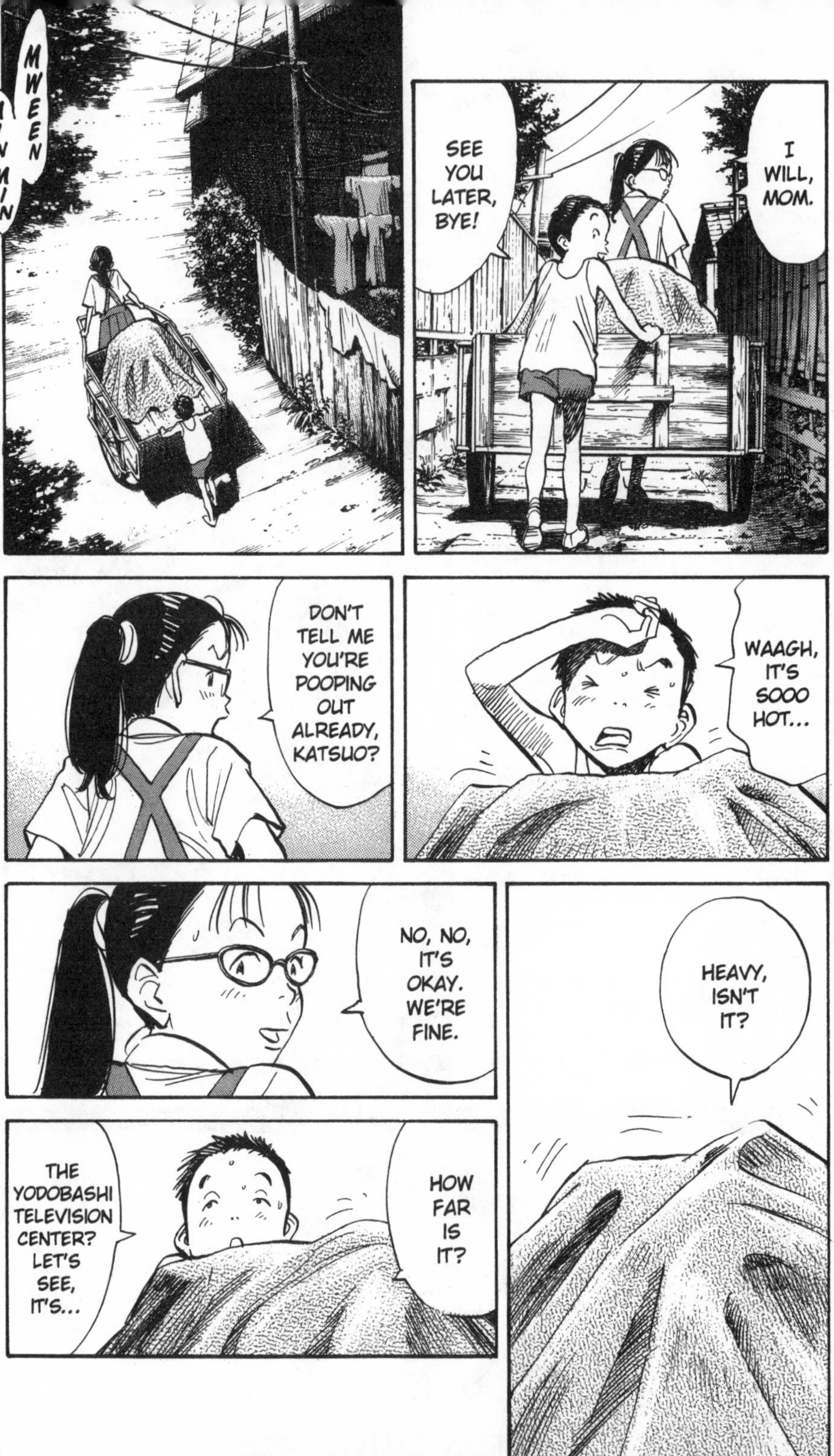
I WILL, MOM.
SEE YOU LATER, BYE!
MWEEN
MIN MIN
WAAGH, IT'S SOOO HOT...
DON'T TELL ME YOU'RE POOPING OUT ALREADY, KATSUO?
HEAVY, ISN'T IT?
NO, NO, IT'S OKAY. WE'RE FINE.
HOW FAR IS IT?
THE YODOBASHI TELEVISION CENTER? LET'S SEE, IT'S...

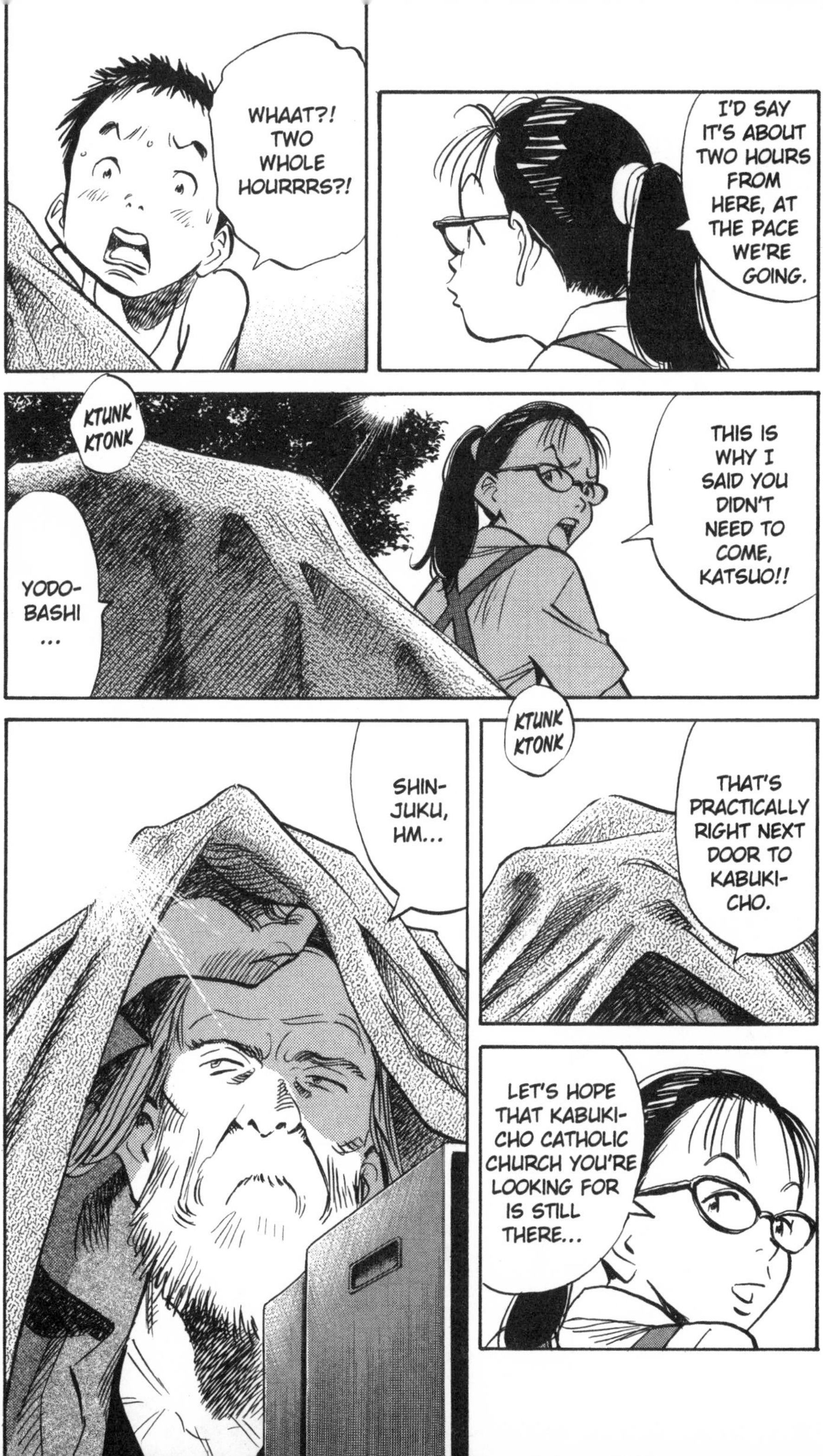
I'D SAY IT'S ABOUT TWO HOURS FROM HERE, AT THE PACE WE'RE GOING.
WHAAT?! TWO WHOLE HOURRRS?!
THIS IS WHY I SAID YOU DIDN'T NEED TO COME, KATSUO!!
KTUNK KTONK
YODO-BASHI ...
KTUNK KTONK
THAT'S PRACTICALLY RIGHT NEXT DOOR TO KABUKI-CHO.
LET'S HOPE THAT KABUKI-CHO CATHOLIC CHURCH YOU'RE LOOKING FOR IS STILL THERE...
SHIN-JUKU, HM...

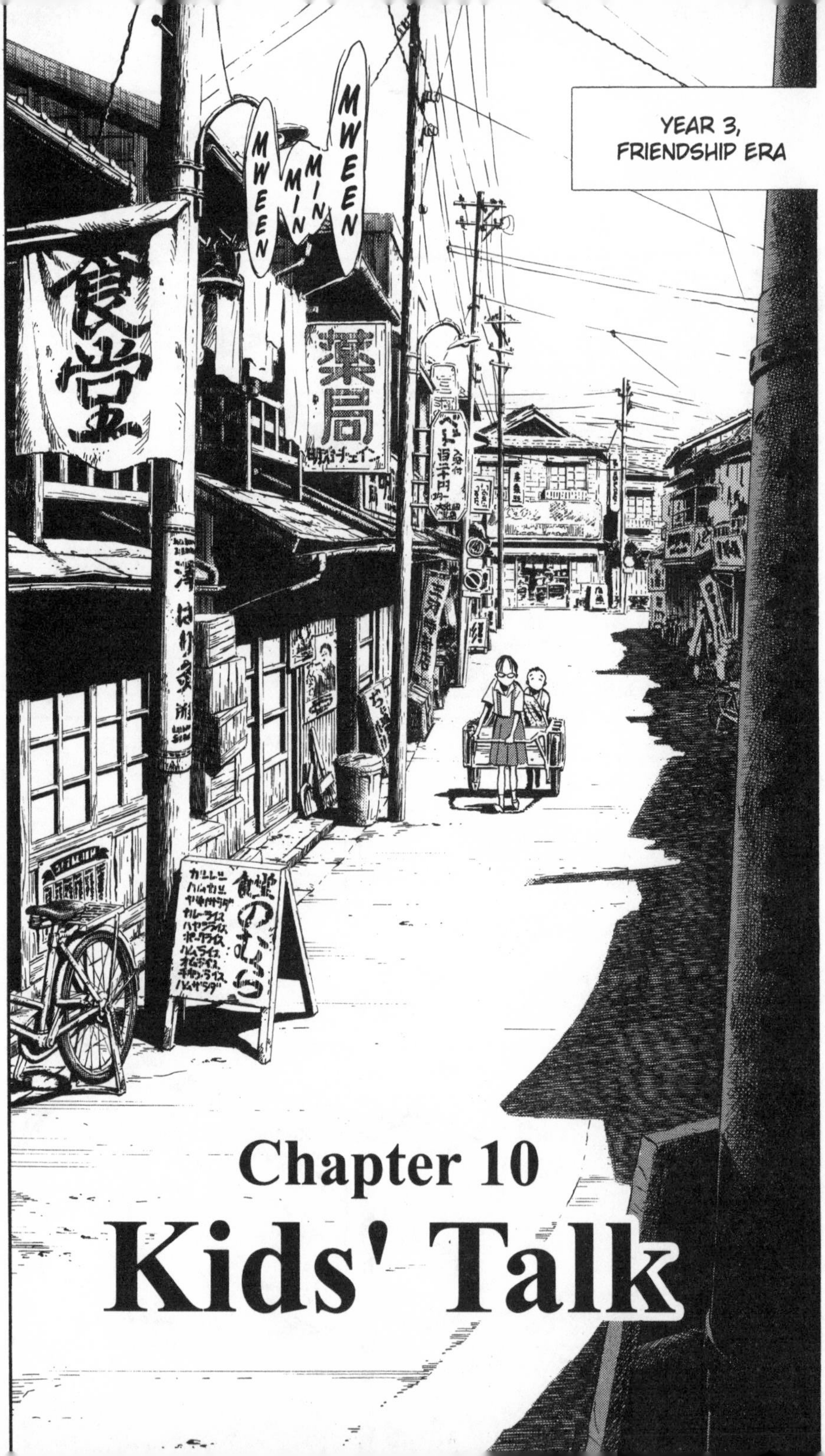
YEAR 3,
FRIENDSHIP ERA
MWEEN
MIN MIN
MWEEN
食堂
薬局

Chapter 10
Kids' Talk

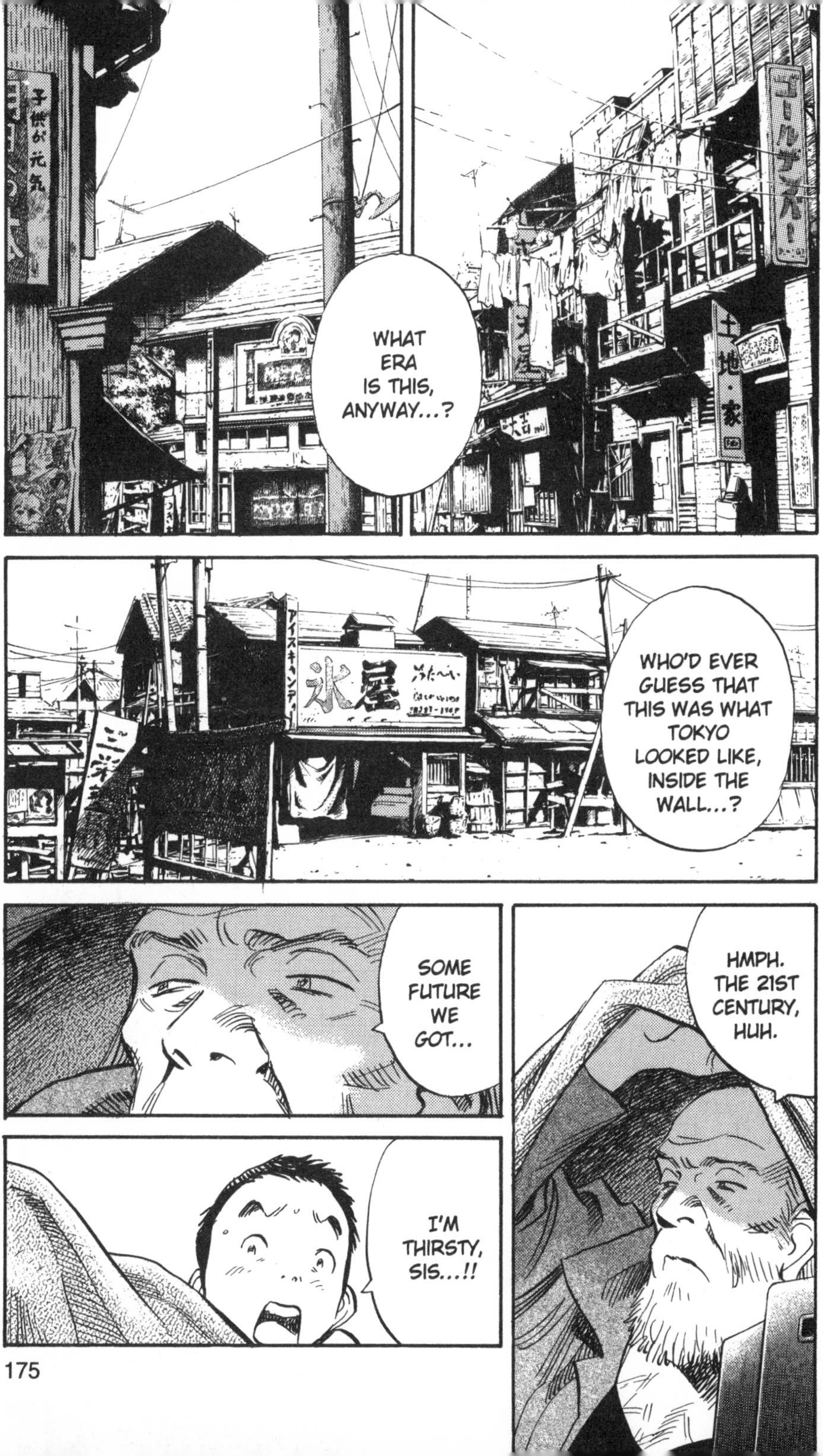

子供が元気
WHAT ERA IS THIS, ANYWAY...?
氷屋
WHO'D EVER GUESS THAT THIS WAS WHAT TOKYO LOOKED LIKE, INSIDE THE WALL...?
HMPH. THE 21ST CENTURY, HUH.
SOME FUTURE WE GOT...
I'M THIRSTY, SIS...!!

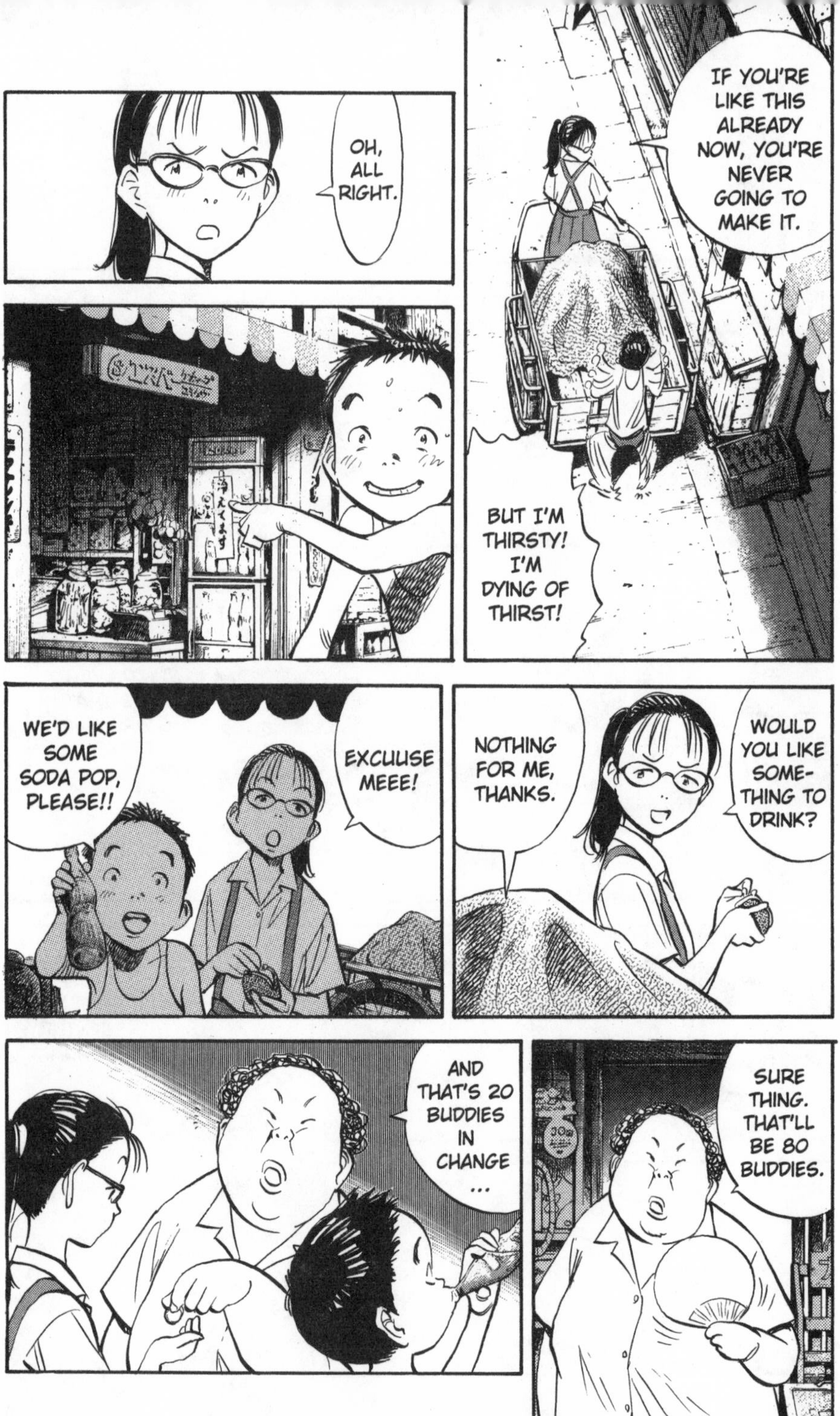
IF YOU'RE LIKE THIS ALREADY NOW, YOU'RE NEVER GOING TO MAKE IT.
BUT I'M THIRSTY! I'M DYING OF THIRST!
OH, ALL RIGHT.
WOULD YOU LIKE SOME-THING TO DRINK?
NOTHING FOR ME, THANKS.
EXCUUSE MEEE!
WE'D LIKE SOME SODA POP, PLEASE!!
SURE THING. THAT'LL BE 80 BUDDIES.
AND THAT'S 20 BUDDIES IN CHANGE ...

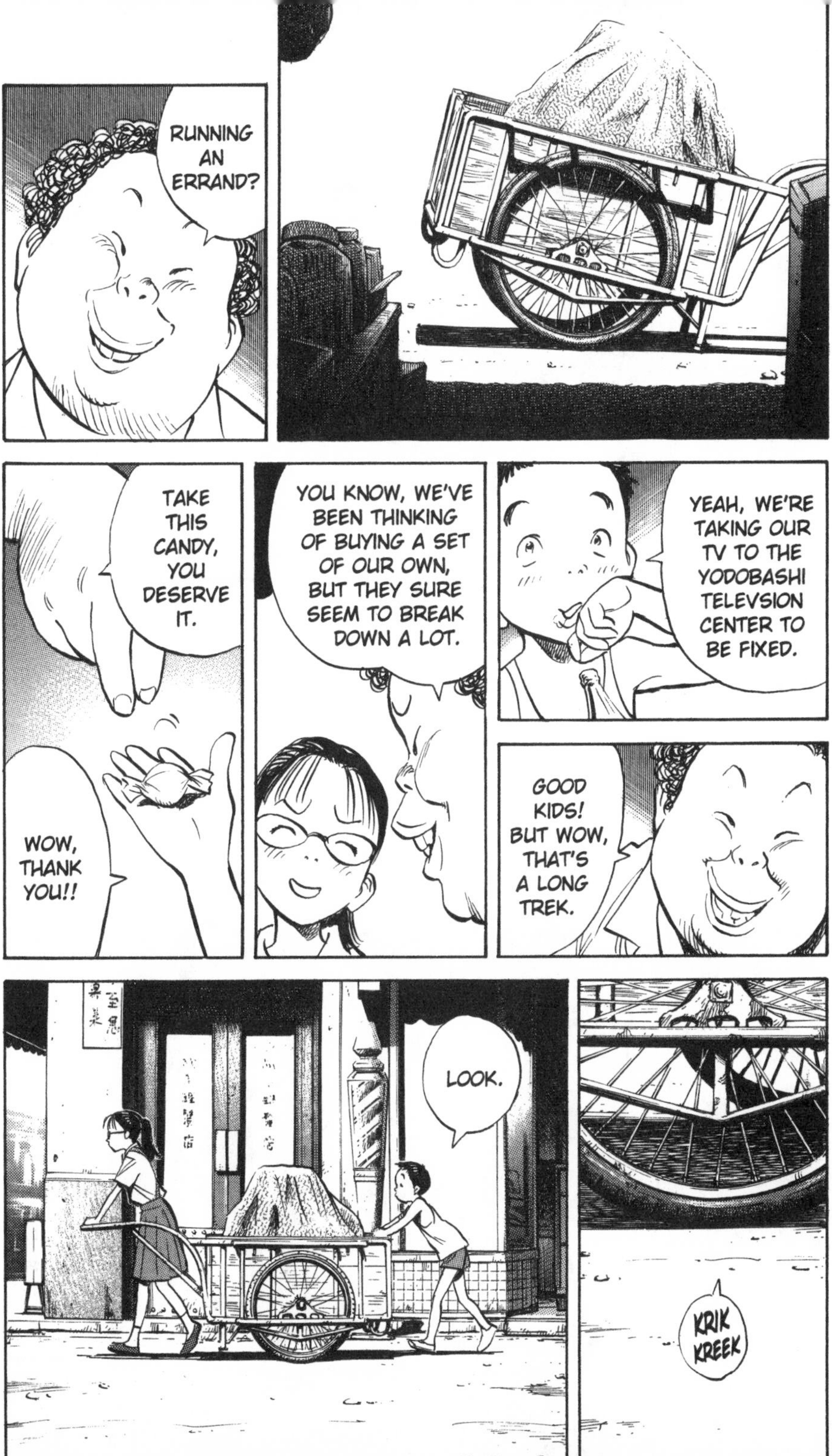
RUNNING AN ERRAND?
YEAH, WE'RE TAKING OUR TV TO THE YODOBASHI TELEVSION CENTER TO BE FIXED.
GOOD KIDS! BUT WOW, THAT'S A LONG TREK.
YOU KNOW, WE'VE BEEN THINKING OF BUYING A SET OF OUR OWN, BUT THEY SURE SEEM TO BREAK DOWN A LOT.
TAKE THIS CANDY, YOU DESERVE IT.
WOW, THANK YOU!!
KRIK KREEK
LOOK.

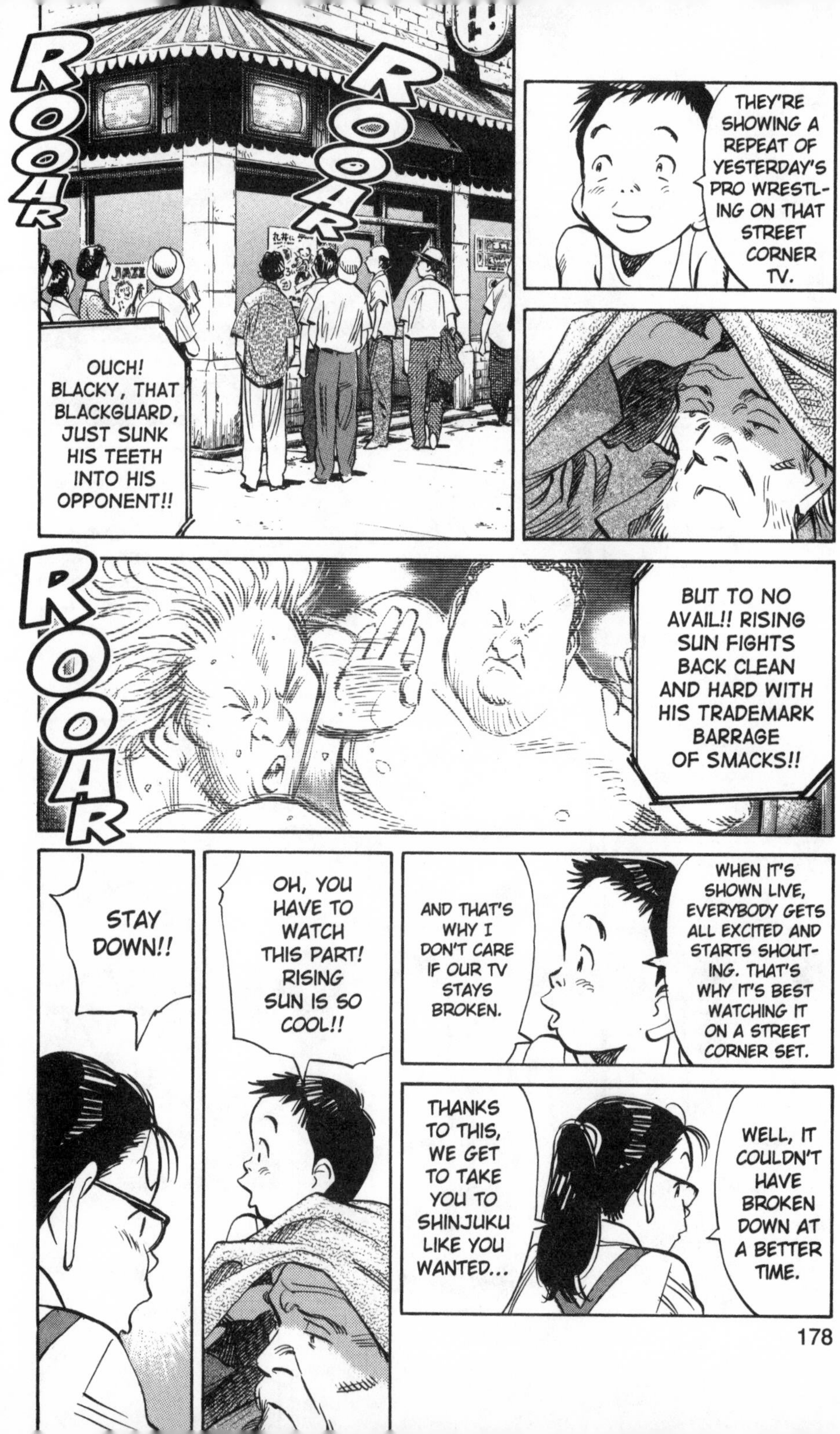
THEY'RE SHOWING A REPEAT OF YESTERDAY'S PRO WRESTL-ING ON THAT STREET CORNER TV.
ROOAR
ROOAR
OUCH! BLACKY, THAT BLACKGUARD, JUST SUNK HIS TEETH INTO HIS OPPONENT!!
ROOAR
BUT TO NO AVAIL!! RISING SUN FIGHTS BACK CLEAN AND HARD WITH HIS TRADEMARK BARRAGE OF SMACKS!!
WHEN IT'S SHOWN LIVE, EVERYBODY GETS ALL EXCITED AND STARTS SHOUT-ING. THAT'S WHY IT'S BEST WATCHING IT ON A STREET CORNER SET.
AND THAT'S WHY I DON'T CARE IF OUR TV STAYS BROKEN.
WELL, IT COULDN'T HAVE BROKEN DOWN AT A BETTER TIME.
THANKS TO THIS, WE GET TO TAKE YOU TO SHINJUKU LIKE YOU WANTED...
OH, YOU HAVE TO WATCH THIS PART! RISING SUN IS SO COOL!!
STAY DOWN!!

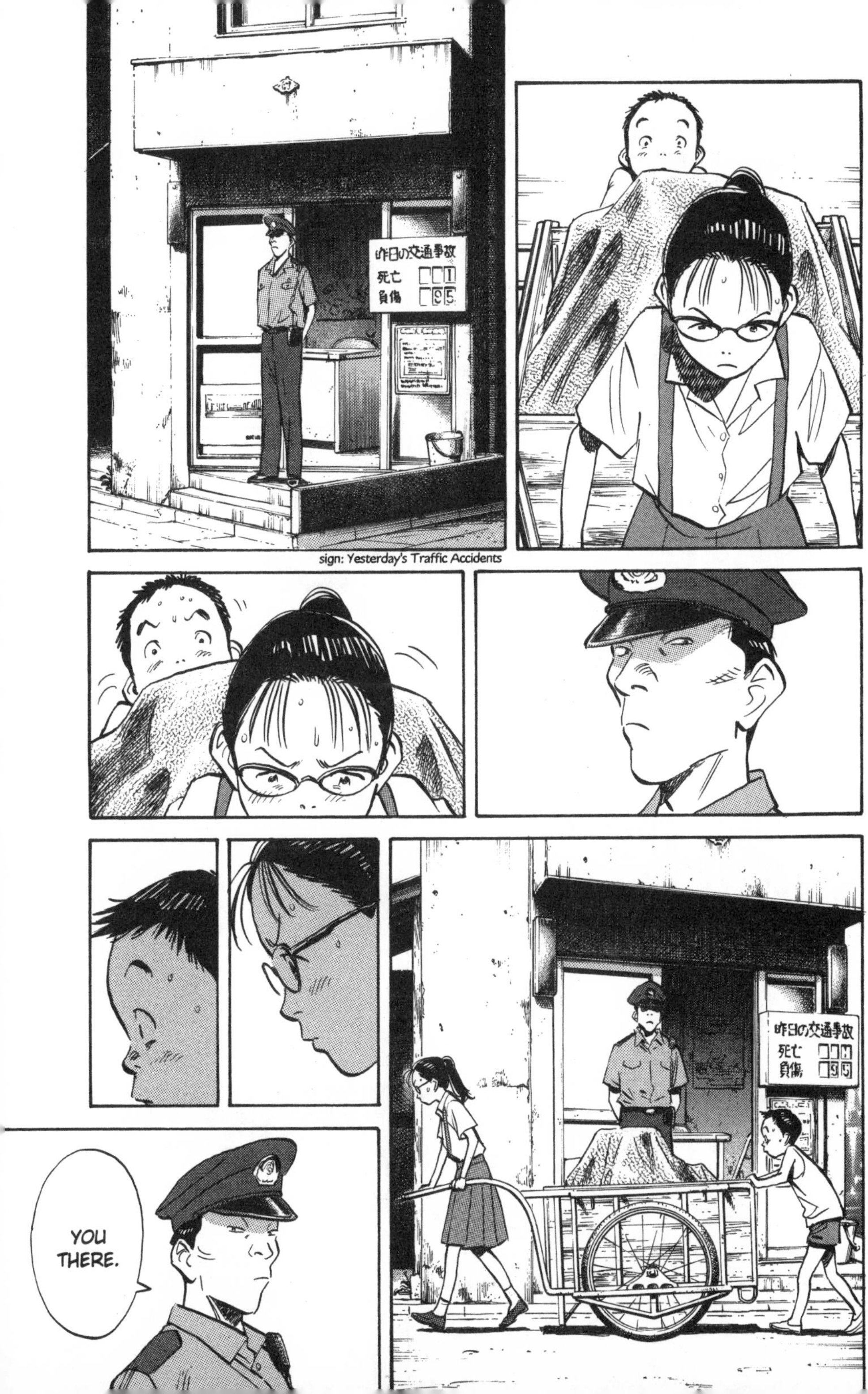
昨日の交通事故
死亡
負傷
sign: Yesterday's Traffic Accidents
昨日の交通事故
死亡
負傷
YOU THERE.

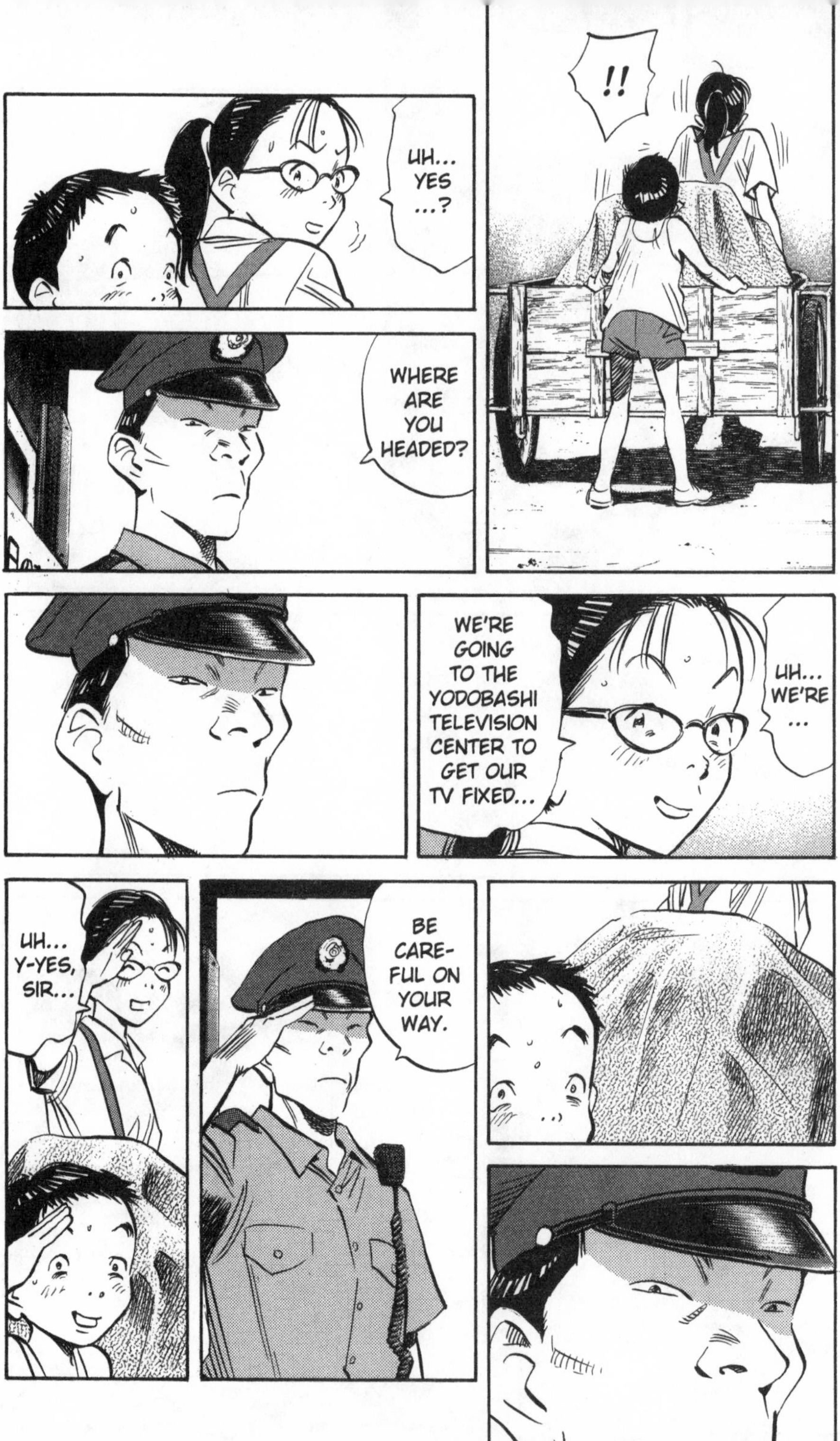
!!
UH... YES ...?
WHERE ARE YOU HEADED?
UH... WE'RE ...
WE'RE GOING TO THE YODOBASHI TELEVISION CENTER TO GET OUR TV FIXED...
...
BE CARE-FUL ON YOUR WAY.
UH... Y-YES, SIR...

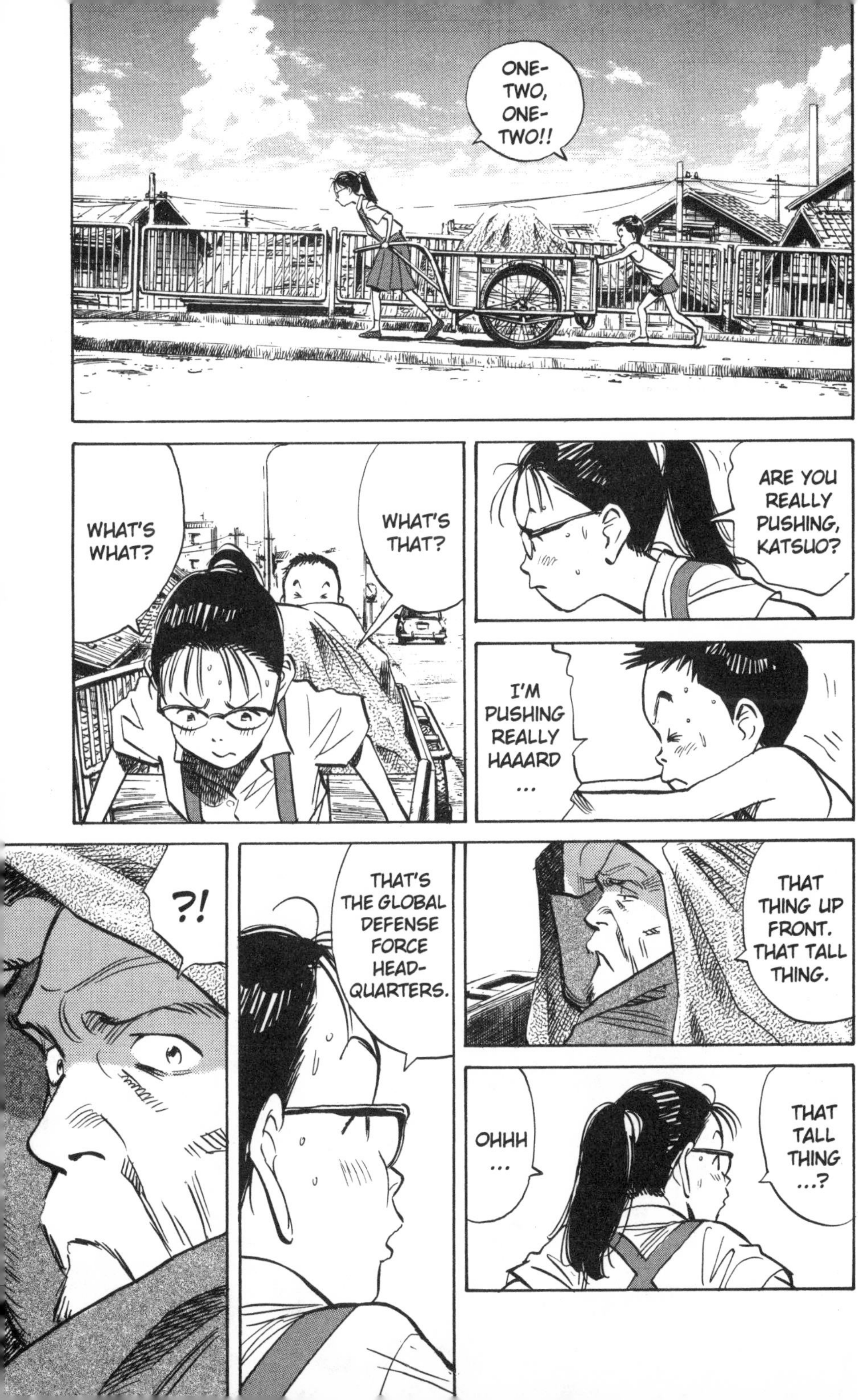
ONE-TWO, ONE-TWO!!
ARE YOU REALLY PUSHING, KATSUO?
I'M PUSHING REALLY HAAARD ...
WHAT'S THAT?
WHAT'S WHAT?
THAT THING UP FRONT. THAT TALL THING.
THAT TALL THING ...?
OHHH ...
THAT'S THE GLOBAL DEFENSE FORCE HEAD-QUARTERS.
?!

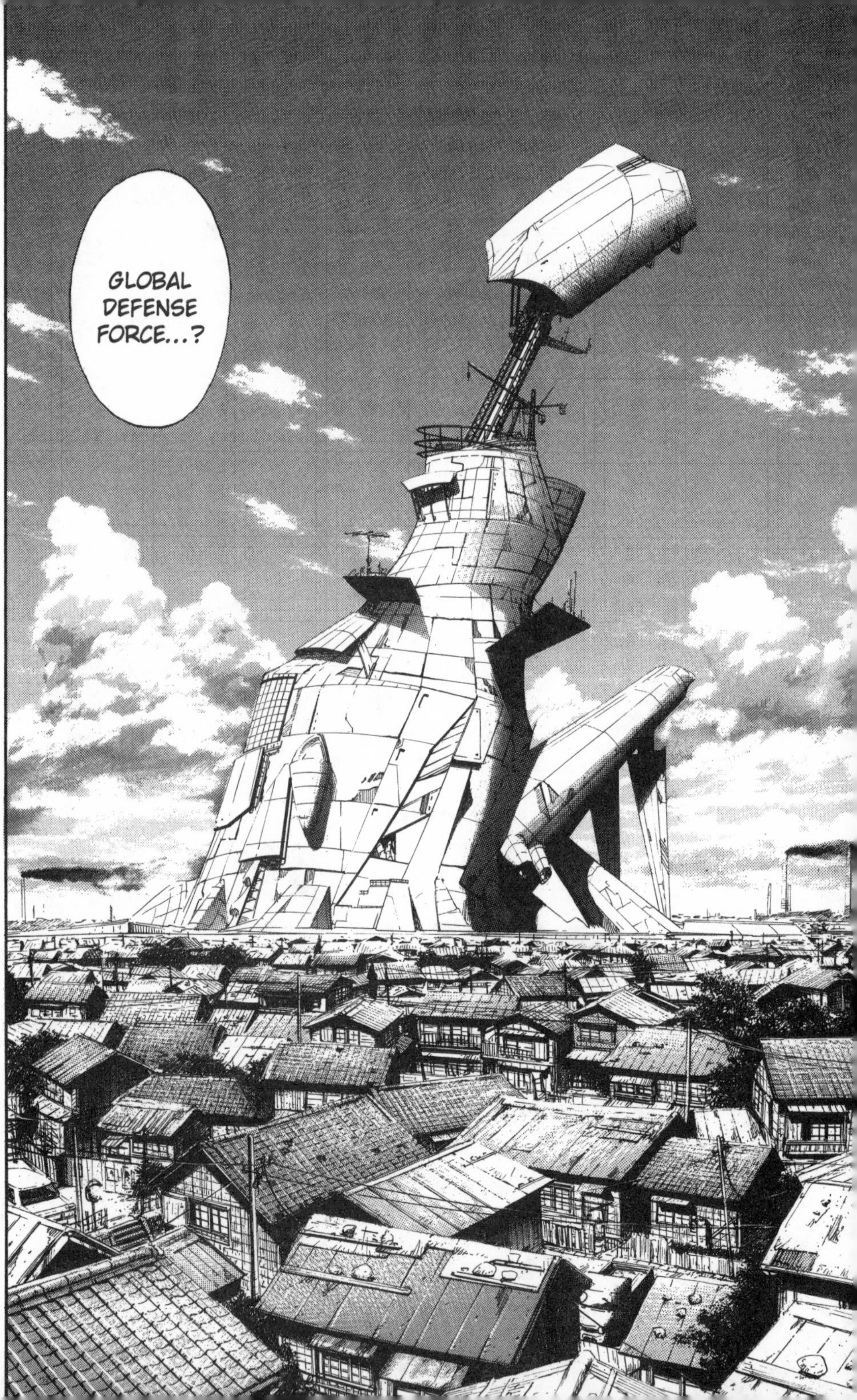
GLOBAL DEFENSE FORCE...?

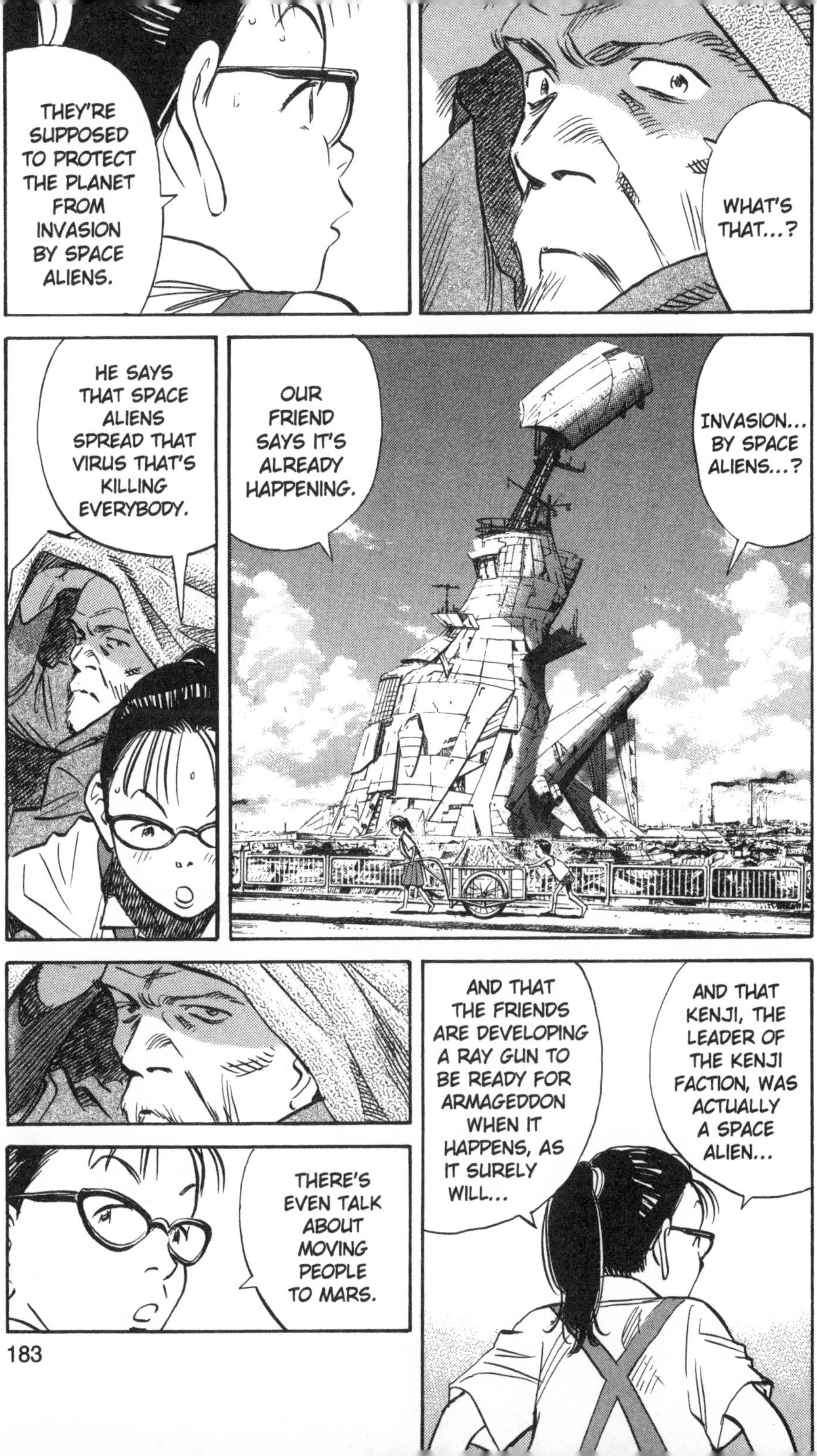
WHAT'S THAT...?
THEY'RE SUPPOSED TO PROTECT THE PLANET FROM INVASION BY SPACE ALIENS.
INVASION... BY SPACE ALIENS...?
OUR FRIEND SAYS IT'S ALREADY HAPPENING.
HE SAYS THAT SPACE ALIENS SPREAD THAT VIRUS THAT'S KILLING EVERYBODY.
AND THAT KENJI, THE LEADER OF THE KENJI FACTION, WAS ACTUALLY A SPACE ALIEN...
AND THAT THE FRIENDS ARE DEVELOPING A RAY GUN TO BE READY FOR ARMAGEDDON WHEN IT HAPPENS, AS IT SURELY WILL...
THERE'S EVEN TALK ABOUT MOVING PEOPLE TO MARS.

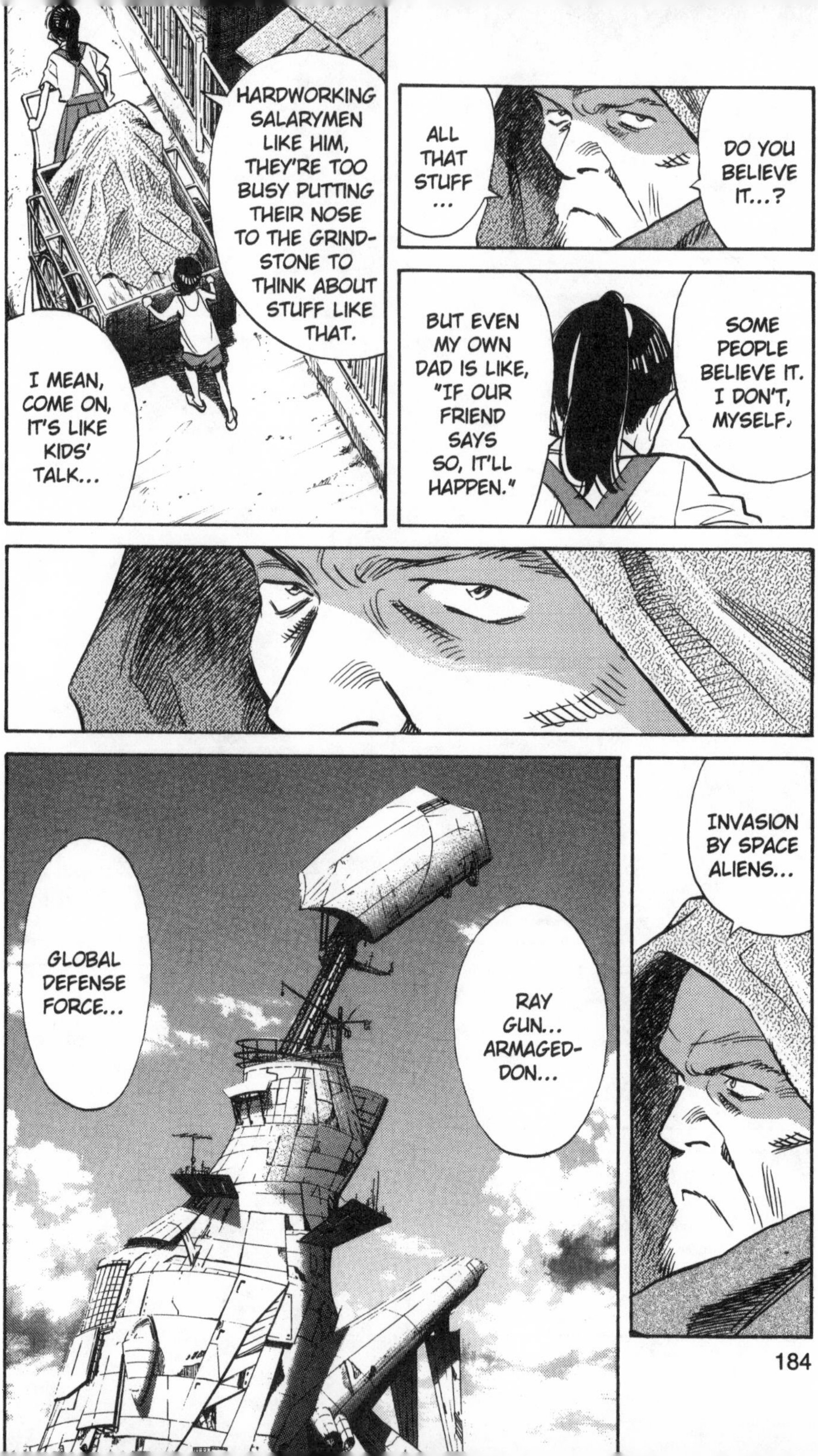
DO YOU BELIEVE IT...?
ALL THAT STUFF...
SOME PEOPLE BELIEVE IT. I DON'T, MYSELF.
BUT EVEN MY OWN DAD IS LIKE, "IF OUR FRIEND SAYS SO, IT'LL HAPPEN."
HARDWORKING SALARYMEN LIKE HIM, THEY'RE TOO BUSY PUTTING THEIR NOSE TO THE GRIND-STONE TO THINK ABOUT STUFF LIKE THAT.
I MEAN, COME ON, IT'S LIKE KIDS' TALK...
INVASION BY SPACE ALIENS...
RAY GUN... ARMAGED-DON...
GLOBAL DEFENSE FORCE...

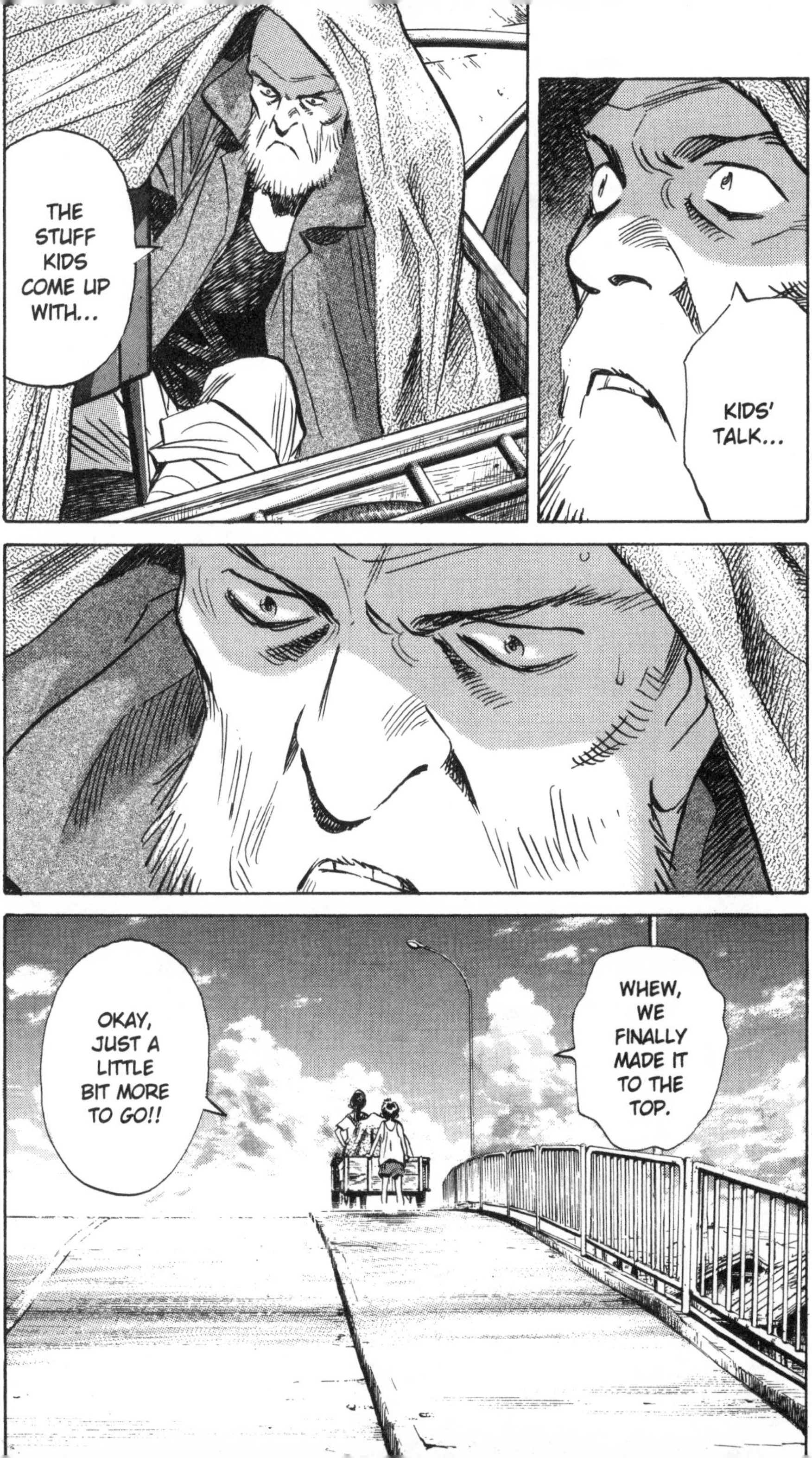
KIDS' TALK...
THE STUFF KIDS COME UP WITH...
WHEW, WE FINALLY MADE IT TO THE TOP.
OKAY, JUST A LITTLE BIT MORE TO GO!!

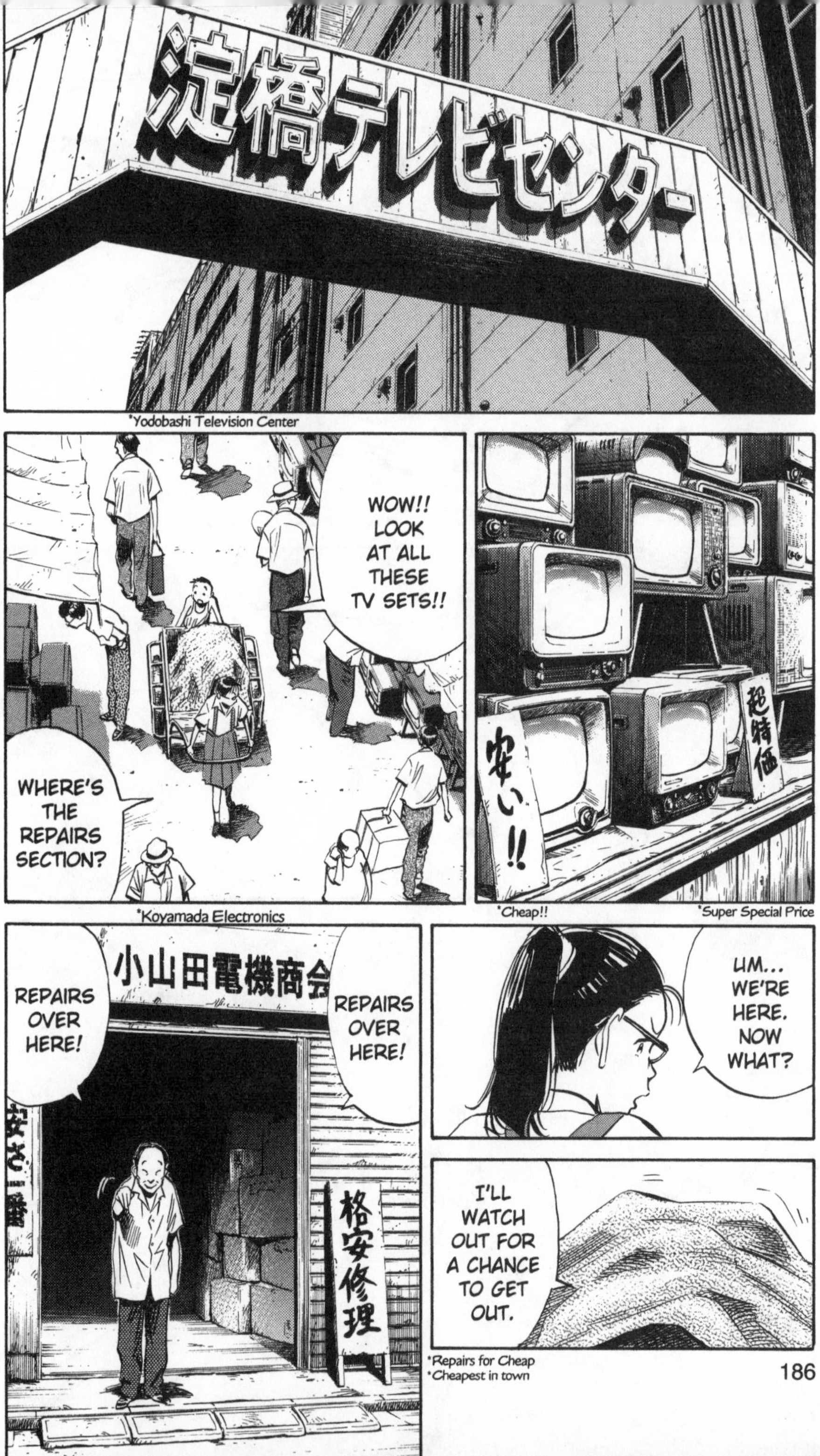

淀橋テレビセンター
超特価
安い!!
WOW!! LOOK AT ALL THESE TV SETS!!
WHERE'S THE REPAIRS SECTION?
UM... WE'RE HERE. NOW WHAT?
I'LL WATCH OUT FOR A CHANCE TO GET OUT.
小山田電機商会
REPAIRS OVER HERE!
REPAIRS OVER HERE!
格安修理

*Yodobashi Television Center

*Super Special Price

*Cheap!!

*Koyamada Electronics

*Repairs for Cheap

*Cheapest in town

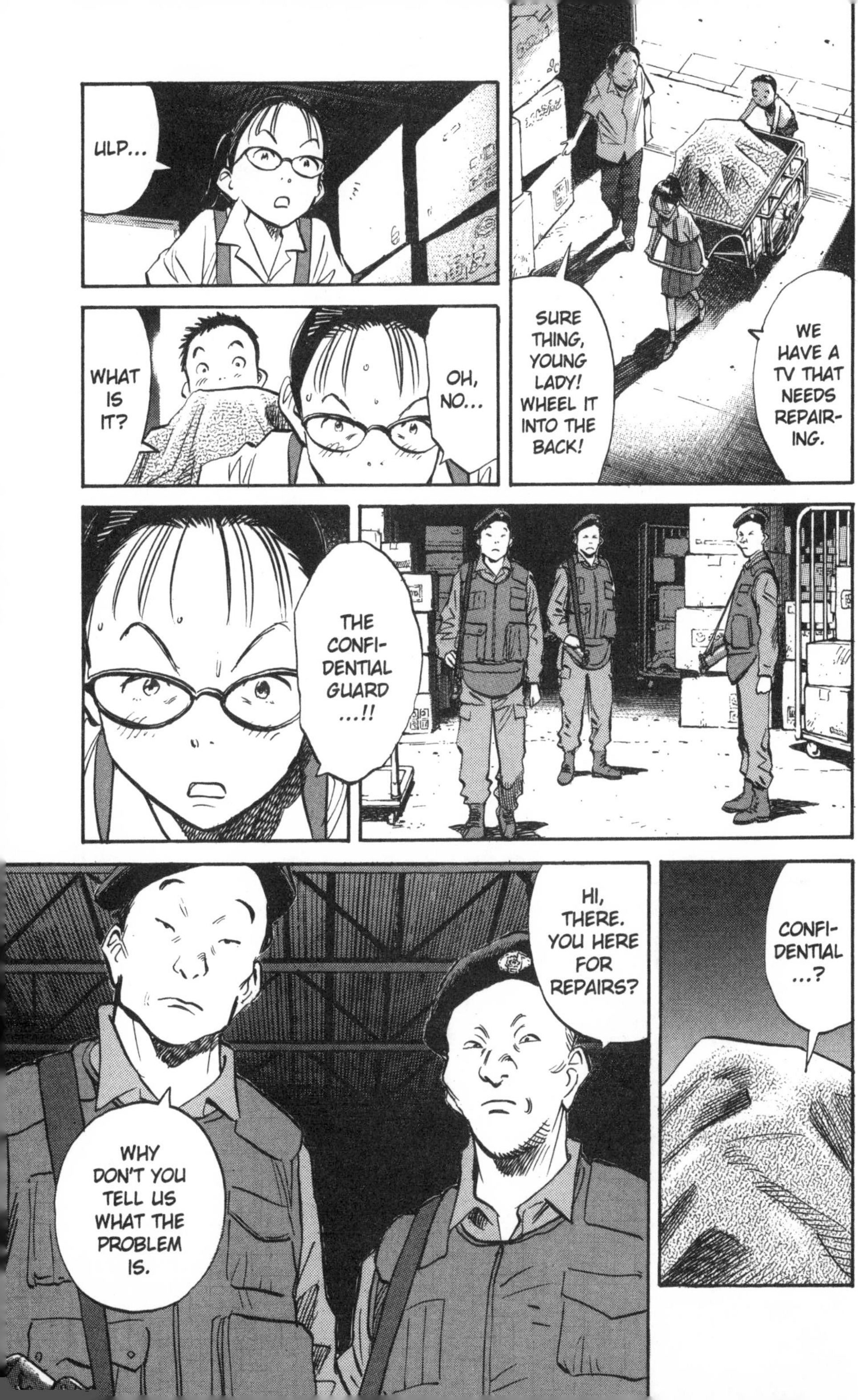
WE HAVE A TV THAT NEEDS REPAIR-ING.
SURE THING, YOUNG LADY! WHEEL IT INTO THE BACK!
ULP...
OH, NO...
WHAT IS IT?
THE CONFI-DENTIAL GUARD ...!!
CONFI-DENTIAL ...?
HI, THERE. YOU HERE FOR REPAIRS?
WHY DON'T YOU TELL US WHAT THE PROBLEM IS.

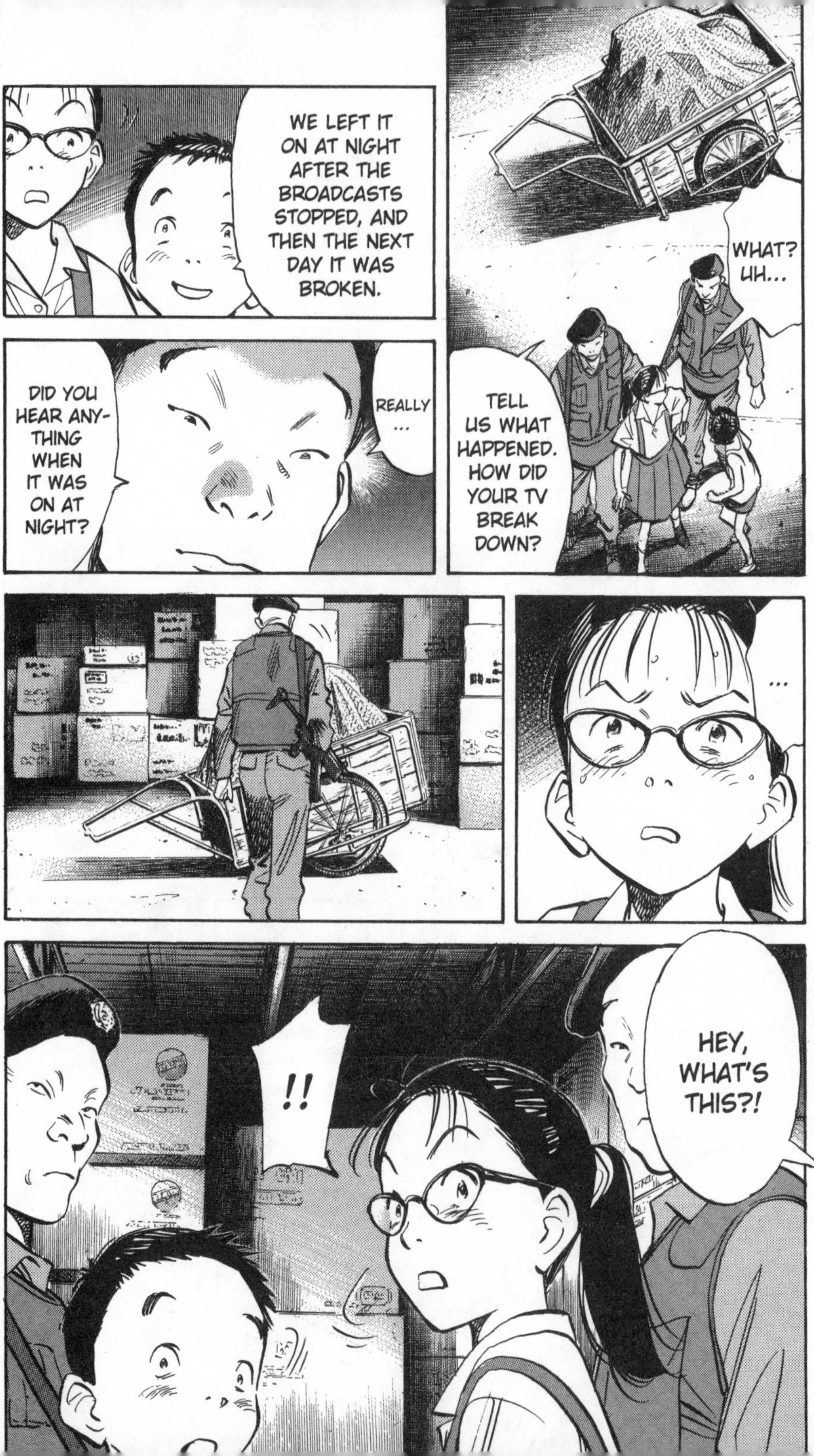
WHAT? UH...
TELL US WHAT HAPPENED. HOW DID YOUR TV BREAK DOWN?
WE LEFT IT ON AT NIGHT AFTER THE BROADCASTS STOPPED, AND THEN THE NEXT DAY IT WAS BROKEN.
REALLY ...
DID YOU HEAR ANYTHING WHEN IT WAS ON AT NIGHT?
...
HEY, WHAT'S THIS?!
!!

Chapter 11 Toy Chest

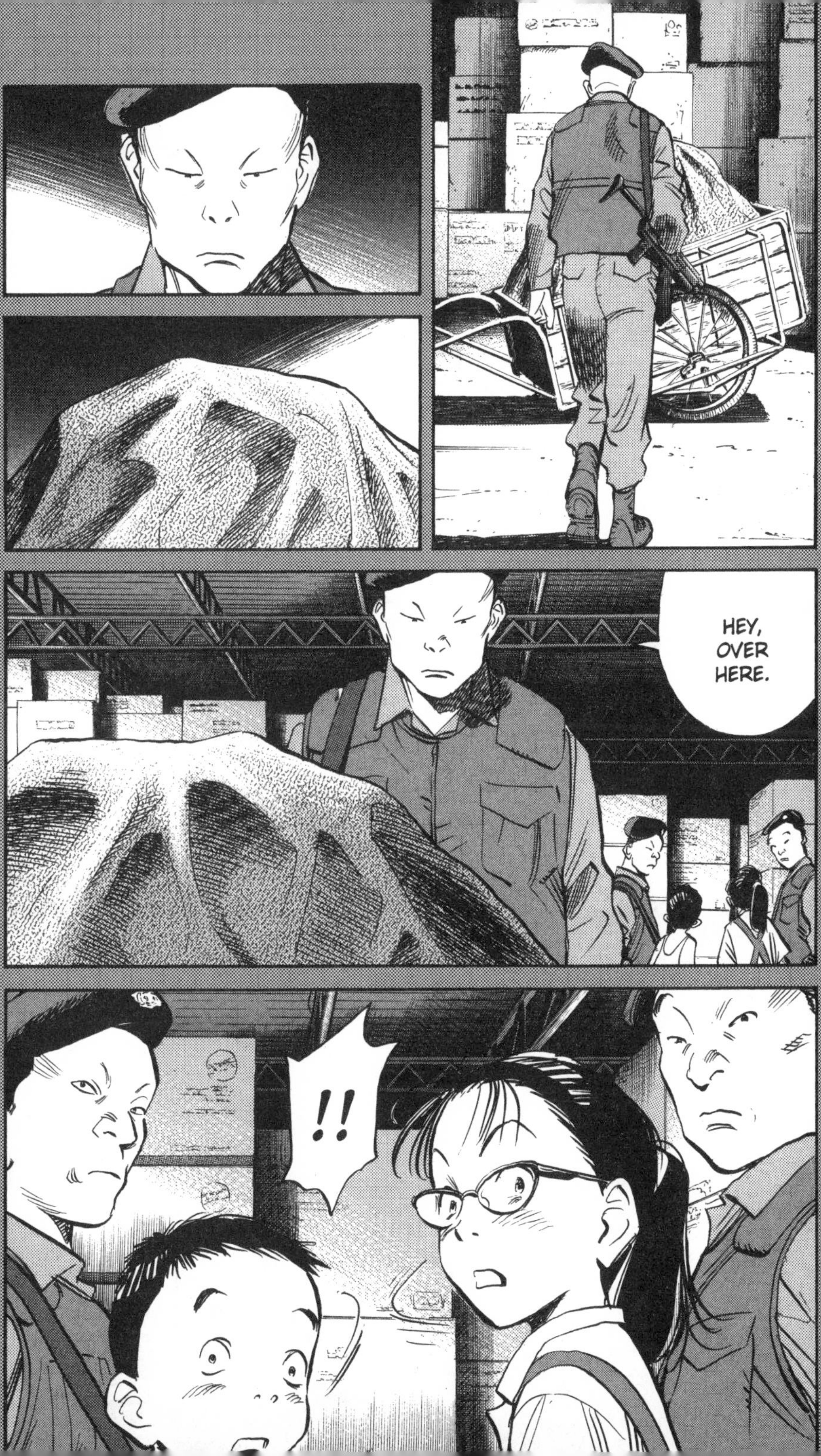
HEY, OVER HERE.
!!

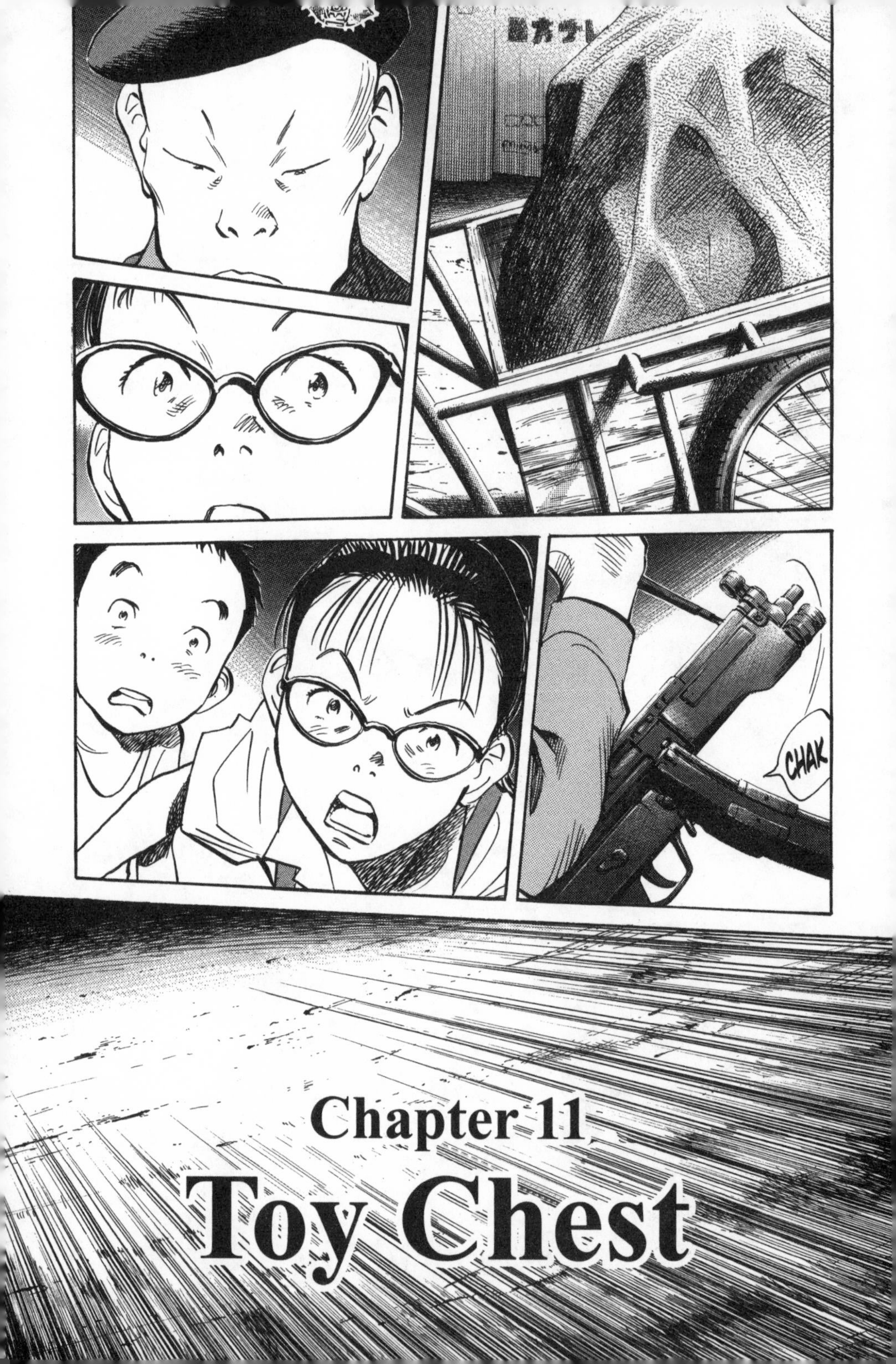
CHAK

Chapter 11

Toy Chest

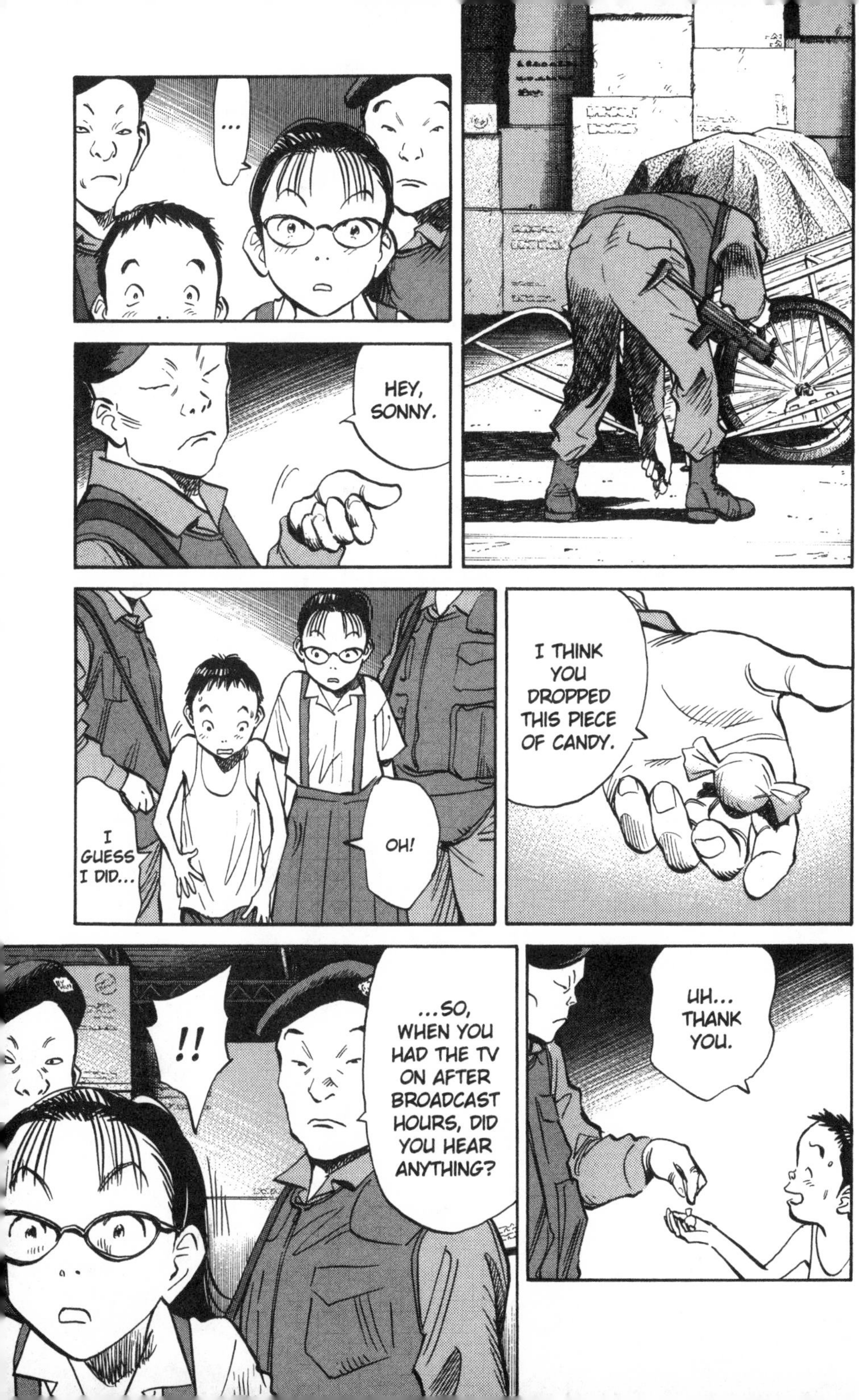
...
HEY, SONNY.
I THINK YOU DROPPED THIS PIECE OF CANDY.
OH!
I GUESS I DID...
UH... THANK YOU.
...SO, WHEN YOU HAD THE TV ON AFTER BROADCAST HOURS, DID YOU HEAR ANYTHING?
!!

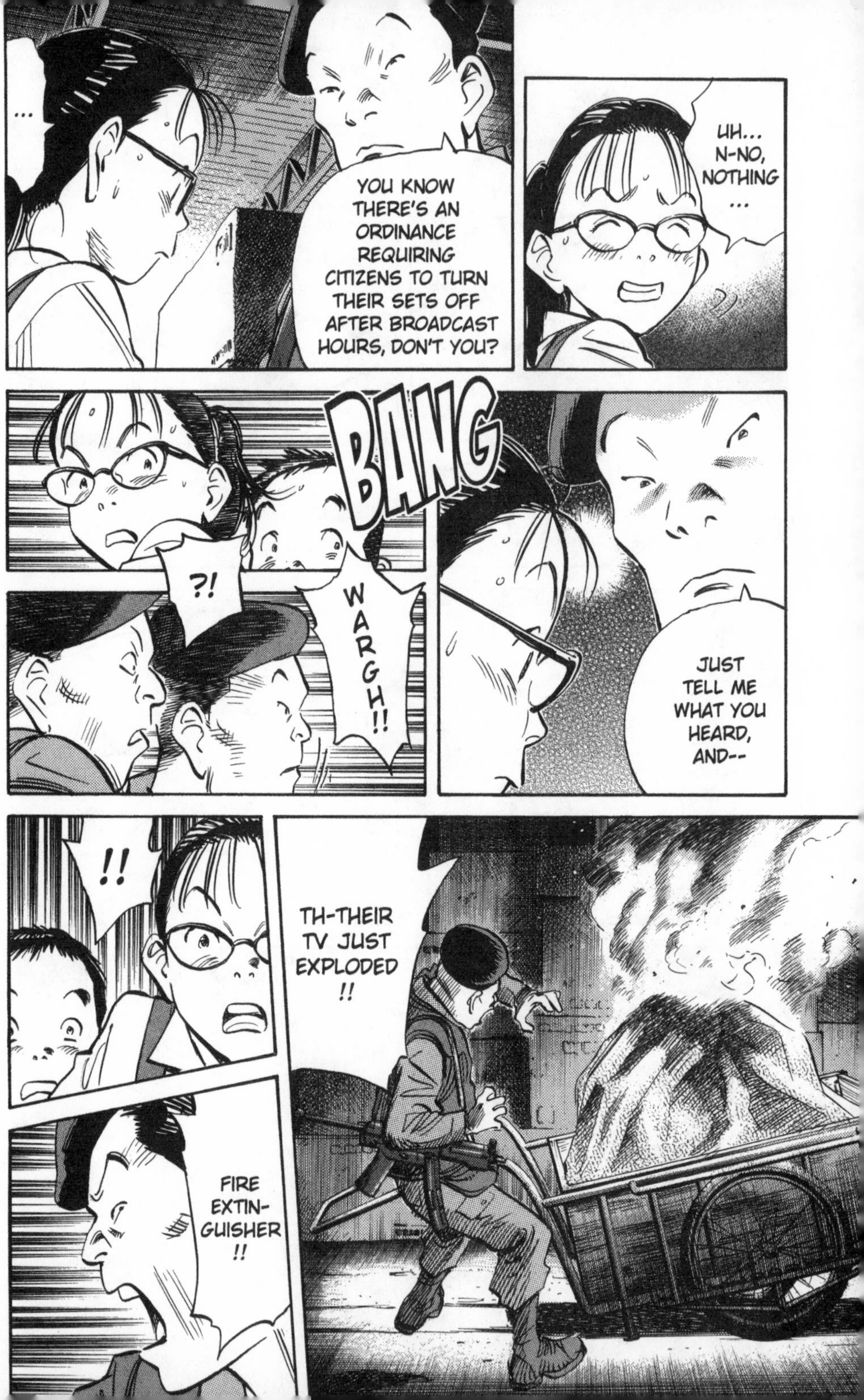
UH... N-NO, NOTHING...
YOU KNOW THERE'S AN ORDINANCE REQUIRING CITIZENS TO TURN THEIR SETS OFF AFTER BROADCAST HOURS, DON'T YOU?
...
JUST TELL ME WHAT YOU HEARD, AND--
BANG
?!
WARGH!!
TH-THEIR TV JUST EXPLODED!!
!!
FIRE EXTIN-GUISHER!!

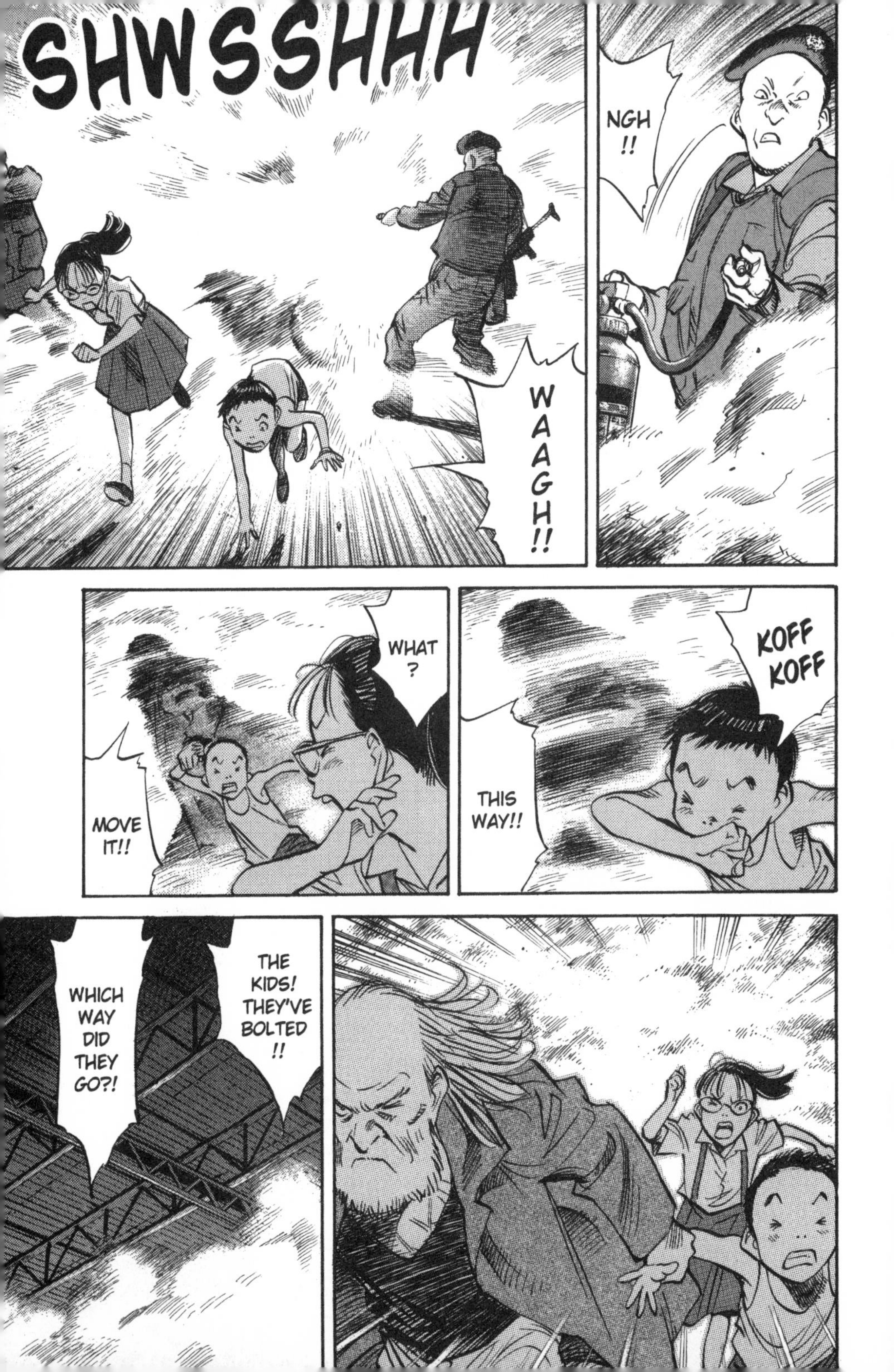
NGH!!
SHWSSHHH
WAAGH!!
KOFF KOFF
THIS WAY!!
WHAT?
MOVE IT!!
THE KIDS! THEY'VE BOLTED!!
WHICH WAY DID THEY GO?!

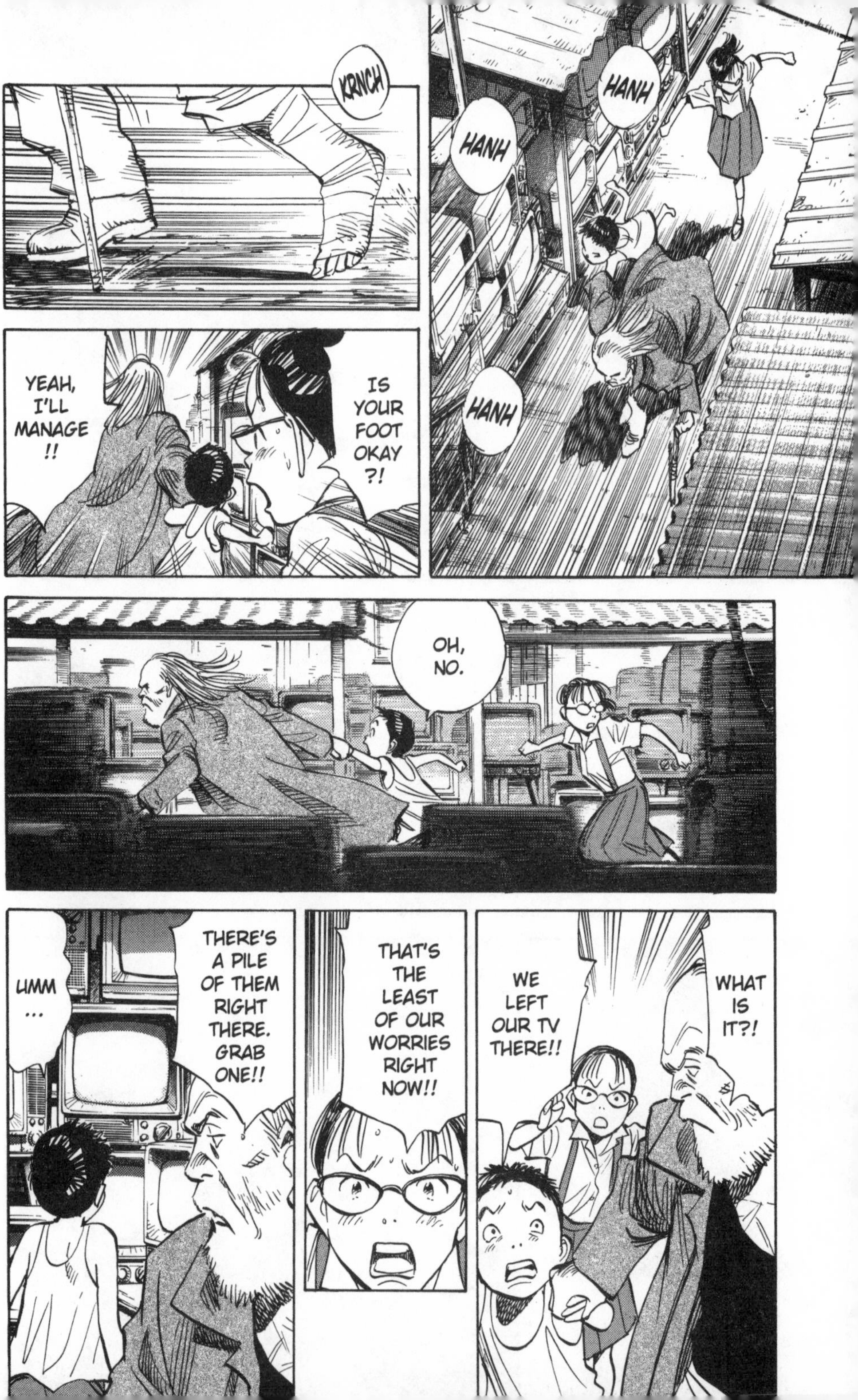
HANH
HANH
HANH
KRNCH
IS YOUR FOOT OKAY?!
YEAH, I'LL MANAGE!!
OH, NO.
WHAT IS IT?!
WE LEFT OUR TV THERE!!
THAT'S THE LEAST OF OUR WORRIES RIGHT NOW!!
THERE'S A PILE OF THEM RIGHT THERE. GRAB ONE!!
UMM ...

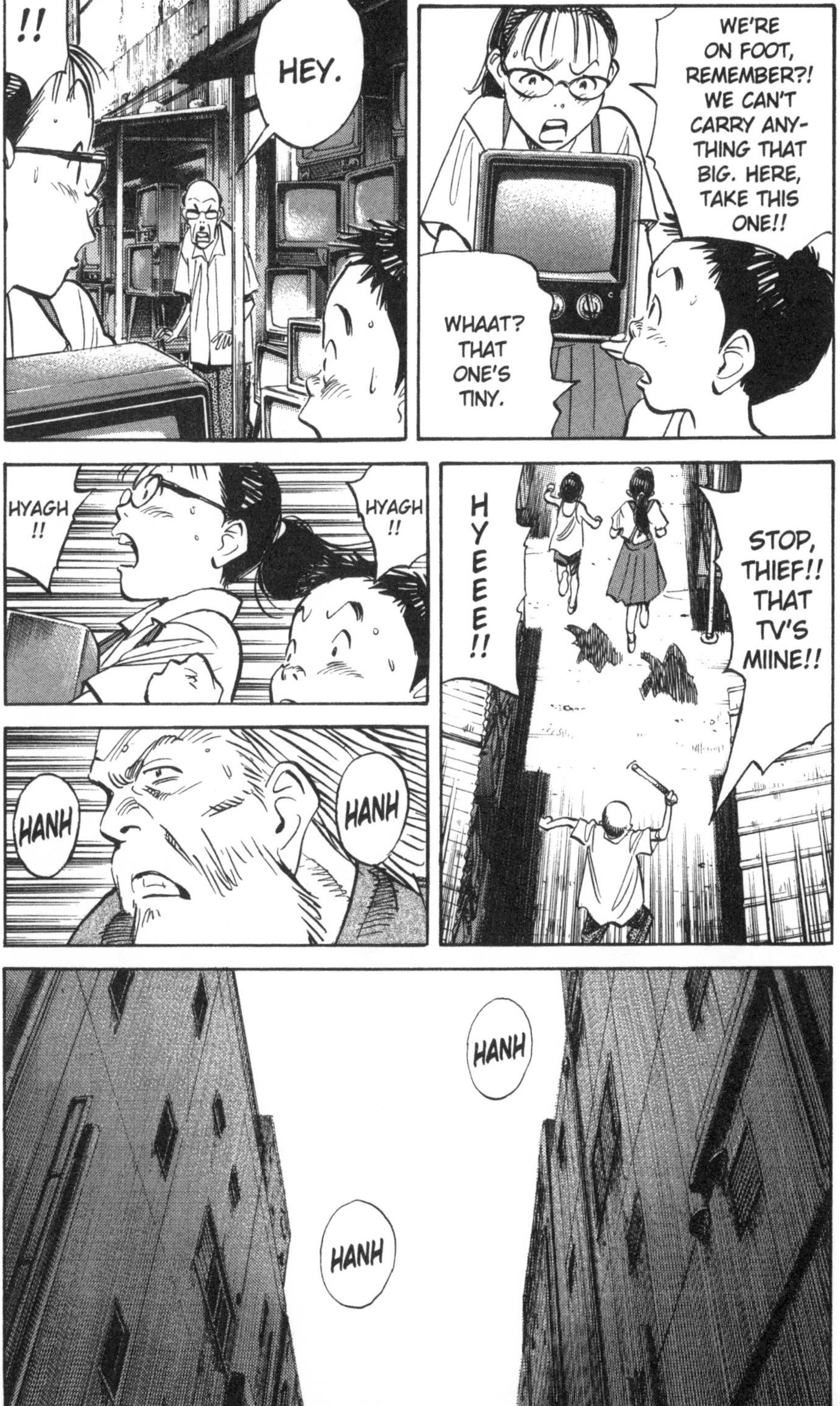
WE'RE ON FOOT, REMEMBER?! WE CAN'T CARRY ANY-THING THAT BIG. HERE, TAKE THIS ONE!!
WHAAT? THAT ONE'S TINY.
HEY.
!!
HYEEE!!
STOP, THIEF!! THAT TV'S MIINE!!
HYAGH !!
HYAGH !!
HANH
HANH
HANH
HANH

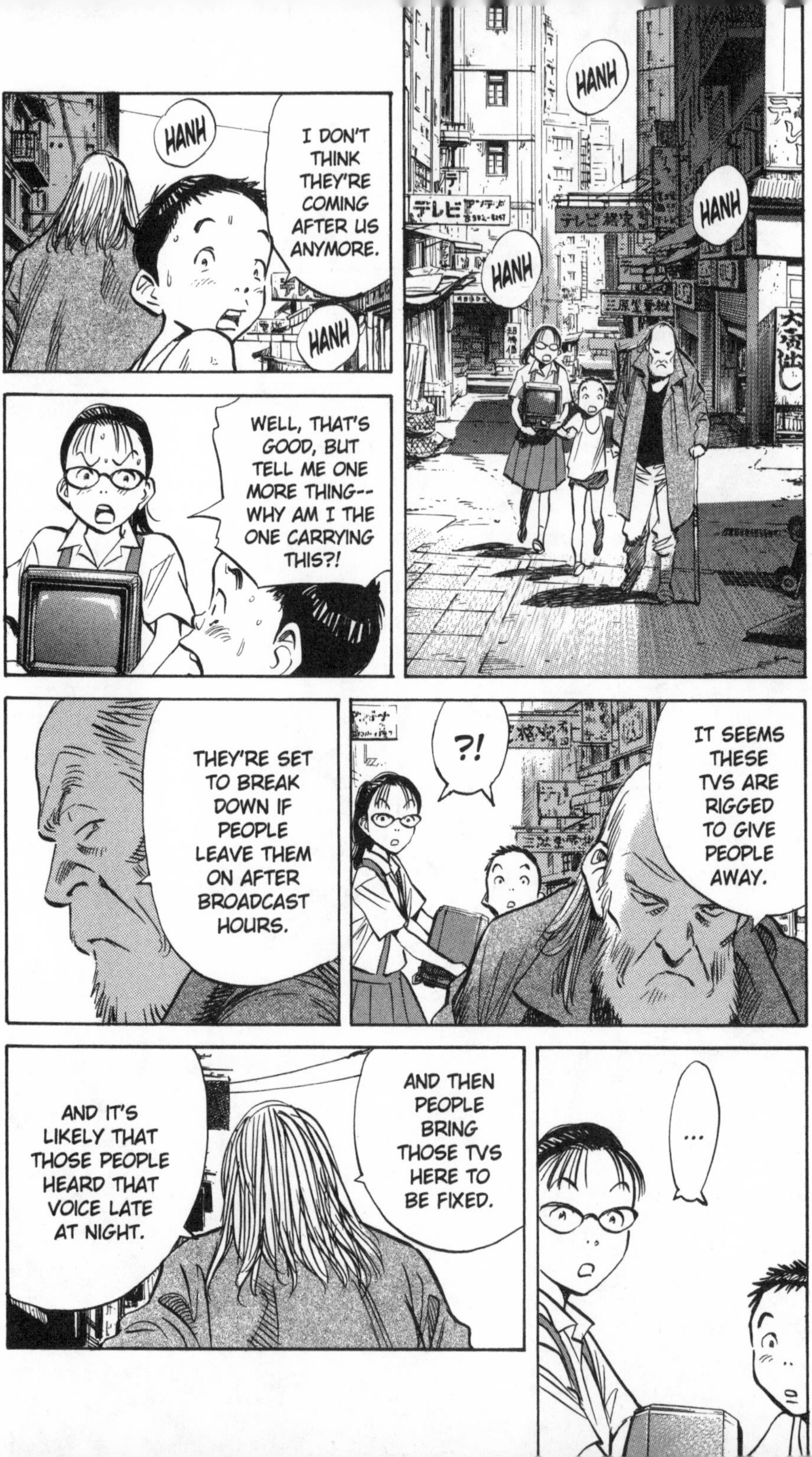
HANH
HANH
HANH
HANH
I DON'T THINK THEY'RE COMING AFTER US ANYMORE.
HANH
WELL, THAT'S GOOD, BUT TELL ME ONE MORE THING-- WHY AM I THE ONE CARRYING THIS?!
IT SEEMS THESE TVS ARE RIGGED TO GIVE PEOPLE AWAY.
?!
THEY'RE SET TO BREAK DOWN IF PEOPLE LEAVE THEM ON AFTER BROADCAST HOURS.
...
AND THEN PEOPLE BRING THOSE TVS HERE TO BE FIXED.
AND IT'S LIKELY THAT THOSE PEOPLE HEARD THAT VOICE LATE AT NIGHT.

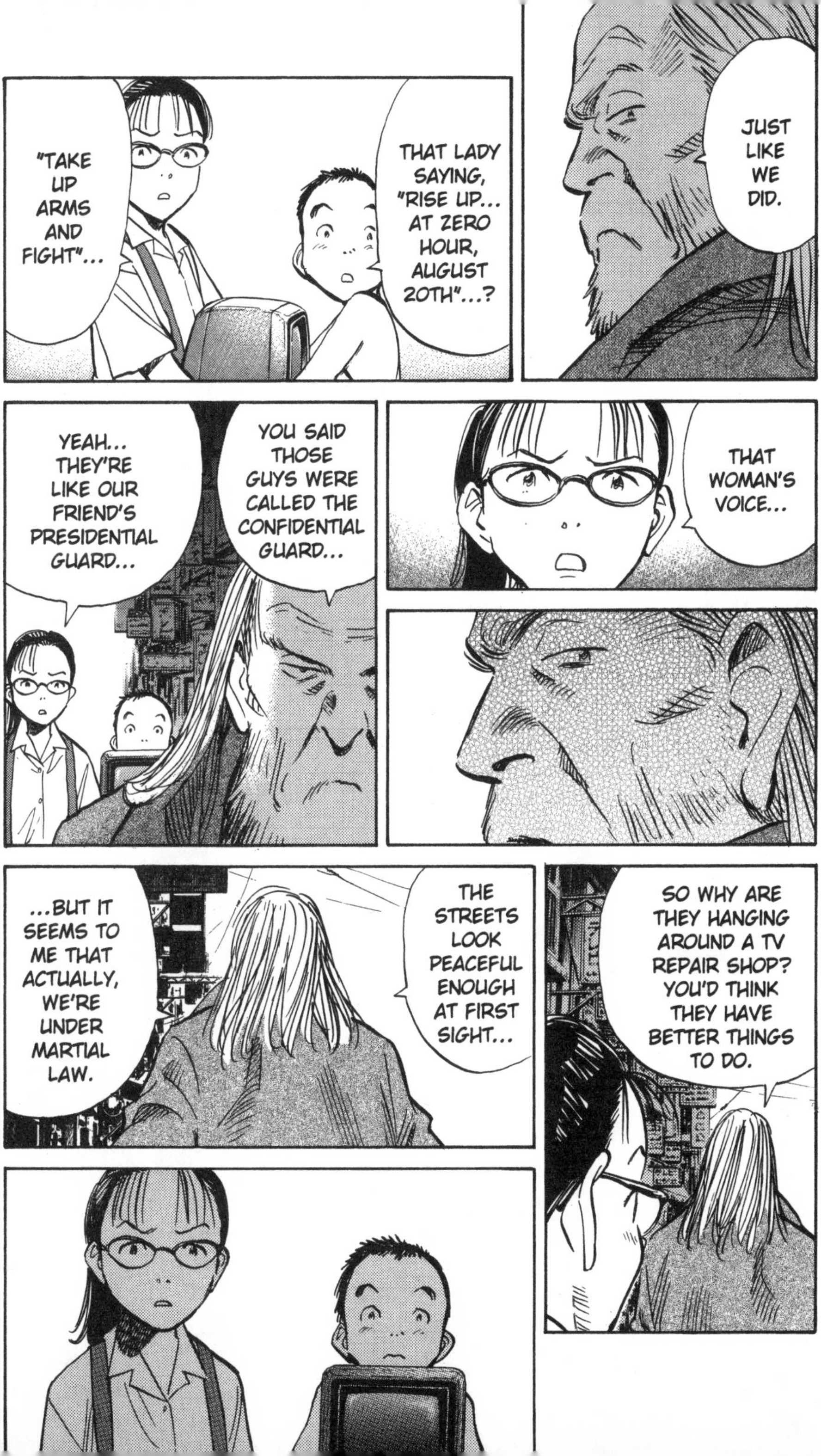
JUST LIKE WE DID.
THAT LADY SAYING, "RISE UP... AT ZERO HOUR, AUGUST 20TH"...?
"TAKE UP ARMS AND FIGHT"...
THAT WOMAN'S VOICE...
YOU SAID THOSE GUYS WERE CALLED THE CONFIDENTIAL GUARD...
YEAH... THEY'RE LIKE OUR FRIEND'S PRESIDENTIAL GUARD...
SO WHY ARE THEY HANGING AROUND A TV REPAIR SHOP? YOU'D THINK THEY HAVE BETTER THINGS TO DO.
THE STREETS LOOK PEACEFUL ENOUGH AT FIRST SIGHT...
...BUT IT SEEMS TO ME THAT ACTUALLY, WE'RE UNDER MARTIAL LAW.

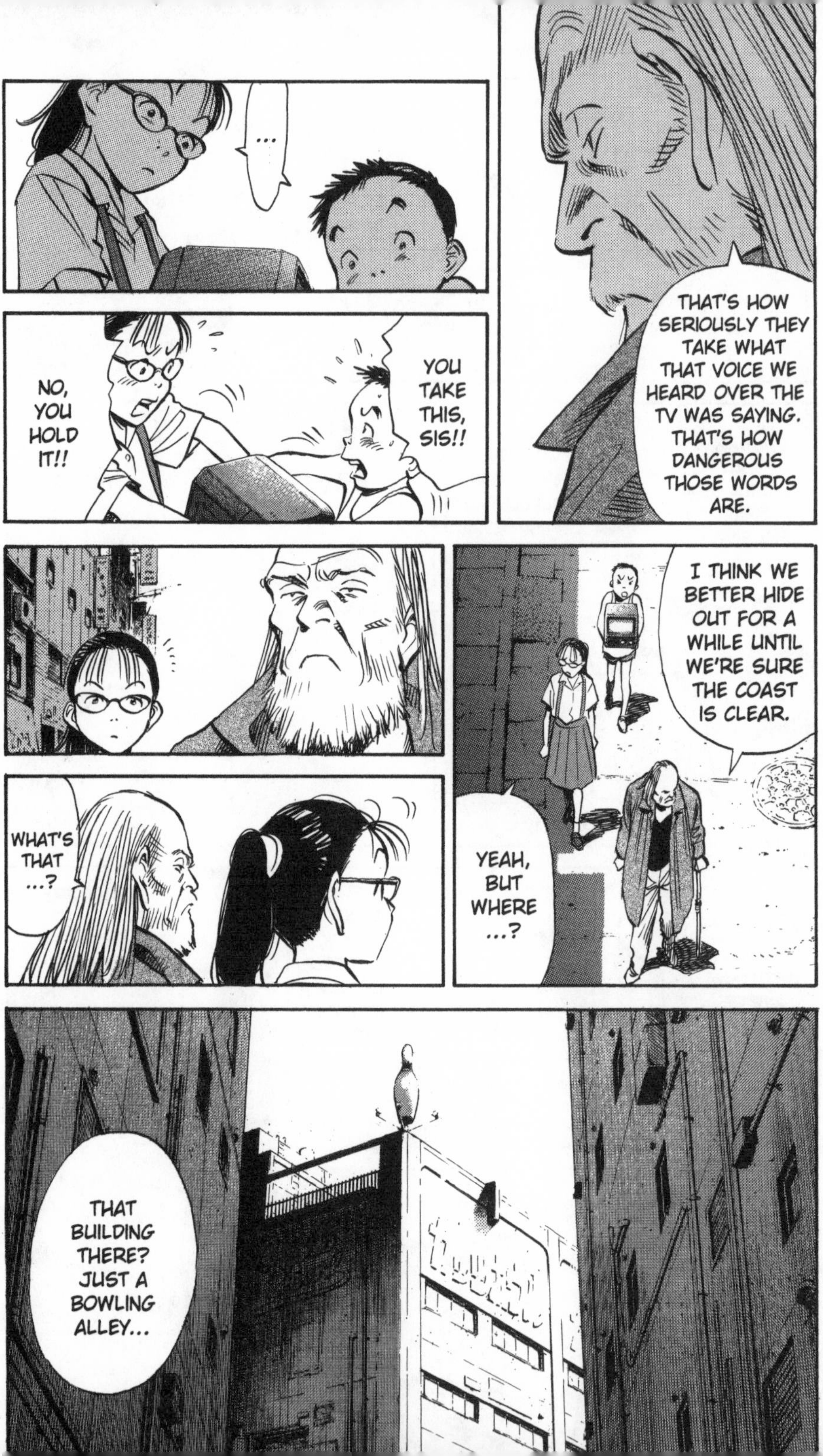
THAT'S HOW SERIOUSLY THEY TAKE WHAT THAT VOICE WE HEARD OVER THE TV WAS SAYING. THAT'S HOW DANGEROUS THOSE WORDS ARE.
...
YOU TAKE THIS, SIS!!
NO, YOU HOLD IT!!
I THINK WE BETTER HIDE OUT FOR A WHILE UNTIL WE'RE SURE THE COAST IS CLEAR.
YEAH, BUT WHERE ...?
WHAT'S THAT ...?
THAT BUILDING THERE? JUST A BOWLING ALLEY...

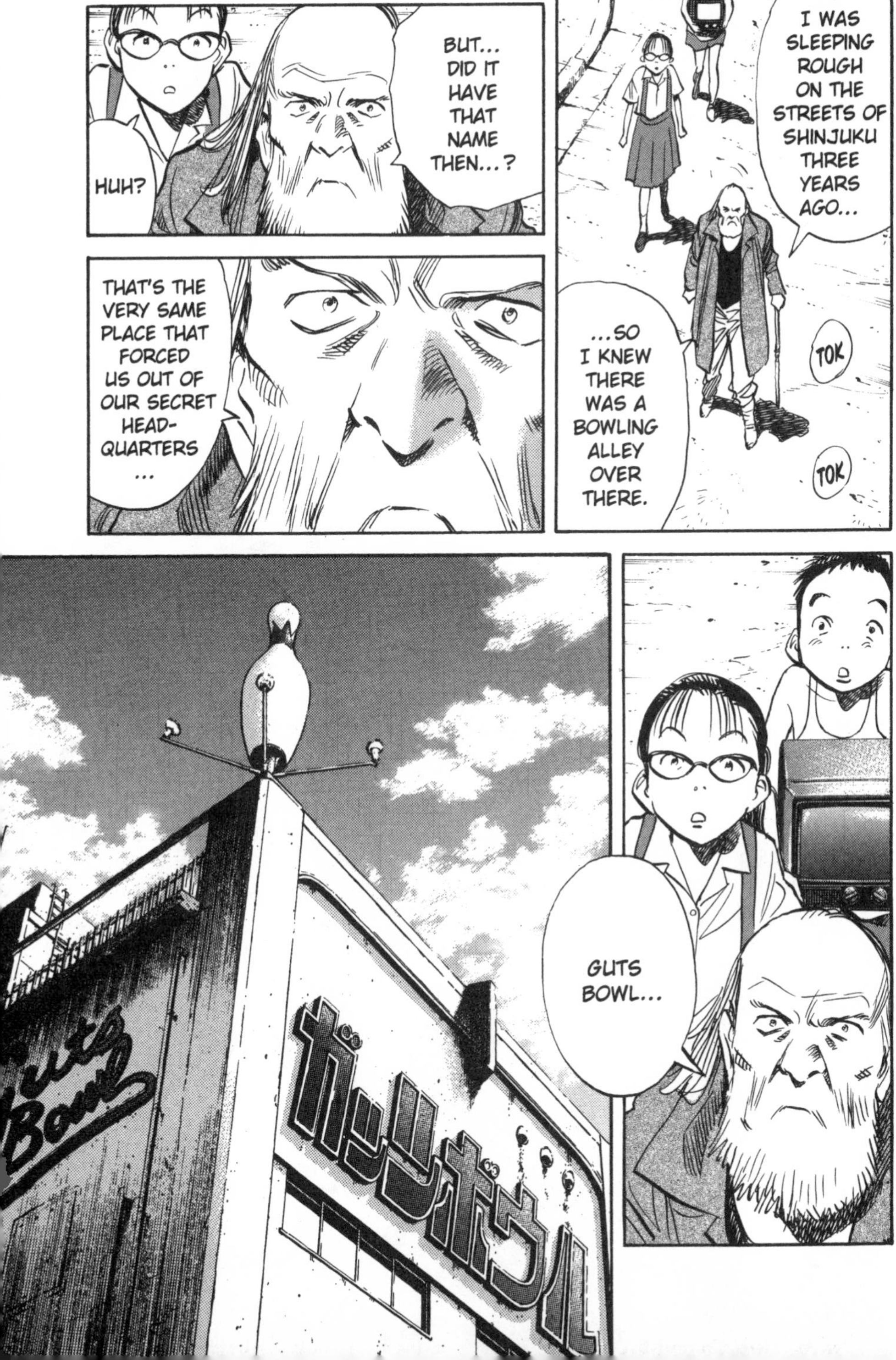
I WAS SLEEPING ROUGH ON THE STREETS OF SHINJUKU THREE YEARS AGO...
TOK
...SO I KNEW THERE WAS A BOWLING ALLEY OVER THERE.
TOK
BUT... DID IT HAVE THAT NAME THEN...?
HUH?
THAT'S THE VERY SAME PLACE THAT FORCED US OUT OF OUR SECRET HEAD-QUARTERS...
GUTS BOWL...
ガッツボウル
Guts Bowl

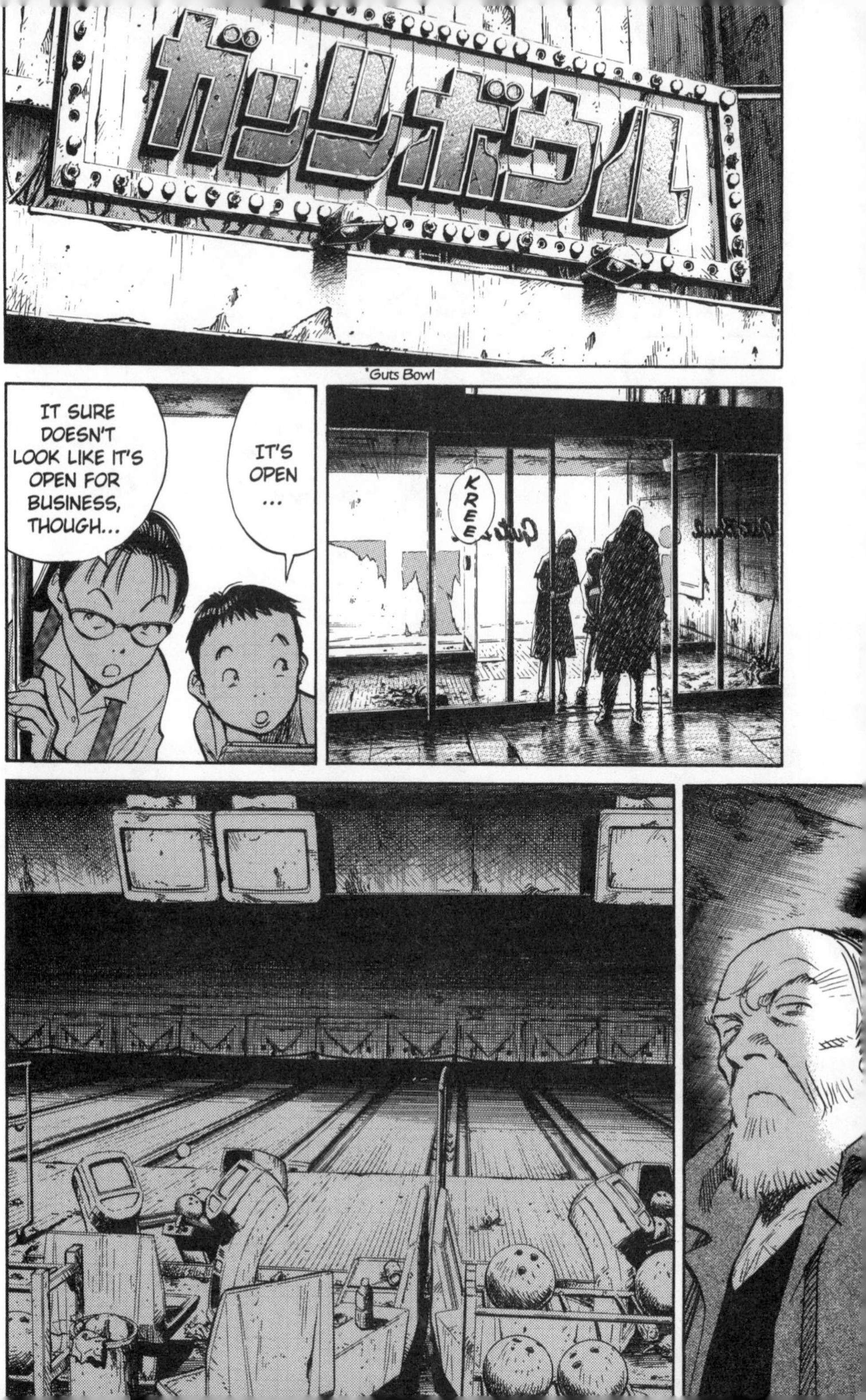
ガッツボウル
*Guts Bowl
KREE
IT'S OPEN ...
IT SURE DOESN'T LOOK LIKE IT'S OPEN FOR BUSINESS, THOUGH...

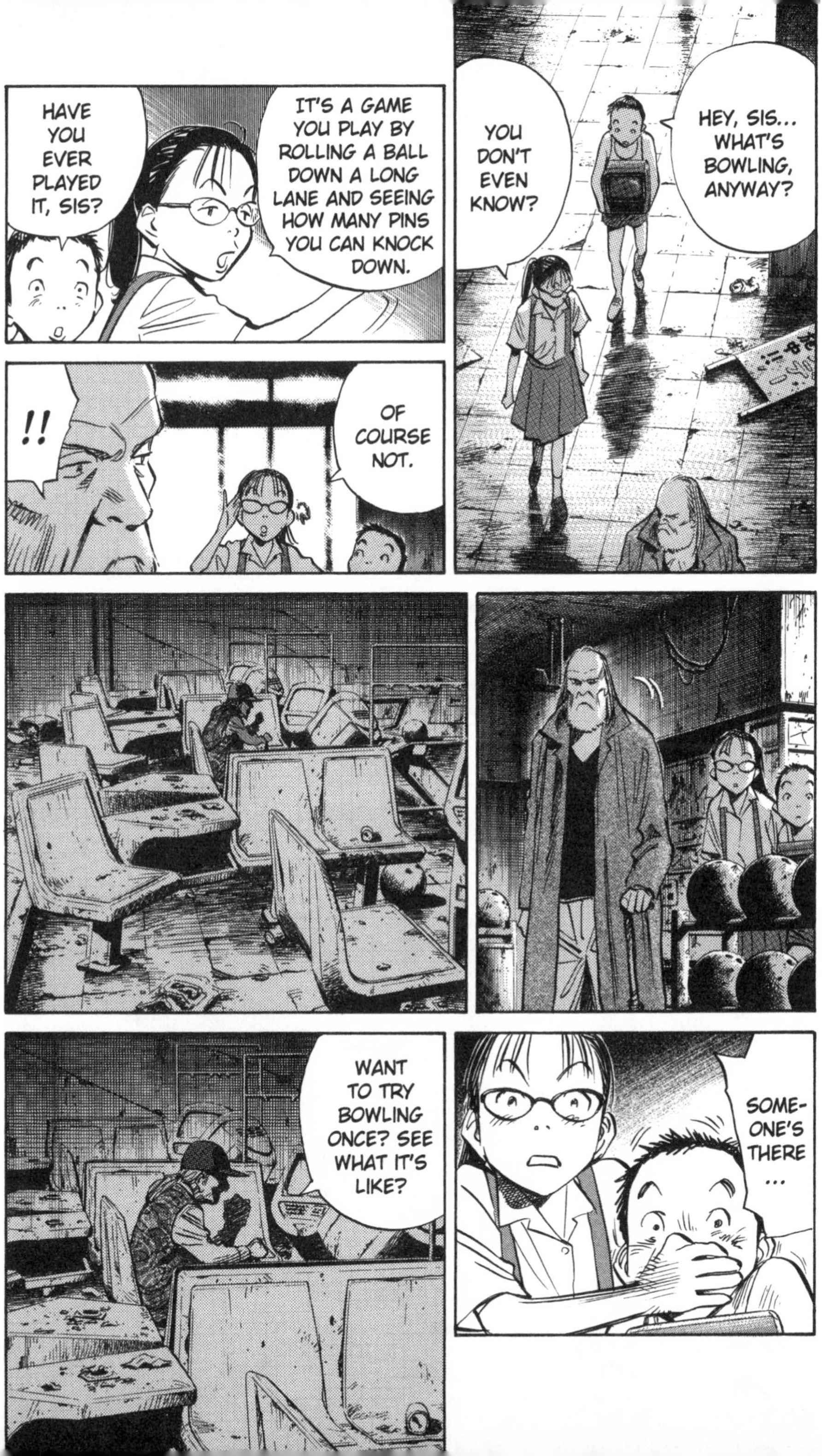
HEY, SIS... WHAT'S BOWLING, ANYWAY?
YOU DON'T EVEN KNOW?
IT'S A GAME YOU PLAY BY ROLLING A BALL DOWN A LONG LANE AND SEEING HOW MANY PINS YOU CAN KNOCK DOWN.
HAVE YOU EVER PLAYED IT, SIS?
OF COURSE NOT.
!!
SOME-ONE'S THERE ...
WANT TO TRY BOWLING ONCE? SEE WHAT IT'S LIKE?

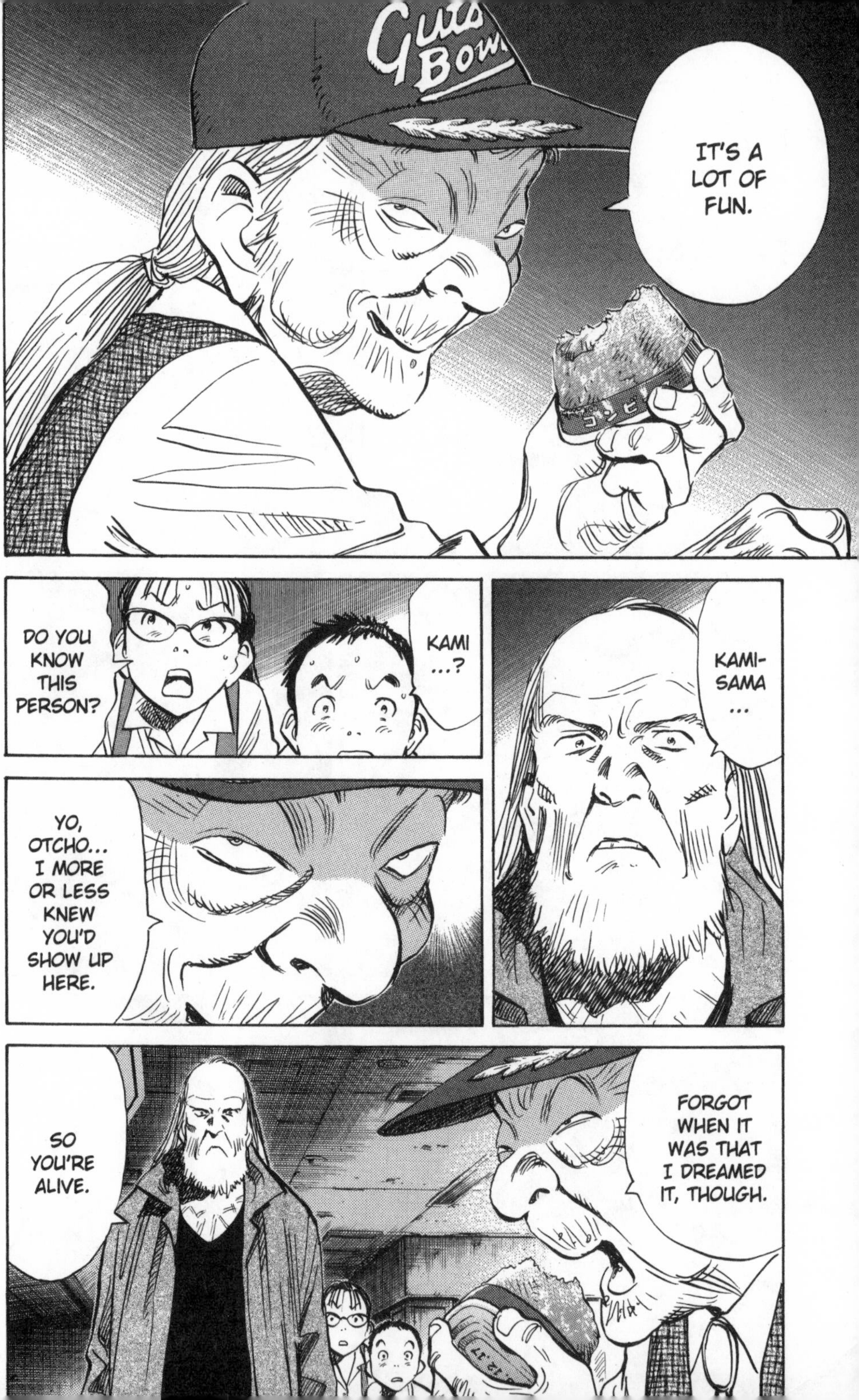
IT'S A LOT OF FUN.
KAMI-SAMA...
KAMI ...?
DO YOU KNOW THIS PERSON?
YO, OTCHO... I MORE OR LESS KNEW YOU'D SHOW UP HERE.
FORGOT WHEN IT WAS THAT I DREAMED IT, THOUGH.
SO YOU'RE ALIVE.

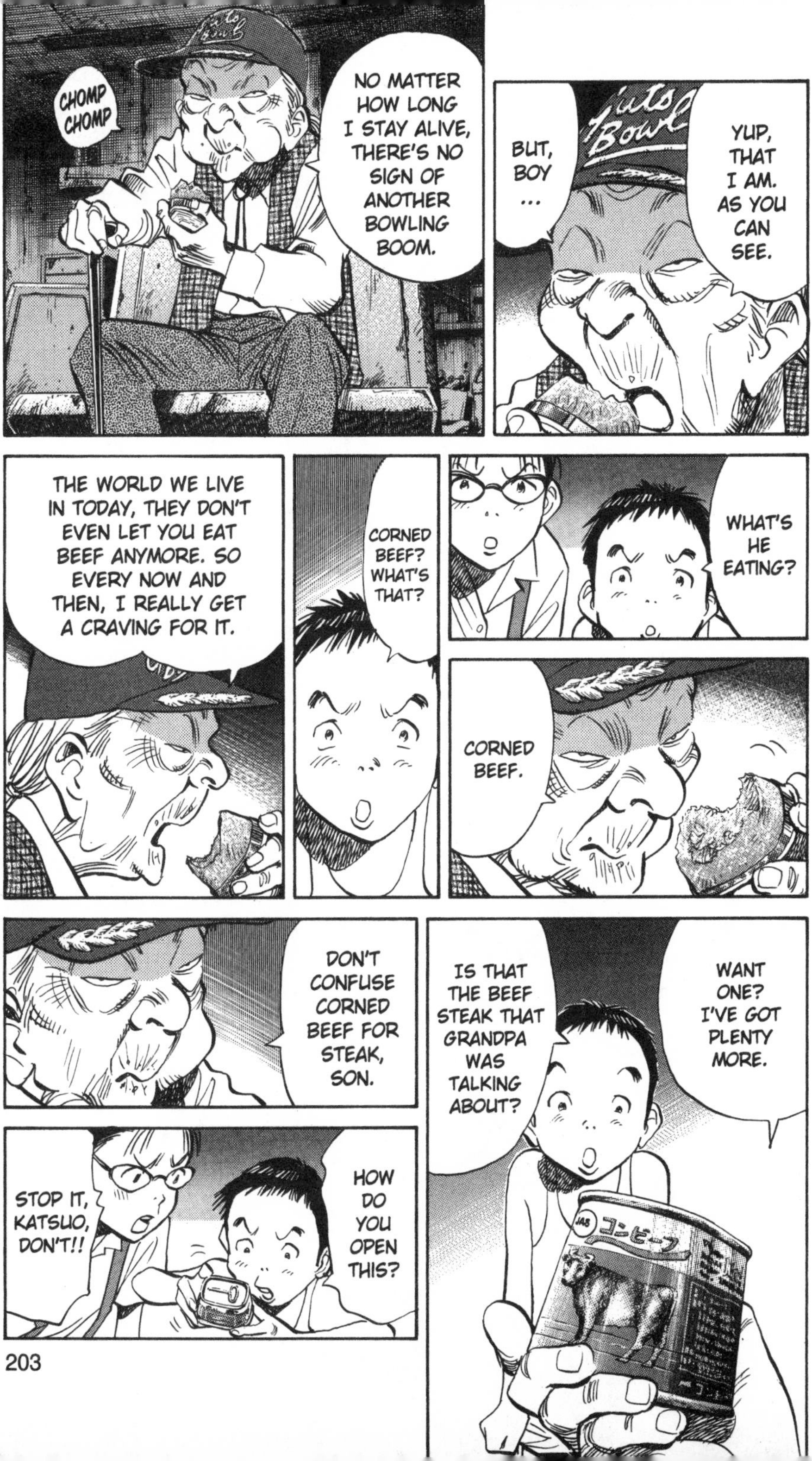
YUP, THAT I AM. AS YOU CAN SEE.
BUT, BOY ...
NO MATTER HOW LONG I STAY ALIVE, THERE'S NO SIGN OF ANOTHER BOWLING BOOM.
CHOMP CHOMP
WHAT'S HE EATING?
CORNED BEEF.
CORNED BEEF? WHAT'S THAT?
THE WORLD WE LIVE IN TODAY, THEY DON'T EVEN LET YOU EAT BEEF ANYMORE. SO EVERY NOW AND THEN, I REALLY GET A CRAVING FOR IT.
WANT ONE? I'VE GOT PLENTY MORE.
IS THAT THE BEEF STEAK THAT GRANDPA WAS TALKING ABOUT?
DON'T CONFUSE CORNED BEEF FOR STEAK, SON.
HOW DO YOU OPEN THIS?
STOP IT, KATSUO, DON'T!!

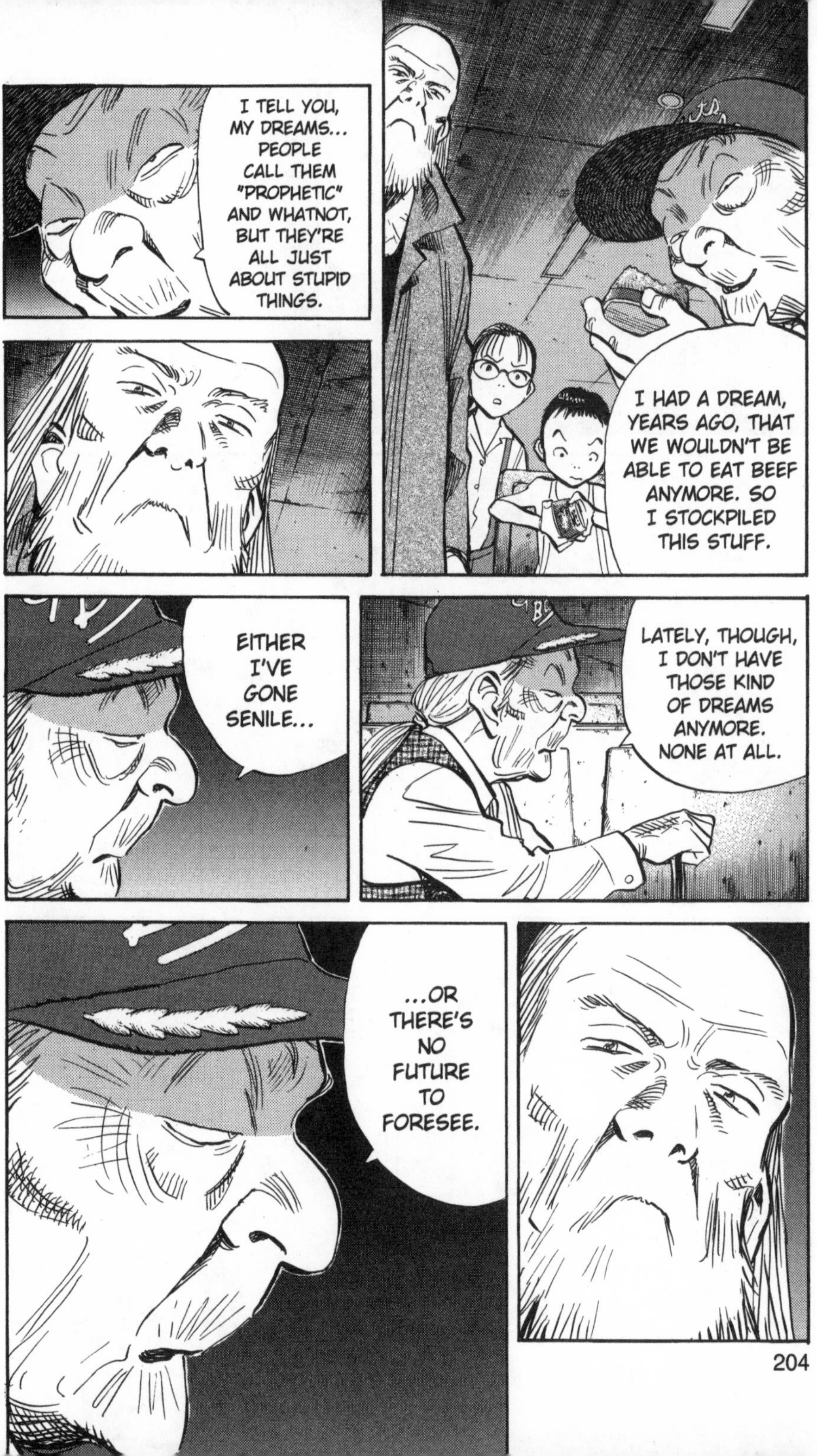
I HAD A DREAM, YEARS AGO, THAT WE WOULDN'T BE ABLE TO EAT BEEF ANYMORE. SO I STOCKPILED THIS STUFF.
I TELL YOU, MY DREAMS... PEOPLE CALL THEM "PROPHETIC" AND WHATNOT, BUT THEY'RE ALL JUST ABOUT STUPID THINGS.
LATELY, THOUGH, I DON'T HAVE THOSE KIND OF DREAMS ANYMORE. NONE AT ALL.
EITHER I'VE GONE SENILE...
...OR THERE'S NO FUTURE TO FORESEE.

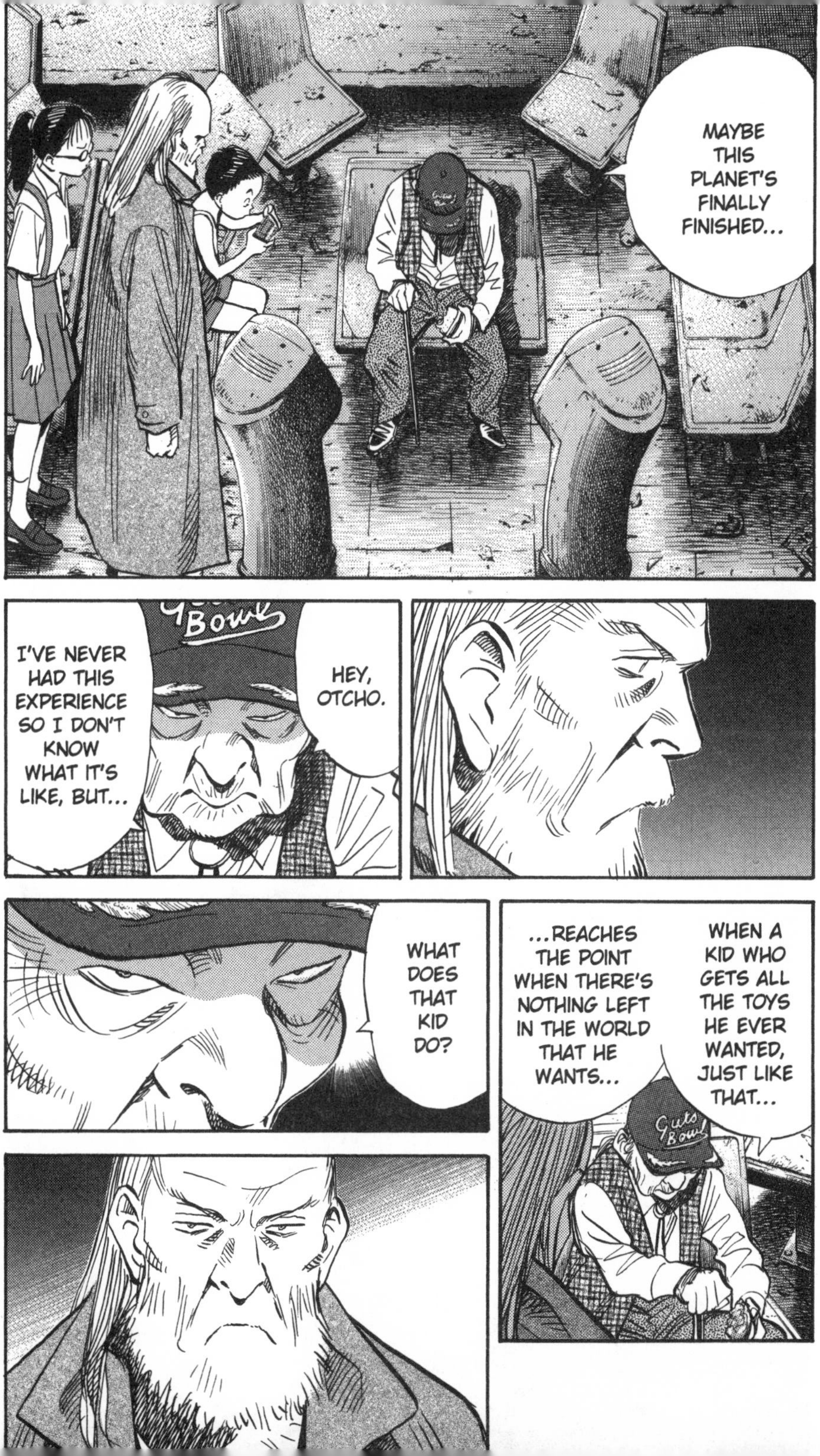
MAYBE THIS PLANET'S FINALLY FINISHED...
HEY, OTCHO.
I'VE NEVER HAD THIS EXPERIENCE SO I DON'T KNOW WHAT IT'S LIKE, BUT...
WHEN A KID WHO GETS ALL THE TOYS HE EVER WANTED, JUST LIKE THAT...
...REACHES THE POINT WHEN THERE'S NOTHING LEFT IN THE WORLD THAT HE WANTS...
WHAT DOES THAT KID DO?

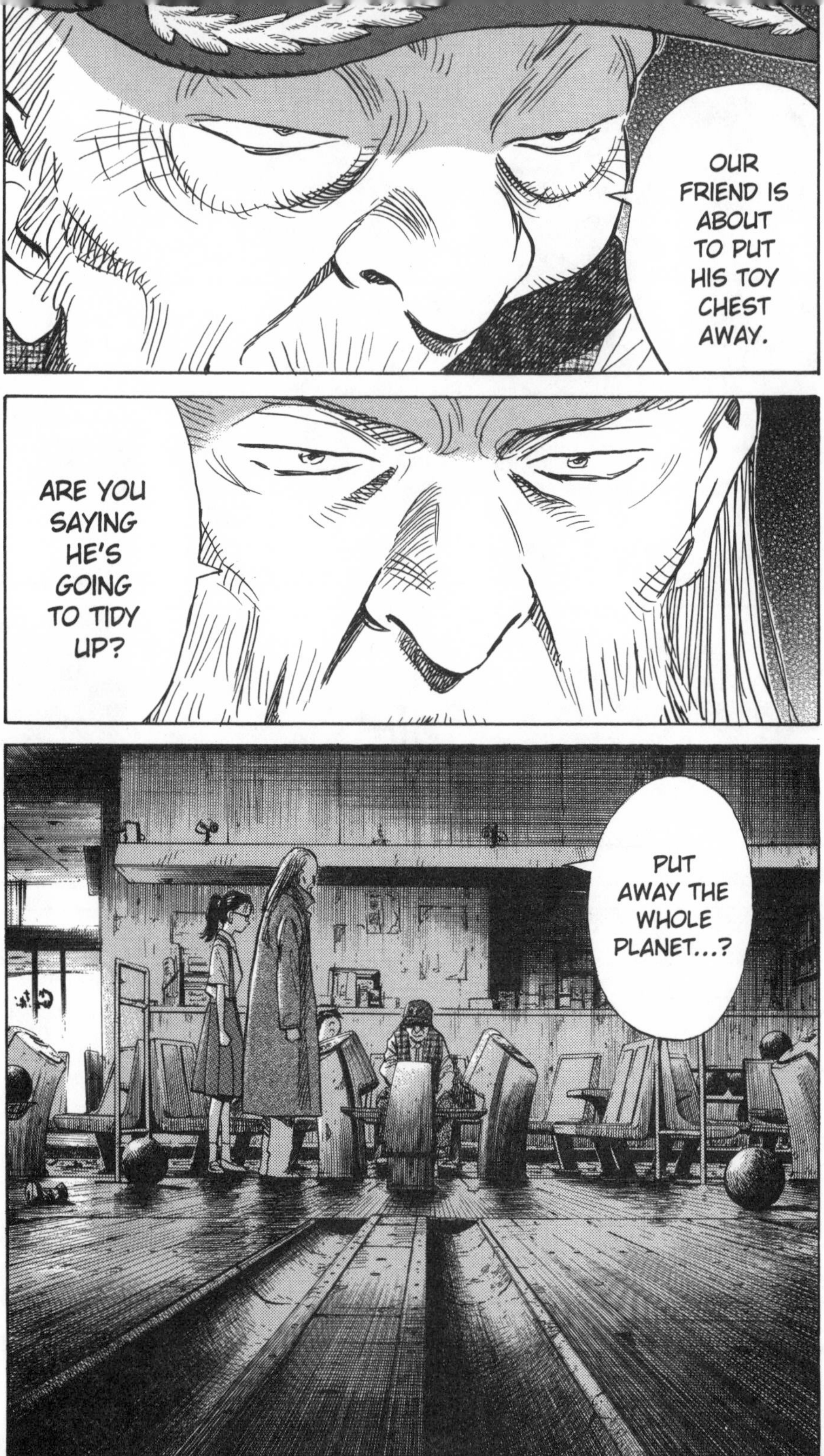
OUR FRIEND IS ABOUT TO PUT HIS TOY CHEST AWAY.
ARE YOU SAYING HE'S GOING TO TIDY UP?
PUT AWAY THE WHOLE PLANET...?

NOTES FROM THE TRANSLATOR

This series follows the Japanese naming convention, with a character's family name followed by their given name. Honorifics such as -*san* and -*kun* are also preserved.

Page 150: Minamoto Yoshitsune was a famous general from the 12th century. "Genji" is an alternate reading of the kanji characters for "Minamoto family."

Naoki Urasawa's
20th Century Boys
Volume 16

VIZ Signature Edition

STORY AND ART BY NAOKI URASAWA

20 SEIKI SHONEN 16 by Naoki URASAWA/Studio Nuts
© 2004 Naoki URASAWA/Studio Nuts
With the cooperation of Takashi NAGASAKI
All rights reserved. Original Japanese
edition published in 2004 by Shogakukan Inc., Tokyo.

English Adaptation/Akemi Wegmüller
Touch-up Art & Lettering/Freeman Wong
Cover & Interior Design/Sam Elzway
Editor/Kit Fox, Andy Nakatani

The rights of the author(s) of the work(s) in this
publication to be so identified have been asserted in
accordance with the Copyright, Designs and Patents
Act 1988. A CIP catalogue record for this book is
available from the British Library.

Printed in Canada

Published by VIZ Media, LLC
P.O. Box 77010
San Francisco, CA 94107

10 9 8 7 6 5 4 3 2 1
First printing, August 2011